Contents at a Glance

Table of Contents

Introduction

*T*he fact that you've taken this book off the shelf or been given it as a gift is a good indication that you're seriously thinking about starting or expanding your business, and you realise that you're going to need some other believers, in the form of lenders, investors and facilitators, to accompany you on your roller-coaster journey. Firstly, well done for thinking outside the box, and secondly, congratulations for realising that help is at hand and you don't have to do everything on your own.

Whatever your reason for dipping into the pages that follow, it's safe to assume that you have an inkling that luck and a fair wind are not enough to enable you to achieve funding success for your business, and you want to find out as much as you can in order to ensure that you come out with the best result for you and your business.

This book starts with the premise that a good idea, better-than-average skills and hard work are not enough for you to raise the finance you need to create a viable business – one with growing revenue, healthy profit margins and a good rate of return on investment. It brings together information and examples from a wide variety of sources, some essential knowledge, and some tips, hints and guidelines for maximising your efforts to achieve funding success, no matter what the economic backdrop is.

About This Book

Half of the businesses that start this year will fail. Of those that survive, few will reach the scale necessary to make a significant impact on the UK economy as a whole. Everyone in the business community wants to see this situation improve, and it's clear that some extra help is required.

One area that's been identified as a stumbling block to business growth is accessing appropriate business finance (you can find out more in the government-commissioned Scale-Up Report). Many smaller businesses aren't aware of the full range of external funding options on the market. However, you can find a good deal of funding out there, and like water trickling down and through, it'll find its level. This funding is looking for good business deals to invest in, but not just any old deal flow; it wants good, solid businesses with amazing teams and a product or service that has a growing and sustainable market. It's up to you to find the right funds at the right time and for the right price.

If this isn't happening, it may be due to:

- ✔ The lack of a strong business foundation to approach funders from
- ✔ A lack of awareness about what funding products are in the market, or where to find them
- ✔ A lack of education and practical understanding as to how to effectively prepare and successfully approach and obtain funding
- ✔ Entrepreneurs and business owners feeling overwhelmed in the face of the changing funding landscape, which now has technology-enabled platforms adding a new dimension to the receding traditional offering

This book gives you help in all these areas.

In addition, every business needs a business plan, an eye-catching pitch deck, an impressive investment memorandum or opportunity note, and a short, sharp, crystal-clear executive summary. You also need a well-researched and thought-out story that covers how much money you need, what you'll use it for and what you'll provide in return to a funder that has the faith and conviction to back you, your team and your credible plan and idea.

This book is also invaluable to the inventors and innovators among you. If you're researching or developing some groundbreaking or life-changing product or service, you may benefit from the down-to-earth business advice and guidance I provide, as well as the unearthing of possible financial support, be it tax credits, grants or competitions. Your discoveries may mean the difference between your next big thing languishing in the bottom drawer or successfully travelling from the lab to the light of the public gaze.

Business Funding For Dummies, UK Edition, can help you succeed no matter what stage of funding you're seeking. Whether you're about to take your first plunge into funding or you're an experienced entrepreneur, you can always discover something new. This has never been more relevant than in the current funding climate, where alternative finance is really finding its voice and creating many challengers to traditional providers, and the lines between investment rounds made by equity providers are blurring, opening up avenues that may have previously been closed to you.

This book is set out to allow you to dip in and out of it to suit your situation and needs, no matter what stage you're in:

✔ If you've not started your business yet and want to be as well-informed as possible, consider starting at the beginning of this book and working your way through each chapter.

✔ If you're already up and running, and you've had a bit of funding to get you started, you may want to pick and choose the areas where you're less knowledgeable, or have knowledge gaps, as a starting point, radiating out from there as you go along.

✔ If you're further along and more confident in your funding knowledge and experience, you can find a particular topic that enhances your knowledge and also serves as a review or refresher guide.

✔ If you prefer to learn by example, the True Story and Warning icons may be good ways to shed a little light, using other people's experiences as a guide.

✔ If you're familiar with the more traditional forms of business funding but only just beginning to explore some of the new funding methods, check the relevant chapters for topics to improve your knowledge and confidence levels as you begin to explore whether they're appropriate for your business needs.

Foolish Assumptions

This book brings together essential, go-to information about getting your business funded. It assumes that you're either just starting your funding journey and want to see where you stand now as well as the road ahead or that you're somewhere on the road already and want to find out what's out there that will work for your business at every stage along the way.

You may find yourself in need of this book for a number of reasons:

✔ You've been given a gift or an inheritance that provides enough to get you started on realising a long-held dream or ambition, and you want to spend it wisely – as well as see what other funding you may need to go with it.

✔ You've finally been cut loose from the drudge of the day job that you've disliked for years, with a financial incentive to soften the blow, but you have a feeling that this leaving present may not be quite enough to launch your world-dominating enterprise, so you need to explore additional funding options.

✔ You may have already made a start on your business, and to the surprise of everyone, including you, it's doing so well that you can't keep up with the finance it demands! If so, you need to discover more about what your options are and how to secure additional funding.

✔ You can see the potential for your business to become a world leader, or the next big thing, and you're curious as to what that journey to your island retirement may look like in funding terms.

✔ You've read about how well the UK economy is doing, and the great environment for supporting small- and medium-sized enterprises (SMEs) seeking finance – tax incentives, mentors galore, business support schemes, export programmes and a plethora of funders – so you thought you'd find out what all the fuss is about and get on board the funding train.

This is a book for a business that has or will have products and services that people want to buy so your business can grow and access a variety of funding options. This book has chapters that point you in the direction of potential guidance and advice, and assumes that everyone has something to learn.

I don't assume that you know everything about how to go about funding your business, or that you're less of a businessperson if you have some knowledge gaps. What matters is that you're eager to learn and willing to make a start.

Icons Used in This Book

All *For Dummies* books use icons to highlight especially interesting, important or sometimes dangerous information. In this book, I use the following icons:

The Tip icon draws your attention to useful and practical points or information.

This icon alerts you to a potentially precarious or dangerous situation, and reminds you to stop, look and listen and proceed with caution.

The Remember icon gives you a gentle reminder that this bit of information topic is important enough for you to note it down.

 The True Story icon lets you know that I'm referring to a real-life business example that shows you how another entrepreneur handled a situation or topic that you may encounter yourself one day.

The Technical Stuff icon is next to information that number-crunchers may like but that isn't necessary to understand the topic at hand.

Beyond the Book

As you embark on and travel further along your funding journey, you can add to or supplement what you've read here by checking out some of the 24/7 extra information hosted online. You can access bonus articles and an extra Part of Tens chapter by going to www.dummies.com/extras/businessfundinguk or discover the book's online cheat sheet at www.dummies.com/cheatsheet/businessfundinguk.

Where to Go From Here

Resist the need to feel that you must sit down and read this book from cover to cover unless that works for you. You don't need to read the chapters in order to get all you need from it – you can make à la carte selections rather than being stuck with the set menu. Don't turn what's an enjoyable and exciting voyage of discovery into a boring, mundane walk.

Start by taking a few minutes to read through the table of contents and get familiar and comfortable with the topics this book covers. Perhaps select a chapter that takes your fancy, piques your curiosity or hits the particular nail on the head that you need to hammer home most urgently. This may be looking into the various debt products on the market or strategies for coping with family members who want to invest in your business. Start anywhere that interests you and see where it takes you. Alternatively, you can head to Chapter 3, which offers an overview of the process of raising funds.

Wherever you start and wherever you end up, I hope your business is the better for it.

Part I

Getting Started on Funding Your Business

For Dummies can help you get started with lots of subjects. Visit www.dummies.com to learn more and do more with *For Dummies*.

In this part . . .

- ✔ Use your knowledge of business principles and cycles to give your business the best chance of obtaining funding in a changing and challenging economic environment.

- ✔ Understand the stages and cycles of your business and how each impacts your funding options.

- ✔ Lay the foundations to help you successfully raise funding for your business.

- ✔ Assess your skills and readiness to go for and accept funding for your business.

Chapter 1

Preparing for Funding at Any Stage of Growth

*W*hen you're embarking on the mission to fund your business, you need to carry out the same level of preparation as you would for any important mission: advanced reconnaissance, tactical thinking, logical planning for any eventuality – and add a large dollop of courage and confidence in the abilities of yourself and your team to survive and thrive.

You may have a fantastic business idea that you've nurtured, protected and evangelised about, but the fact is that however great you think your brain child is, it may never receive a penny of funding. Or it may be the exact opposite – and funders get your idea, think it's a winner and pour money into it. But you now need to deal with all the challenges and responsibilities that getting funded brings.

The UK is currently experiencing a period of economic growth that surpasses that of the pre-2008 crash – unemployment is down, and tech businesses are the new black, receiving millions of pounds of investment from the four corners of the Earth – but the number of people choosing to go it alone is also up, and competition for all forms of funding is on the rise.

The unfortunate reality is that many new businesses don't survive the first year, and many others don't grow beyond a *lifestyle business* that generates enough income to let you enjoy a good standard of living but doesn't aspire to ambitious revenue goals. Getting the right form of funding at the right time can be the thing that makes your business one of the winners in this competitive landscape. Equipping yourself with as much knowledge, awareness and resources as you possibly can will go a long way to helping you to determine your funding needs and to know when and where to go to look for the appropriate solution.

When it comes to funding, your bank manager is no longer your only option. Traditional funders are nestling alongside a new breed of alternative financiers challenging the status quo, and everyone is jockeying for position. It's a brave new world in some respects, and it's full of promise and exciting opportunities for your business. Technology has been a game changer when it comes to business funding, and it's a constantly changing scene – whether it's a platform, a crowd or a direct lending application. The supply of finance is now more diverse and accessible than it's been in a long time, so explore, but proceed with caution and advice.

In fact, you can now find so many options to fund your business that you need to stay networked, stay alert and stay updated if you're going to maximise the finance in your business and get it at a good price.

How you prepare and how you implement your funding plan can make the difference between success and failure. This chapter sets the scene to make sure that you're well-prepared for the exciting, and hopefully rewarding, journey ahead.

Understanding the Accepted Wisdom of Business Strategy

When you're consumed with passion and enthusiasm for your new business or growth idea, and you're convinced that it's as obvious as the nose on your face that someone just needs to throw money at you for it to be a huge success, it's sometimes hard to see the bigger economic, business and funding picture that surrounds you. If you're going to be a player, you'd better make sure that you know the rules of the game.

Establishing and positioning your business within your industry and giving it a loose, but logical, framework early on gives your business a structure to hold it together and to grow on. You can tighten and refine your structure as your business grows.

I'm not talking about constricting your innovative concepts into a box; I'm talking about keeping a loose lid on the box, so everything that's good and useful doesn't escape.

A framework helps you and your business stay focused and be clear about what differentiates you from the rest of the herd. It gives you an easily recognisable and understandable means of communicating within your organisation and to your financiers.

Staying focused and informed

Recently a very well-known business investor asked me why Americans think a business plan is still relevant to a funding application; he doesn't think they are. I didn't hesitate for one second in saying, 'Maybe it's something to do with knowing where the business is going and showing an investor or a lender that you know', which is what I genuinely feel. I also think a business plan helps you to get focused and – when used properly – to stay focused.

I've lost track of the number of times I've read or heard successful business-people harp on about the need for focus in order to achieve your goals and success. Sorry to disappoint if you were expecting me to say 'Rubbish. What do they know?' Because I have to agree, especially when it comes to raising money for your business. You need to be fully engaged with, and focused on, the process and achieving your outcomes with regard to both getting the funding and hitting all the targets and milestones linked to the money along the way. And sometimes, just writing the plan opens your eyes to the things you haven't thought about or potential problem areas you overlooked.

As it is with anything that demands unbroken concentration, it's not uncommon to lose your focus over time and have to rediscover what your core purpose is, especially if your funding is linked to this purpose.

In your business, focus takes on a number of forms, in both the business process as well as in your team. Maybe it shows up in pricing strategies, product differentiation or cost-cutting exercises, but it will always be something to keep your eye on. When you're in the throes of running your growing business, it's easy to take your eye off the ball or forget some of the reasons you did this in the first place.

Refocusing and rebranding

Sometimes, staying focussed on what it does best can lead a business to make significant changes, going so far as to change its name. For example:

✔ Winkler Plastic made the decision to rebrand itself as Nuconic Packaging – a clever way of making what it does sound like its name. What Nuconic does best is make new containers and plastic. The name change was an effort to redefine and safeguard its position in what is a highly competitive food-packaging market. Nuconic invested in new technology and capabilities and certification and created razor-sharp customer service to differentiate itself.

✔ When 37 Signals, the web application development business, changed its name to Basecamp, the name of its most popular product, it regained its focus and co-ordinated its vision, doing more business with a smaller, more focused team.

Appreciating the forces at work in your sector

Having a general understanding of the principles behind business strategy, and a focused idea of how strategy and business planning affect your funding efforts, is a good starting point in your preparation stage.

The next thing you want to do is go a bit deeper, and look at the drivers in your specific industry or sector. You want to be able to clearly differentiate yourself and see off your competition while simultaneously maximising opportunities in every area of your business – from supply chain to end-user. You want to keep as much cash in your business as you can while continually strengthening and monitoring the key performance areas that underpin your ability to successfully raise finance at all stages of your business.

As you consider your business sector, keep these points in mind:

- Identify a gap in your market and prove demand – figure out the problem and what your solution is.
- To succeed, you must do something better or do it differently to your competitors. Know what's unique about your business and what your value-add for the customer is.
- Be aware of the impact of external forces on your business – the economy, environment, regulations and so on – and have contingency plans.

And, no matter what sector you're in, use these tips for success:

- Plan for success. Have a business plan and a five-year plan that includes funding needs and financials.
- Find funding. Do your research, use your networks, and allow plenty of time.
- Get a great team together with all the skills – make them amazing!
- Be ready to take calculated risks and prepare for things to go wrong.

Recognising the first-to-market fallacy

It's okay not to be the first to the party, as long as you're fashionably late and make a noticeable entrance. It's no accident that you find sayings such as 'fools rush in where angels fear to tread', or that you can usually remember the runner-up in the talent contests and not the winner. Rushing headlong into a new business, or a new business area, without proper planning, preparation and funding, is a recipe for disaster.

Don't feel the pressure to launch prematurely; it's always better to learn from someone else's mistakes, capitalise on his educating the market, and discover the ways to do it cheaper, faster and better by analysing his mistakes. Funders will appreciate your pragmatic and more mature approach. If, however, you're the first to market and you fail, learn your lessons well and come back fighting.

The strategy of being first to market is often over-hyped, but of course you do see advantages: You have little competition, you can make a greater impact and you may become a household name. Think Ford and automobiles, Gillette and razors, Hoover and vacuums and Xerox and photocopiers. All these brands were first movers and spawned successful businesses and, in some cases, industries.

You do, however, have the burden of developing a market for the first movers – *proof of concept,* or being able to demonstrate that your idea is feasible and has business potential, can be painful and expensive, and sometimes you're too early or just plain wrong.

If you don't have the following, there really isn't any point in crossing the finish line first:

- A well-researched, good idea

- A dream team of partners or employees who are either experienced or qualified, have unique skills and all come together to create the perfect combination for your business

- Enough cash to give your idea time and room to catch on

- A way to listen to your customers while you get some early traction

In 'The Half-Truth of First-Mover Advantage', published in the *Harvard Business Review,* authors Fernando Suarez and Gianvito Lanzolla argue that first-mover advantage is dependent on the pace of the market and technology. A slow market is good for first-mover advantage; a rapidly changing market makes it harder to gain first-mover advantage. Think of Motorola and BlackBerry (first movers in a slow market), and then Samsung and Apple (who both surpassed BlackBerry in a fast-moving market).

Some famous first-to-market failures

First to market doesn't mean staying in the market, as these examples prove:

✔ **PalmPilot:** At one point, *PalmPilot* for personal digital assistants (the precursor to smartphones) was like *Hoover* for vacuum cleaners – the go-to generic term for a handheld personal data device. Today, who talks about them or remembers

them? iPhones and Androids are all the rage.

✔ **Atari:** Nintendo has a great console and okay games, but it overtook first-to-market Atari quickly.

The lesson? Innovation is key in certain business areas.

Getting in Shape to Start Up

You need to get in shape to start or grow a business. I'm not talking about going on a diet and working out (although I believe that a healthy body helps you perform better and stay focused) – it's more about making sure that you have the skills and knowledge you need for your business, or know how to find and activate such sources of expertise.

You may not have all the skills, expertise and knowledge you need to run the business and raise the funds yourself. Chapter 8 introduces you to the myriad of agencies and advisers that can help fill in the gaps in your expertise.

Assessing your abilities

Before you begin what will be a challenging and demanding funding journey, have a frank and honest discussion with yourself on the subject of your ability to actually start on this road and see it through to the end. Better to stare yourself in your internal mirror before you start than at some point down the line when you feel like you're drowning and you're looking for someone to throw you a lifeline.

Of course, you can't know everything before you start – but knowing a good part of it, and also knowing what you don't know, can be very useful. Address the following points before you set out:

✔ **Know why you're looking to fund a business.** Your patience, commitment and constitution will be tested, so it's good to remind yourself why you're doing it in the first place. What was it that made you decide to strike out on your own, or buddy up with your best mates and go out and change the world? Was it the money? The independence? To do what you love instead of what you have to do? To work with family or friends? Because other doors are closed to you? An opportunity to do it better than your boss? Or maybe to be the next billionaire with a social conscience?

✔ **Assess your skills and knowledge.** Once you've determined the why, it's a good idea to assess your knowledge and skills, because both will come into play when you're trying to raise funds.

Make a frank assessment of yourself and your CV, and be brutally honest about your management skills, your financial skills and your industry knowledge. Identify any gaps or areas that you need to improve on or get help with:

- Ask yourself if you fully understand all the things that make your business tick – what drives it, how to measure performance and whether you and your team have the skill set for the job ahead.

- Decide whether you have the leadership skills needed to create effective working relationships, run a tight ship and keep order to a high enough standard to withstand external scrutiny from funders.

- Match your current skills and expertise against your necessary-skills list, and identify any gaps.

   Decide on a way to plug any gaps, either with people, knowledge or expertise.

Ask someone you respect, like a mentor or an adviser, to help you identify gaps, offering an objective and unemotional opinion.

You also need to ask yourself if you want a lifestyle business that gives you enough money to be comfortable or a business that you can scale and make a great return on. The type of business you aim for affects the way funders see you and your business.

✔ **Understand how much funding you need.** As you ready your business to go forward and seek funding, you need to understand what you need to risk and what you need to do to get funders on board. You have to assess the amount and the use, but also prove to potential funders that you can control and monitor any money you receive and give them a great return. (I offer advice on estimating your financial needs in Chapter 3.)

This soul searching isn't meant to put you off. On the contrary, if you're reading this book, you're probably 99 per cent of the way to getting started on funding, whether it's the start of your venture or further along. My aim is to make you think and take stock, plan and make any adjustments before diving in to a pool that has both dolphins and sharks in it.

Discovering a genuine need

Every time I experience poor customer service, excessively high prices or the lack of a product in the market, I hear a little voice in my head say 'I could do that better', or 'Why don't I bring that to the UK; there's obviously a demand for it'. At some point, I ask myself how much money I'd need and who else I could rope into my cunning plan. Enthusiasm and blind ambition are admirable qualities in an entrepreneur, but your opinions are not enough to go on until you find out if there's a real need for your fantastic solution.

Before you start asking for money to get your brilliant idea off the ground, ask yourself these questions:

- Is there a problem in the market that you can clearly define?
- Do you have a unique solution to this problem that customers will want to pay for?
- How much will it cost to get out there and satisfy this need?
- Are you and your team able to bring the solution to market and turn a good profit?
- How do you plan to reach your target market?
- How much revenue and profit will that generate?

You need to consider what drives people to buy into a product or a service, no matter what the cost, and then see if you've got what it takes. The reason may be:

- Convenience
- Need, requirement or legal reasons
- Specialist products or services that are hard to find
- Fear
- Luxury

Checking how you fit the bill

When you have a good business idea and are confident that you have the skills and knowledge to make it a reality, you need to ask yourself one final, two-part question: Will this business suit me and my goals, and what am I prepared to live with in order to make it a success? This may also include the question: What am I prepared to ask my family to put up with in order to achieve my dreams?

For example, you may love baking biscuits at home, but would you love getting up at 2:30 a.m., abiding by strict health and safety regulations and relying on staff to get your biscuits to your customers every day, as well as making sure you can repay your loan or generate the return an investor expects?

 Have a frank conversation with yourself about what it is that you want from embarking on this journey, and what you're prepared to put up with – whether that's working long hours, travelling, doing the accounts, or meeting with and dealing with people. Make sure that you and your chosen industry or sector are a good match. When you take someone else's money, you can't pick and choose when it comes to the tasks that get the job done.

Confirming Viability

In a well-known cartoon magazine, a cartoon shows two cavemen with a square wheel. The caption reads, 'I call my invention "The Wheel", but so far I've been unable to attract any venture capital'.

An idea or product that may be the basis for a business, however unique, isn't a business in and of itself. A bare idea certainly won't convince someone to give you money. It's a great place to start, but before you give up the day job and raid the biscuit tin where you keep your savings, explore the steps in the following sections so that you don't have to go crawling back to that job or live on bread and water.

Researching the market

Before you go forth unprepared and ill-informed and wind up speaking in broad brush strokes without really saying anything about the realistic size, characteristics, approach and financial return from your market, discover as much as possible about the market and put that knowledge into an intelligible format for funders. Don't look for funding on the basis that you and a couple of your mates think you've got a great idea or ignore the glaring examples of those who have gone before you and failed, because this won't wash with funders.

One of the best ways to explore your market is to conduct and/or commission some market research, using secondary sources of already published information, and primary sources of first-hand, fresh or new data that you gather from your potential market. Some things to look at include:

✔ **Your customers or clients:** What are their characteristics and what is the value-add offering from you?

- **Your product or service:** What is it, what problem does it solve, and what's unique about it?

- **Your price:** Have you got your margins right? What price will the market bear? Will you get repeat, sustainable business?

- **Promotion:** How will you promote your goods and services, at what cost and for what return?

- **Partners:** Whom can you partner with to get your goods and services out in the market?

- **Competitors:** Who are they? What do they do well? Where can you take advantage of a weakness? Who is a real threat?

You can find additional resources in *Marketing Research Kit For Dummies* by Michael Hyman and Jeremy Sierra (Wiley).

You need to consider the whole of the market versus your share of the market. When it comes to funding, don't talk about the universe if your business is concerned with only one or two planets in the galaxy. It just puts people off and tells them that you haven't figured out how large your potential piece of the celestial pie is. Having a UK market of £5 billion is terrific, but if you're only going after £1.5 million of that, why are you even talking about it like you own it? You need to drill down on which part of the market, at what spend, over what time frame is likely to be yours so that you can outline a realistic plan of attack.

Crunching the numbers

You've sorted out the product or service, and you know you're on to a winner. You've looked yourself, and your team, straight in the eye and seen your good and not-so-good points and put a plan in place for improvement. Now the question is: Can you raise the money to make this dream a reality?

Before you make one phone call or send one email to a funder of any sort, you need to do a few things first in order to make sure that your idea is financially viable. Some of the things to consider include:

- Cash flow forecasts
- How much money and effort it'll take to get to the *breakeven point* – where there's no loss, but still no gain
- Profit and loss statements and projections
- Balance sheets and projections
- Funding need and uses
- The likely financial rewards for funders

I discuss financial documents and projections in Chapter 3.

Raising capital for your start-up is no mean feat, but it's ten times harder if you haven't done your financial homework and aren't able to tell a convincing and realistic story. If you lack confidence or experience with any of your funding documents, do what you'd do with anything that's unpleasant but essential: Get help if you need it, and then get comfortable with your documents and presentation. You need to be in control of them.

Raising the money

Broadly speaking, a business can access two different types of money at various stages on its journey – debt and equity. A third, lesser known option, alternative finance, has experienced explosive growth over the past few years, and is rapidly becoming more mainstream.

The basics features of each type of funding are:

- ✔ **Debt** is money that you borrow, most commonly from a bank but also from newly created online peer-to-peer lending platforms, where unrelated individuals or institutions lend money to your business through an intermediary. You have to repay these funds, and, during the time you use the money for your business, you have a cost to pay, usually in the form of interest on the loan amount. I look more closely at debt funding in Chapter 12.

- ✔ **Equity** is money that people put in to become a shareholder in your business. The business owner or proprietor probably has an equity stake. Unlike debt, you don't have to repay this money, but the shareholders expect to get a return or increase the value of their shares. If you decide to offer shares to the wider public, they'll expect dividends as well. Check Chapter 13 for information on equity funding.

- ✔ **Alternative finance** typically describes any finance that's not stocks and shares, cash or bonds. In the past few years, this category has become a bit broader due to the influence of technology, which has enabled the creation of online platforms, such as crowdfunding sites, that have stretched the definitions of equity and debt. Alternative finance also includes competitions, grants, awards, and family and friends. Chapter 14 covers alternative finance.

Raising the funding you need is usually more challenging in the early stages of a business than in later stages. You may wind up asking yourself why you even started down this road in the first place on more than one occasion during the early stages. Fear not, intrepid entrepreneur, you're not the first and you certainly won't be the last person asking that question. If you're on to something good and do your homework and preparation, you most probably can find and secure the funding you need. Be aware that funding may not come from the place you thought it would; it may also come with a few too many strings for your liking, but, hey, no one ever said this would be easy.

One of the things about raising money that's often overlooked or ignored by entrepreneurs is just how long the whole process can take. Unless you have access to a very wealthy benefactor or have your own deep pockets, raising funds for your business can take months. You need to factor the time and effort into your plans and schedules. If you're a procrastinator by nature, you may want to get someone who's a bit more get it done now involved in helping you with the preparation.

Writing up the business plan

When it comes to getting funding for your business, a business plan is still an essential. Along with the other documents I cover in Chapter 5, your business plan is your company's calling card and road map. After potential funders get a taste of your funding proposal in your investment memorandum or your pitch deck, your business plan makes them want to come back for seconds. Any potential backer will ask to see the detail once the niceties are over.

Your business plan is a living document that needs updating as your business evolves so that you're ready for every opportunity that comes your way. Fundraising can often be a time-consuming and lengthy process, and you don't want to have to drop everything and write a plan from scratch or make major changes at the exact time you need to present it.

Your plan includes financial forecasts that you may need for a quick decision from a web-based funder, for example. You need it for different reasons at different times, but you do need it. It needs to cover three to five years, depending on the type of finance that you're looking to raise, and funders should be able to see what's in it for them in exchange for giving you the money.

Investors and funders of all kinds receive literally hundreds of business plans every week, so in order to make sure that they read and genuinely consider yours, it needs to stand out from the crowd. Some things to think about include:

✔ Don't try to flimflam investors with deep or amusing quotes and eye-catching headlines – it's about what you do, why you're the best, and why someone wants to buy your product or service. Get straight to the point, be clear and concise, and choose your words wisely so that they have meaning as well as impact.

✔ There's no *I* in team – make sure that you highlight the balance of skills and experience in your team and identify roles. Remember to include advisers and non-executive directors, who may be well-known in your industry and create an additional layer of credibility.

✔ Have credible, believable financial projections. Even if you feel your numbers are a bit shaky after the first year of your three- or five-year projections, make sure that your logic and thought processes are sound and explained.

✔ Clearly outline the market size and how your proposition fits within it – no one gets 100 per cent of the market, and you will have competition.

✔ For debt, make sure that you show how you will repay it and in what time frame; for equity, what is the return and when will funders see it?

Going for Growth

People start a business thinking that they want to see it grow from an idea they gave birth to, to become a fully grown adult, with all the growing pains in between – exactly as for a parent watching a child grow. The reality is that a relatively small number of small and medium-sized enterprises (SMEs) reach the highest percentile in terms of revenue and staff, and the majority stay somewhere in the adolescence to early-adult stage of growth, achieving admirable success for themselves and their employees.

In Britain in 2013, there were around 450,000 new start-ups. Over 40 per cent of new businesses close within three years of starting up. Only 6.6 per cent of businesses in the period from 2010 to 2013 had ten or more employees and were considered high-growth businesses. It's a positive that the majority of these businesses grow to a decent turnover and employ a good number of people and keep the economic engine turning.

Most businesses that survive follow a similar pattern of growth: The excitement of the start-up to the initial dip or plateau, and then a surge in growth followed by a longer plateau within five to seven years, which precedes consolidation. Not surprisingly, you get corresponding stages of financing growth, which I explore in the chapters in Part III.

Gaining economies of scale

When it comes to attracting funders, one of the attractions of a high-growth business is its ability to optimise its buying power while saving money and increasing profit margins at the same time. It's usually in the later funding rounds that your business becomes this competitive – poised for a final push before an investor exit or maybe a public listing, allowing the public to share in the spoils.

Your business may eventually achieve *economies of scale* – cost advantages that come with being able to negotiate better deals because your purchases are larger. Some of the areas you may see this reward for aggressive but managed growth are:

- ✔ **Marketing:** If you have more to spend on attracting a larger share of the market for your business, you can negotiate hard to secure savings on things like databases or promotional campaigns, and get a wider exposure for your business. This includes both domestic and foreign markets. If you're accessing a wider network, the cost of adding a new user comes down considerably and the value of a customer increases as he transacts in your business network.

- ✔ **Technical:** More efficient machinery to make your products or better IT (information technology) systems may save you time and labour.

- ✔ **Resources and skills:** You may not want a team of hundreds, but if you're serious about growth, you need to get beyond a couple of handfuls of people. Your people need to be well trained and skilled so that your business can compete effectively. You need to develop leadership skills as well, which can sometimes be easier said than done.

- ✔ **Administrative or associated infrastructure:** If you're able to share the cost of joined-up systems, you save money and gain efficiency, both of which are attractive to funders.

- ✔ **Purchasing:** Bulk buying has its benefits in terms of cost savings, which is good for your bottom line.

- ✔ **Financial:** You'll be able to access the right kinds of finance for your business at the time you need it, and you may also be able to achieve savings by being able to access finance more cheaply because you have more assets to secure more borrowings.

Getting to a minimum standard in all these areas is essential for growth. Taken in parts, they're unlikely to achieve a significantly stronger whole.

Securing a competitive advantage

When you present your business to potential funders, one of the early slides in your pitch deck looks at your product or service in the marketplace, and what is unique about it so that price takes a back seat in a customer's decision to engage with you. This is pretty powerful stuff, and has an impact on your ability to create sustainable, profitable revenue streams and keep the competition at bay.

Successful businesses manage to simultaneously optimise a number of functions and activities, including marketing, production, distribution, finance, customer service and other activities that are unique to your business or industry. However, a true competitive advantage usually comes down to doing one or two of these areas really well, giving you the edge over your competition. Being known and respected for doing something well can be the long-term making of your business and provide the focus that a funder needs to see.

If you're looking to define your competitive advantage, take a good look at some of the following areas:

- ✔ **People and product resources:** What you have now, how much more capacity you have, and what you can identify in the mix that's unique to your business, ties in with your overall strategy and can be used to your advantage.

- ✔ **Customers or clients:** Profile them and find a way to communicate with each segment in your market. Ask them what they want, listen closely to the answers and then translate that into products and services that they can't get from your competitors. Once you know what your customers want and need, you can give it to them in a way that keeps them engaged for the long term and helps you build a sustainable, high-growth business.

- ✔ **Competition:** Be it direct or indirect, don't ignore what your competition is doing or planning. Acknowledge their strengths and look to exploit their weaknesses by creating opportunities to gain an advantage over them, while gaining market share.

When thinking about your place in the market, ask yourself the following questions. If the answer isn't 'yes', work to get it there.

- ✔ Is the business and target market clearly defined and segmented?

- ✔ Are we communicating regularly and effectively with customers?

- ✔ Do we know what financial return we expect from our efforts?

- ✔ Do we have an identifiable and recognisable business strategy that touches all areas of the business?

- ✔ Do we know how we compare with our competitors?

- ✔ Are we taking advantage of competitors' weak spots and creating a positive opportunity for our business?

- ✔ Are our products or services priced competitively and do they have any extra added value for our clients?

- ✔ Is our customer service red hot and well-regarded?

Keep one eye on the present and one eye on the future to stay one step ahead of the competition and make your business attractive to anyone who may be thinking of offering funding.

Retaining key staff

Conventional business wisdom says that the true cost of losing and replacing a key member of staff is much more than the recruitment fee to replace him. The cost includes the time to train someone new, the impact on client relationships, the productivity slowdown caused by the impact on the rest of the staff and so on. Logically, you want to hold on to your best employees for as long as possible. *Constant turnover,* or a revolving door in the area of one of your key performance measures, is not good for your business or your funding prospects, as it sends out the wrong signals. It rings alarm bells with regard to your management abilities, the potential for confidential and valuable data to walk off and the bottom line costs. In short, losing staff doesn't make good business or financial sense.

Money isn't the only incentive for employees to remain loyal to a business – variety, reward, praise and development are all vital to keeping the troops happy.

Identifying, nurturing and empowering up-and-coming managers helps them realise their potential, earn higher salaries and stay with you for longer, while helping to grow your business and your bottom line.

If you take on equity funders, they may have ideas about who in your team should stay, should go or should be supplanted by an outsider of their choice. Be prepared for this, and be aware that this cull may include you, if the funders don't think you're up to the bigger growth task.

Gaining critical mass

You often hear that bigger is better, and most of the time, this can be true. In business, getting to a stage where you have enough money, staff, customers and brand recognition to run efficiently, effectively and competitively – in other words, when you've gained *critical mass* – bigger can get you noticed and help you weather economic storms.

This critical mass is music to a later-stage funders' ears. They can work with what you have achieved and tighten it up ready for that big, final push to exit.

However, if you're too reliant on one product or service or a couple of key customers, and a hostile competitor enters your space, you may find yourself in a tricky situation – one that's been known to bring a business to its knees, and in a quick time frame.

Of course, your business is usually more than one product or service, and you try to avoid depending on a few of your customers for most of your business. But often, and especially at the start-up stage, it's the idea or invention of the entrepreneur that makes up the business. As you move along, the development of product ranges or service lines can help to deflect the inevitable uncomfortable questions around vulnerability from finance providers, and create a more secure, long-lasting business that deserves their money and time.

Chapter 2

Recognising the Stages of Business Funding

*P*eople often talk about the funding escalator or funding ladder, with each step or rung you take upwards representing a higher amount of equity funding and involving more complicated processes, agreements and working arrangements. I don't deny that this is a great graphic, but for a minute . . . well, for a chapter . . . I'd like you to think of your equity rounds starting at the *top* of the ladder, or, indeed, the peak of a roller coaster: it's scary at the top, and you know that you're in for the ride of your life. You know the ride will have lots of twists and turns and a few stomach-dropping moments, but you also know that eventually you'll get to the wide open spaces at the end of the ride, and then the exit – a bit like your equity journey.

You start the ride with a small number of investors, perhaps just your friends and family, and gradually expand your investor base. Investors exit the ride at different stages, with some staying for the whole journey.

You may even ride a loop-the-loop, opening out into a wide arc and take on dozens if not hundreds of investors via a crowdfunding platform, all the time moving on to more sophisticated venture capital and private equity investors with deep pockets who want to buy the tickets for other people's cars on the ride, even if they don't sit in them.

Finally, the end is in sight, and the long, straight track leads to your exit. The gut-wrenching, stomach-turning fear and trepidation you felt at the top is now gone. It's time to make room in your cars, and look at options like a public offering to give other members of the public the chance to join you on the ride before you get off and head home, feeling like you've conquered the world and ready for your next adventure.

As you start assessing your funding needs, keep an open mind and do your research. You may have heard horror stories from friends or family members who've had bad experiences with certain forms of finance, but pre-determining what is right for your business is dangerous and can become very costly.

Looking at Funding Needs and Risk Levels

Whether you're at the start of your business, feeling the financial squeeze that comes with meteoric growth, or on the cliff edge staring into the precipice of decline, each stage has its own funding options and solutions.

The reasons for raising funds at different stages are varied, but some universally recognised staging points for all businesses include:

- The costs associated with starting a business that occur in your start-up phase.

- Purchasing equipment or physical assets, which can take place at the start-up phase of your business as well as throughout your growth and expansion stages.

- Filling working capital gaps to ensure that you can pay the essential day-to-day costs of running your business for a few months. You may find yourself in this situation during periods of very active growth, as well as in the initial start-up phase of your business.

- Refinancing expensive or inappropriate finance, such as debt with very high interest rates. As your business grows and takes on piecemeal funding, you may arrive at the point where the cost of financing your existing debt is too high, and it makes sense to refinance your current finances.

- Renovating or refurbishing business premises. As your business grows and expands, fixtures and fittings will need to be replaced or upgraded.

- Revamping your brand image and all the associated marketing materials.

- Expanding your business, either physically or online. During your expansion phase, you may need to move into larger or more efficient premises, and you'll very likely need to upgrade and improve your website, e-commerce store and so on.

✔ Preparing your business for a sale or public stock exchange listing. In the later stages of your business, as you prepare to exit, you have a variety of options, but all of them come with significant financial demands.

As diverse as your needs for finance are, so, too, are the solutions. The trick is to know which form of finance is the right one for which need and at each stage. This assessment and decision requires a good level of skill, a sprinkling of instinct and a dusting of luck that what you need is known and available to you at the exact time that you need it. It also usually requires that you get some outside help in the form of an experienced business advisor with a financial speciality. You may get this advice from your accountant along with input from a mentor or other trusted and educated source. (See Chapter 16 for advice on finding a mentor.)

Figure 2-1 shows the stages and types of funding.

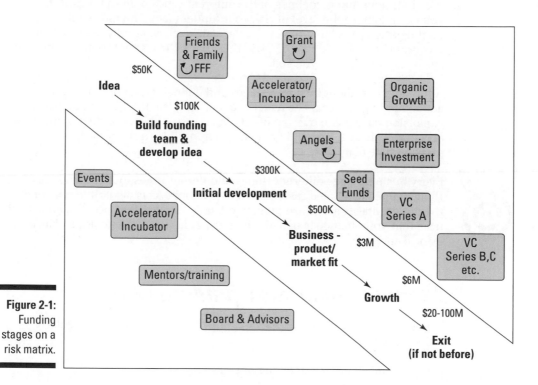

Figure 2-1:
Funding stages on a risk matrix.

Checking risk levels

Depending what stage your business is in, the levels of perceived and actual risk differ depending on the type and amount of funding you're considering. Not surprisingly, funding the earlier stages of a business is seen as more risky than funding at later, more established stages. The earlier the stage you're in, the higher the risk because you've yet to prove you can achieve your goals, aims and targets. This can have an upwards effect on the cost of funding. Conversely, once you have an established track record, you're seen as less of a risk, and you're in a better position to negotiate on the cost of funding. Investors sleep better at night knowing that the uncertainty around making repayments or returning on investment is diminishing day by day.

Risk appetite also varies depending on the type of funding you're looking for. Risk appetite is low for debt funding, where the goal is to make loan repayments, and higher for equity funding, where the aim is to provide a significant return to investors in the shortest period of time, requiring a healthy appetite for risk on the part of investors.

The level of risk your business holds has an impact on the type and cost of funds that you can tap into, and so it follows that the more you understand the limitations and guidelines of the different types of funding, and the more you can minimise the level of risk your funders face, the more you open up the options available to you. Lower risk levels generally lead to a more favourable cost to the funding, whether that's through interest or a percentage of ownership that you sell.

Although I talk about business stages and defined types of funding, the actual funding landscape is never that cut and dried. All stages of growth and expansion have some overlap of funding types, which is perfectly normal and acceptable. In fact, it would be nigh-on impossible to run your business on just one type of money.

 Every business does different things at different times, but rarely does anything happen in a linear fashion and in isolation. As is also often true of life, the middle stages are those most in crisis, and it's at that point in your business that your finance is usually the most complex and as colourful as it's ever likely to be.

Planning your next funding rounds

No matter where you are in your funding journey, you should regularly ask yourself:

- ✔ How much money does the business need?
- ✔ Why does it need funds? What will we spend it on?
- ✔ Does the business only need money or do we need some additional skills, contacts or know-how?
- ✔ If we take this money, what's the impact on existing investors?

Forestalling the time thief in raising funds

In the Lewis Carroll story of Alice in Wonderland, the King says to the White Rabbit, 'Begin at the beginning and go on till you come to the end: then stop.' Well, in your quest to raise finance – be it a small or significant amount – you'll sometimes ask yourself if it will ever end and wonder why you began in the first place.

I've lost track of the number of times I've heard entrepreneurs and business owners say 'Raising funds is a full-time business! I have no time to run my business.' Heed the warning. Raising funds *is* almost a full-time business, and it can make you take your eye off the fundamentals of running your business to disastrous effect if you don't take steps to avoid this outcome.

If you haven't already gone through it, you'll soon know what it feels like to run your growing business, assess the funding gaps, research and evaluate your funding options, prepare all the documentation (substantial enough to warrant more than one chapter in this book) and then go out and actually raise the funds. In some cases many months go by and you still don't have the money you need, and suddenly you realise that you're another year older, sporting a few more grey hairs and you're still nowhere near the end of your fundraising story.

You can make the funding process a bit easier and minimise the time lost and ease the strain of effectively running two businesses at the same time by using these tips:

✔ **Keep your documentation up to date.** I can't stress enough how important it is that you update all the documentation you need for funding on a regular basis. Keep your business plan, your financial forecasts and actual figures (all covered in Chapter 5), your pitch deck and your executive summary and investment memorandum (check out Chapter 6 for these) ready to use.

Don't put off updating your presentation materials until you have some down time or a holiday, because you need to take a break from time to time and you won't do it then anyway. Schedule these tasks into your monthly calendar and stick to the schedule. If you don't update regularly you won't be ready when an opportunity presents itself. If you need to stop whatever you're doing when a funding opportunity presents itself, you don't do either your business job or your funding job well. Trust me – I've seen it so many times. I want you to be the exception. Does that make you exceptional? It does in my book.

✔ **Update your funder database.** Continually update your database of funders so you know who's putting money where and roughly how much they have left to give. You need to keep on top of who's moved on or changed roles and what the current contact details are. This can save you hours of phone calls and emails later on.

✔ **Check your credit profile.** Check your credit profile regularly. It's not unusual to be unaware of a problem in your credit file, and you don't want to find that you have a problem when a funder checks you out. I've known company directors to have County Court Judgements against them without knowing it because they moved without redirecting their post, and so never received any notices. A poor credit profile obviously delays or in some cases eliminates some funding options, so always know where you stand.

(continued)

(continued)

> ✔ **Make use of your advisors.** Whenever you're looking to raise money, consult your mentor or advisor or seek out other professional advice. People who've been there and done it many times can save you a lot of time and possibly a lot of money.
>
> Even if you get help, you still need to know what your documentation says because you're the one pitching to funders. Ignorance is not a defence in this case, and quite rightly so.

You and your investors know when you need to start actively planning your next funding round, You know that it takes a good deal of time and effort to get ready to go for another round, and that you need to start sooner rather than later, even if some of your current investors are likely to stay on.

Starting with Seed Stage

When your business is still just the seed of an idea that you decide to plant, nurture and see what grows, you're at the *seed stage* of your business, when you're taking your idea and turning it into a product that's market ready.

The seed stage can be broken down into three phases:

- ✔ **Pre-trading:** Before you officially open to the public for business.

- ✔ **Pre-revenue:** You've probably had funds in from family, friends and yourself, but you may be using this small amount of money for research and development and initial running costs before you have a product or service that generates income.

- ✔ **Pre-profit:** At this point, your business is generating income or revenue, so you've started to prove that your business model works. You're not, however, making any profit on your sales yet.

You aren't ready to go and find seed funding until you put some order and some planning on to your unique idea, and come up with a business plan, some financial forecasts and a projection of how much money you'll need and what you need it for in order to make your baby grow. (I talk about business plans in Chapter 5.)

Check Figure 2-2 for an overview of funding stages, funding challenges and appropriate funding sources and method.

	Seed finance	Angel finance	Equity crowdfunding	Venture capital	Corporate venture	Private equity	IPO/Public offering	Start-up loan	Overdraft	Loan/Peer-to-peer lending	Bond	Asset-based finance	Leasing & hire purchase	Export finance	Trade finance	Mezzanine
Pre-trading	●							●								
Pre-profit	●	●	●	●	●			●	●				●		●	
Profitable growing business		●		●	●	●	●		●	●	●	●	●		●	●
Established & steadily growing		●				●	●		●	●	●	●	●		●	●
Established stable business							●		●	●	●	●	●		●	
Launching new product /service/ brand							●			●	●	●				
Making acquisitions						●	●			●	●	●	●			●
Expanding into new territories						●	●			●	●	●		●		
Investing in new facilities						●	●			●	●	●	●			
Looking to refinance			●							●	●	●	●			
In need of capital restructuring			●							●	●	●	●			

Figure 2-2: The funding needs and sources matrix.

© *John Wiley & Sons, Ltd.*

Seeking funds for activities and phases

Because the seed stage can kick in as early as the idea or concept stage of your business, financing at this stage helps you to develop the concept and build prototypes, and gives you time for research and for writing the business plan.

You frequently hear people talk about *bootstrapping* – surviving without outside investment – at this stage. It's possible to rein in the spending and do your laces up tightly in order to spend as little as possible and stay as lean as possible.

Seed stage activities that may need funding include:

- **Research and development (R&D):** If you're investigating or creating new or innovative products and processes before your business starts trading, it can be a drain on both your time and finances. If you're creating a product that will be patented, funding is needed to get you through the R&D phase, as well as to pay for the patent applications.

- **Product testing:** If you've created a product but it's in its beta or testing stage and not yet generating income, it needs funding to get your product to a customer-ready phase.

- **Technology:** Whether it's technology you're developing in the form of software, for example, or technology you need to purchase to operate your business, you need to lay the money out before your product or service starts to generate a return.

Getting funding at any stage involves crafting a very good story on your part, assembling as much supporting evidence as possible, and inspiring an enormous belief on the part of the lender or investor, because generally speaking you won't have much to go on yet.

Maximising your funding resources

In seed stage, your business can be in the pre-trading stage, and definitely in the pre-profit stage, and so accessing funding at this early stage can sometimes be challenging.

Seed stage funding options include:

- **Yourself:** You know you have to stump up a bit of cash yourself, so be prepared to throw your savings or your redundancy payout into the kitty. You may go even further and take out a start-up loan, sticking your neck out and claiming to be able to pay it back with money from the business.

- ✔ **Friends and family:** Getting funding is often highly dependent on you as the entrepreneur being able to summon up a mammoth amount of charisma, peppered with a generous helping of chutzpah in order to convince your nearest and dearest to part with any spare cash they can afford to lose. Your family and friends know that you're planting the seeds of a great business, which you hopefully grow into a mighty oak tree of a successful business, and they usually want to help.

- ✔ **Incubators or accelerators:** You may choose to be part of an *accelerator* – a fixed-term, fast-track business development and support programme that invests a small amount of money and a good deal of mentoring in exchange for a single digit percentage of equity shares – or an *incubator,* which is a fixed-term business support programme that uses external management teams to help you bring your business idea to business reality, ready for your client market. Incubators have been known not to take equity shares, but more often than not they take a double-digit percentage of equity in exchange for their business input and physical space (see Chapter 8 for more on both programmes). Through them, you can tap into valuable resources that go beyond just money and help you take your idea and turn it into a viable and desirable product or service, ready to face the market.

- ✔ **Grants and awards:** You may be fortunate enough to come across a big corporation or a grant awarding organisation that understands your idea and has money, people, technology and contacts to contribute. Corporations and grant givers like the idea of taking you into their family and watching you grow.

- ✔ **Competitions:** Often found in the areas of science and technology, a variety of competitions come with cash prizes, as well as mentoring and/or office space.

An early infusion of funds can help you achieve lift-off and paves the way for established funders to take the same leap of faith. If you can get a working product or service to market at this stage, it's an immense help to getting funding. (Chapter 10 talks more about early stage funding.)

Whichever combination and amount you decide on, know that this is the first step of many on your business-funding journey. Do your best to keep your records up to date, your understanding of what finance is available current and your wits about you from here on in, because this will be one ride you'll never forget.

Understanding the Start-Up Stage

In the *start-up stage* you're beginning to reap the rewards of watering, feeding and nurturing your idea, and you can see the first green shoots coming through. If you prefer the life cycle analogy, your business is now a toddler and starting to walk, talk and get around.

You're generating revenue, albeit probably only a small amount, and you have some traction in your marketplace, with new customers coming on board all the time. If you've done your calculations properly, your profit margins are good, and you're on target for achieving your goals and milestones. Your systems are in place, your accounts are up to date – mostly – and although your time's a bit squeezed, you can see where your business is going.

You've made good use of the money you had in your seed round, but this surge in growth means that you now need some additional funding, and this time you need to be a bit more serious.

Funding start-up activities

Start-up stage activities that may need funding include:

- **Building the team:** As with any start-up organisation, a key, and sometimes significant, cost is that of recruiting, hiring and paying the core team members. The right team is essential to creating growth in your business and to attracting funding.

- **Developing minimum viable product:** Getting your idea to the point where a customer sees the unique value in your product or service and is happy to pay for it, developing your *minimum viable product* takes time and money and is an essential step in your start-up phase.

- **Marketing:** Marketing in your start-up phase takes many forms, and almost all of them cost money. Your website development, social media, direct promotion, online and offline marketing materials, events and collaborations all cost money and are essential in helping potential customers find your business.

- **Overheads:** Although you try to run a lean, mean start-up machine, you still have costs associated with your business overheads, such as rent, deposits, telecoms, travel, dues, subscriptions and so on. Although you have some control over these costs – you can pick and choose your suppliers – they still eat up some of your finances, and as such, need to be included in any funding calculation. At some point, around three to six months after you receive funding, your business needs to cover these costs from the money you make by selling your product or service.

- **Legal costs:** Protecting the intellectual property or registering the design rights of your product is critical to protecting the asset that earns your business income. You need professional legal help with this and you may also need help with employment contracts and supplier contracts, if you have these in the early phase of your business.

✔ **Technology:** Your business, be it technology-based, design-inspired, manufacturing a product or delivering a service, requires hardware in the form of laptops, possibly desktops and servers and smartphones. Depending on the type of business you have, you may also need sophisticated software, like Salesforce for managing your client information or Shopify for handling your integrated e-commerce data, which can represent a significant cost.

✔ **Capital expenses:** Depending on the type of business you have, you may need to purchase or lease expensive equipment, such as vans, kitchen equipment, hair salon materials and so forth. The costs of these high-value, long-term capital items can be very onerous when you're starting out. To minimise the amount of funding needed, always investigate the more cost-effective leasing options for equipment versus making outright purchases.

✔ **Qualifications, training and quality certificates:** Certain businesses, such as hair and beauty salons and personal training, require you to have professional qualifications before you open for business and to update and maintain these skills as you go on. Some other businesses, such as beauty and food products, for example, also ask you to have health-and-safety and product certifications at the start of your business. These qualifications and certifications vary in cost, but all come out of your funding before you generate a penny in revenue.

Most of these expenses continue as your business moves forward, changing in amounts and application to suit the needs of your growing business and developing products and teams.

The amount that each start-up business requires varies depending on the type of business and the projected pace of growth. If your business is *capital intensive,* meaning you have a cafe that needs ovens, tables and chairs, exhaust systems and so on, you clearly need more upfront funding than a hypnotherapist who works from home.

Predicting your funding needs

Contrary to popular opinion, forecasting your funding need is not a mystical, magical monetary tour, nor does it demand the finance skills of the Governor of The Bank of England, especially at the very start of your business. However, it does mean that you have to get to grips with an Excel spreadsheet and that you need to do some research into costs, potential income and so on.

You're not looking to fund the whole first year, unless your business has a very long lead time as part of its natural business cycle. The idea is to get enough money on board to allow you to launch your business and get it to the point where it starts to wash its own face. Generally, if it can't do that within three to six months, you have to ask yourself if you've really thought this through.

Bearing in mind that you're most likely to be using other peoples' money at this point, it should also be obvious that you need to deploy it well and make it work hard and smart.

Equally, you don't want to set the amount you need too low. I often see businesses that have been trading for a year or two experience severe cash-flow problems because they didn't start out with enough money to take them from the start-up to growth phase. They run the risk of having to close the business they worked so hard to set up due to a lack of cash.

It's human nature to not want to put yourself in stressful situations, which is how some people view investment or debt, but it is even more stressful to try to run a business on the thinnest of shoestrings, setting yourself up to fall at the first hurdle.

Good financial forecasting coupled with a heavy dose of realistic thinking helps you to estimate the most appropriate funding need for your business.

After you decide the amount of funding you need and how long you'll need it for, it's time to identify, understand, prepare for and approach potential funding sources.

Attracting funding sources

Sourcing additional funding at this start-up stage show you the increasing, and potentially confusing, array of funding options open to your business. You also get a sense of just how much of your time is required to find the necessary money – time that takes you away from running your fledgling business.

At this point, you may begin to look for advice and guidance to help you identify genuine finance options and avoid wasting too much time going down blind alleys. A mentor, which I talk about in Chapter 16, can come in handy.

Proving your concept and showing some growth means that you have many more options open to you with regard to funding:

✔ Your **bank** may be open now to providing you with a small overdraft, depending on your business cycle.

✔ You can take advantage of **invoice** or **export financing,** unlocking cash that's tied up in unpaid invoices. (I talk about these in Chapter 14.)

✔ You can **sell shares** in your business and offer early stage equity. An individual investor, a few investors, or a whole crowd of investors may be the answer for you. (Equity funding is covered in Chapter 13.)

✔ Catching the eye of a **venture capitalist,** someone who represents an investment fund and invests large amounts of money, may be an option if you have the next best thing since sliced bread. A very early-stage venture capital investor may see you as the next *unicorn,* a company that has a £1 billion valuation even before it starts trading, steaming ahead of your competition.

I talk about all these finance options in the chapters in Part III. Whatever funding you choose, remember that the preparation and completion always take much longer than you think they will and take more of your time than you think they will, and that sometimes you need a few attempts in the preparation stage to get the amount and the timing right.

Moving into Your Growth Phase

Having made it through the early years, your baby is now a young child; starting to get around on its own, knocking a few things over and sometimes leaving little messes in its wake. Typically, revenue and customers are increasing, profits are good, the team is expanding and you know your business model works. But it's not all smooth sailing, and the sharks, in the form of competitors in the market, are circling.

As it is for first-time parents, the growth phase of a business can be a testing time for management. You require a more formal approach to running the business and to making the almighty leap into delegating versus micro-managing. Systems and plans come under strain from your increased business activity and need to be shored up and continually reviewed to remain robust. This includes your financial plans and funding needs.

Whether you're considering human physical growth, emotional growth or business growth, all have one thing in common: The taller, stronger and more developed you become, the more money and resources you need to continue to grow. As your business grows, you need to be thinking ahead and trying to see where the likely funding gaps will arise. You also need to prepare the groundwork to raise appropriate funds so that you're not caught on the back foot and left scrambling around for finance.

Identifying your funding needs

One of the cruel ironies when it comes to growth is that the better you run your business and the more sales you make, the more cash you run out of. Growth is like a furnace that needs fuel to stoke the fires and keep them burning.

Some reasons you may need additional funding in your growth stage include:

- **Equipment and inventory:** If you have products, you may need to get more inventory; if you've got a van for deliveries and your business is growing, you may need another one and also some more people to drive it, take orders and so on.

- **Infrastructure:** Perhaps you need to upgrade your equipment in order to be more efficient. If growth means that your team has outgrown your space and you need to move to bigger, more prestigious premises that require a deposit upfront, perhaps one of the digital lenders can come to your rescue with a short-term loan. I discuss digital lenders in Chapter 14.

- **Accounts receivables:** If you have larger clients with bigger ticket invoices, you may need to make that invoice liquid. If an increasing number of customers who don't pay upfront is putting a strain on working capital, the solution may be as simple as an overdraft or an invoice factoring arrangement, which I discuss in Chapter 14.

- **International markets:** You may want to outsource some of your manufacturing to another country. Or you may want to expand your business to sell your product or service to foreign markets.

- **Personnel:** You may need to hire more people as your business becomes ever more successful.

- **Building the brand:** You may need to refresh or update your brand identity or further expand and exploit your brand recognition, both online and off; domestically as well as internationally.

In the fast-paced phase when your business is growing in leaps and bounds, identifying your funding need means taking a good look at where the gaps are emerging and what type of funding is needed to plug these gaps. You need to decide what needs are short term and which are longer, and the right funding instrument for each. Your financial forecasting can give you a steer in the right direction.

As tempting as it is to use one source of funding to address all your funding challenges, this is the first time that you'll really have to look at matching short-term needs with short-term finance, and longer term needs with its appropriate longer term finance. Learn this lesson early on and it will serve you well as your business continues to grow.

You may want to harness the power of the crowd to sell some shares of your hot artisan brewed-tea venture or use a tax-efficient incentive scheme to fund your growth and increase market share. Equally, you may decide that it's time to bask in the protective aura of a business angel. The choices you make have significant impact on your business. Whether it's debt, equity or alternative finance – or combinations of them all – you need to educate yourself as to what's available now and what it means for your future funding needs as well.

I explain the types of funding available in the chapters in Part III.

Coping with the financial pressure of growth

The irony of growth is that the more you grow, the bigger the strain on your finances. Growth is often one of the most dangerous times for your business with regard to holding on to enough cash. You need to do a few things at this stage to stay on top of this growing pressure so the lid doesn't blow:

- ✔ Update and check your forecasts versus actual figures.
- ✔ Monitor your payment times and terms closely.
- ✔ Think and plan a few steps ahead to avoid hitting icebergs.
- ✔ Keep your financial providers in the picture so that they aren't taken by surprise.

This is the time you're most likely to utilise a variety of debt products, from overdrafts to revolving cash facilities or peer-to-peer loans – perhaps you need the money to lease a shiny new machine or bigger business premises, for example.

As your infrastructure grows, you may be able to access government grants to upgrade your premises, make environmental improvements or pump up the Internet connection for your growing team. Some of these options are relatively quick and easy to source and arrange; others take more time, requiring leg work and comparison shopping. You may also need to provide proof that your growth is sustainable before you can get hold of government funds.

At this stage, your business is less fragile than it was before, and your systems and your approach to running it are more robust, too. Your business is also beginning to be more susceptible to changes in the economy, to new competitors entering your market, or to changing customer tastes, and so your hands will be full with just trying to run it well, let alone stopping to raise funds.

You may have a mentor or possibly a non-executive director on board; this may cost you even more money, but it will pay dividends if you've chosen wisely.

Go to as many events as you can to create useful financial networks, maximise online social media and business groups and fully exploit your mentors' connections. You want to have funding relationships, not one-night stands, and so you need to start early.

Focusing on Improvement: The Established Stage

At this stage, your business has matured and growth is on a solid, steady trajectory. Your growth falls just short of explosive, and your business is stable enough, but you wonder whether it's strong enough to withstand the increasing demand on all its systems. You have time to consider questions like this and to investigate some more serious growth finance options.

Your place in your market is secure, you have a loyal customer base and you could just sit back and put your feet up for a while and enjoy some steady, organic growth that provides a decent but not spectacular return for your early investors and a decent living for you and your team. On the other hand, if you have more ambitious growth goals and objectives, this is no time to rest on your laurels and pat yourself on the back.

This is no time to forget about the bigger picture and everything that's going on around you in the great, wide world. It mattered before, but external factors such as economic shifts, customer appetite for change and encroaching foreign competition really matter now, and so you need to stay alert. Assuming that you have ambitions to grow your business, you may require some additional, heavyweight finance to:

- Improve or upgrade your systems
- Take on and train more staff
- Expand to a second outlet or a franchise
- Step up the way you outsource your manufacturing
- Increase the level of exporting you do

You may still need some of the basic types of funding, such as loans, to tide you over while you wait for a big payment or complete your equity paperwork, and your overdraft may still be in place. Be aware that you may be able to refinance debt at a cheaper rate of interest or on better terms, perhaps making use of the government-backed enterprise finance scheme. It's a great time to explore your options because you have more to bring to the table and a bit more bargaining power. In a sense, your business is a young adult now and more mature in the eyes of funders.

You may be thinking about another round of equity finance if you've already had one, looking at your first round of funding from business angels or considering early stage venture capital if you haven't supped at this particular table yet. You can explore these options in more depth in Chapters 13 and 14.

You may also be looking at more exotic forms of debt finance, such as *asset finance* for large purchases, *mezzanine debt* if you need something between debt and equity, or *venture and convertible debt* if you want to delay parting with shares but need some money now.

Responding to the Signs of the Expansion Stage

At this stage your business – your baby – is now all grown up; it's an adult. You're poised for significant growth in new markets, possibly with new product development and distribution channels. Expansion may include making some acquisitions, opening offices abroad or taking on large numbers of employees to meet the demands of large contracts with some serious clients.

 You're at that point where you can see some pretty seismic shifts in your business – it's important that you keep your focus and don't wander off into what look like exciting new directions that can be a distraction and a drain on finances. It's also time to understand and accept that you may need some bigger funding guns in order to hit that next milestone, and that you may therefore need some equity. It's that moment where you know that having a smaller piece of a really amazing pie makes more sense than having a large piece of a not-so-tasty pie.

If your goal is to offer shares in your business on the open markets, you need to set up the final stretch of years of hard work and focus to make your proposition as attractive as possible to new investors, current investors, employees and the public. On the other hand, you may be considering ramping up your business with a joint venture or acquisitions, or by starting a franchise operation because your long-term goal is a trade sale and you want as much industry clout as possible.

Your funding options are also changing in this stage. They're expanding, and although some of this growth can be done using more exotic debt products (which I look at in Chapter 12), your equity options are stepping up a gear. You may be considering venture capital funding or even private equity, depending on how much funding and fresh expertise you need.

Planning funding requests

Researching, identifying and deciding what type of funding to go for always takes longer than you think, and you need to plan ahead as much as possible. Whatever your stage, and whether you're shouldering the total responsibility or being supported by advisors, other directors or mentors, it's still a long and winding road, and you need a full tank of petrol to motor your way to your final destination.

You need to keep one eye on the present and the other one on the future – you don't want to suddenly realise a month down the road that your business needs a funding fix because you probably won't get it. When I meet a business owner who says she needs money as soon as possible, I know I've met someone who wasn't looking and planning ahead, and is now like a swan – calm for all the world to see and treading water furiously below the waterline. Unless it's a couple of weeks until the year-end tax deadline, when an investor may have an incentive to off-load some funds – and even that's a stretch – you're not likely to get money in a hurry and when you need it. Funding is a process that ends in an event, not the other way around.

Responding quickly to negative cash flow

One of the tools you use to measure your business performance is your cash flow spreadsheet, which I talk about in Chapter 15. Cash flow figures are especially useful when raising funds, but they have a number of other uses that are equally valuable for you as your business grows. One of these uses is to act as a warning sign when you're heading for a negative cash position. In some instances, they give you an indication of some of the ways out of the impending hole.

When you're heading towards negative cash flow, you need to act and react quickly and to be aware of the types of funding available to you to pull your business back from the edge, and how best to utilise them for your specific situation.

Your business can get into a sticky cash flow situation for a number of reasons – some of them better than others with regard to your skills and judgement:

✓ **Overtrading:** Ironically, a precarious cash-flow situation can sometimes come from being very good at what you do. You can run out of cash if you're selling so much that you're unable to keep up with demand but need to keep making your goods or providing your service, even though you don't have enough money coming in at a quick enough pace to pay for growth.

The most obvious solution here is better sales planning and being realistic about what you can achieve with the resources you have. One of the outcomes of better planning is that you can forecast high demand and make arrangements to cover it ahead of time. You may need to look at upping your production or your number of team members if the demand is sustainable by borrowing or raising enough funds to cover these needs. Throwing short-term, usually expensive, money at a problem only makes the problem worse if it's something that ultimately needs to be rebalanced.

✓ **Declining sales:** For whatever reason – the general economy, competitors entering the market, changes in technology – if your business experiences even a small step down in sales volume, it can have a significant impact on your bottom line and on your working capital. If you've not done any what-if scenarios as to the impact various events can have on your business and made provisions for them, it may have devastating effects. Declining sales also highlight potential problems with your sales process or your business process that you need to address as swiftly as possible.

To help avoid being ill-prepared for the negative impact of declining sales, take pre-emptive steps by doing what's known as *sensitivity analyses* – creating hypothetical cash-flow forecasts to see the impact of dropping sales levels by 10 and 20 per cent, while maintaining the same level of fixed costs. You can then decide on some pre-emptive action plans and possibly some product or service diversification plans.

If drooping sales numbers are due to something beyond your control, such as the economic crash of 2008, you can do little more than have a cash reserve, diversify your product ranges to spread the risk and keep a very close eye on your cash flow movements so that you can react quickly.

✓ **Poor pricing:** If you're just not pricing correctly, you end up with more outgoing than incoming cash, and your business model and margins aren't correct. This is a fundamental problem, and the solution isn't to throw more money at it, but to go back to stage one and perform a bit of forensic analysis and some basic restructuring to regain control of your business.

✓ **Experiencing peaks and troughs:** In some industries business runs in cycles, and you experience peaks and troughs in your cash flows. It's just part and parcel of what you do. You can see this in the jewellery industry, where holiday gifting sees a spike in December, and marriage proposals turn into engagement rings in January. So the third quarter of the year sees a real strain on stock, and the last quarter and first quarter of the next year see cash coming in.

If peaks and troughs are part of the fibre of your business, you need to prepare ahead of time, especially in the early years of your business when you may not have a cash cushion. Secure overdrafts or cash facilities that you can draw down on when needed, but not pay for when they're not in use. Temporary needs call for temporary finance solutions, so keep your cash-flow forecasts updated and speak to the bank or other finance providers earlier rather than later to avoid panic. Also try to draw out your payment terms to suppliers for as long as possible, whilst getting money from customers as quickly as possible, in order to keep cash in the business.

✔ **Holding too much inventory:** If you make a product, you may get overly excited and ambitious when you order stock, or get a good price for bulk buying, bring a lot of stock in, and tie up too much cash in inventory sitting in your warehouse. Better planning and a closer eye on managing inventory levels can help avoid this situation.

✔ **Paying yourself generously:** Even though you feel as if all you do is work, be careful not to take too much money out of your business for yourself until the business can sustain it. Don't starve yourself, but also don't go wild and take more than the minimum you need until your business is on an even and predictable keel. Equally, check yourself when it comes to the suppliers you use, and always review your outgoings to make sure that you're not paying over the odds for essential goods and services or wasting money on non-essentials. If you determine that you need more money to breakeven (not making a profit or a loss), you can seek to raise that money in debt or equity to get you to the break-even point so that you're able to concentrate undistracted on the job in hand.

✔ **Carrying expensive debt:** When your business has debt, the assumption is that you can service the interest and principal repayments from the money in working capital. If you're paying too high a rate of interest or you're on very tight terms for your debt it can put a real strain on your cash flow, indicating that you're servicing debt that's beyond your means or that you have too much debt.

One solution is to look for better terms elsewhere and refinance your debt into a better solution. Government-backed loan schemes or peer-to-peer debt platforms may prove a better solution to your debt problems.

✔ **Spending too much on capital expenditure:** Spending too much of the wrong kind of money on capital expenditure can leave you cash poor. For example, heavy equipment – vehicles, machinery and so on – isn't a candidate for short-term funding need and shouldn't be funded out of working capital. Asset finance and lease finance products are better suited to a long-term funding need like equipment purchases.

✔ **Unbalanced debtor and creditor terms:** One very common reason for a problematic cash flow situation is not getting paid quickly enough by your customers or perhaps not taking enough money upfront, depending on your business model. Aim to enforce your payment terms so that you don't inadvertently wind up providing your clients with a free loan and putting a strain on your own cash position.

If you have larger invoice payments due to you from reputable clients, look at selling them on to a financier who can advance you the money and possibly collect the payment for you, like an invoice finance company. This improves your cash position and also takes some of the burden of chasing payment off your back.

In the same way that you may be getting paid too slowly, you may be paying your invoices too quickly and therefore have more money going out than coming in. Negotiate the best terms you can on your payments so that you always have more coming in than going out.

✔ **Funding gaps:** Even when you're successful in raising funds, there can be a delay in actually getting the money into your account, which can have an impact on your cash flow. Waiting for funds to come in or plugging a gap when you come up short in raising equity funds may mean you need a temporary solution while you wait for the funds to come in. For example, a *bridging loan,* or temporary finance to tide you over until your next round of agreed funding arrives in your bank account, can help ease a pressing situation.

Interest rates can be very high on short-term loans, and they come with additional fees attached, and so you need to make sure that you can afford to take them on.

Preparing for the Exit Stage

Don't let the door hit you on the way out, whether it's a lucrative exit or a less-than-profitable closing down sale. This is the lead up to the moment when, hopefully, all your hard work pays off and you're able to sell up and cash in on all the years of blood, sweat and tears. It's time for your fully grown and independent adult of a business to leave you with an empty nest and presumably a full bank account and to go on to its next adventure.

Exiting on your own

In reality, planning and preparing for your business exit starts years before the actual event. In most cases, it starts even before the business opens its doors, or at the very latest in the first couple of years, because you need to know your destination before you set out on the funding journey. Otherwise it's just aimless wandering, which may not give you or your investors the desired return.

Having a destination helps you to figure out the road map – to see where the road widens and narrows, where money is plentiful and where it's tight and what hazards and obstacles you can head off at the pass or plan for on the road ahead.

Having some idea of what your exit looks like drives you to hit certain goals and milestones, push for better margins, influence the speed of product development and put a rein on expanding too quickly. It helps you to decide what's worth measuring, including your financial performance. When you hit a fork in the road, your exit plan guides you to the right funding road for that moment and the times that follow, signposting you to explore different paths along the way. It also helps to ensure that both you and your shareholders get the return you hoped for, because the exit is the final destination in a journey that takes years to complete.

Contrary to popular opinion, this isn't a time of clear sailing and little effort on your part. A number of challenges and decisions may keep you awake at night because you want to make sure you're happy with the end result. Plus, depending on how you choose to exit, you may be sticking around for another year or two, which means that you'll be living with the consequences of your decisions in a very real way.

Sometimes, the stage preceding a business exit is when a private equity firm gets on board, bringing in cash and considerable expertise and reach in order to really take your business to another level. Often the equity firm may take your business to a global level in order to maximise the share value on sale or public listing, depending on what your aim is.

The sums involved here are usually in the tens of millions upwards, and you recognise that you're going to have to give up a reasonable amount of control if they're going to be able to ready your business for sale. They'll tighten up your operations, stretch your management's abilities, or even replace some of the management team if they're not up to scratch. A private equity firm makes sure that you're crossing the t's and dotting the i's when it comes to compliance, corporate governance and company law. You need to do a bit of work to get your business over this last big hurdle, so don't pull out the pipe and slippers just yet.

You won't be doing this all on your own, and as it was in the very early stages of your business, now is the time to start interviewing professional advisors like accountants and lawyers in order to get this stage right. They'll help you sort out the tax implications, the documentation and also work with you to get your final valuation right.

Checklist for exiting your business

Exiting your business is mostly in the timing. Try to time your exit for the moment that your profits are on the up and you can prove that this growth will continue. If your business is cyclical, try to time your exit during a peak time and avoid the trough. Go out on a high!

Other tips include:

✔ Make sure that you have a strong management team in place. Keep in mind that this may not be the same team that was with you at the start of your business. The skills of the founding team members may not be strong enough to guide the business as it grows, so make sure you have a team in place that can take the business to its highest success levels.

✔ Make sure that all your registrations, patents, compliance certificates, updates and accreditations are up to date.

✔ Ensure that all your commercial and employee contracts are agreed and up to date.

✔ Enlist the aid of professional advisors for tax, legal and valuation discussions.

✔ Check that you understand the tax implications, both business and personal, of a sale.

✔ Update and audit your accounts.

✔ Budget for all the fees and costs you'll encounter along the way.

Most importantly, keep it real. Don't let your ego or your pride get in the way of a good exit.

Creating an opportunity to cash in

Although the popular media may give you the impression that a trade sale or a public listing on a stock exchange are the most obvious ways to cash in your chips and sail off into the sunset, you have other options and opportunities to exit your business. And, sorry to disappoint, but a number of exit strategies require that you hang around for a while, because your rewards are tied into making the transition a success.

 Although a trade sale is the most likely exit for many small- and medium-sized business (SME) founders, the following list shows a number of ways to create a more liquid cash position at this stage. Seek advice on the best alternatives and the optimal timing for you and your business to cash in.

Among your exit options are:

✔ **Trade sale:** Being sold to a trade buyer, who you probably know as a bigger player in your industry, is often an exit of choice. You negotiate the price and agree the terms, and hopefully get the fit right, and so what you worked so hard for can continue to grow instead of being run into the ground.

It may be a logical fit, but it may not be plain sailing and you may have to stick around for a year or two afterwards to ensure a smooth transition. This is harder than it sounds, and it can get quite emotional because you need to let go of the reins.

✔ **Merger:** Merging with another business that creates a new super business or a new market for a complementary business is another option. You receive a payment for merging what you bring into the creation of a brand new entity.

You may not be asked to stay on in the same role or capacity – as two companies become one, some people inevitably go. Too many cooks spoil the broth, if you see what I mean.

✔ **Joint venture:** If you see a potential partner who can leverage her ability to open up new markets, save you both loads of money in product development or research or take something that's been a bit of a sideline for your business and develop it into a moneymaker, you may consider an alliance of sorts in the form of a joint venture. It's a bit tricky because one of you is inevitably in the top position, but it can provide you with some cash and perhaps a gateway to a full exit later on.

✔ **Sale to family:** This is especially useful if you run a family business and want to ensure that the succession is smooth. You may be more amenable to staged payments in this arrangement, which can have an impact on what you take away at the time of sale.

A family transfer can be fraught with emotion, as you can choose your friends, but not your family!

✔ **Management buy-in:** An external management team buys into a business that they don't work at. This type of transition can be great, but can also cause some friction with your current employees and senior team, as it's likely that some of the fat will be trimmed by the new owners, and a few heads will bang over differences of opinion.

✔ **Management buyout:** In this scenario, your current managers think that they can do it better than you, and they buy you out. The new owners may use a combination of debt and equity to make the purchase, and so there may be a slight delay in receiving all your money while they wait for the equity to come in. If external funding is involved, be ready to bargain hard.

✔ **Initial public offering (IPO):** Offering your shares to the public is a very costly, time-consuming option, and puts your company under the microscope of regulated affairs. It's not all glitz and glamour.

Bleeding the company dry is an exit strategy I do not recommend!

You can find more information on all these exit options in Chapter 17.

Chapter 3

Preparing the Groundwork for Raising Funds

*O*ne of the most often quoted warnings when starting out or shifting up a gear in business is the familiar phrase by the scholar, statesman and inventor Benjamin Franklin: 'By failing to prepare, you are preparing to fail'.

Nowhere does this ring more true than in the need to prepare the groundwork for funding before you thrust your business – and yourself – out onto the open market, exposed and vulnerable. It's up to you give yourself the best chance of fundraising success – to put in the hours preparing the documentation, yourself and your team before you make the first call or send the first email to potential funders.

Investors and lenders want to know that your business is built on solid foundations, that you know how to scale and grow and that their money is in safe hands.

When you're looking for funding, you need to consider many aspects of your business. Your business plan, which I talk about in Chapter 5, is one. In this chapter, I look at the plan and how your strategies are manifested in a clear, concise and cohesive business planning document in more detail.

Consider this logic:

- ✔ A **business model** defines where you want to and need to take your business.

- ✔ A **value proposition** illustrates your understanding of your customers' needs and how your unique business offering provides a solution to their problems.

- ✔ A **business plan** outlines the steps to get you where your model wants to take you, incorporating the essence of your value proposition every step of the way.

Maintain the link between your business model, your value proposition and the practical steps that connect them when you're preparing to approach funders. Very often entrepreneurs are so focused on the actual fundraise that there's a disconnect between their business model and the overall strategic aims behind the actions in their business plans. You don't want your strategy to come across as no more than a fuzzy afterthought, or something you've dusted off and freshened up from an old document, hoping it passes for a cohesive and aligned strategy.

Setting Out a Clear Value Proposition

As you prepare to go forward for funding, you need to ensure you have a strong business model that will yield a good return while minimising risks, a clear _value proposition_ that shows how the unique selling points of your product or service will attract customers and a business plan that sets out your strategy and the timetable of actions you'll take that will convince a funder that you've done your homework.

Your business plan identifies your customers in segments and explains how you plan to bring your product or service to market. It also illustrates the things that set you apart from your competitors and shows that there's room for you in the market.

You also need to reassure funders that you have or can get a team with the necessary experience and skills required to deliver the actions in your plan.

In the following sections, I lay out some of the key aspects of preparing for funding. In Part II, I cover some of the documents and practical considerations you need to get started.

Sharing your business model

Inherent in any preparation for meeting funders and for any discussion about your company's value proposition is the way you bring your proposition to market – in other words, your *business model*. How do you create a product or a service your customers want, find a way to get it to them, add that extra value and make sure that you get paid? That last bit about making sure that you get paid is particularly important to funders, as they want to get paid, too.

Equally important, funders want to know that you've thought it through and come up with the best way to embody your vision, with all your unique value adds, in an easily understood and executable way. They want to be sure that you recognise that you don't have unlimited resources, and that you know that to be successful, you have to get your product or service to market. Now, that's something a funder can get excited about.

How you actually bring this model to life may take a variety of forms:

- ✔ Sell directly to your end consumer.
- ✔ License someone else to sell it on your behalf and just take a bit on each sale.
- ✔ Buddy up with someone in a joint venture or other co-working arrangement.
- ✔ Sell your idea to someone else for a nice price and let him deal with getting it to market.

Some of these methods bring you riches sooner; some take much longer; some involve a lot of your time; others give you more time to develop the business further; some minimise your risk and exposure by spreading the load; others put heavy demands on your negotiating and selling skills in order to get what you deserve; some require a significant injection of cash to get going; others only need a seed from which to grow. The one common theme is that you need money to implement any of them.

Whatever you decide to do, be very clear what your business model is and how it works before you step in front of funders. If you aren't clear on this point, you lose all credibility and interest.

After you decide which model is best for you, you need to look at the resources, relationships, distribution channels, customer segmentation, costs to achieve your model, resulting revenue streams, and of course, what the value proposition looks like. I look at some of these topics in Chapter 5, and another good source is *Starting Your Business For Dummies* by Colin Barrow (Wiley).

Defining and expressing your value proposition

Much has been written on value proposition – what it is, how to write one, why you need one and so on. The term is generally credited to a 1988 research paper by Michael Lanning and Edward Michaels. The authors define *value proposition* as 'a clear, simple statement of the benefits, both tangible and intangible, that the company will provide, along with the approximate price it will charge each customer segment for those benefits'. Simple enough, but when you start to think about it, not always so simple to articulate and explain.

Your value proposition is a clear expression of what's unique about the way your business adds value to the customer journey, so much so that your customers make the cost of your product or service a secondary consideration.

Your value proposition should leave no doubt as to why customers want your product or service. This opinion should be formed, in part, by what they've told you that they want from your business.

Avoid making your value proposition sound phoney and paying lip service to what you think funders want to hear. It needs to have genuine meaning for you and your business and communicate why you're in the business you're in. It should figure highly in your push for sales.

A value proposition can be particularly useful if it's harder to communicate the benefits or value added from your business, like it might be in the IT industry, so writing it can do you a very big favour.

If you're in the start-up phase of your business, you've done some customer research and possibly carried out focus groups, surveys and interviews to get customer input. If you're further along you can incorporate the lessons you've learned over time.

Your value proposition may not be something you've deeply explored or tested so far on your business journey. You may not have considered customer segmentation needs in depth or given any real thought to addressing these needs in a meaningful way. Preparing to seek funding is a great opportunity to right this commercial wrong.

Your company value proposition needs to be precise about the benefits for your customers. Be sure to include what you charge relative to your competition, and make it simple enough for you to remember without too much thinking, or else it'll feel false.

Because your company's value proposition may not be as obvious as the nose on your face, here are a few thoughts to ponder to help you focus your mind and make a start on formulating it:

✔ Think about what you want your company to stand for and what you want it to be known for. How do you define your company vision?

✔ Ask whether what you stand for is enough for your clients to choose you over your competitors or whether you need to add extra value.

✔ All your customers or clients are important to you, but determine which ones are the most valuable to your business, and what it is about them that makes you say that.

✔ Every business likes to think that it offers a value-added service or product, but apart from shouting that from the mountain tops, how do you actually measure the value that you add to a customer transaction?

✔ How do you get your product or service out to your customers? How do they easily access this terrific offering that so perfectly meets their needs?

These interrelated questions can be seen as tools working to produce a value proposition that paves the way for sustainable sales growth. They also highlight the need to take into account all the people involved in the way your offering gets to market. If you use subcontractors or sell through a distributor, your value proposition needs to reflect their importance in the chain. In turn, this helps to ensure that you get goodwill from them as they sell the product on.

Bringing in Marketing and Sales

Funders are keen to see your sales forecasts because income from sales is an important part of making sure they get a return on their investment. They're also keen to see that you have a very good understanding of your market place, its size, its peaks and troughs, customer segments and behaviours and how you plan to attract customers to spend money with your business. They want to see how you stack up against your competition, and where you excel. They look for any gaps that need filling, threats to your position in the market, and opportunities that will benefit your business and their interests. Funders want to see what's so unique about your solution to a customer problem that the cost of your product or service is a secondary consideration for customers when choosing whom to spend their money with.

Funders want to see that you have a clear plan for how to create your product or service, make sure it's easy for customers to access and pay for and that your plans and procedures are robust. Funders also want to know that you've gathered enough information on how your customers feel about your product or services, whether that's at your very early testing stage or after you release your offering on to the market, and that you've gathered this feedback with a minimal amount of money and risk.

Expressing your unique value add

Defining your value proposition is always a good lens from which to view your company USP (that is, its unique selling point or points). Remember, your value proposition is what makes the customer consider you first and the cost of your offering second. If your funders can see that you've achieved that, they can see why they should invest in your product or service.

Be very clear about what unique features and benefits make your company value proposition so good. They need to be easy to grasp and understand, as you want to stop customers in their tracks and make them realise that they want what you're offering. Your USPs have to differentiate you in the marketplace; after all, what's unique about offering the same thing your customers can get elsewhere? Don't forget to base your USPs on what your customers want – there's no point in shouting about your unique product if no one's interested in it!

While formulating your value proposition, consider every aspect of your business and identify – or include – the value-adds at every stage of getting your product to your customer. Identify your USPs and how your solution uniquely addresses a client's pain point. By doing these things, you can be precise about how your customer benefits and why that's good for your funders.

Investors want to know if your USP is genuine, and not just something that sounds good but has no substance. Whether it's your concept, prototype or test product or your minimum viable product, something that you've started testing in the market with little risk, each stage sees investors looking for the unique aspects of your business that make a customer spend money with you.

Demonstrating that You Have a Minimum Viable Product

Every great product or service starts with an idea – a light-bulb moment. Wherever you have your Eureka moment and whatever it is, it's a raw idea, and you can't go to market with a virtual product idea. However, you can go with a minimum viable product and get customers to tell you what they think. A *minimum viable product (MVP)* is the version of your product that you can release on the market in order to gather information about your clients or customers with the least amount of financial or reputational risk.

Getting a working prototype in the market

An investor wants to see an MVP that can bring the highest return on his investment risk. This doesn't mean that you guarantee that every member of your family will buy it. It means that you've bargained with suppliers, got your best price on raw materials, resisted competitors' threats in the market and sold your product or service to a genuine, bona fide, hopefully repeat purchase customer who's prepared to pay top dollar.

Generating sales already

When you're preparing the groundwork for raising funds, you're preparing your business to be attractive to funders, and one of the sure-fire ways to do this is to be able to show what's known in the trade as *traction* in that you're able to gather evidence in enough quantity to show that you've got market demand.

If you've already taken your MVP to market and have repeat customers generating sales and bringing in revenue that looks like it'll be sustainable and repeatable, you're ahead of the game. You've proven that your idea works and your passion is justified in the most time-honoured business way possible – someone's paid you money for it. This outcome is a great indicator to the market, to funders and to yourself that you're on to something. It shows that with a bit of money you can replicate and expand upon your success and create a win-win situation for you and your investors.

Actual sales is the best proof of viability that you can have, so don't underplay it. It also gives you access to a great resource: customer feedback! Make sure that you tap that resource and listen to what your customers want from you.

Once your value proposition, unique selling points and a viable product are clear, you need to assure investors that you've identified the best route to market and that you understand the needs of your customers and how to sell to them in convincing detail. Actual sales are the best evidence of this assurance, but if you don't have sales yet, then your research and your evidence that you've listened to your customers when designing your products or services needs to be strong.

Including your customers

As an entrepreneur, customer feedback is the most valuable data you can gather, but only if you collect it consistently and use it correctly. In order to gather, collate and interpret this prized data in a measurable and useful way, you need to identify the component parts of your customer profile so that you can incorporate your findings into meaningful customer interactions. After all, your customers usually have more than one point of contact with your business, even if one of them is just looking at your website.

After your customers tell you what they want, tell them that you're listening, and then deliver on what they asked for. This shows that you're responsive and also lays the foundations for more valuable feedback from your customers in future. Potential funders want to see that you've listened to your market and not made important decisions in isolation.

Consider the following to help you think of how you can identify and include your customers in your decision-making process:

- **Target market:** What is your precise customer base? You can't be all things to all people; you need to focus.

- **Characteristics:** What is unique about your preferred customers? What are their buying behaviours and what do they respond to? Are they price or time sensitive?

- **Lifestyle:** What do your customers earn? Where do they live? Are they globetrotters or homebodies? Are they aspirational or have they already arrived?

- **Segmentation:** Can you break down your customer base into sub-categories so that you can target your segments, thus increasing your chances for successful sales?

Outlining your route to market

It's a wonderful thing to create a fantastic product or service that meets an identified need, and have a team that can deliver it, but if you can't get your product or service to the end-user, there really isn't much point. Knowing your customers and why they buy is one thing. Finding the best and most profitable route to them is another thing.

Perhaps some of the funding you're asking for is to take your product or service to market, so you'd better outline that route to market for a potential funder, for yourself and for your team.

Your route to market can be long or short and may be complicated or complex, leading from the brilliant idea in your head to a real spot in the marketplace, but at each step in the road, your insubstantial idea becomes more tangible and solid.

Missing out some of the steps on your route may mean compromising the integrity of your offering, so start at the beginning and build that road as you go.

Make sure that you can justify the choices you've made with regard to how and where you make or create your product or service: are the costs reasonable or can you improve on margins; is your idea or process – your *intellectual property* – protected; are you controlling all the logistical and delivery problems that you can control; what have you done to minimise any risk factors that you can't control? Think about how your money will flow – delivery and payment cycles – and how reliable they are.

Be able to show how your customers can reach you in the marketplace. Perhaps you can utilise existing channels for distribution or perhaps you need a platform of your own. Do you plan to target direct sales? How big do you expect them to be? How will direct clients pay? What are your plans for targeting the big spenders in your field? Do you prefer to pick the low-hanging fruit, achieving less return but at a lower cost and with less risk? Is it worth considering a licensing arrangement, rather than taking your product or service to market independently?

Once you're available in the marketplace, how will you build market share? Consider costs for marketing, public relations (PR) and advertising. How will you fulfil all these needs? With employees, or partner organisations or a mix of the two? How much will that cost?

Thinking about every facet of what you're offering, and making sure that you know the answers to all the relevant questions, is how you determine your route to market.

Sizing Up Your Market

A very important part of the groundwork for approaching funders is your knowledge and awareness of your market size, characteristics, dynamics, metrics, opportunities and players. This is, after all, the stage on which your business will play its greatest role. Your customers are your paying audience and they want to be wowed by your performance. Your critics come from all corners and are just waiting for you to trip up and forget your lines. Your MVP is your opening act, and you're looking for backers to give your show a long run. You need to know and be able to size up your market and your role within it.

You need to be able to see your market opportunity, be fully conversant in its size, history, quirks and idiosyncrasies, how it measures its success and where you fit before and after you approach a funder. You also need to be able to convince someone that the market has sufficient potential for you to sell enough products and services to live up to your forecasts in both revenue and profit and that you see additional growth potential to give investors a meaningful scale and an exceptional return on their money.

Whether a potential funder is familiar with your market or not, he wants to know that you have a rigorous understanding of the market you're trying to penetrate. Questions about your market are absolutely key for an investor to identify whether you can deliver what he needs, so expect to be asked everything about your intentions. Some questions you may be asked include:

- ✔ What is the size of the market that you can address? You don't want to throw out a number that represents a global population so large that you can't possibly reach them all.

- ✔ What percentage of the market do you plan to attract and over what period of time? Are you really going for 75 per cent of a market or the 25 per cent that's being overlooked or underserved?

- ✔ How did you arrive at the sales figures for your industry and its growth rate?

- ✔ Are you already running trials that prove your product solves a problem?

- ✔ How do you plan to scale your business?

- ✔ Why does your company have high growth potential?

Being vague or evasive in answering these questions can send potential investors running a mile. Having a 360-degree understanding of your market comes down to knowing your customer and knowing your competition.

Identifying customers

Before you can actually go to market, you need to understand who your customers are and how you're going to reach them. Knowing them doesn't just mean being able to point at them in the marketplace; it means understanding what's important to them, and so being able to predict their behaviour to some extent. Doing this job well is the most important safeguard of the funds you spend on marketing your product or service. (*Marketing For Dummies* by Alexander Hiam, published by Wiley, can help with understanding customers.)

Try walking in your customers' shoes to understand their characteristics, their hobbies, their needs, their concerns and how much they're willing to pay to address these. Then get back in your own shoes and think about where your customers live, both literally and metaphorically, and how you can make sure that they see you in these places.

When you're breaking down your customer profile, approach it in a way that's relevant to your sector and business. Remember that your goal is to focus your attention on the customer segment, behaviour and feedback that's most valuable to your enterprise. Being able to target your customers precisely is a great first step in marketing, and reaps rewards for both you and your funders.

When you've identified your most likely customers, you may discover that they're also aware of companies offering a similar solution to their problem, albeit not as unique as yours. Funders need to be reassured that there's room for you alongside these other rivals in your marketplace, or that you've identified ways in which to displace your rivals.

Recognising your competition

You've done all the prep work and managed to get an appointment with a lender or an investor. They like what they've seen so far, and it's all going very well. You get to that point in the discussion where you're talking about the market, your place in it, your USP, your competition, and you utter those four words that tell the audience that you've either not done enough research or you have an artificially inflated opinion of yourself and your business: 'We have no competition'. Boom! You just threw all your hard work into jeopardy.

Be smart, heed the warning and don't let that happen to you. Acknowledge that you have some competition and demonstrate that you know your enemy. Make it clear that you're diligent and thinking several steps ahead.

Maybe you really have struck upon an idea that's not yet in the marketplace – rare though those are. If it's a good idea, someone is likely to at least be starting to work on it. Be sure you start thinking about who that may be.

When you're preparing to meet funders, be able to identify who's in a position to launch something similar or who has a ready-made customer database to access. Have clear ideas on how you can protect your business against this threat. More likely, you have some clear competitors fulfilling the same need that you want to address. Be clear-sighted and realistic about who they are; research what they have in their favour; think about what advantages you have over them, or the ways that you're meaningfully different and whether that is a virtue in your favour. Glossing over the details won't fool your potential funders, and it won't impress them either.

Checking out the competition

In a similar way to how you work to understand your customer, you also need to be able identify and understand your competitors. Your competitors may be *direct* and doing a version of the same thing you're doing, or *indirect* and offering an alternative way to spend the same money. Either way, you'd best find out all you can about them.

I'm not saying that you need to sit and worry about your competitors, but you need to know where they're stronger than you and what weaknesses they have that you can turn to your advantage. Funders will be thinking about and asking the same things.

Even if, by some miracle, you're in the truly rare position of having a product or a service that no one has hit upon yet, potential investors and lenders will be scratching their heads and thinking about who may be sniffing around the edges or getting close to being a viable threat.

Assess what competitors offer

Researching your competitors is easier than it may seem. For example, you can simply collect any flyers and price lists they produce for customers, read their online material and even buy their products and services to compare them with your own. You can talk to suppliers you both use, attend industry events and network or subscribe to and read trade journals. If you meet a prospect who's working with one of your competitors, that's a fantastic opportunity to get some direct customer feedback with regard to what you're up against.

Analyse what they do better than you

Once you know who your competitors are, you need to know how they operate and why that makes them your competition:

- Are they *low margin high volume,* so they make less profit on each sale and have to sell large numbers of products? If your business has a higher margin on each product and sells fewer items, then you'll probably minimise the competition by selling to different ends of the market.

- Are they too niche to impact you significantly or are they agile and able to pivot into your area? Sometimes being focused on a narrow product or service area limits a competitor's ability to respond quickly to changes in the marketplace, meaning it isn't able to effortlessly expand into other customer segments.

- Are their products of a higher quality? If they offer better products, can you upgrade yours or can you make up for the lesser quality by providing better customers service or more competitive pricing?

- Is their customer service more efficient?

- Is there a potential chink in their armour that you can capitalise on? If you spot an area of weakness in your competition, like a long-winded ordering process on an e-commerce site, then use this knowledge to make your site simple, efficient and a pleasurable experience, and you may capture some of their market share.

Being critical of your own business and taking inspiration from your competitors can help you be more competitive.

Do a SWOT analysis

Although SWOT sounds like something you should use to shoo away pesky irritants, taking a swipe at your competitors is not a good idea – however satisfying it may feel in certain situations!

On the other hand, doing a *SWOT analysis* (looking at Strengths, Weaknesses, Opportunities and Threats) is very useful when it comes to looking at what you do well, and not so well, in relation to your competitors. You can use this data to increase your competitive advantage.

When creating your SWOT analysis, apply the exact same process you use to create your value proposition for your competitors. (Refer to the section 'Setting Out a Clear Value Proposition' earlier in this chapter.) You develop your value proposition design as a way of exploring opportunities and threats for your business.

Not requiring any special skills to create and readily understood by the funding community at large, a SWOT analysis is a great way to succinctly pull together all the competitor intelligence you gather and see how it matches up against you and your business. You can use a number of formats to compare data – a chart, spreadsheet, matrix or any way that you're most comfortable looking at information – that can help you formulate a competitive strategy.

Table 3-1 shows an example of a completed SWOT for an educational technology business. It illustrates the type of content funders expect to see. You're looking at the strengths and weaknesses of not only your own business but those of your competitors; highlighting the threat competitors may pose and areas where you see opportunities to outdo them.

Table 3-1	A Sample SWOT Analysis			
	Strengths	*Weaknesses*	*Your Opportunities*	*Threats Posed to You by Competitors*
You	Team of teachers and experienced technical people Patented technology Low-cost development Key English hubs engaged and Department for Education supports us Building a great teaching resource source	Lack of funds Relatively unknown in the marketplace Team is at full capacity Schools are on very tight budgets that are vulnerable to cuts Lead times to sales are very long impacting income	To raise funds To hire more people To offer a freemium model and sell add-ons To maximise the commercial opportunity of the data we collect To expand into other subject areas To create an app to go with our desktop product	New entrants to market will catch up with our technology We run out of money before we can get to income generation We lose staff to employers who pay more

(continued)

Table 3-1 *(continued)*

	Strengths	*Weaknesses*	*Your Opportunities*	*Threats Posed to You by Competitors*
Your Competitor	Established player in the market Well-funded Experienced team of people Already a global player	Not as agile due to size Limited to one subject area Locked into long-term, low paying contracts due to legacy agreements		

A *freemium* is the offer of a no-cost product or service tied to a full version that the freemium recipient is encouraged to buy.

Using your market data to enhance your proposition

No doubt you can find copious amounts of data published on your market, as well as the data you gather and analyse directly from clients, prospects, suppliers and so on. It's great having all this information at your fingertips, but it's valuable only if you can use it to enhance your proposition and your market penetration, and then communicate that to your potential funders.

Everyone talks about the value of data – big data, targeted data, primary data gathered directly and secondary data from published sources – and you can spend a lot of time trawling through oceans of data that may never be of use to you. You need to understand your audience(s) and create customer segments when you're analysing and acting on market data and insights, and be able to illustrate this in your value proposition.

You want to get to grips with what triggers a positive response in your customers and how you can get that message out on every channel – both online and offline – that you use to get in touch with them. Use the data to reinforce your marketing strategy and justify some of your assumptions regarding the potential size of your market, your penetration, the cost of getting and retaining a new customer and what that means for your bottom line.

Explaining Barriers and Intellectual Property

Funders appreciate your enthusiasm and sometimes evangelical belief in what your business can achieve, but they know that every business has barriers and obstacles to overcome in order to gain a foothold in a market.

It's important that you explain any factors that need to be considered and overcome in order to enter your market, be they legal, financial, linguistic or other. Funders want to know what you've done to ensure that your products or services have been cleared by the proper authorities, if this applies to your business, and that you have the documentation to prove this. If you have intellectual property (IP), be able to show that it's protected from competitors or would-be competitors trying to copy it.

This preparation doesn't present insurmountable obstacles, but it has varying levels of cost associated with it, and it needs to be done in a timely manner, so don't delay these practicalities.

Barriers to entry

Barriers to entry come in a variety of shapes and sizes, and they exist in all business sectors. A *barrier to entry* is essentially any factor that makes it difficult or prevents a company from entering a market.

These barriers can be technical, distribution-related, geographical, property-driven, financial, legal or competitive. Their very existence serves to make a market less competitive, because they make it harder for new businesses to enter and grab a share of the market, which is definitely a hurdle for your business if you need to overcome barriers in order to raise finance.

If you want to be the next big widget manufacturer, you need to raise a few million to buy and equip your widget factory, patent the new thread system on your widget and find a way to deliver widgets that eliminates the need to drive through a treacherous mountain pass in the middle of winter – in other words, overcome a few barriers to entry.

An important part of researching and truly understanding your industry before asking for funding is knowing how far and wide these barriers stretch so that you know what makes it harder for you, and your competition, to enter the market. If you're looking to raise funds to open a chain of nail bars, the barriers to entry are pretty high due to the need for prime real estate and qualified, reliable staff. If you're looking to raise money to start a mobile manicure business, the barriers to entry are pretty low because you need qualified staff, insurance, some tools of the trade and a good social media plan in order to get a foothold in the marketplace, but you don't need to find the money for expensive real estate, furniture and fittings. From a funding point of view, it's two different appetites for risk.

The lowest point of a barrier to entry gives you, and a funder, a good idea of how long it will take and how easy it will be for additional competitors to enter your market and take potentially valuable market share and revenue.

Consider your competitors when preparing the groundwork regarding barriers to entry. If there's a large, dominant player in your market, and it's beyond your risk appetite to be the David who challenges and slays this Goliath, you can still look to nip at its heels by developing a niche business in the same sector. Buying a language book from a well-known online retailer may be cheaper, but it isn't the same as going to a cosy, friendly foreign-language bookshop, sampling some of the food from that country and taking part in a weekly informal language exchange with real live people. Bigger is not always necessarily better.

Researching and exploring entry barriers in your chosen marketplace can save you a great deal of time and money, and sends a signal to a potential funder that you've thought it through and aren't acting in ill-informed haste.

Outlining regulatory, technical and language barriers

Barriers to entry come in a variety of shapes and sizes, but the main three relate to regulations, technical capability and language or communication hurdles:

- ✔ **Regulatory:** These barriers can come about as a result of legislation, government intervention, or legislation and guidelines. If you already have a foothold in a market and are compliant with the current regulations for your industry, you're in a good place, but be careful not to become complacent. Keep your ear to the ground, think ahead and make sure you touch on this point when preparing and presenting to funders.

- ✔ **Technical:** Some naturally occurring barriers, such as a process or a product that's beyond your technical reach or is already patented by a competitor, can prevent you from competing on a level playing field. You may be approaching funders with a view to their investment helping to overcome this barrier, and they may even have the talent or resources in their own stable that can help overcome this hurdle.

✔ **Language:** If launching or running a business on your home turf is a challenge, dealing with language and cultural barriers in another country exaggerates the struggles and strains of clear communication with customers, suppliers, officials and staff. To put a funder's mind at ease, demonstrate how you've worked to overcome this barrier by using translators, interpreters, visual communications and so on. A slip of the tongue in the wrong direction can prove very costly for you and your funders, so be sure to let them know that you're on top of it.

Protecting your idea and maintaining confidentiality

Confidential information can be one of the most valuable assets in your business, so it's important that you can show funders how you protect not only your own information but that of your customers and employees. You have a business case for this, but also a legal and ethical argument as well.

Requiring non-disclosure agreements (NDAs)

Most of the time, you and the potential funders aren't known to each other before you start the funding process, and you may be understandably reluctant to share your information without some form of assurance that it won't be made public or fall into the wrong hands – the hands of your competitors, for example. The funding process can be lengthy, and you'll be sharing sensitive information over a period of time, so to help alleviate some of your fear, you can ask anyone reading the plan to sign an NDA (non-disclosure agreement) or a letter of confidentiality to ensure that your information is treated as strictly confidential and that it's only used for the purposes of investigating and determining your business-investment readiness and suitability.

Requiring confidentiality shows investors that you're aware of the value and also the threat of proprietary information falling into the wrong hands and that you're minimising that risk.

Two of the most common NDAs are:

✔ A **one-way non-disclosure agreement** is used when you want somebody to agree that the information or documents that you share with him will be kept confidential.

✔ A **mutual NDA** is used when the person you're sharing information with is also sharing information with you that he wants to be treated as confidential.

You can find a guide to NDAs at www.gov.uk/government/publications/ non-disclosure-agreements. You can find some NDAs online for free; some websites charge a minimal fee. For an annual fee of £99.00 at the time of writing, LawBite at www.lawbite.co.uk allows unlimited downloads.

Meeting regulations (such as the Data Protection Act 1998)

The general public's awareness of protecting personal data and how their data is used and stored has been heightened due to the rise in online transacting and data breaches.

Businesses that collect and use customer data on a daily basis are subject to the Data Protection Act 1998, which protects and safeguards the way in which personal data is used by organisations, businesses and governments.

Everyone responsible for using data has to follow strict rules called *data protection principles* to make sure that personal information is:

- Used fairly and lawfully
- Used for limited, specifically stated purposes
- Used in a way that is adequate, relevant and not excessive
- Accurate
- Kept for no longer than is absolutely necessary
- Handled according to people's data protection rights
- Kept safe and secure
- Not transferred outside the UK without adequate protection

You can find out more about the Data Protection Act and your business at www.gov.uk/data-protection/the-data-protection-act.

Protecting your intellectual property

Intellectual property, or IP, is the ownership of ideas and concepts rather than things you can touch, see or feel. The success or failure of some businesses hangs on whether or not their IP is protected. If you have one of these businesses, you'd best protect this precious asset before approaching funders or anyone in the public domain.

Whether you've developed a new payment technology or a new fashion fabric, it's vital to protect your IP as it's a golden ticket in the lottery of funding. For many companies, their IP is a key to their success, and it's certainly something that eagle-eyed investors pay very close attention to.

The following lists generally accepted methods for protecting IP:

- ✔ **Patent:** In a nutshell, a patent protects processes, methods and inventions that serve a real use and illustrate a real advance that no one has made before or that hasn't been seen as existing in this form in the market before.

  In applying for a patent, an inventor agrees to make public details of his invention so that the patent office can decide if it's a real advance and grant a patent that gives the patent holder a 20-year monopoly on selling, using or making an invention.

  The application process is long – over two years – and it's complicated, complex and costly (searches at different levels range from £500 to £1,500 plus application fees). Inventors often use patent agents, lawyers or other professionals.

  Don't disclose your idea without protecting its confidentiality. Sharing your invention may be viewed as publishing it, which makes it not new. Make sure that you know your timing and submit your application before you speak to anyone.

  From a funder's point of view, patents are golden tickets for you. If someone else can come along and legally copy or use something critical to your business success, you won't be successful in raising funds. It's a deal breaker, so don't scrimp and save money here. Bite the bullet and get it done before you approach funders.

- ✔ **Copyright:** A copyright gives the holder an exclusive protection against the unlicensed copying of artistic and creative works such as literary works, art, photography, films, television broadcasts, music, web content and computer programmes, engineering drawings, architectural works and sound recordings. Only the creator can modify, copy, perform or display it. It doesn't protect ideas, but rather the expression of ideas. You show your claim on the copyright by displaying the © symbol along with the author's name and date of the claim. You don't need to do anything else if the copyright is relevant and used in your business.

  For further guidance and information see the Intellectual Property Office website (www.ipo.gov.uk/types/copy.htm).

  Fortunately, copyrights don't die with the creator of the work; unfortunately, however, they aren't an evergreen thing, and last between 25 and 70 years after the creator's death.

- ✔ **Design registration:** You can register a design, shape, pattern, colours, or decorative feature that's never been seen before or applied to the product you have in mind for it and is aimed at products that will be produced in numbers of more than 50. To register a design you need to apply to the Design Registry at www.ipo.gov.uk/types/design.htm

and send a photo or sample specimen with a fee of about £60 for the first one and £40 for each additional design. If you want to protect your design abroad, you need to register it in each country on your list.

- **Trademarks:** A trademark is indicated by the TM symbol that identifies a product or other goods as belonging to a particular business. It can cover product names, logos, jingles and so on.

Make your trademark distinctive – everyone recognises the Coca-Cola script, for example. Often the font or spelling makes a logo eligible for trademarking.

A trademark lasts indefinitely if the company continues to trade and use it on products or services, but expires if the product or service is retired. You apply at the Intellectual Property Office (www.ipo.gov.uk/types/copy.htm), and pay a fee of £170 with your intention to use it, and then get your full registration later on.

More than one type of protection can be linked to a single product. For example, you can:

- Register the business name and logo as a trademark.
- Protect a product's unique shape as a registered design.
- Patent a completely new working part.
- Use copyright to protect drawings of the product.

None of these methods is perfect, but all are necessary if they apply to you and you're trying to get someone to invest in your business.

One of the most common reasons for rejection by investors is the inability to protect your product or service from being copied by others. Therefore, you must make sure that you apply for patent or design registration to protect your IP before you start talking to funders. If your product or process isn't unique or isn't innovative enough and doesn't tick all the boxes required to obtain protection, you must be able to explain why you're confident that your business doesn't present any risks on this front. *Patents, Copyrights and Trademarks For Dummies* by Henri J. A. Charmasson and John Buchaca (Wiley) offers more information on this topic.

Keeping trade secrets close

Some IP, such as a trade secret, isn't eligible for protection. So if you have a 200-year-old soup recipe or the elixir to a long life, but you can't get a patent on it, make sure you keep it secret! If you have to share some aspects of it in order to get it to market, make sure that you get a non-disclosure agreement signed, but know that there's always a risk that someone will try to analyse the formula or figure it out to reproduce it – and there's not much you can do about that. You also run the risk that an employee may try to steal the formula, which is a legal offense, so lock it up somewhere safe, and never tell anyone the whole formula or where it's held.

Obtaining patents and registrations

You can see a line in your cash flow forecast for legal and professional services – this exists for expenses associated with protecting your IP.

If your business depends on the IP you've created to ensure its success, you absolutely must do all you can to protect it and get the certificates to prove it's untouchable without a fight. Allow money in your budget for this, and don't even think about not making provision for it on an ongoing basis. Not setting money aside to obtain patents and registrations is just foolhardy.

Experienced investors know that you'll lose your competitive advantage and market share if you don't obtain patents and registrations. Failing to get the necessary protections will put them off funding your proposition. It also brings your ability as a leader into question. Since management is a key decider for whether or not a funder will get on board, you want to do all you can to put yourself and your team in the best light.

Chapter 8 looks at sources of help. It has contacts for patent and design applications and registration. Use those or contacts gained through your network or other support organisations to get in touch with qualified professionals in this area who can advise and assist you with your applications, both in the UK and on a worldwide basis, if need be.

Be sure to leave plenty of time to prepare and submit your documentation, and remember to bring copies of these documents to your pitch presentations or funder meetings in case potential investors ask to see them.

When you're thinking about laying the groundwork with regard to funders and IP, consider what may be running through a funders' mind:

- ✔ Does this business have its key IP protected? This includes patents, patents pending, copyrights, trade secrets, trademarks and domain names.

- ✔ Are they protected only in the UK, EU and/or America, or on a global basis?

- ✔ How and who developed the IP? Do the IP rights lie with the business or with an individual within the business, a third-party developer or a manufacturer in the supply chain? Who is the true owner of the IP?

- ✔ Does a previous employer or co-developer have a potential claim to the company's IP?

If you're open to copycats, you have no way to protect yourself from competitors muscling in on your market, which is a risk that most funders aren't prepared to take.

Introducing Management and the Team

When funders receive your business plan, if they like what they see in your business model and plan so far, they skip to the financials and then hop back to the section on management because the team is critical when it comes to preparing for and raising funds.

Experienced funders know that the team, be they all full-time employees or a combination of employees and advisors, are the key ingredient in turning the model and the plan into a successful working reality. A well-balanced team with different strengths and skills is music to funders' ears. After all, they're putting their faith in and their financial future with you.

At any stage of growth, success or failure in raising funds often hinges on the same thing – the management. In the start-up phase, the management is especially important because in the absence of any trading history, it's one of two essential influences on funders; the other is how the business makes money.

As a business grows and takes more people on, it's important that the management team has the skills to get the best out of the growing workforce and to navigate the choppy waters caused by the stresses and strains of growth. Everyone needs to be responsible for his own area of expertise.

You may want to keep the team structure as democratic as it was on the day you all decided to set the business up over beer and pizza, but every team needs a leader if it's going to survive, so a certain level of hierarchy needs to creep in. Funders like to know that the buck ultimately stops with one of you.

Be prepared to defend the decisions you make regarding your management team, especially when it comes to the chief executive officer (CEO) or equivalent, as this is the most high-profile and strategic role in the business.

Detailing employment history and experience

Raising funds is not a job interview, but it does have some of the same characteristics. For example, you need to provide some background information that gives potential funders an understanding of the skills, experience and network of the management team, and of the roles they've had in the past that are relevant to your business.

Be sure to include voluntary or unpaid jobs, as they can sometimes offer the most responsible roles to an otherwise inexperienced entrepreneur and strengthen your management skill base.

If you're older, highlight your useful and relevant experience instead of every role you've ever had.

CVs are not always requested by funders, but if they are, include them in the appendix of any documentation for funding. Short bios are good for the main body of your business plan and pitch deck, and even shorter summaries are used in executive summaries and investment memoranda.

This segmentation of information is very good practice for really honing in on why the mix of skills and experience you have in the team works well and why the parts add value to the sum.

Defining roles and responsibilities

I often hear from the team running a start-up, 'It's chaos; everybody is doing everybody else's job because we're a start-up'. Frankly, that's ridiculous. I encourage a business at any stage to have clearly defined roles and responsibilities. Without them, you risk duplicating tasks – or worse, having things slip through the net. Make sure everyone's skills are being utilised in the best possible way and that you know where the gaps are.

A chaotic management system tells an investor that you're disorganised and inefficient.

Start as you mean to go on: Make sure that each member of your team has a proper job description and *person specification,* detailing the skills and qualities you require. Organise clear procedures and policies that are easy for anyone to pick up and that will hold up under the scrutiny of governance. After you take funding on board, you have much stricter reporting guidelines, so you may as well get used to it and impress a funder at the same time.

Introducing the team

The team is critical at any stage in your funding journey, but is particularly important in the early stages when you may have little or no traction in the market.

In preparing your business to attract funding, make sure that you assemble a great, well-rounded team. If you're a relatively inexperienced founder who's failed to recruit to plug your skills gap, it adds to getting a 'no' from funders, who need to know that the team at the helm of their investment is more than capable.

Great teams come in a variety of shapes and sizes – especially at the early stage of your business, when you may not have a fully-fledged, complete and one hundred per cent pay as you earn, or PAYE, team on the payroll.

You can do quite a bit to make up for any gaps, shortcomings or lack of experience in the team by recruiting valuable advisors, board members or committed mentors to present a united and substantial front to funders.

Explaining why your team is amazing

Not surprisingly, it's not enough to just have a team, you need to have an amazing team and to be able to tell potential funders and investors exactly what makes it amazing. Keep in mind that it's not just work experience that makes a team amazing – although it helps if you've got some great technical or financial minds on the team, accompanied by some marketing gurus and design wizards, for example. But, people can be amazing in other ways.

Someone who's run ten marathons for charity, swum the Channel or climbed Everest, all with his hands tied behind his back, is a pretty amazing individual. Okay, maybe that's a bit extreme, but you get the idea. Having committed people on board who can focus single-mindedly on achieving a goal – who have the strength of an individual accompanied by the support of a team – not only makes for a good read, but also means you have great businesspeople and team players.

Be sure not to overlook or downplay some of the non-work achievements and successes of the people on your team when putting your bios together for the pitch deck (which I talk about in Chapter 6).

The following gives you a flavour of how investors size up the team. People are key, so ask yourself what matters most:

- ✔ **A team, A product:** This combination gives funders the absolute best chance of a successful return on their investment.

- ✔ **A team, B product:** Very good chance of making a good investment and a pretty sure chance of getting their money back.

- ✔ **B team, A product:** Average chance of getting a return, and a very good chance of losing part or all of their investment.

- ✔ **B team, B product:** Every chance of throwing their money down the toilet.

Creating Financials

When preparing your financials for potential funders, you need to include a number of standard documents, which I explain in the next sections.

If you're starting out, you may have very basic and limited numbers, so the quality of your assumptions really matters. Use credible research, hard facts and historical data to back up your positions, and make sure that your forecasts are believable. I look at number crunching in more detail in Chapter 4.

Your natural inclination as an entrepreneur may be to paint the most positive and amazing financial picture, but funders want to see realism, which may vary for each of their positions. If it's debt funding, they want you to err on the side of caution; if it's equity, they want you to be aggressive in your projections, but not off the wall. There's a difference between rapid growth and impossible growth. (I talk about the types of funding in the chapters in Part III.)

Whoever you're approaching no doubt has thousands, if not millions, of pounds already invested in a variety of industry sectors and sizes, so he 'didn't come down with rain', as my mother used to say. Investors have a pretty good idea of what is realistic and achievable.

When giving funders an idea of how much you think your business is worth before and after you receive investment, be careful not to overvalue your business, and don't open yourself up for an argument on this point. Investors like realism and a good defence for your valuation.

Predicting your profit and loss

I look at preparing your profit and loss statements for your business plan in Chapter 5. What's important at this point is to recognise that a *profit and loss statement,* or P&L, looks at a snapshot of your business at one moment in time. It can be your month end or your year end.

It looks at your income minus your expenses, and lets you know if you've made a profit or a loss. It also shows you your *profit margins,* which are the indicators of the financial health of your business, and will be of interest to any potential funder. If the margins aren't right, you'll never be profitable, and therefore you'll never be fundable.

Forecasting cash flow figures

Investors and funders want to see your *cash flow forecast,* or your projected income and expenses with resulting cash position, for at least three years – five years if your loan or your investment is still active within that time frame. I look at how to utilise a forecast when testing your financial assumptions and presenting to funders in Chapter 4. Check out *Accounting For Dummies* by John A Tracy, published by Wiley, for clarification about cash-flow numbers.

A funder looks for the impact on working capital his investment will make. Make sure that you tell funders the assumptions you made to arrive at your figures and be prepared to defend your assumptions.

Compiling a balance sheet

A *balance sheet* helps investors understand how much your company is worth. Figure 3-1 shows a sample. The balance sheet is often overlooked, but it has meaning for equity investors. It helps you keep track of finances and ensure that what you owe doesn't exceed what's due to you. It reports on

- ✔ Your **liabilities,** or how much your company owes.
- ✔ Your **assets,** or how much you own that can be turned into cash.
- ✔ Your **retained earnings,** which is the money held in the company; the cumulative total amount of profits earned minus all the money paid to shareholders in dividends.

Your balance sheet gives an investor a good idea of the financial health of your business. To keep the balance, it's divided into two halves – assets on one side, and liabilities plus shareholder's equity on the other side. The sum of your assets equals the sum of your liabilities plus equity because everything that your business owns (assets) is bought with money that comes from shareholders or lenders (liabilities) when you first start your business. There are a number of ratios or calculations that tell you how well you're doing in balancing your assets and liabilities, and funders look at these. I cover these in Chapter 20.

Listing your personal assets and liabilities

Some entrepreneurs are uncomfortable having their personal finances scrutinised for a business funding application and don't understand why it's necessary. But your finances are especially important for debt funding. You're

			2014		2013	
	Notes	£	£	£	£	£
Fixed Assets						
Tangible assets	3		4,467		3,509	
Current Assets						
Trade Debtors	5	17,930		17,782		
Cash at bank and in hand		92,516		92,516		
Other Debtors	5	109,862		109,862		
		220,308		220,160		
Creditors: amounts falling due within one year	6	(121,152)		(120,136)		
Net current assets			99,156		100,024	
Total assets less current liabilities			103,623		103,533	
Creditors: amounts falling due after more than one year	7		(6,096)		(6,096)	
Net assets			97,527		97,437	
Capital and reserves						
Profit and loss account	8		89		51,438	
Shareholders' funds			89		51,438	

Test3 Ltd

Abbreviated balance sheet
as of 8 May 2013

The directors' statements required by Sections 475(2) and (3) are shown on the following page which forms part of this Balance Sheet.

Figure 3-1:
A sample balance sheet – a game of two halves.

© John Wiley & Sons, Ltd.

almost certainly going to be asked to provide some kind of personal guarantee and/or security in case the business is unable to make the loan repayments, so your own circumstances take on a greater importance.

It's a good idea to prepare your own personal *ALIE statement* – Assets, Liabilities, Income and Expenses – as well as provide financial information about your business. You definitely need it for debt funding, but it also helps to focus your mind on what you really need to make this business work for you.

An ALIE lists your personal assets that can be used to repay your debt; your liabilities, so a funder can see what your financial commitments are and how they impact being able to service new debt; your income; and your expenses – and most importantly, what's left over when you subtract one from the other! Figure 3-2 shows a sample – and fictional – ALIE.

WARNING!

Ask as many questions as you need to in order to understand what you're personally guaranteeing when it comes to funding. You want to make an intelligent and informed decision and understand both the upsides and downsides of entering into a binding financial agreement.

Assets Liabilities Income & Expenditure

sardison Ⓢ

Name of Business

Household income/expenditure (excluding business commitments)
Only complete one form for husband and wife

Name of bank which holds your personal current account

Full Name(s) shown on passport

Sort Code   Personal current account number

Monthly Income

Income from Business	£0
Spouse/Partner's income	£0
Other incomes	
(specify)	£0
Income Subtotal (A)	£0
(specify)	£0
(specify)	£0
Income Subtotal (B)	£0
Total Income (A+B)	£0

Monthly Household

Cost of Mortgage/Rent

Mortgage Payment/Rent	£0
Endowment/Pension	£0
Buildings/Contents Insurance	£0
Subtotal (A)	£0

Other Credit Commitments

Loans/Hire Purchase	£0
Credit/Store Cards	£0
Subtotal (B)	£0
Maintenance Payments (C)	£0
Total Financial Commitment (A+B+C=D)	£0

Other Regular Commitments

Council Tax/Water Rates	£0
Domestic Fuel	£0
Telephone	£0
Travel Costs	£0
Car Tax/Car Insurance	£0
Food	£0
Clothing/Hobbies/Leisure	£0
Other Regular Commitments	£0
Subtotal (E)	£0
Expenditure Total (D+E)	£0

Property Details — **Value & Mort o/s**

1. Address	£0 v
Mortgage Lender	£0 o/s
2. Address	£0 v
Mortgage Lender	£0 o/s
3. Address	£0 v
Mortgage Lender	£0 o/s
4. Address	£0 v
Mortgage Lender	£0 o/s

Asset

Use schedule of assets if you have more than four properties

Total Property Value (from above)	£0
Cash Savings	£0
Other Savings	£0
Total Savings	£0
Stocks and Shares	£0
Life Policies (surrender value)	£0
Total Investments	£0
TOTAL ASSETS	£0

Liabilities
Continue on separate sheet if necessary   Name of Lender   Balance Outstanding

Total Mortgage outstanding (from above)			£0
Bank/Building Soc. Loans	Schedule		£0
Hire Purchase			£0
Other Loans			£0
Credit Card held	Yes ☐	No ☐	£0
Other Credit/Store Cards	Yes ☐	No ☐	£0
		TOTAL LIABILITIES	£0

Figure 3-2:
A sample
ALIE.

Chapter 4

Becoming Investment Ready

Investment readiness in everyday business use is a relatively new term generally used when talking about raising external equity finance. However, the thought process, framework and procedures, as well as the majority of the content you produce, can be similar as for dealing with debt and for some grant funding.

In this chapter, I take you through the investing process – from acquiring the right mindset and approach to finding and meeting with potential investors or stakeholders.

Exploring the Basics of Investment Readiness

Investment readiness refers to the preparation needed before the actual process of fundraising begins, when you, hopefully, acquire investment. It looks at how suitable a business is to receive investment, how open the owners are to parting with some of the ownership of the business and the preparation of the materials used to present a proposition for investment. It also looks at how you attract and hold the attention of investors and get them interested in investing in your business. As I discuss in Chapter 6, you need to know what makes your investor audience tick and how to maximise your chances of success by playing to your strengths in these areas.

Not surprisingly, investment readiness also means doing your homework on your possible investors. You need to find out

- ✔ The risk and reward appetite of your preferred investors.

- ✔ The investments potential investors have already made and what's still missing from their portfolios. If the potential return on their investment sees you offering a good return, you may just be that missing link.

You may have everything in place for a textbook investment opportunity – a great plan, a terrific executive summary, an even better digital presentation in the form of slide pitch deck and an opportunity that, at least on paper, is a knockout, but that doesn't necessarily mean that you're investor ready. You have the content (Chapters 5 and 6 tell you how to prepare), and now you need to practise and rehearse your presentation, so that it's captivating, believable, real and convincing.

Show investors that you're on the same page. As the entrepreneur, you naturally think about what matters to you when taking on investment. But you need to take the time to find out what's important to your investors. Try to discover why they rejected some businesses as well as why they said 'yes' to others. Show them that you're able to see the bigger picture and able grow your business to the point where all the risk turns into rewards for everyone involved.

You also need to convince investors that you're comfortable with selling them some of your equity, and open to the possibility of receiving more than just financial input from funders or investors. They can also bring valuable skills, knowledge and networks.

There's a pretty well-worn structure to what you put in front of investors. Pretty much all investors consider the same things when they evaluate a potential investment. These include:

- ✔ **How you make money:** The business model and what you've done to date.

- ✔ **Who's on your team:** What kind of experience, functional strengths, skills and vision do your people have?

- ✔ **What your product or service is:** What's so wow that they just have to invest in it? If it includes intellectual property, is it legally protected?

- ✔ **Who your competition is:** Who's in the same market, and why are you better?

- ✔ **Where your money goes:** What are you going to do with the money lent or invested and over what period of time?

- ✔ **What's the potential for a return:** Can you show future growth, an ability to provide a return and a clear view to a possible exit?

I look at these in more detail in Chapter 13 when I talk about equity funding.

Looking at types of investors

Not all investors have the same background and experience, and not all have the same amount of money to invest or the same expectations of a return on their investment.

Depending on the stage of your business development and the amount of money required to get your business to the next growth phase, some types of investors may be more suitable than others. The types of investor include:

- **Friends and family:** Those nearest to you who you may persuade to help you get your company off the ground with their early financial support.

- **A business person with a small amount of spare cash:** These investors are often former city workers, accountants or lawyers, so they're not necessarily sophisticated, experienced investors like business angels, but they may have a spare £10,000 or so and want to invest in other businesses. They may do this individually or in groups, known as *syndicates*.

- **Business angels:** An individual or group of individuals that metaphorically comes to the rescue – like an angel – and invests in your business, usually in the earlier stages. I look at them in more detail in Chapter 13.

  Some types of investors in the angel community are:

  - **The successful ex-entrepreneur who invests just money:** This successful entrepreneur has exited her business, made a good amount of money and invests in your business with no further involvement. Typically, this investor enters in the earlier stages of your business and generally invests up to a maximum of £400,000.

  - **The successful ex-entrepreneur who invests money and time:** This entrepreneur has had a successful exit and wants to invest funds, but also wants to roll up her sleeves and take an operational role in your business.

  - **The business person with a large amount of money to invest:** This type of investor may be a city worker, finance professional or just a wealthy person with business experience who has a healthy amount of spare cash she wants to put to good use.

  - **The career investor:** This investor looks to have a portfolio of companies she invests in, either on her own or as part of an angel group or network.

✔ **Institutional investors:** These investors represent a fund versus individual or networked angels. They usually invest larger amounts and at later stages in your business. I talk more about them in Chapter 13. Institutional investors come in two types:

- **Venture capital firms:** These are usually fund managers of small- to medium-sized funds that invest in your business in its later growth stages.

- **Private equity houses:** These are managers of much larger funds, who invest at the later stages of your established and stable business, often in anticipation of your business listing on a public stock exchange.

✔ **Debt funders:** Although I'm looking at equity investors, it's worth mentioning that certain types of debt funders lend debt funds to your business after it receives equity investment. This type of lending has an accompanying equity provision for the lender written into the contract upon repayment of the debt. This is sometimes known as *venture debt* or *mezzanine debt*. I look at this in more detail in Chapter 12.

Beware of consultants or individuals who say that they're investors, but who are really looking for fees or entry into a start-up without investing any cash.

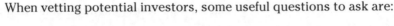

When vetting potential investors, some useful questions to ask are:

✔ How many investments have you made in total?

✔ How many in the past 12 or 24 months?

✔ Can I have company/founder names of businesses you've invested in, and is it okay for me to contact them?

✔ In addition to cash, what can you offer my business?

✔ If you invested in my business, would you prefer to be the lead investor or follow others who invest first?

Resigning yourself to the process

You may start to wonder how long the funding process will take; how many frogs you have to kiss before you find the prince of your dreams; how many doors you have to push open; how many rejection emails you need to read.

When you're planning, remember to take into account how much time you need to write and/or polish up your business plan and pitch materials. If you need to get help with this, make sure you retain control over the process and the material, or you'll find it difficult to present it in a convincing way.

Before making a presentation or talking to an investor, review your materials:

- ✔ Check and double-check your facts.
- ✔ Include all the key points and areas of interest.
- ✔ Be sure the valuation you arrived at is realistic.

Even before you do the basics, you need to think about when you actually need the money and create a timeline to get the funds with time to spare. It's not uncommon for businesses to need their investment yesterday, but unless you know someone who is super wealthy and ready to write you a cheque today, you need to be aware of how long the investment process takes and plan accordingly.

Competition for investment is fierce, and there are no guarantees that you'll be successful. Prepare to spend three to eight months for the whole process of finding an investor to receiving your investment. There will be many emails, presentations, meetings and negotiations that require your patience and stamina.

Don't tell a potential investor that you need the money in two weeks' time – it highlights your ignorance of the process and raises a red flag as to your financial planning and control skills.

Preparing to kiss a lot of frogs

The following example from Mark Thomas, CEO and founder of Reesio, a real estate transaction software business that raised just over $1 million in 2013, as written in a Quora blog on 31 May, 2014, nicely illustrates the potential filtering and whittling down of opportunities and investors on a fundraising journey. (Quora is a question-and-answer website where content is curated by users.)

When he raised a $1.096m seed round in 2013, this was his funnel:

- ✔ 160 potential investors contacted
- ✔ 50 face-to-face meetings
- ✔ 12 investors who invested

So roughly one-third of outreaches turned into meetings and about one-quarter of the meetings turned into investments, so one-in-twelve outreaches became an investment. Other factors such as time of year and at what point in the funding journey new contacts were made (it's always easier to get someone to join in when the party's in full swing) also have an impact, but to a large extent, it's a numbers game.

In addition to realising that you'll need to kiss a lot of frogs before you find your investors, you also have ample opportunities to learn from your mistakes and to develop a very thick skin!

Evaluating Your Attitude to Receiving Investment

Before embarking on your journey to attract and obtain investment, take a long, hard look at the person staring back at you in the mirror and deep into your metaphorical soul. You need to make sure that you're ready, willing and able to receive any investment that comes your way. If seeking investors is something that you do reluctantly or unwillingly, it'll never feel right and both you and your potential investors will see and feel this.

Talk to other entrepreneurs who've already taken on investment to get a better idea of the upsides and the potential pitfalls. They can help you to go into the relationship with your eyes wide open and your expectations set to *realistic* on your entrepreneurial dial.

Weirdly, receiving money can often be more uncomfortable than giving it, and if you're that way inclined in the rest of your life, you have even more of a reason to have some checks and balances in place before you start forging relationships.

Make sure you're seeking investment for the right reasons and that you're completely comfortable with using other people's money in a responsible way. If it makes you feel undue pressure, this may not be the right course of action for you and your business. It should empower you, not destroy you. To get a handle on your state of investment readiness, ask yourself:

- ✔ If you're a founder or an entrepreneur, is it just about the buzz of the setup and getting it off the ground, or are you looking to grow a successful business?

- ✔ Have you considered the implications for you, your team and on your financials that come with taking on investment?

- ✔ Are you creating a business that will stand on its own, whether you stay with it or not?

- ✔ Do you break out into a cold sweat at the thought of someone else having a say in how you run your business?

After answering these questions, if you feel you aren't ready to take on investment, then you may want to continue fine-tuning your proposition whilst looking at other sources of funding, such as grants or awards that don't involve sharing company ownership. Or, you may find a role in a company that's already received investment and see what it's like to actually work in that situation. Whatever you decide to do, keep networking with the investment community and build a good support system of advisers and mentors to help you when you feel ready to accept external investment.

Determining your readiness to share ownership

If you decide that taking on investment is a good idea, you need to be aware of and comfortable with the reality of exchanging a share of the ownership of your business in exchange for the money invested.

If you're going to take on an equity investor, you need to be totally comfortable with sharing the risks and the rewards.

As the youngest girl in a family of six children, I got used to sharing very early on in life. I shared my room, my food, my clothes and any quiet space that existed in our overcrowded house. I accepted sharing as a part of life and could see the benefits of strength in numbers and running a lean household. I'm not saying I always liked it or that I always got on with my fellow sharers, but I learned to understand and appreciate how sharing can lighten the workload for everyone involved in an enterprise, resulting in a stronger overall performance and a more cohesive community.

I approached my businesses with the same attitude, but I couldn't always find the right people to share the risk and the rewards. Believe me, there were times when I was carrying a very heavy load, both mentally and financially, and it would have been a great relief to have an *equity investor* – someone with a stake in the business – to shoulder some of the responsibility. I think if you ask my husband, who was an indirect investor in my second business, he'd agree!

The desire to have all the marbles isn't unusual. Most business owners, and in particular first-time entrepreneurs, are understandably reluctant to surrender any ownership or control of their businesses, seeing it as giving away part of what they worked so hard to create.

You may believe that by giving away a share in your business you're somehow leaving yourself in the position of being controlled by an outside force. You may not find it easy to step back and take the view that having a part of something that's making money is better than having the whole of something that's not making any or as much money. You may assume investors will ride rough shod over you and take you for all you're worth. Keep in mind that you have a choice in who invests in you, and you can seek out a potential investor you feel comfortable with.

Don't set yourself up to feel like a victim. See the act of taking on investment as a positive step towards growth – both yours and the business's.

Measuring the depth of your knowledge of the funding process

Years ago, getting funding for your business consisted largely of popping down to your friendly bank manager's office and getting a loan with little or no bother. It was rare to find someone in your circle taking on equity investment unless you moved in circles where high-net-worth individuals and fund managers were the norm. You still needed to understand what you were signing and what the implications were, but like most things in a bygone era, things were simpler then.

The funding process is no longer such a blissfully straightforward process for many entrepreneurs. In addition to the changing financial and economic environment, you now have all sorts of funding options – debt, equity and crowdfunding, to name but a few. (I talk about funding options in more detail in the chapters in Part III.) And, these funding options come in all sorts of sizes and shapes with differing terms and conditions, tax implications and long-term implications that can have very beneficial or very detrimental effects on you and your business.

Wading through the options can be especially scary if you're not financially experienced or have a condition, such as dyspraxia or dyslexia, that makes it physically difficult to work with figures. Making the final decision can be a very daunting experience, so don't be too hard on yourself if you start fumbling around. Make sure you find out as much as you can, seek advice and support (I look at organizations to help you in Chapter 8) and ask plenty of questions.

If you're the sensitive type or have a fear of rejection, put on your thickest coat before you go seeking investors or don't go to market for funding. Because as sure as eggs is eggs, you will be rejected. Hopefully, you'll learn from it and get better each time you ask for investment funds.

To help separate the wheat from the investor-readiness chaff, use the following checklist as a starting point in determining whether your business is investor-ready:

✔ You can deliver an *elevator pitch* – a short, concise and punchy verbal summary of your funding proposition. (I talk about constructing your pitch in Chapter 6.) Your pitch needs to be no longer than three minutes and shouldn't use complicated terminology or jargon. It should get your key market, product/service, team and financial points across succinctly, and still hold your audience's attention.

✔ You're able to prove that there's a market need for your product or service. You identified the problem, and you have the solution.

✔ You know the size of your market and the rough percentage of the market you're likely to capture both now and in five years' time, when an investor is most likely to exit. (Head to Chapter 13 for more on timing issues.)

✔ You can show proof that the intellectual property rights of your idea are protected and that you've applied for any registrations, patents or trademarks required. (See *Patents, Copyrights and Trademarks For Dummies* by Henri J. A. Charmasson and John Buchaca [Wiley]).

✔ You can lay out your clear route to market and explain how you plan to get your product or service out there. Strategic partnerships add some oomph to your proposition as they instantly widen your reach and help to strengthen any sales or marketing forecasts.

✔ You can demonstrate that you have proven your concept, launched a minimum viable product (MVP) and tested your business model. This adds significant weight to your argument for needing funds, but in the very early seed stage or pre-launch phase of your business, it's a bonus more than a necessity. As you move further along, however, it becomes a non-negotiable requirement. If you have market validation, it's a good idea to have some documentation to hand to prove sales, contracts and so on.

✔ You can speak intelligently about your competition, backed up by facts and figures, and explain what makes your business superior and how you'll handle competition.

✔ You've assembled a crack team, with experience and a depth of skill in all the key business areas, and you can demonstrate why your people are an investor's dream team.

✔ You can provide evidence that you're invested in your own business – that you have skin in the game. If you have other investors, be prepared to show that they're committed as well.

✔ You can show that you have a registered entity with a shareholders' agreement, an advisery board (partial or whole), commercial legal agreements, VAT registration if needed, tax incentive approval (or pending approval) from Her Majesty's Revenue and Customs (HMRC), if appropriate, and an accountant in the wings.

✔ You know how much money you need, for what period of time and exactly how you plan to spend it. You can point to concrete milestones and results you expect to achieve and what return your investor can look forward to.

✔ You're open to sharing your ownership in the business, to taking advice and constructive criticism, to being flexible and agile and to pushing the envelope just that little bit beyond your perceived reach.

✔ You can articulate a number of possible exit scenarios. (Head to Chapter 17 for a rundown of exit strategies.)

You're unlikely to be investment ready if

✔ You have an okay business plan, a pitch deck based on a PowerPoint template and nothing that tells a compelling or interesting story.

✔ You can't prove – with facts – that there's a real need for your product or service.

✔ You can't show an in-depth knowledge of your market at a moment's notice.

✔ Your team is just ordinary instead of extraordinary.

✔ You shiver and shake when you think of giving up a stake in your business.

✔ You're a steady-Betty type, content with slow-and-steady progress, not looking for rapid growth. Investors want to see that you can offer growth levels of at least eight to ten times their investment within five years.

✔ You're unable to deliver an effective pitch.

✔ You don't understand the basic mechanics of the investment process.

Approaching Investors

When you feel ready to approach investors, you need to ask yourself what kind of investors you want and how you'll find and approach them.

In the past, entrepreneurs felt as if they needed to be a member of a secret society or a very well-connected individual in a moneyed network in order to find or attract investors. You can thank the popularity of the Internet and the wave of tech businesses, often founded by bright young things with little or no connections, for democratising the investment process and making it open and accessible to any business owner with a great idea and a plan for taking it forward. The angel and early stage venture industries have been truly revolutionised by the advent of the Internet.

This isn't to say that finding investors is just a matter of going online, tapping a few keys, and hey presto you have an investor, but the Internet does make it easier to do your research, to network and to book useful events where you can meet with and question investors and get your face and your business known on the scene.

It used to be that you'd attempt to find debt funding for your fledging business, then after some time, you might approach an angel investor (who may or may not have been called that). You'd eventually move on to venture capital, and possibly for a few, private equity investors if you were looking for a few million to £10 or £20 million pounds. The path is no longer so straight, and the lines in the middle of the road are no longer so clearly marked out. Also, you need to recognise that some investors travel in packs, some are lone wolves and some prefer to join a crowd and go with the wave of public opinion.

There's no right or wrong road to follow when looking for investors. You just have to be thorough, well informed and logical when considering what's best for you and your business.

Finding the perfect space

JustPark (www.justpark.com) is a terrific example of how the right investor fit makes all the difference to the growth of an investee business. JustPark is a company that uses technology to enable customers to pre-book parking spaces and other customers to rent out parking spaces.

Having secured millions of pounds of equity investment from BMW Ventures and Index Ventures, a private equity house, JustPark went on to raise £3.7 million from thousands of investors on Crowdcube, the crowdfunding website, with the blessing of their original investors. The investors knew that despite diluting their shares, it was the best thing for the business to raise funds with crowdfunding and agreed with the JustPark management team on the strategy.

Not all investors are created equal, and you want to create your own checklist for evaluating who's a good fit for you and your business. Some of the areas that you want to look at are:

- **Level of involvement:** Look at how involved potential investors want to be and see how that makes you feel. Are you comfortable with someone potentially checking your work, guiding your decisions and making suggestions and demands, or do you want an investor who stays at arm's length, makes introductions and isn't an executive-director type?

- **Reason for investing:** Figure out why an investor is interested in investing. Is she merely looking for a tax-efficient vehicle or is she really interested in what you're doing? Do you care either way?

  Is a successful exit so important to your investor that she will crack the whip in order to get the most profitable end game, even if you don't think that's in the best interest of the business? Along the same lines, does she have strong feelings about how and when both of you should exit? Does she want to take tighter control over the process? You may be more comfortable with an investor who's relaxed, happy to be in the game with quite a few others and not fixed on a pre-determined exit strategy.

- **Working style:** Working effectively and interacting with your investor is important. Do you want someone who's relaxed and informal in the way she deals with you and your team, or do you think you need a more structured, procedural approach that holds you accountable on a regular basis?

- **Depth of scrutiny:** You need to determine whether you're comfortable with someone going to unplumbed depths in your financial history and background or prefer a lighter touch that's less focused on you and more on your products and services. Due diligence, or *due dil*, as it's known in the trade, forms part of every investor's assessment of you and your business. During the *due diligence* process, a potential investor investigates the material facts surrounding your financial and legal areas of your business in order to help her make an investment decision. You have to decide how deep you're prepared to go.

Finding Investors

After deciding on the type of investor you want, it's time to put yourself out there and start meeting a few of these heretofore mythical beings. These meetings may happen in the freezer section of your local supermarket, during the cocktail hour of your best friend's wedding reception or at some other chance gathering, but in order to really make it happen, you need to do all you can to remove the random coincidence from the process. Just as you do when looking for a job, or a house or a place to study (and some would say when looking for a mate), you need a game plan with strategic tactics and alliances and a time frame in which to achieve a successful outcome.

Expect to be out almost every evening – and not in pubs, clubs and bars unless that's where your investor prefers to meet. You're more likely to be in hubs, workspaces, offices, and *hangouts,* a common term in the start-up community for beer and pizza meet-ups, which is where most investor information and pitch events take place.

In addition to events, workshops, seminars and talks, investors also live online, and sometimes in the places that are, or should be, familiar to you from other areas of your business – networking sites, meeting sites and contact databases. What follows are some of the more familiar online locations:

✔ **LinkedIn (**www.linkedin.com**):** In Chapter 16, I look at the value of mentoring, and in the case of finding and approaching investors, your personal and business network is key. I recently heard James Sore, the head of investments from Syndicate Room, an investor-led crowdfunding platform, recommend using LinkedIn connections to make contact, find out about and attend events and develop relationships with potential investors.

You don't want to overwhelm LinkedIn contacts to the point of making them feel they're being stalked. And, it's wise not to offer up too much information when you first meet a potential investor in person. Asking questions such as 'Have you come on your motorbike?' can make you appear just a wee bit overzealous in your personal research. On the other hand, if you both share the same hobby or outlet, this can be a very good bonding topic. You have to play it by ear.

In addition to making direct contact, you can join and participate in countless LinkedIn groups on any number of topics. By doing so, you raise your profile, get your point of view across and extend your reach. Some groups run on an invite-and-acceptance basis, but others are open to all. If you can't find one you like, then you can start your own. (*LinkedIn For Dummies* by Joel Elad can fill in any knowledge gaps for you.)

✔ **Meetup (**www.meetup.com**):** My first experience of Meetup involved being forcibly dragged along by a friend who had a thing for French women to a French ex-pat event in London. I have to admit I was a bit dubious as to what I was getting myself into. I don't know what the French for *wingman* (or wingwoman) is, but that was my role. Since that first social meet-up years ago, I've attended a number of business meet-ups, and have been impressed.

You can find many industry categories on Meetup, so you need to do your research. Perhaps attend some that are purely financial and some that are in your industry sector in order to get a good cross-section of contacts.

Many of the business and finance meet-ups include investors and pitching opportunities, and also provide a good opportunity to meet other business owners who have received funding, know funders and can point you to once-removed contacts.

Like most open platforms, your success, or lack of it, is down to how much you make the process work for you and your business. The more proactive you are, the better the outcome. The events may be free or very low cost, but the real cost is in your time, so there's no point in attending and then being a wallflower. Get stuck in and make it work for you.

✔ **Databases:** You can trawl through many databases and lists of investors on the Internet. Do your research as to what's out there and who's particularly interested in your business sector, using both online and offline sources.

A few of the best-known sites for both investors and listed deals are

- **Angel List (**www.angel.co**):** One of the first places for both start-up founders and investors to register their investment intentions and the type of deals they're looking for.

- **CrunchBase (**www.crunchbase.com**):** Established in 2007 in the United States, CrunchBase is arguably the world's most comprehensive data source for tracking tech-based start-up activity, and it's open to all. To date, it has over half a million profiles of people and companies listed on the website. The profiles can be edited by company owners, investors, and others with a registered user profile. In essence, it's a crowdsourced database that depends on the community to keep it updated. You can list your company here and also see which venture firms, incubators, accelerators and investors are working with other companies.

- **Gust (**https://gust.com**):** Established in 2004 and still based in New York City (with an office in London), Gust (originally Angelsoft) is a privately owned, global funding platform set up to source and manage the funding journey of early-stage investments.

  Using its hugely respected intelligent software, Gust simplifies what can be a very frustrating experience and a very complex relationship. Gust makes it possible for entrepreneurs to collaborate with investors and angel investor networks by providing virtual support at all stages of the investment relationship from initial pitch to successful exit. Regularly endorsed by the world's leading business angel and venture capital associations, it powers over 1,000 investment organizations in more than 80 countries.

Additional online resources include:

- **BVCA, British Venture Capital Association (**www.bvca.co.uk**):** To give its full name, the British Private Equity & Venture Capital Association is the industry trade body and voice for influencing public policy in the private equity and venture capital industries in the UK. It has over 500 members who work to provide capital and expertise to growing businesses. It has a great calendar of events with expert speakers on topics that matter to both investors and entrepreneurs as well as research publications and training opportunities.

- **UKBAA, UK Business Angels Association (**www.ukbusinessangels association.org.uk**):** A membership-based organization, UKBAA is the national trade body in the UK representing angel and early-stage investors. UKBAA promotes its activities and standards in the industry, acting as a voice for the industry in policy areas, offering training to both members and entrepreneurs and providing members with a closed platform where they can co-invest and manage a number of investments at the same time. It's also very active in raising awareness of what's happening in the community, and hosts a number of showcases and social events that are highlights in the investor calendar each year.

- **EBAN, European Business Angel Network (**www.eban.org**):** The trade body for European early-stage investors, EBAN has over 150 members. EBAN aims to foster the relationship between early-stage investors and entrepreneurs, creating a bridge between the two and fostering opportunities to create links, promote education around investing and offer insights, advisory and benchmarking services to help all parties make a success of the process. Like UKBAA, it holds a number of annual events that are great for networking and developing relationships with investors and also for getting a glimpse into future trends and developments in Europe, the Middle East and Africa.

Assessing How Much Money You Need

Needing £100,000 and asking for £200,000 just to be sure is not a good idea. This poor logic sends the signal that you haven't done enough planning or forecasting, that you don't know how much the money you're looking to raise will cost in fees and other expenses and that you don't understand the impact on your bottom line.

An equally bad idea is asking for enough money for six months, and stating that you're already prepared to go through this extremely time-consuming, sometimes soul-destroying, always draining process again in six months because you don't want to take too much money.

Work out what you need for a decent run, know what the limits are for your chosen group of investors and then match the two. A decent run of time is enough time to achieve the objectives you set out in your business plan. The earlier you are in your business stage, the shorter your time frame will be. If you're in the very early stage, the runway can be one year; if your business is further on, then it can be 18 months to two years.

Do your research, create your cash-flow forecasts, run your best- and worst-case scenarios and arrive at the optimum figure for the amount you need. I help you look at this in more detail in Chapter 3, but for now, just be sure that the amount you require is not some random figure plucked from the air or based on what feels like enough. Base it on as much fact as you can bring to the table, pepper it with a dose of calculated risk and reward projections and wrap it up in a bit of gut instinct.

For most SME (small- and medium-sized enterprise) owners, the realisation that you don't have enough money to survive the next three months, or to launch your next product or carry out necessary expansions triggers an immediate assumption that you need an injection of cash. This may be the case, but in the same way that you don't know what gems are hidden up in the loft until you investigate, you may be overlooking funds that are right in front of your face.

Part of being ready to receive investment is being fully conversant and confident in how finance functions in your business. It pays to know where you can free up some cash in your business for things like working capital before going to the market cup in hand.

Some areas to look at within your business are

- ✔ **Payment terms:** The longer you give someone to pay you, the longer you become her lender. You provide people who owe you with money while depriving your own cash-strapped business of income. Ask yourself why you want to offer credit terms to your suppliers and then pay interest or give equity to someone else to cover your own costs. Police your payment terms and take care of your own business.

- ✔ **Invoice factoring:** Depending on the type of business you're in, you may have some large invoices out to some very stable clients or suppliers who take a longer time than usual to pay. Local authorities, the NHS, large department stores and multi-nationals tend to set a 90-day minimum for paying their suppliers. Depending on how many of these clients you work with, this waiting game can cripple your business, and in some cases, take it under. You need to think of alternative ways to get these funds into your cash flow more quickly.

I look at alternative finance in Chapter 14, but one relevant alternative finance product is *invoice factoring*. In simple terms, a financier buys the invoice you're awaiting payment on and advances you the majority of the value of the invoice upfront, thereby bumping up your cash flow position and easing the strain on your day-to-day finances. When the remainder of the money comes in, you receive the rest of the money that's due to you, minus the fees involved. This approach suits certain types of invoices and companies more than others (I look at these types of invoice and companies in Chapter 12), but it's something you should explore before you go begging. An investor wants to know that you've looked at all the options before asking for outside assistance.

✔ **Renegotiating interest rates/terms on existing credit:** As busy a business owner or entrepreneur, it's easy to forget the details after you arrange a loan or a credit facility. As all these things change in line with the economy and financial environment, it's good practice to regularly revisit any existing funding agreements and see whether you can get a better deal with your current funder or with their competitors. The difference a few interest percentage points can make to your cash flow can be significant. The ability to extend a payment plan to additional months or years, thereby lowering your monthly payment, can make all the difference if you're trying to tighten your financial belt. As the saying goes, 'if you don't ask, you don't get'. And as your mother may say, 'What's the worst that can happen? They can only say "no".' If they do, you can go to their competition! What's important is that you keep on top of these agreements and make sure you aren't paying over the current odds.

✔ **Green funds:** Depending on your business sector, you may be eligible for some grant or rebate funding for green or eco-friendly initiatives. If you're in the restaurant trade, you may be able to tap into some waste disposal grants from your local authority. These can all save you money as well as generate some income, so take some time to do a bit of research that may bring valuable rewards.

You may look at your bank balance and think 'kerching!' if you see a healthy chunk of change in there, but having cash in the bank doesn't necessarily mean you have healthy finances within your business. You need to plan ahead and make sure that you can pay your upcoming invoices, have a buffer for unexpected events and, ideally, have enough money to cover three months of running costs. Money in the bank is not a signal to plan your next holiday, and potential investors and funders want to know that you understand this.

Sometimes the most successful businesses go under, even though they're healthy and trading, because they didn't consider the increased demand on cash that results from an increase in trade, and they literally run out of money. Frequently, the entrepreneur reaches out to the investment community to throw her a lifeline at this point. However, this poor cash management sends the wrong signal to any funders, so best to get a grip on it early on.

You can maximise the amount of cash in your business, while at the same time letting investors and lenders know that you know how to manage your finances, by being prudent in your spending decisions and having monitoring and reporting systems in place that you update regularly and can share with your financiers at a moment's notice.

You need to know how much money you require to run the business on a regular basis – what's called *working capital* – and when it's time to look externally for funding. Master these skills to have a successful business. The knowledge these skills give you helps your business stand up under intense scrutiny if you take on investors as your business grows.

Stress Testing Your Financial Plan

People often talk about doing *sensitivity analyses* on financial forecasts to see what would happen to the bottom line if sales dropped by 10 or 20 per cent while fixed costs remained the same. You can also do the same type of analysis for a 10 or 20 per cent increase because growth comes with its own challenges. But, generally, you look at a downward sales trend when testing for robustness.

You can imagine that SME owners carrying out this exercise in 2008 may have done a 20 per cent drop, but I very much doubt anyone was testing a 70 per cent or 80 per cent decline, so it's not foolproof (or, indeed, recession- or crisis-proof). Use sensitivity analyses as a guide only. Financial sensitivity analysis gives you one method of testing your theory, but there are other things to look at when testing the strength of your plan.

A useful tool to help with financial sensitivity analysis is an Excel spreadsheet; you can find one at www.excel-easy.com/data-analysis/what-if-analysis.html.

Areas that aren't specifically about finances include your strategy, plans for implementing it, having the skills needed to make it a reality and what may get in the way of making it a success.

Following is a checklist to go through when considering how your business copes under pressure. These points are worth spending some time pondering and planning for, as they can be the difference between make or break:

- ✔ Research your business strategy and run it by an industry expert to validate the perceived opportunity.

✔ Plan thoroughly at each stage of your implementation plan.

✔ Identify and recognise the hidden barriers to the implementation of your business and financial plans.

✔ Pre-plan the steps you will take to overcome these barriers.

✔ Ensure your team has the best possible skill sets to overcome any barriers.

✔ Make sure you have a development plan for all employees in your business.

Business Planning Essentials For Dummies by Veechi Curtis (Wiley) can help you round out your plan.

Finding out if you can make money

You've done your research, and you're certain that you've hit upon an idea for your business that solves a genuine problem in a unique or better way than anything else on the market. You know who your target customers are and what they're willing to pay. Your next step in finding out if you can make money is to determine whether you have the right model for your type of business to be profitable and to work out how much money you need to put into your business to plug your funding gap.

Chapter 3 looks at sample cash-flow forecasts, and this tool is incredibly helpful for determining the viability of your business. Creating a spreadsheet that gives you a place to experiment with different sales forecasts, costings, pricing structures and expense scenarios – including the amount you need to earn to survive – is a huge help when it comes to making your final decisions on whether you can make money, at what point your business will wash its own face (breakeven) and how much funding you need to inject into the business at certain points in time if your forecasts are to become a reality.

I know this may seem like a time-consuming and somewhat tedious process when you just want to get out there and sell, sell, sell, but the time spent on it now can save you a lot of heartbreak and sleepless nights later on, and it may also save you a lot of money!

Estimating costs

If you're like most people, a good percentage of your common sense goes out the window when you enter into areas of your personal or business life that you're not very familiar with or are used to approaching from a different angle. This is frequently the case for business owners when estimating costs.

It's not unusual for me to hear, 'How can I possibly know how much it'll cost me to make my product or resource my service until I start doing it? How can I know how much my public liability insurance will cost or my mobile phone bill will be?' But, how can you *not* know what these rough costs are before you open for business? Don't you research some of these same types of costs in your personal life using the Internet, your network, directories and bricks-and-mortar shops? You need to do the same for your business.

Throughout this book, I talk about using your network, mentors, trade associations, membership groups, libraries and small-business resource centres, many of which have an online presence, so it's no different to the types of things you'd do in your personal life when you need a costing or a quote. You don't suddenly have to become the font of all knowledge with precise figures at your fingertips just because it's for your business. You don't need to know the exact cost down to the last pound, but an estimate that's close enough to what the real cost may be is enough to guide you through your financial forecasts and test your assumptions. These figures are your starting guide, and eventually, your forecasted data turns into your actual costs and you can use this now-historic data to adjust, amend and plan more accurately going forward.

Forecasting sales

Forecasting your business sales may feel a bit like gazing into a crystal ball. You struggle with the concept of being able to see into the future with any real accuracy and feel like you're making it up as you go along. Well, you can pack up the supernatural paraphernalia and fix your gaze firmly on some very useful and readily available sources of information to help make forecasting your sales more of a science and less of an unpredictable art form.

It's very likely that you went into or are considering going into a business in an industry you worked in before or that you know a bit about from friends or family. So you probably have some idea of what sales levels are possible in your own head or within your close groups. You can supplement this information by doing a bit of library or online research into the historical data of companies in the same industry and size categories.

People who work in research love to help you learn, so use them as a valuable and respected resource.

If your business area has an industry body or association, it can offer a terrific range of historic data gathered from its members. It may have industry and policy reports that you can download from a website to help fill in some of the gaps in your knowledge. In other words, you can tap into a number of really useful resources to ground your forecasts in reality and give you a baseline to work from.

Don't overlook the obvious. Whenever possible, try to observe and experience your industry from a competitor's point of view and do some *primary,* or firsthand, research. For example, if you're going to open a café on the high street, sit outside across the road from a café in the same area and count how many customers go in and out at different times in the day and night, then go inside to listen and get a sense of how much the average customer spends. This is very useful, and relatively free, information. You probably need to buy a tea or coffee during each visit as well as spend some of your valuable time, but there's nothing like grassroots data to show you what really goes on in a business.

The other obvious source of information to inform your forecast is to sit down, either face-to-face or virtually, with a group of your potential customers and ask them what they want, how often they want it and how much they'd be willing to pay for it.

For at least the first two years of a three-year forecast and the first three years of a five-year forecast, you want to be as close to a reasonable truth as you can be. All forecasts and estimate are just that – a best guess scenario based on research, intelligence gathering and market trends, and it's rare that anyone is ever bang on target with her figures. You do the best you can.

When assembling numbers for your forecasts, start with your costs because they're the easiest part of the equation to uncover. Start with something that makes you feel you're making progress and gives you confidence to move onto the trickier bits.

When you know what your monthly costs are, you know the minimum amount of sales revenue you need to cover those costs. So far, so good. No one goes into business to cover costs, so set yourself a target that makes profit.

The other key indicator that most entrepreneurs often overlook is the average amount of a customer spends and how often she spends it. This tells you how many customer purchases you need to achieve your sales target, which then helps shape your marketing. Everything is linked into a beautifully virtuous circle. In a café, for example, you probably have lots of small transactions but many customers who come in every day or every week. If you're setting up a dental practice, you have fewer, larger receipts repeated once or twice a year, so you need to keep introducing new services and products and continually find new customers.

Exceeding breakeven

Every sales forecast has a *good, better, best* version, varying from very conservative to pretty realistic on to extremely optimistic. In doing the forecasting, you'll be able to see when your business arrives at its *breakeven point,* the point at which you're not making any profit, but you're not losing any money either. (For more information on breakeven, see Chapter 20.)

When you're talking to investors, the breakeven point is a particularly important calculation. It's a tipping point – a watershed for your business – and it signals the moment that you're primed and ready to tip over into profit.

The breakeven point is different for different businesses, and you should get to know your own. But wouldn't it be great if you could not only illustrate the point at which you'll arrive at breakeven, but go one better and show potential investors that, with their investment and support, you can exceed that target and go into profit ahead of your anticipated time frame?

In order to do this, you need to look at the different variables that affect your breakeven point, and how you can manipulate them to create different outcomes. For example, you can

- Run a scenario that illustrates the impact of manufacturing part or all of your products abroad, where it's cheaper, thereby lowering your direct costs to market.

- Decide not to hire so many PAYE (pay as you earn) people, but to outsource some work to subcontractors who lower your overall costs to deliver a service.

- Develop or share a partnership with some cutting-edge technology sources, thereby lowering your direct costs. This also allows you to charge more while you're the only one with this technology – making hay while the sun shines with regard to the retail cost of your product.

There are a number of ways to arrive at profit sooner than later, and potential investors will appreciate your ingenuity and forward thinking as long as it isn't unrealistic and unachievable.

Determining Your Best Source of Finance

Determining the best source of finance for you and your business has to do with the stage your business is at, the investment you've already received, your company structure and what you can achieve in your network and with your raw materials. That said, if more SME owners and entrepreneurs were better educated as to the implications of different types of finance for business growth and development, there would be more use of the variety of funding options on offer – and perhaps more would consider alternative forms of funding as well as equity funding. You need to keep an open mind when considering the options and parameters for financing your business.

If you approach funders at the wrong time, it gives a bad impression of you as a leader and wastes an awful lot of your valuable time. As a business owner, it's your responsibility to be as educated, informed and networked as you can be. Knowing when you're fully ready and able to receive investment is key.

Identifying your stage of funding need

At different stages in your company's growth, you need different types of funding and investment, and sometimes more than one type at the same time. You need to know what stage your business is at so that you can narrow your search for funders and target those looking to invest in companies at your stage of business growth. For each stage, be it early growth, significant revenue growth, established and expanding, growing too fast and hitting the buffers or preparing to exit, there are funders who want to invest in your business.

Decide what stage you're at using the guidelines in Chapter 2, and if you need some help deciding, consult your mentors and advisers before approaching funders.

You also need to be sure that your company fits the investor's criteria and investment parameters. There's little point in approaching a private equity house looking to invest £20 million if you're a relatively new company needing £150,000.

Reviewing your finance options

Being investor-ready means you not only understand what makes an investor tick but that you have options in how you raise your funds. Sometimes the obvious choice is not the best choice at a specific point in time.

You need to recognise the relationship between the various stages of funding and the impact one round has on the next. As Chapter 2 talks about, each stage of business growth has certain funding solutions associated with it, and sometimes these solutions overlap. The skill is in knowing what finance option is right for your business at a particular stage, and understanding the implications for the road ahead.

If you're a drinks company, crowdfunding may be a good option because you're likely to need debt in the future, and you won't have large equity investors to consider. Similarly, if you're a tech business with an aggressive growth plan, your late-stage equity investors may be put off by having to buy out 478 small crowd-sourced investors, preferring to invest only in companies that have sophisticated investors at the earlier stages.

You need to do your homework and find the right solution for the stage you're currently at, but also think ahead to the next stage and consider the impact of your decision on future funding rounds.

Going for debt

The readiness principle holds when debt is the right type of funding for your business, with some notable differences.

Depending on the time frame and the specific need for funding, debt is sometimes the more appropriate option for your business. Unlike equity, you don't give any of the business away, but you need to be able to pay the money back with interest, and your cash flow projections should bear that out. In terms of investment readiness, lenders are not usually interested in helping you shape and hone your business strategy, where an equity investor has a selfish interest in doing exactly that.

Debt is often, but not exclusively, used for short-term or one-off funding situations. In general, minimising the risk of defaulting on repayment outweighs the risk associated with the high-growth reward trajectory that an equity investor seeks, so what you present to funders and how you pitch the opportunity is more about good growth, usually maximum 20 per cent year on year – not the meteoric growth you'd present for equity.

Sharing with investors

Equity investors take a risk acquiring shares in your business, and they look to the business's growth to give them a return in good dividends and rising share prices before they get a final big return when they exit the business.

As the business owner, you dilute your shares when you take investors on, and you just have to accept that as part of the package. On the plus side, if you find the right investors, they may be interested in funding future stages of your business growth in follow-up rounds, which can save you a lot of time, money and headaches going forward. Sharing has its benefits.

Finding free money

A variety of grants and competition awards may be right for your business – I look at them in detail in Chapter 9. This type of funding can be particularly useful at the start of your business, when you've yet to prove that you can generate decent sales. You can also use so-called free money at critical stages in the development of new products or services, which often require a substantial cash injection to bring them to life.

Reviewing Your Current Documentation

When I talk to funders in my network, one of the most often quoted reasons for rejecting an approach for funding is a lack of readiness in terms of the materials to showcase and represent the business seeking finance. You may have the best business and proposition in the world, but if it looks like an untidy and unwieldy mess when you present it to funders, you've just blown that opportunity. You need to be clear and concise about what is on offer, how it makes money and what the risk and rewards look like. Make your proposition come to life in both the written and interactive formats.

Raising money is time-consuming process, so you need to do anything you can to make it more efficient. You never know when an opportunity to pitch may present itself, so you want to be completely investment ready.

Writing your investment executive summary

Your investment executive summary gives potential investors an overview of your business as well as an overview of the investment opportunity you're putting in front of them. The summary should give investors a complete understanding of how your business works and how their investment is used in order to generate a good return.

The investment executive summary is approximately two pages in length and covers your business description, market overview, team, how the business works in practical terms, financial projections and investment required, the specific uses of the money and possible exit and potential investor rewards.

Your business plan also has an executive summary that gives an overview of your business, with a mention of the funding requirement and your intended use of the funds, but it goes into less detail about the possible exit and return on investment. The business plan executive summary is roughly one page in length. It covers your business description, market overview, team, financial forecast summary, investment required, brief description of how the money will be used and a couple of lines on the potential exit for an investor.

Revisiting your business plan

Time to dust off your business plan and see where it needs updating and improving, because believe me, it needs both before presenting it to potential funders. It may also require a hard pruning back, as you may have previously planted very flowery beds and overflowing borders, which is now full of weeds and seems overgrown to your fresh eyes – no 56-page business plans at this point. Be cruel to be kind! (I talk more about business plans in Chapter 5.)

Assessing your pitching materials

Although you may have had only PowerPoint available to you when creating your original presentation, the progress of technology marches on. You can now take advantage of a number of reputable presentation software packages and websites, incorporating video, live streaming, social media and so on. It's important to find the tool that works best for your business rather than relying on one solution. Make sure your pitch materials represent the century you live in.

You need to grab an investor's attention and keep it for as long as possible, so the way you present yourself and your business can be as important as what you present.

Not everyone – including yours truly – is a dab hand at using technology and equipment, so if you feel unable to tackle all this on your own, there's no shame in getting some help from your nearest ten-year-old or outsourcing some of the actual pitch creation from the content you write. Just make sure you know how to access and use it on your pitch day!

Clearly, what you put into your pitch is terms of content is equally if not more important than the way you present it. (I look at pitches and presentations in Chapter 6.) Don't fill your pitch with fluff or with an endless amount of statistics and data. Do your research and know your business universe, but whittle down all the reams of information to a focused and topical pitch deck for your audience. You want to cover the business background, the market, your team, the financials and the exit strategy.

Before you share your presentation with potential investors, get an experienced but objective eye to review it. Don't get precious about suggested cuts and amendments. You can have too much information, and death by PowerPoint is never pleasant.

Updating your investment memorandum

An investment memorandum (IM) is a great way to quickly introduce your business and funding proposition to potential investors, helping to tease interest out of them and prompt them to ask for more detailed information or even better, a meeting.

Essentially, an *investment memorandum* provides an investor with an overview of the business and the management team, the marketplace you run in and your plans for the future. It has a breakdown of the funds you need to make your plans a reality. It outlines the risks and rewards for the investor, with a route to exit in five years. An IM also has a sidebar listing a series of highlights and milestones for your business. This sidebar acts as a kind of shorthand for the short attention spans and time constraints of most active investors.

The sidebar contains essential information about your company, including

- ✔ A **summary** section that includes
  - The company name and address.
  - A one-sentence description about what the company does.
  - A link to the company website.
- ✔ The **general information** section gives specific details about the business, including
  - The sector your business is in.
  - The stage of your business. (I talk about business stages in the chapters in Part III.)
  - The year the business was established.
  - Number of staff.
  - Current turnover.
  - Revenue growth by quarter or by year.
  - Total market size, including how much money is spent in your sector each year.
  - The business's EIS/SEIS (Enterprise Investment Scheme and Seed Enterprise Investment Scheme) eligibility.
- ✔ The **key achievements** section lists high points for your company so far and includes

- How far your product or service has been developed – whether it's a prototype or a fully fledged product, for example.

- Research and development you're doing that's significant to company growth and investment.

- Mention any pilot studies you've done or will do.

- List key existing clients.

- List key contracts the business has won.

- State growth in turnover over a quarter, a year or other time period.

- State any previous investment amounts and types.

- State any awards or competitions the business has won or been shortlisted for.

- State any grants awarded, their source and amount.

The main body of your IM has the following sections:

- ✔ **Business overview:** A short summary about what the company does, the market problem it solves, its unique selling points (USPs), your current stage, current revenue and existing clients, the business sales model, brief product information (if relevant), how the business can scale up in the future and the company's global ambitions.

- ✔ **Market information:** Information on market size, trends and competition.

- ✔ **Management team:** Give the management team's background and credentials as well as expertise of any advisers or non-executive directors (NEDs).

- ✔ **Investment requirement:** State the amount of funding needed and what it's required for. Detail any subsequent rounds of funding you anticipate and mention your eligibility for SEIS or EIS.

- ✔ **Exit strategy:** This very brief statement describes the anticipated exit route and timescale.

Figure 4-1 shows a sample IM.

After you create your first IM, treat it as a living, breathing document. Keep it up to date and ready to send at all times.

Raising money is a time-consuming process, and anything you can do to make it more efficient, you should do. You never know when an opportunity to pitch may present itself, so you want to be completely investment ready.

SUMMARY

[Insert company name]

[Insert a one sentence description about what the company does]

[Insert link to website]

Office address:

General information:

[Sector]
[Stage]
[Year established]
[Number of staff]
[Current turnover]
[Revenue growth]
[Total market size]
[EIS/SEIS eligibility]

Key achievements:

- [Development phases]
- [R&D]
- [Pilot studies]
- [Existing clients]
- [Contract wins]
- [Growth in turnover]
- [Previous investment]
- [Award wins]
- [Competition wins]
- [Grants]

BUSINESS OVERVIEW

A short summary about what the company does, what market pain it serves, USPs, current stage, revenue, existing clients, sales model, brief product information (if relevant), scalability, global ambitions

MARKET INFORMATION

Information on market size, trends, competition

MANAGEMENT TEAM

Information on management team's background and credentials as well as any advisers or NEDs

INVESTMENT REQUIREMENT

Amount of funding needed, what it is required for, details on any subsequent rounds anticipated, eligibility for SEIS or EIS

EXIT STRATEGY

Very brief statement on the anticipated exit route and timescale

Figure 4-1:
A sample investment memorandum.

Part II

Creating a Compelling Funding Proposition

Five Tips for Composing Your Pitch

- ✔ **Check and double-check the language you use.** Use plain, clear, jargon-free English.

- ✔ **Be mindful of the number the pages or slides.** You want to be able to flick back and forth effortlessly when you need to.

- ✔ **Limit the amount of text on each slide.** The slide is a guide for the audience and a prompt for you. It should contain key words that don't overload the page.

- ✔ **Limit the number of points on each slide.** Avoid too many points on one slide and limit the number of times information slides in or drops down. Crowded slides and too much activity can be very distracting.

- ✔ **Stick to one or two basic fonts and avoid lots of different colours.** Use familiar fonts such as Arial because they're easier to read and keep your colour palette simple.

Visit www.dummies.com/extras/businessfundinguk to learn more about the pros and cons of a crowdfunding video pitch versus a face-to-face pitch.

In this part . . .

✔ Put together a knock-out business plan.

✔ Create a winning pitch.

✔ Improve your funding success rate.

✔ Access various sources of help and advice.

Chapter 5

Loving the Paperwork: Preparing Your Business Plan

● ●

In This Chapter

▶ Answering 'why write a business plan?'

▶ Assembling the parts of the plan

▶ Reviewing planning software

▶ Making your presentation

● ●

*P*ossibly the most important activity in preparing to raise funds for your business is the research, planning and construction of your business plan. If the numerous websites and download-ready business plan templates on the Internet are anything to go by, I'm not alone in my opinion. Your business plan gives you a place to record and store your goals, your strategy, your objectives, assumptions and your needs, and in this case, your financial needs as well. It provides you with a platform for letting the funding world know what problem you solve and why you do it better than anyone else. It tells the reader why your red-hot team is worth trusting with their money, and how you'll make their investment generate their desired return.

Be under no illusion. It takes time to write your business plan, but it's time well-spent as the act of writing crystallises your thoughts and helps you focus on and clearly explain your financial requirements and uses. In addition to an extremely useful funding tool, it's also a rite of passage. By writing a business plan, you show the world your serious about making your plans or ideas a reality, and that you're not wasting anybody's time. This core document becomes the foundation for charting your business changes as you grow.

Your fundraising toolkit may eventually contain not just a business plan, but an investment memorandum (or opportunity note) and a pitch deck (or presentation) too (as I discuss in Chapter 6). In this chapter, I focus on the business plan, as it's the common denominator in all funding propositions.

Establishing Why You Need a Business Plan

If I had a pound for every time someone asked why he needs a business plan whether or not he needed to raise funds, I'd be relaxing on a secluded beach, sipping piña coladas and enjoying early retirement instead of writing this book. You've probably heard the old adage, 'failing to plan is planning to fail', and in business this often rings true; it's definitely true when it comes to writing a business plan to raise business funding.

Contrary to popular belief, raising funds isn't the only reason to write a business plan, but it's a very good one. Other reasons include proving to yourself that the opportunity exists, providing a guide for the direction of your business, confirming that your team can deliver, establishing how you can monitor progress, holding yourself accountable and attracting others to invest in your business. By offering a solid business plan, you show potential investors that your business knows where it's going and that it's mapped out how it's going to get there.

The act of writing up the business plan forces you to face some cold hard facts and to focus on considering the key areas of your plan all at the same time:

✔ What your actual proposition is

✔ How you're bringing your business to market

✔ The practicalities of how the business operates

✔ How much money your business needs and how much money it will make

Without a plan, the tendency is to see these inter-connected areas in isolation, which is where problems start to arise. It's one thing to say 'we want 10,000 customers by the end of the year' and another thing to think about how much you need to spend (on marketing your product or service and getting it to customers) in order to achieve this.

Your plan needs to prove to funders that you:

✔ Have a feasible proposition

✔ Can bring that proposition to market

✔ Have some idea of how you can deliver, in practical terms – and that you have a team in place to do so

✔ Have clear financial systems, projections and targets

✔ Can give a return on investment (ROI) or repay the loan

Building confidence

Writing – and completing – your business plan boosts both your confidence and that of your investors. The business plan gives you a road map to success; you feel more in control of the venture, knowing that you have a plan to follow. It also helps you to attract the talent you need to deliver what you say you can.

A good business plan shows investors that you've done your research and you can prove that there's a market for your service or product, and that you have the skills to get this product or service to customers. Your business plan lays out how the business will give a return to investors, repay its loans and so on.

Some investors may be investing in a business for the first time, and so they also need to feel confident, as well as have a point of comparison to other opportunities they may encounter in the future as they sign that cheque.

As with any plan, things can and do go wrong. Anticipating some of the potential bumps in the road when you're writing your business plan can help you feel more able to deal with any unexpected hiccups along the way.

Structuring your business plan

Despite the fact that business has sometimes been compared to war, writing a business plan is not *War and Peace*. Your plan doesn't need to be 56 pages long, and you don't have to be a Pulitzer Prize-winning writer to guarantee success. You do, however, need to be organised and succinct in your writing, and brutal with your editing, so that you wind up with a compelling and informative road map to successful funding.

Although nothing's set in stone, the universally accepted format for a basic business plan looks like this:

- ✔ **Executive summary:** The executive summary is exactly what it says on the tin – it's a summary of all the parts of your business plan, including the financials, and is usually only a page or so long.

  Resist the temptation to write your executive summary first – even though it's the first thing your audience reads. It can be the most difficult section to write because it forces you to pull out the highlights of your plan, and is, therefore, the last thing you write. The clue is in the name – executive *summary* – you can't write a summary if you haven't written the rest of the plan.

- ✔ **Marketing:** The marketing section follows the executive summary and covers the size and behaviour of your market, your route to market, your USP (unique selling points), your marketing strategy, your action plan and any collateral that you require, such as point of sale materials, leaflets and so on. You can find more information on this topic in *Marketing For Dummies* by Alexander Hiam (Wiley).

✔ **Operations:** Up next is the operations section, which provides the nuts and bolts of your plan. Here you cover what your business does, how you do it, where you do it and who does what. You also include any design, prototyping, manufacture, logistics and distribution information here.

✔ **Financials:** The financials section needs to contain your actual up-to-date financial position, as well as believable three- to five-year growth projections. Include cash flow, profit and loss, and balance sheets, plus any supporting facts, explanations or hypotheses that led you to your projected growth figures. In addition to these spreadsheets and financial documents, include an illustration of the impact the investment will have on your business and the return investors can expect to make. Help with the financial and operation sections of your business plan can be found in *Starting a Business For Dummies,* UK Edition, by Colin Barrow (Wiley).

✔ **Appendices:** Instead of cluttering up the body of the plan with CVs, sales emails, sample marketing materials, training plans, contracts and so on, put them in the appendices, which is where you include any supporting documentation.

Showing how much money you need

Given that you want to raise funding for your business, your business plan needs to show how much money you need, when you need it and for how long, what you intend to spend it on, and what the long-term return will be. You need to present this information using detailed financial documents because, when raising funds, detail matters. If you underestimate the funding need, investors can spot that immediately; if you overestimate, with no obvious reason for doing so, investors will see this too. The trick is to think your financials through carefully, cost things accurately and come up with the optimum figure to achieve your milestones and targets.

Whatever your reason for seeking funding – taking on staff, prototyping, launching your product overseas – you need to do your research, talk to people who have experience and connect with your market. Use agencies to get salary costs, search your business networks to find people a year ahead of you, get advice from those who have printed a 3-D product successfully . . . in short, do your homework to ensure that you get accurate figures to put into your plan.

Your investment need isn't what your business start-up costs overall – it's what you need to spend and when. For example, when you hire staff, you don't need to have a full year's salary in the bank at the start of each year – you just need to cover a few months of their hard work before their efforts start paying for themselves. Don't ask an investor for a full year of wages.

Be very rigorous. If your figures have gaps, shortfalls or sensitivities, investors become wary and lose confidence that you're on top of your proposition.

Consider how various scenarios may affect your need for funding. What factors may increase the amount you need – landing larger customers sooner than expected, regulatory changes, your competition changing tack? Make sure that you know how much more money you need and when you'd need it in case feasible scenarios occur and create the need for additional investment. If you need less money than you thought, great. If you may need more, it's good that you – and your investors – know and understand why from the start.

Testing your idea

You need to prove that your proposition can succeed and give a return, and it makes good business sense to take a systematic approach to testing your ideas before you go to market. Decide on the best *business model* – the way you intend to get your product or service to market and get paid for it. (*Business Models For Dummies* by Jim Muehlhausen has good information.) Find your best approach and test it out on prospects and customers to get valuable feedback on how they see your concept, product or service. I look at market testing and your business model in Chapter 3, and you can also consult *Starting a Business For Dummies,* UK Edition, by Colin Barrow.

Writing your business plan forces you to test your approach to market over and over again: to research customers; to test prices; and to check and double-check costings, anticipating every overhead, and understanding how your costs are all connected to each other and the impact of any one of them not being on point.

As one entrepreneur confided in me, 'I had no idea that revenue was not the same as profit, and breakeven didn't even enter my vocabulary. It was a sobering moment when I realised that my overheads were just way too high for my business, and all my numbers were out.'

You need to make sure that your business model works, and that it compares well to other businesses succeeding in the marketplace and winning investment. Is it the best? It needs to be.

Satisfying financiers' concerns

When faced with a situation where you're desperate for a positive outcome, you can sometimes forget the obvious. Remember that when you're raising finance you need to find out and understand what financiers want and expect from you if you're going to be successful at getting them to fund your business. (For more information on successfully approaching funders, see Chapter 4.)

Not a day goes by when some newspaper or online blog doesn't bemoan the fact that no one is lending any money – or says that no one is funding anything but technology businesses. But, this isn't the case. If you put together a good proposition, have a top-notch management team with an excellent business plan and supporting material and aim for the right investors, at the right time, you have every chance of getting in front of funders who are looking for what you offer.

Lack of available funding is nowhere near one of the most common reasons for a business not being funded. Reasons funding isn't forthcoming include: no evidence of demand and/or a growing market; unrealistic financial forecasts; no ownership or protection of IP (intellectual property); no minimum viable product (which I talk about in Chapter 3) already in the market and generating income; and a weak business model. You can also find additional information in *Patents, Copyrights and Trademarks For Dummies* by Henri J A Charmasson and John Buchaca (Wiley).

It may take longer than you anticipate to raise funds, but a well-researched, well-written and effectively presented business plan gives you the best chance of success.

Writing Up Your Business Plan

In this section, I share some useful guidelines to help you create a knock-out business plan that captures the attention of potential funders and gets your business funded where others fail. Thousands of businesses start each year, while others take their first tentative steps towards growth; some businesses pull back to consolidate and strengthen what they have, while a small number experience significant growth, taking on vast sums of money for global expansion. Whatever your stage of growth or need for funding, making your business plan and its supporting material the best that they can be gives it – and you – the best chance to stand out from the crowd and raise those funds.

Defining your audience

As any good actor can tell you, you play to the audience in front of you. The same rule applies when looking for funding for your business. A business plan is most effective when you write it for the audience that you intend to show and present it to, and so you need to define your audience's characteristics and adjust your business plan accordingly.

Traditionally, bankers – the trusted guardians of the public's money – are notoriously risk averse, and don't respond well to a business plan that has high risk and unrealistic projections written all over it. On the other hand, venture capitalists (VCs) are used to taking risks and know that higher-risk investments often produce the highest returns in the shortest amount of time – thus creating a lucrative exit.

Although the fundamentals are the same for any audience, in order to write a winning business plan you first need to decide whom you're writing it for, examine their characteristics and understand what makes them tick. You therefore need to create a number of versions of your business plan, adjusting each to suit the risk appetite and desired outcome for each audience.

Creating the plan

Business plan formats can vary, but time, experience and results show that certain styles are more successful than others.

Your business plan may need all, more or fewer of these headings, as they are generic and don't take into account all the subtle nuances of every industry. But this broad structure provides a well-worn, readily accepted and robust format that you can adjust for your specific business needs:

- ✔ **Title page:** This page contains a brief statement about what the business does and what its current funding need is. Include the name and physical address of your business, your name, your contact information (including your email address, phone number[s] and fax if you have one), and your Twitter handle, Facebook page and website URL. Include the date for this particular version of your plan as well.

- ✔ **Table of contents:** This is the reader's guide to your plan, and as such it needs to clearly indicate the headings and subheadings for each section of your plan, with corresponding page references. Number each heading and subheading hierarchically; for example, as section 1, section 1.1, section 1.2, section 2, section 2.1 and so on.

- ✔ **Executive summary:** You ideally aim to keep your executive summary to one page, but if necessary it can spill over into another paragraph or so on the next page. This summary is your first impression, and so you need to use it to get the reader excited about what follows and to ensure that he's keen to keep reading.

   You break down your executive summary into sections that correspond to the four main sections of your full business plan:

   - • You start with a description of what your company does, its products or services, any patents or trademarks, when it was established, by whom, where and what its current trading position is. This information comes mainly from the fuller operations section of your business plan.

- Next, you state the company position within its marketplace, roughly how big the market place is, why customers need this product or service, what is unique about it, and provide some indication of how much growth you anticipate. You will have covered this information in detail in the marketing section of your business plan.

- Following on from that is a summary of your financial forecasts of longer-term sales revenue and profit (look at three to five years), together with your short-term forecasts and how you aim to achieve these.

- Last, you need to state how much money you're looking to raise, what you plan to use it for and what benefits you can offer to the provider of this finance. Both your forecasts and your funding requirement/use are covered in more detail in the finance section of your business plan.

✔ **Marketing:** The marketing section has a few distinct areas that you can break down into:

- An overview of the market size

- Key market characteristics and any areas of segmentation

- A strategy for capturing a share of this market

- The increase in market share you hope to achieve

- Key competitors

- An action plan for implementing your strategy that includes your marketing costs, your promotion and distribution channels, the intended location for your marketing efforts and any potential partnerships or joint-working arrangements

✔ **Operations:** The operations section provides the nuts and bolts of your business plan. It tells funders how you do what you do. This section gives the what, how, where and who of your business and includes:

- **What you actually do and how you do it:** Repeat what it is that you actually do – for example, explain the consultation service that you provide or describe the product that you manufacture.

- **Where you're located:** State where your business operates. If you have multiple locations, put them all in the plan and explain what happens at each site.

- **Who's in your team:** Give details of who is in the team and the roles and responsibilities of each person. Include mention of human resources (HR) information such as your employee handbook, equal opportunity (EO) policy, training plans, retention strategies and any reward systems.

  You put your team's curriculum vitaes (CVs, or résumés) in the appendices section, and so you only provide a short description here of who's who.

You also include the following operational business information in this section of your business plan:

- **Health and safety and quality assurance:** Include any certificates, assurances and policies that your business has and indicate whether these are required or desirable.

- **Legal requirements:** Include mention of any legal considerations if you have any contracts or specific legal requirements/agreements. Place full copies of any relevant legal documents in the appendices section.

✔ **Financials:** The financials section of your plan summarises the key financial documents, data and ratios for your business with a description of your methods of monitoring and controlling financial performance. Some of the documents you summarise, with both forecasted and actual (if your business has trading figures already) figures, include:

- Cash flow

- Profit and loss

- Balance sheet

You include full financial documentation at the back of the financials section of your plan, rather than in your appendices section unless they're very detailed, as they are for larger amounts in later growth stages, in which case, you put them in an appendix.

In addition, your financials section may include:

- **Sensitivity analysis:** To illustrate that you're aware that forecasts can be out by a reasonable amount (in either a positive or negative direction), show what the effect on the bottom line may be if things improve or decline by 10 and 20 per cent in either direction – four scenarios in total.

- **Average customer spend:** Estimate the typical amount a customer spends each time he engages with your business. This helps to show investors how many clients or repeat purchases you need to achieve your revenue projections.

- **Financing requirements:** Include the amount of finance you require to achieve your currently planned goals and objectives, along with how long you need it for and what the impact on your business will be if you don't raise the money.

- **Risk assessment:** Whether your business plan is for a lender or an investor, identifying and minimising risk is at the forefront of a funder's mind. Use this section to show that you've anticipated potential risks and that you have a solution or a strategy to minimise these risks if they occur – or to avoid them altogether.

- **Valuation and impact of investment:** The company valuation is a bit of art meets science. You can use online tools to help you get a fairly accurate picture of your valuation, and to illustrate the valuation both before and after any money is invested. Good examples of these tools are bizequity (www.bizequity.com) and D-RISK IT (www.drisk.it).

✔ **Exit route:** *Business angels,* individuals or networked groups of individuals who invest in start-up and early stage businesses or VCs typically look to realise their investment and exit the business within three to seven years. Your business plan needs to show them how much money they can expect to make from their investment and approximately in what time frame. If you're looking for a longer-term, paced investment, explain who the likely buyers of the business are or at what point you think you can take the business to a public listing on a stock exchange.

✔ **Appendices:** Include CVs of all key people in the business, which can also include advisers, accountants and consultants. Include details on patents, design copyright, design specifications, technical data, examples of confirmed or intended orders and so on.

Writing, drafting and editing

The first version of your business plan won't be the last. Like paying taxes and dying, this is something I am prepared to guarantee. The first draft of your plan compiles your notes, research, team input, ideas, thoughts, opinions and randomly gathered facts. It ignores correct grammar, spelling, formatting and layout – and that's okay. As you speak to advisers, people in your business networks, researchers, other entrepreneurs and possible investors, you refine the draft into your final version, ready for editing.

It's in the editing stage that grammar, spelling, tone, style and layout become all important. You can expect your finished product to be 15 to 25 pages all in, and you may want to make use of online or freelance editing services if you struggle to cut to the chase. (You can find some resources in Chapter 8, where I cover getting help.)

Bear in mind the following points as you format your business plan:

✔ **Ensure readability:** Layout and font are very important for making your plan visually appealing to the reader.

- **Font:** Use clear fonts that are a good size – Times New Roman at 11 or 12 point, for example – in order to avoid eye fatigue and take the strain off the reader. For funders past age 50 who are using bifocals or reading glasses, steer clear of any point size below 12. Avoid fancy fonts that are difficult to read, and make use of bold text to clearly separate out headings.

- **Layout:** Bullet points and the prudent use of white space all add to the ease of reading and create a favourable impression. Keep your margins wide enough for readers to make notes, and use single- and double-line spacing, as appropriate.

✔ **Include visuals:** Too much block text can be difficult for readers to absorb, and an image can often be much more effective at conveying meaning than words. Images, graphs, charts, pictures and tables can summarise and convey large amounts of complicated data in an easily understandable way as well as provide a great way to hold the reader's interest and attention.

✔ **Present the physical plan:** No hard-and-fast rules apply for how you package up and present your plan, but be sure to keep it simple. Make sure that readers can easily flip from one section to another.

A simple bound-edge binder with a clear plastic cover in front and a card cover at the back is always a safe bet. The covers make the paper document more robust so that it can withstand all the handling it will get.

Using Business Planning Software

The explosion in the use of online resources (and the number of professionals wanting to monetise their business knowledge) has created a startling array of business planning software, both free and fee-based. You may want to think about whether you can save some time and frustration by using one of the packages on the market. You can also find a business plan template at `www.dummies.com/extras/businessfundinguk`.

Avoid the 'one size fits all' option, or one that gives you 500 business plans to choose from. Chances are it won't be suitable for your business, and may wind up resulting in a generic, dull and lifeless business plan. Funding professionals can see right through these generic constructions, and you may find it hard to present the plan as your own to funders.

Whenever possible, try to find a template for your industry or sector written by people who have experience and insight into what the plan needs to include. Unless the plan is created by someone in your industry, the designer probably knows less than you do – and you may be lulled into a false sense of security and not check the quality as closely as you need to.

When considering using a business planning software package, some useful capabilities and content to look out for in a product include

✔ Industry profiles by experienced professionals

✔ Market research provided for your sector

✔ Examples of financials for different target audiences

✔ Ability to import from Microsoft Word and Excel

✔ Investor insight and information guide

✔ Valuation tools

✔ Enables team collaboration for amendments and updates online

✔ Easy to customise

✔ The ability to automatically generate charts and graphs from text

✔ Easy to export to presentations

✔ Simple to use – no MBA required

Reviewing the packages

You can find hundreds of different software packages offered by a variety of sources. Most of these packages come from one of three sources:

✔ **Bank:** Your bank may offer you a free solution in order to give you a warm and fuzzy feeling before it approaches you to pay for additional optional services. All the high street banks offer their own versions of business planning software that cover the text or written sections of the plan as well as the financials. They sometimes incorporate accounting software, such as Sage, and usually provide examples. Examples can be found and downloaded on high street bank websites, such as www.barclaysbank. co.uk/startupsupport or www.bankofscotlandbusiness.co.uk.

A good starting point for a start-up business, these packages encourage low-risk strategies and emphasise maintaining a positive cash position, as these are banking concerns, so they may not be suitable when you prepare for equity funding.

✔ **Business advisers or enterprises:** These often want to get you hooked via a sample for a commercial service that requires payment later on. In contrast to banking software, enterprise and adviser templates or down-loads are aimed at preparing for and raising funds in the wider commercial and funder marketplace, and as such, are more useful from start-up to later growth stages of your business.

Example of these packages can be found on sites from independent advisers and consultants, as well as enterprise support agencies, and the list of potential URLs is very big. A good place to get an overview of a number of business planning software packages is http://business-plan-software-review.toptenreviews.com, where you can see up-to-date comparisons of the most popular plans such as Live Plan, Business Plan Pro and Business Magic Plan. And, you can refer to Chapter 8, where you can find helpful reference links.

Recognising the limits

Business planning software helps you get started if the alternative is staring at a blank piece of paper. Software can also provide a useful framework in which to drop your information as you and your team develop and amend your business plan.

Business planning software often comes with pre-programmed spreadsheets, which takes the hassle out of creating formulae or relying on friends to help you with unfamiliar financial programmes. These spreadsheets can offer a first step to a financial dialogue with your bank, for example, which provides its own branded software that comes with your account, and is most suited to that bank, but not necessarily to other types of funders, such as business angels, so be aware that this package my have limited uses.

If you rely on the software to do all the work for you, it's easy to forget that it doesn't have the ability to create a unique, compelling and authentic representation of you and your business – which is what you need to add as meat on the bones of an off-the-shelf solution.

Computers don't make mistakes, it's the people who operate them; your computer can only work with the information that you put into the programme to generate your results. The universally accepted computer truism GIGO – garbage in equals garbage out – also applies to computer software packages.

Recognise these limitations, and see business planning software programmes as starter kits for building the plan of your dreams. Ignore this advice and you may do more harm than good, which may ultimately see you wasting a good deal of time and effort.

Presenting Your Plan

Dale Carnegie became famous for his work helping people become accustomed to and good at public speaking. He is the author of the very well-known *How to Win Friends and Influence People,* and is often quoted when it comes to presentation advice. For the purposes of presenting your plan to potential funders, you'd be wise to consider this gem: 'A talk is a voyage. It must be charted. The speaker who starts nowhere usually gets there.'

In other words, you need to prepare, practise and take the audience along on your journey to success. This journey can start in a number of ways, such as emailing your plan, or your executive summary, to your potential funders to familiarise them with your proposition before sitting down for a more detailed face-to-face discussion or verbally presenting your plan at investor open pitch evening.

Your business plan is one of the prerequisites you present to funders to show that you're serious and that you've charted your business journey and funding need. When you get to present your plan to a small panel of funders or to a large room full of equity investors, your plan has given you passage to the next phase of the funding journey.

If you're unaccustomed to formal – or informal, but public – speaking, there's no time like the present to learn to love, or at the very least, like the process: formally introducing yourself, your team and your plan to funders and investors, who are likely to be experienced audience members. Funders have read and been pitched many business plans – perhaps they've made presentations themselves – and can spot someone winging it from miles away. They're also human – they know that nerves can be very difficult to tame, and they expect some minor hiccups, but they won't be impressed by a presentation that stumbles from one section to the next. They'll expect you to be well-prepared, well-rehearsed but still natural and ready to answer questions and respond to challenges in a calm, professional and thorough manner.

When it comes time to bringing your text to life, your manner, your look, your pace and how you respond to criticism are all key. Everyone screams at the television set when entrepreneurs go into meltdown on a television programme such as the BBC's *Dragons' Den,* and so heed the warning when it's your turn to get up from your armchair.

Dr Albert Mehrabian, author of *Silent Messages* (Wadsworth), conducted several studies on nonverbal communication. He found that just 7 per cent of any message is conveyed through words, 38 per cent through certain vocal elements, and 55 per cent through nonverbal elements (facial expressions, gestures, posture and so on). Therefore, get feedback on your presentation from people with an interest in seeing you succeed so that you can work on any distracting gestures or tics before presenting yourself to funders. *Presentations For Dummies* by Malcolm Kushner (Wiley) offers useful pointers.

Highlighting key points

Prepare, prepare and then prepare some more! You've done it before – hairbrush as a microphone in front of the bathroom mirror, practising until you're perfect. The same thing applies when presenting your plan to potential funders and investors. As important as preparation, and why you must write your own plan yourself, is being able to talk your way around your plan from any page at any time with confidence and ownership of the facts, including the numbers. You want the words to roll off your tongue naturally as a result of many hours of unnatural practice and polishing!

To make your presentation memorable in the best possible way, use these tips:

✔ **Dress for success.** You may be a tech genius and every day is dress-down Friday in your office, but your audience is expecting something close to a suit to give you a solid, trustworthy, business-like look. After all, the subject is money, maybe quite a bit of it, and you want to impress.

✔ **Master your nerves.** If you find presenting akin to walking on hot coals and don't have an identical twin to come to your rescue, you have to work with what you have. Get some advice on presenting, or maybe take an acting workshop at a local college to help put you at ease and give you hints and tips. Whether it's a panel of three or a roomful of angel investors, it may feel like Wembley Stadium to you.

One way to put yourself at ease is to find someone you can make eye contact with and imagine that he's the only person in the room. Some people imagine that everyone is naked, which puts you all on equal and exposed footing. Whatever your tactic is, you need to come across as measured and at ease, with a confident tone in your voice, good eye contact and an effective use of body language (which accounts for the largest part of listening). Shouting, mumbling, staring at the floor or the ceiling, standing with folded arms, or almost laying horizontal are extremes to be avoided.

✔ **Use visual aids.** If you have a product, prototype, model or diagram to demonstrate your idea, bring it in; if you've been featured in the press, set up press boards; if you have highlights from a film or recorded interview, play it. As with most things, a picture or an image is worth a thousand words. Just make sure to test any technology you need to show these things beforehand in order to avoid embarrassing slip-ups.

✔ **Make sure your information is accurate and up-to-date.** More often than not, the third-party facts and stats in your plan are based on the most up-to-date published information. If you can supplement them with any newer, up-to-the-minute facts and figures to enhance your presentation, be sure to do so – but make sure that they're accurate. Accuracy is also essential for your own financials, forecasts, sales information and milestones. Check them and double-check them, and make sure that they've been updated as near to the date of your presentation as possible so that you have an accurate picture of the state of your business.

✔ **Anticipate and allow time for questions.** Whether you allow for questions throughout your presentation or just at the end, make sure you leave enough time for them.

Anticipate and prepare answers for typical questions. Ask trusted but objective sources to listen to you rehearse, and see what questions they have. You can also think through potential questions yourself.

Answer questions calmly and sincerely, and under no circumstances get defensive or fob a question off as not valid. It's the right of the investors to get all the information they need.

Handling feedback

Receiving what you feel is negative feedback, or indeed a rejection of your plan or idea, is an inevitable part of presenting your plan when raising funds. Take it in your stride and learn from it. It's all part of the process, and as the saying goes, 'you can't please all the people all of the time'.

Many household names were turned down before they found fame and fortune, so don't be disheartened. The hugely successful entrepreneur Shaun Palfrey, who came up with the hair product Tangle Teezer, was famously turned down by Dragon's Den, citing a lack of a need for his product. He's gone on to win two Queen's Awards for Export and Enterprise and to revenues in the tens of millions. Harland David Sanders, better known as Colonel Sanders, had his famous Kentucky Fried Chicken secret recipe turned down over 1,000 times before he found fame and fortune.

Some of the business angel networks I work with regularly turn down 140 applications every week, and VC firms reject a similar number. You mustn't be surprised if you get turned down. What you need to do, however, is learn from the rejection.

Often, plans are rejected because potential funders aren't convinced that the team is up to the job or they can't see how the business can make money (and therefore provide either repayments to lenders or a lucrative enough exit for investors). Ironically, these reasons are usually the same when a plan is successful – albeit with the opposite supporting information.

So, what can you do to help make good use of feedback and minimise the chance of rejection? Use these tips:

- ✔ **Sharpen your listening skills.** Try to listen carefully during your presentation – easier said than done, I know – and to read the signs. If you can listen to and process the information in real time, you may be able to rephrase or explain something more fully, and bring it back from the brink of failure.

  If it's too late, and you sense that you're on the road to rejection, be mature enough to ask, 'why?' and 'what could I have done better or differently?' so that you can adjust your presentation to get a more positive outcome the next time.

- ✔ **Make sure that you have the right plan for the right audience.** Different funders have different appetites for risk – for example, banks are risk-averse, while VCs are open to high-risk opportunities. You need to have different business plans and approaches ready for each audience, and to address the right audience at the right time for your funding need. A common mistake is for businesses in the early stages of development to pitch to VCs when what they really need are business angels. Another mistake is to use the same pitch and presentation for a bank as for an angel community.

You need to pitch your presentation to the audience most likely to fund you. So pay attention to investors' appetite for risk, the appropriateness of the funding vehicle and the timing of your approach.

✔ **Revisit your plan.** When you know why your proposition was rejected, go back over the plan and see whether you can make any adjustments that can improve your chances of getting funding. For example, maybe you don't really need that million all upfront and in one lump sum. In your enthusiasm, it's easy to misjudge the real funding need and ignore the positive knock-on effect of an investment three or six months down the line.

Be careful not to present an unnecessarily risky or amateurish view of your financial projections, or to present a plan that's haemorrhaging funds before any sales revenue comes in. If you seem oblivious to apparent risks, you may put investors off.

Chapter 6

Creating a Winning Pitch

In This Chapter

▶ Looking at the parts of a pitch

▶ Designing the essential ingredients for a winning pitch

▶ Using video to its best effect

*N*ever underestimate the value in creating and delivering a winning pitch. A *pitch* is essentially a summary of your business idea and the business plan that brings your idea to life put into a slide format and presented to a panel of funders or investors. The presentation may be face-to-face or online.

The purpose of a pitch is to interest funders in your business and your team so that they invite you to a follow-on meeting to find out more of the details in order to enable them to make a decision to invest or not. You want the pitch to result in an instant investment decision, but in reality, that rarely happens.

Everybody loves a winner, and winners like to surround themselves with other winners in one virtuous winners circle. Giving your pitch is one of those times where winning matters more than the taking part, although taking part is good practice where pitching is concerned!

In this chapter, I talk about the parts of a pitch and how to compose one – or several – that can effectively help you find the funding you're looking for.

Exploring the Elements of a Winning Pitch

A great pitch is much more than just an informative speech, peppered here and there with some well-placed funny anecdotes. It needs to be a balance between captivating content and imaginative storytelling. A truly great pitch has a universal and easily understood structure, although it varies in content depending whether you're pitching for debt or equity, to a panel of investors or to the crowd on a crowdfunding website using video, animation and so forth. Also, if you're going to stand a chance at success, you must include content specific to your audience.

The mechanics of a winning pitch can be split into three areas:

✔ Preparing both the materials and yourself

✔ Creating the actual pitch materials

✔ Lots and lots of practice

If you're using your pitch for crowdfunding, there's an additional element of promotion as you need to bring a certain amount of the crowd to fund your proposition.

Common to all winning pitches is an often overlooked but mightily important characteristic: honesty. This isn't the time to inflate your figures, to over egg the team or to come up with a wildly outrageous valuation. This isn't the time to boast or gloat. Of course, a pitch is a selling tool, so you need to have some passion and a way to make the audience believe that you can achieve what you say you can achieve, but you can never tell lies. You'll be found out, and you may burn very useful bridges.

Picking up on this theme, I'm not going to lie to you and say that it's as easy as one, two, three to come up with a winning pitch. It's a team effort, and you'll go through a number of versions before you arrive at the version you're happy to present to the investing world at large. If you're not used to writing and delivering a pitch, it can be a pretty daunting experience, so maximise the expertise in your network and practice until you can't stand the sound of your own voice anymore.

Follow these guidelines when composing your pitch:

✔ **Check and double-check the language you use.** Use plain, clear, jargon-free English. Eliminate industry jargon, slang, swear words, colloquial or street vocabulary. In addition, check for variety, repetition, relevance and correct use of all the language you use.

Your audience may or may not have experience in your market, and although they may have done a little research ahead of time, it's not wise to baffle them with acronyms, abbreviations and industry-specific slang or unexplained vocabulary, because they'll just lose interest and switch off.

✔ **Number the pages or slides.** You want to be able to flick back and forth effortlessly when you need to.

- ✔ **Limit the amount of text on each slide.** The slide is a guide for the audience and a prompt for you. It should contain key words that don't overload the page. The font size should be large enough for people to easily see – 28 to 32 points for the body of the slide and 36 to 44 for the headings, for example. It's not a book or something to be read out word for word. Lots of text is distracting, and people start reading it instead of listening to you.

- ✔ **Limit the number of points on each slide.** Avoid too many points on one slide and limit the number of times information slides in or drops down. Crowded slides and too much activity can be very distracting.

- ✔ **Stick to one or two basic fonts.** Use familiar fonts such as Arial because they're easier to read. As tempting as it is to jazz up the words, stretchy fonts or curly-whirlys are hard to read.

- ✔ **Stay away from lots of different colours.** A range of colours may look pretty, but they can be hard to read at a distance and certain colours fade into the background. Also, not everyone in your audience may see colours in the same way due to a visual impairment, so keep to as simple a palette as possible.

Some golden rules for presenting a winning pitch include:

- ✔ **Dress for success.** Make sure you're well-groomed and all cleaned up. Seriously, dress for your industry and your audience, but make sure you're presentable and that you smell good without being overpowering. Remember, you're pitching yourself too.

- ✔ **Do a technical check beforehand.** Know your way around all your equipment, and make sure it's functioning properly. Make sure the room is well ventilated, well lit, and everyone is comfortable. There's nothing worse than not being able to breathe in a hot and stuffy room, straining your eyes in dim lighting and being shoved into a small space with a lot of people.

- ✔ **Speak in the first person – *I*.** You're making the case for your business, not letting someone else talk for you. The language you use says something about you.

- ✔ **Sell your compelling vision.** Give your audience just the core commercial points – not the full *Encyclopaedia Britannica!* Don't overpower your audience with endless facts and figures. Just use what helps sell your story.

- ✔ **Tell a story.** Investors are people just like you, and they like to hear a real person's story. You may have a funny or moving story about why you came to be standing in front of them. This can be a terrific secret weapon in your pitching armoury.

✔ **Be specific about your market, competition and customers.** Be prepared to answer questions on all these areas.

✔ **Ask for a realistic amount of money.** Be able to explain what you want to do with it and what it will achieve.

✔ **Never make the claim that you won't need a future round of funding.** This is naive and shortsighted, and if you're going for equity, you probably will need additional funding. If possible, provide a positive milestone when more funds will be needed; for example, 'These funds will let us capture the UK market, but to realise our potential in Europe, we'll need . . .'.

✔ **Tailor your pitch to your audience.** Do your research, know your audience and tailor your pitch. If you're pitching to investors, know what's already in their portfolios, where their industry knowledge lies and what kind of appetite they have for risk. If you're talking to lenders, be aware of the industry sectors they shy away from, check the news for stories that shed light on industries they're happy to get involved in, and be aware that financial institutions tend to have a less aggressive attitude towards risk than investors. Be aware that you'll most likely need different versions of your pitch for different types of audience.

✔ **Ask for feedback.** If the opportunity presents itself, you can ask during or right after your presentation. If not at the time, then ask later on. It's a great learning experience that can help make you better the next time.

✔ **Be at your optimal point of readiness.** Try not to over-prepare – or for that matter, under-prepare. The aim is to get to the point where you're rehearsed but still natural. You can and should listen to all the advice that comes from reliable sources, but you're the one standing up there so you need to make the presentation your own.

You've heard the advice to keep it simple, but when the heat is on, the natural tendency is to fall back to a safe place and witter on about what you know well. This is why it's important to practice.

As Guy Kawasaki of Garage Technology Ventures said, 'If you experience great difficulty in raising money, it's not because VCs (venture capitalists) are idiots and cannot comprehend your curve-jumping, paradigm-shifting, revolutionary product. It's because you either have a piece of crap or you are not effectively communicating what you have. Both of these are your fault.'

Preparing Your Materials

An investment memorandum, an executive summary and a pitch deck are the three elements you need to have ready to send at any time to a funder meeting, the invitation to pitch, the request for the business plan, or all of the above! The next sections cover each in turn.

Drumming up investor interest with an investment memorandum

Before you get to actually pitch in person, potential funders and investors discover whether they're interested in you and your business through an investment memorandum, sometimes also referred to as an *opportunity note, or investment note.* Whatever it's called an *investment memorandum* or *IM,* it provides a comprehensive overview of:

- ✓ What your business does
- ✓ The market it functions in
- ✓ The way it gets out to its customers and makes money
- ✓ How much money it makes or will make
- ✓ How much money you need from funders to make your vision a reality
- ✓ The risk to funders and their reward for having faith in your team and your idea

It also gives you a place to point out any highlights or milestones, and to toot your own horn if you've won or been a finalist in any relevant competitions or awards. (Chapter 4 walks through the parts of an IM.)

An investment memorandum is a great tool for drumming up investor or funder interest in advance of a meeting or an event where you can pitch directly to your investor audience. It's the starter on the menu that whets the appetite and makes funders want to order the main course, or at least start choosing from your à la carte menu. Ultimately, you want to get to the icing on the dessert cake and raise your investment, but, like most aspects of funding your business, you never get to eat the full buffet at one sitting.

When it comes to courting investors, you rarely have an opportunity to pay one price, go to one outlet and gorge yourself on all you can eat. It's more like enjoying a bite-sized taster menu, full of delectable morsels, so accept this, sit back and try to enjoy the feast.

Put yourself in the shoes of your potential funders: If you received and were expected to read up to 200 investment propositions or business plans a week, you'd want a universally accepted shorthand document to cut down on your reading time and help speed your decision-making process. It's just not possible to get through thousands of pages of proposals, particularly if you're not using a known intermediary to filter your introductions. To capture attention, you really need a snappy but informative IM to make an investor stop and take notice and ensure she doesn't miss out on a gem.

Many funders use a network of referral agents and introducers who are familiar with their investment criteria, well versed in their documentation style and requirements and very good at spotting potential investment opportunities. If you can identify and engage with some of these funder-finding professionals, it can help you get past the gatekeepers more quickly.

Preparing an investment memorandum is a team effort. It covers all areas of your business in an abbreviated format, so get input from each member of your team about their areas of responsibility, and then aggregate all the data and information in your style.

Summarising in an executive summary

As an introduction of your business to investors or lenders, your *executive summary* covers all the points in your business plan and most of the points in your IM, but in a reader-friendly, one-page document. The aim of your executive summary is to attract funders with a compelling story that leaves them wanting more.

Just as there is additional value in an IM in the lead up to a pitching event, the same can be said for your executive summary. Different people like to receive information in different formats, and your job is to get them all prepared so that you can respond to any request without having to stop what you're doing and reinvent the wheel in order to meet a deadline. I look at the executive summary for your business plan in Chapter 5.

Your executive summary hits the highlights of your business and doesn't delve too deeply into the details. You can do that later when you actually get a meeting. It should include:

- An overview of your business and of the market
- The operations, or the nuts and bolts of the business
- The finances, including the amount of funding you're seeking
- Some milestones to tease out interest from investors
- Your exit strategy

Assembling your pitch deck

A *pitch deck* gives funders a quick, visually attractive and informative view of your funding proposition without having to trawl through pages of wordy, fluffy, padded business plans before they know if they want to delve into the detail.

Your pitch deck helps sell your company and team to funders and gets them interested in what you want to do with their money and contacts. It starts the ball rolling on creating a rapport between you and the funding community and gets you on the long road to building trust in this critical business relationship. It opens the bonnet a crack so they can get a look at this engine in need of oiling and peek at who's in the driving seat.

It's your chance to tell everyone that you've identified a problem out there, and gone one better by finding the solution to it. Oh, and even better than that, it's actually going to make money for you and them.

A good pitch deck is

- Well prepared and ready to go at a moment's notice
- Personal to you and your business
- Your best performance

What makes your pitch believable is

- The experience and qualities of your team
- Your unique product or service
- Strong customer benefits or cost savings
- Evidence that your business solves a real problem
- Proof of scalability – what the market opportunity is and how you'll be able to scale your business up from start-up
- Strong financials showing what you're going to achieve, when the business will be profitable and your path to profitability
- Proven track record or achievements to date
- Skin in the game – what you've invested so far
- Including how much funding you need
- Laying out an exit strategy for funders

Have someone you trust, but who doesn't know your business, read through the documents looking for jargon and then get jargon busting!

I suppose there's nothing to stop you rocking up to a pitch event with nothing but yourself and a bit of confidence, but I've never seen this go well, so I don't recommend it as an approach. It's best to have a clear, concise and visually attractive pitch deck or slide presentation, using a universally accepted software tool such as PowerPoint, Keynote or Prezi. You need to create an informative, stimulating, no-nonsense presentation containing 1 to 12 slides that cover your key business proposition and funding request points.

What tends to happen when you don't have a presentation mapped out is that your mind and your thoughts start wandering and your mouth starts rambling in all different directions at once. Any logic, structure and cohesion go out the window, decreasing your chances of being heard and ruining your chance of success.

I'm not suggesting that you be stilted and unnatural, following your presentation materials to the letter. But it's generally accepted practice to have a short, sharp presentation to anchor your pitch, and help keep you on track and focused.

You can leave hard copies of your presentation materials with the funders as a reference point going forward, or you can email the materials as a follow-up.

Always send your materials as a PDF (portable document format) file to avoid having someone try to amend or copy them.

Your aim with a pitch presentation is to get that next appointment to drill down into the detail of an investment or loan, depending on where you are on the funding journey. You want to do all you can to make your pitch a winning pitch in every way possible.

Although they follow roughly the same format, there are at least two simple variations of pitches that appeal to different audiences and presenters, depending on the reason for the pitch, the environment and the experience of the presenter:

- **Full pitch:** If you're totally at ease with public speaking, and you're addressing a large group, such as an angel group – Angels Den or Angel Academe – at an angel pitch event or an open demo day, or if your business is on an accelerator programme, then go for the full pitch format, including fancy slides and technology and some of the interesting facts and figures that appear in your appendix.

  This format allows you to be the consummate storyteller, weaving the different threads of your proposition into a tightly knit golden tapestry, holding everyone's attention and eliciting the response that you want from the crowd.

- **Conversational pitch:** If you're less comfortable pitching to a large group, or you're pitching to a panel of two or three funders, give a shorter, more conversational pitch. Use a simple slide layout and minimal technology.

  This style helps to build rapport and gives you more thinking and breathing space, while ensuring a more human interaction instead of a one-directional, downward delivery. If the discussion takes a more detailed direction in any of the areas of your pitch, you can pull up the appropriate slide and use it as a point of reference to help guide you along.

Depending on the size of the group you're pitching to, it's also worth remembering that money is just one of the things you can get from a room full of investors. An investor may decide that you're not right for her, but that you may be suitable for someone in her network.

It's not always easy to ask potential funders for other useful contacts, but you can couch it in terminology such as, 'We're always open to discussions with a variety of contacts that might be helpful in all areas of our business'.

You're part of the pitch, and you want investors and funder to be at ease with you and you with them, to have confidence in your knowledge and skills and to develop trust in your abilities, so go with what feels comfortable and right for you to put your best foot forward. Don't put on a false voice or become a caricature. Funders are people just like you, so don't be something you're not.

Going through your slides

Before you jump into the main pitch slides, your first slide should be a cover slide with:

- **Your company name and strapline:** A *strapline* is a short, easily remembered phrase associated with your company – for example, Little Ondine (company name), Re-imagining nail polish (strapline).

- **Your name and functional business title:** You're the presenter, and the audience wants to know who's talking to them.

- **The purpose of the pitch:** For example, lender presentation, investor presentation, or include the name the group, such as High Street Bank Presentation or Centurion Investor Pitch.

- **The date:** Put it on the presentation and remember to update it!

- **Your company logo:** Also include any awards logos you can use, as well as any thumbnails.

It can be a nice touch and a good icebreaker to get the panel of funders to introduce themselves before you kick off in earnest, but play it by ear. People generally like talking about themselves and their achievements, but it may not be everyone's cup of tea. Decide on the day.

After you show your introductory slide, it's time to get into the meat of the matter. Look at what's included in all winning pitch decks:

- **Your 30-second elevator pitch:** Get your audience interested with a sharp, short overview of your business and the proposition.

  You never know when the opportunity to present your plan to a potential investor may occur, so you need to have versions of your pitch of varying lengths in your memory, ready to use at a moment's notice.

✔ **The problem:** Many businesses start without actually knowing if there's a problem they can solve, which is not a good strategy. In a winning pitch, you make the investor feel the *pain point* – the problem your customers have. Often you can do this to great effect by telling a story, usually one from your or your team's personal experience. Investors are people, too. They respond to a human-interest story. They may even have experience with your problem. Don't assume that though unless you've done your research on them and you know someone on the panel has felt that pain. If not, it can leave a very awkward silence in the room.

Don't go overboard and drown potential backers in statistics and video clips, but make sure they understand the problem and that they feel your passion and energy. It's important to grab their attention early on in the pitch.

✔ **The solution:** After you identify and communicate the problem, it's time to tell potential investors how your business is going to provide the best profit-making solution to this customer woe.

If your solution is technology based, this isn't the time to start waffling on about taxonomy and nanoparticles in great details. You have a short amount of time to focus on how you plan to solve the problem.

If you have a design-based or prototype product, you can show the audience a visual demonstration, provided you're sure it works! I'd use this tactic gingerly because investors are buying equity and lenders are buying certainty, but neither is necessarily buying your product. A demonstration may be more applicable to a crowdfunding pitch, which I look at in Chapter 13.

✔ **The size of your market:** Whether you come in with an approach from the top down, illustrating the bigger picture view of the market and how you're going to capture a share of it, or from the bottom up, presenting your current sales and user traction in the market projected out over time, you need to reference some credible sources to back up your theory. This can be a tricky area, because the temptation can be to say that you have a £5 billion total market size and that you're looking at capturing 5 per cent of that market, but in doing so, you back yourself into a corner of unreality.

Know how your industry works and how success and profitability are measured so that you can discuss it like you know what you're talking about.

It's also useful to describe any significant market changes, either recent or upcoming in the future, as they may provide fruitful opportunities for your business. Just give enough flavour for your audience to know you're in an interesting space.

✔ **How your business makes money:** Tell the money people what your business model is. Surprisingly, this is one area that many entrepreneurs forget to mention in a pitch. You're trying to get someone to put money into your business, so it follows that you should tell investors how to get money back out of it, and tell lenders how they get their loan repaid.

You may have more than one way of making money, or *multiple revenue streams,* but try to focus on the main revenue generators. You can discuss the others in a meeting if the investor is interested.

Make sure you talk about how you price your products or services, and how often customers or clients will come back and buy from you. Don't go over the top with lots of confusing data.

✔ **Financial projections:** Depending on what stage your business is at, you need to include a different number of years of summary financial projections. On average, you need to provide three to five years (the likely exit time for an investor and term time on a loan) of high-level figures – revenue, expenses, margin, EBITDA (earnings before interest, tax, depreciation and amortisation; see Chapter 20 for an explanation of these terms) – that funders need to start the ball rolling.

Remember that an early-stage pitch to a wide investor audience needs more detail than a later-stage pitch to a venture capital investor audience, as the company at the later stage has more of a public track record to back up its claims.

✔ **Your competition:** It's very rare that you're the only game in town solving the problem you've identified, and that's okay. Hopefully, you can do it better, faster, cheaper or more conveniently than your competitors, but you still have some competition. Be sure to identify it and be able to explain it before you get in front of funders.

You also need to identify the barriers to entering the market in your industry. These barriers may include patents, design registrations and the like, and it helps your case to highlight your successes, with one eye to the future so that you can keep your pole position in the race you're competing in.

Be able to explain why you have the edge on your competition, plus the intellectual property protection you need to stay one or two steps ahead of the game. Know who, amongst your competitors, is closest to catching up with you.

This is your opportunity to showcase the inventiveness of your business, and show funders how you're solving the problem differently to everyone else. If you've been featured in the news or publications or touted as an innovative, top business in your field, this recognition is worth mentioning as a point of differentiation.

Under no circumstances do you start knocking your competitors. It just looks like sour grapes and unprofessional behaviour. Give your competitors their due and emphasise your point of differentiation.

Most pitch decks have a slide with a matrix-style quadrant layout, with you in the top right-hand corner. This is a perfectly acceptable graphic, if a little overused. You can also use a chart that illustrates a comparison between your company and its main competitors on a number of key points. Use whichever suits your data best, and has the most impact.

✔ **Your go-to-market strategy:** Tell your audience what your model is, how you're going to enter into your market and capture those all-important customers.

Give potential backers a sense of what you've done so far, and fill them in on how you think this strategy will evolve and pay dividends over time. Are customers paying straightaway? Do they stay with you or do you have to replace customers often? What are you doing to make them stay; to make your site or business *sticky?* How have you decided to measure all this activity and what does your current scorecard look like? Are you using viral or guerrilla marketing techniques?

Investors and funders know that getting and keeping clients or customers is critical to your business success and therefore the return on their investment, so they will quiz you on this.

✔ **Your team:** After you tell your audience about your great idea, it's time to tell them who's going to bring the solution to life. In an ironic twist of investing fate, one of the key reasons investors decide to invest in a business is the team; it's also one of the reasons investors decide not to invest in a business. No one said this was going to be easy!

The experience and attitude of the team is critical to a successful pitch and subsequent funding, and this is the time to make your colleagues shine. You may not have put one penny into your business account, but if you're an experienced team of entrepreneurs with a red-hot skill set and a smoking-hot network, then you may still be strong enough to invest in. If some of your team know your sector well, and others don't have the background, don't gloss over this fact. Put it out there and have a good reason for selecting those who don't come from the same industry. As long as you can stand by your decision and logically explain why you made certain choices, no one will ask for more.

If you're the only full-time member of the team – a frequent situation in many start-ups – it's a good idea to surround yourself with a mix of experienced and active advisers, non-execs and board members. This lets funders know that you're not taking on this mammoth task in quiet solitude but that you're getting help and advice and taking the necessary time to complete the team to a high standard instead of rushing head-long into a future disaster.

You can represent the team in photos on a slide with an organisational chart and put titles under each person's picture. Include CVs only in the appendix in the printed documentation you leave behind. In a pitch setting, it's best to talk through the team bios rather than putting paragraphs of detailed information up on your slides.

✓ **Your current sales/traction and your projections:** If you're in a very early pre-revenue stage, you won't have much to say about your actual traction, but you can discuss what you've done so far in your testing phase and base this part of your pitch on your projections.

However, if you're generating some revenue, this is a good time to tell people about it, perhaps using a graph or other illustration.

You can highlight any key clients or partners. And, this is a good place to mention any awards or competitions you've won or been short-listed for, especially if you've not started actively trading yet.

Point out how you're measuring your growth and success, so people can see that you know what drives your performance.

✓ **Your valuation:** It's often a point of contention and sometimes an out-and-out deal breaker, depending on your flexibility and pragmatism, but include your valuation in the pitch. It usually sits with the financials or just before the exit slide. I discuss methods for arriving at a valuation in Chapter 17.

Your valuation can be a real sticking point in getting an equity investor on board if it feels overinflated to her. *Unicorns,* start-up companies whose valuation exceeds £1 billion, do exist, and there are more of them in the UK now, but they're the exception rather than the rule.

✓ **What you need from the funders or investors:** Given that you're asking someone to give you money, whether it's her own personal money or an entity's money, and that person is expecting to get a positive return as a result of giving you this money, it's crucial that you explain exactly

- What you'll be using the money for

- How much you'll use for each aspect of the business

- Why the funds will help you realise your business potential and provide a return

This shouldn't come as a surprise to you – you'd want the same information if you were giving your money to someone else. You wouldn't give your employees carte blanche to spend a lump sum of your money, and you definitely wouldn't give your children an open cheque book. You and your business become the business associates and investment child of your investors, and they want the same respect and explanations.

Being able to break it down also shows your audience that you've thought it through, you've researched the costs and you've timed the spend.

✔ **Your exit strategy:** You don't need this when you're pitching to lenders because they don't want to know that your business may be gone, sold or absorbed while you're still paying their loan back, but it's essential for pitching to angels, family offices, venture capitalists and equity platforms. Your exit strategy tells the audience how you see the investor achieving a great return on her exit – usually in five years, but not always – by something happening to the ownership of your business. Investors typically expect anything from 8 to 30 times their initial investment as a return, linked to the level of risk they perceive the investment represents.

Your exit strategy may be a sale, an additional round of funding, a joint venture or a listing on a public stock exchange.

If you anticipate selling the business as an exit, don't go into the specifics and name names, even if you have a good idea of who may want to acquire your business. You can allude to potential candidates, but your current purpose is to show that you've thought it through, and that your company operations are linked to the exit strategy, so that all roads are leading to Rome – the exit – which takes years in the planning and execution.

Answering investor questions

Whatever format or audience your pitch involves, expect to be asked a lot of questions – sometimes tough ones. Try to anticipate many of them so you can prepare answers ahead of time.

I can't stress enough that your pitch is not an opportunity for open or heated debate. Don't adopt a defensive stance about being questioned; try to answer each question calmly and in an engaging way. Be clear about your facts and excited about the opportunity.

Use the following examples of typical investor questions to prepare your answers:

✔ What made you start this business?

✔ Exactly when did you set it up?

✔ How did the team come together?

✔ Have you all put money into this (do you all have skin in the game), including your advisers?

✔ Why are you the right team to make this a success?

✔ How much money are you going through every month (what's your *burn rate*)?

✔ Do you have any cash in the bank?

✔ How big is your market?

✔ How much of the market do you need to hit your targets?

✔ How will you capture that market share?

✔ How much does it cost you to get a customer on board?

✔ Are you out there now? Do you have traction or just a minimum viable product?

✔ What makes you so different? And is that difference sustainable?

✔ Why won't you fail?

✔ What challenges keep you awake at night?

✔ How did you come up with your valuation?

✔ Why have you chosen to pitch to me/us?

✔ Who else are you pitching to/talking to?

✔ How long have you been looking for money?

Also to help you along, check www.dummies.com/extras/business fundinguk for an example of a good pitch deck.

Deciding to Use Video

Most pitches delivered directly to an audience don't have video content. Video is more the domain of crowdfunding sites, where your online pitch is the key to your success or failure in raising funds. (Chapter 13 explores crowdfunding in more detail.)

Depending on your type of business, you may have a short video clip to demonstrate your product or service or a particularly impactful client or user testimonial that says more than you can say yourself. Remembering that you need to embed this content in your presentation or know how you're going to quickly access it otherwise, don't use it unless you're confident that you can manage the process and that it adds value to the pitch instead of creating a meaningless distraction.

If you decide to go down this road, or you're definitely going to use crowdfunding, the next sections offer a few helpful tips and hints on how to use video to your advantage.

Planning your content

On average, pitch videos vary between 60 and 120 seconds, so you have just a minute or two to get your point across. Good preparation – and loads of practice – is essential if you're going to get it right. You need to cover the same points you'd cover in a face-to-face pitch, but in an abbreviated way. I often think of this as trying to create a Twitter pitch – with only 140 characters there's no room for any filler, binder or padding!

Think of your video clip as a television commercial when it comes to the structure and timing of your script. Commercials are made in 30-, 60-, 90- and 120-second durations, so that they can be edited to fit different commercial breaks and still make sense no matter how long or how short they are. In a sense, your pitch needs to do the same thing. This is particularly important if you're filming a separate pitch video for crowdfunding, for example.

You need to know your value proposition as discussed in Chapter 3, the summary points of your business plan for reference, the key figures in your financial forecasts, including your valuation and what the rewards are for investors and your potential exit.

It's important to know exactly what you want to say in your pitch video, precisely how long it is, what, if any, additional clips, inserts or throws to another piece of film and exactly what the segments are and what each covers.

Identifying key points

In order to make your pitch video the best it can be, you need to consider and take on board a number of key points. Although still a relatively young industry, many companies have gone before you, made their mistakes and had their glory, so learn from their experiences and maximise your chances of getting fully funded.

What to consider and include in a video clip:

- Make sure you're in your own video.
- Get the right tone and tempo for your audience – voice, speed of speaking and style of speech.
- Check that your background is clean and tidy and shows your premises at their best.
- Make sure you're clean and tidy and looking your best, too.
- Get your logo in the frame so viewers never have to think about who's pitching.

✔ Be sure to pitch and not beg.

✔ Include the important things – your idea, how it makes money, your market and your team. (For more information, refer to the section 'Going through your slides', earlier in this chapter.)

✔ Make sure the team's experience comes across.

✔ State how much money you're looking to raise.

✔ Explain how you'll use the money.

✔ Tell people what they get for investing.

Using good quality equipment

For something as important as your pitch video, it makes sense to use the best quality video and audio equipment you can stretch to and to make sure it's in the hands of someone who really knows how to use it.

More and more people are using smartphones to record videos, but if you're not completely comfortable with this, either go on a short course to improve your skills or put out a request in your network or on university job boards for someone to help.

Universities often have state-of-the-art equipment and students who are looking for real, live projects, so you may be able to get professional filming and editing at a fraction of the going market rate.

Depending on where you're looking to source funds, it's good to keep in mind that the video is very likely to be posted for public viewing, so make sure there's nothing in there you wouldn't want your mum – or a conservative investor – to see.

Check the technical requirements and limitations of the site you're uploading to, because if your video isn't compatible, you'll have wasted a lot of time and possibly money as well as missed out on an opportunity. Some common formats are mov, mp4, avi, mpg, and mpeg, and the files should be no larger than five gigabytes (5GB) in size – otherwise they start to become unwieldy.

Editing wisely

Your video pitch is likely to be between 90 seconds and 120 seconds, so try this as an exercise: Set a stop watch and start talking about something you're passionate about. Go ahead . . . I'll wait. It's not so easy, is it? Sticking to the time limit – even for someone like me, who has been trained for television presenting – is still a challenge. Sifting that much information down to a few salient points and including a whole lot of enthusiasm and passion isn't as easy as you may think it is.

You'll inevitably be well over the time limit on your first few attempts. You need to prepare a pretty tight script to ensure you stick to your time limit, and then use your editor or editing time to pare it right down to the bare bones. Construct the script in separate segments so that each can stand alone to help make editing easier, and get someone with good video editing skills to make the final cuts while keeping the story flowing.

Chapter 7

Making a Successful Pitch

In This Chapter

▶ Rehearsing your presentation

▶ Communicating your vision and your mission

▶ Knowing your audience

*O*ne thing you can say with 100 per cent certainty about your funding journey is that sometime, somewhere, in some place, you will fail to secure the funding you need. On the other hand, you very well may secure the funding you need and then some and be in the enviable position of turning away enthusiastic investors and lenders. Either way, you discover an awful lot about the ins and outs of funding, and learn a few good lessons about business life in general as you navigate your way through the minefield of declines and arrive at your ultimate destination in the funding zone.

In the land of equity, to pitch 60 times and fail 56 is not out of the question. It's all part of the process, and you need to expect it. In general, your success ratio improves as your business grows and becomes more established. You can cut the search time by half, perhaps, but you'll still experience failure. In fact, in some places – the United States, for example – getting turned down is seen almost as a badge of honour or a rite of passage.

In the world of debt, the current tighter criteria and the minimal appetite for risk imply a certain amount of built-in failure. If you're seeking alternative finance, you stepped away from the mainstream for a reason, and so you can anticipate a few knock-backs. Learn from them all and be proactive in updating and improving your material. If you're confident in what you're putting forth, you just need to keep going until you find your Mr or Ms Right.

The other day I heard someone say he doesn't see a glass as half full or half empty; he just sees the water, is thirsty and drinks it. Focus on the task in hand, and remember that thousands of proposals are put in front of funders all the time, and you may not be everyone's cup of tea. It can be personal if the decline is centred around the team, but in general, it's just business, so stay positive, control what you can and keep smiling.

Although it may feel like it, I'm not trying to put you off raising funds for your business – far from it. But, statistically, you will fail a number of times before you successfully raise your funding, and you want your business plan, your pitch deck, your personal brand and your attitude to ooze success. As somebody who's been around funding for a few decades, and seen the ebb and flow of money into the small- and medium-sized enterprise (SME) marketplace, one thing that's very apparent at this moment in time is that there's plenty of money out there, and it comes in all shapes and sizes; it's just searching for the right deals to fund.

In this chapter, I talk about ways to minimise your declines and what feels like failure and maximise your approval rate and what feels like success.

Practising Your Pitch

I don't want to bring up potentially painful memories, but you've probably had the phrase 'practice makes perfect' thrown in your face a number of times throughout your life, and almost always at the precise moment when you were fed up with practising! But, the sad truth is that when it comes to making your pitch the very best it can be, practice does make perfect, and there's no shortcut or get-out clause.

For some people, standing in front of a group of people and presenting your fundraising pitch, be it to a small group or a packed room, is as natural as brushing your teeth or combing your hair. For others, it's as unsettling as fingernails on a chalkboard. You may be somewhere between the two extremes – as if you're making your signature food dish, the one you've made a thousand times, for a local celebrity – you're a little more tense than usual, but you know it's something you can do. The point is, you'll have varying degrees of confidence and familiarity with the process, but this can also be the reason that you start to ignore the basics of what makes a successful pitch, and start down the slippery slope to the land of declines.

Once you've created your pitch, which I cover in Chapter 6, do yourself a huge favour and make all that work pay off in a successful fund raise by practising it over and over and over again. You'll be sick of hearing it, and possibly of hearing yourself, but it'll be worth it in the end.

 Don't practise your pitch just in front of the mirror. Try filming yourself, or get someone else to film you, so you can actually see how you come across to other people. A recording helps you hear yourself using specialist vocabulary that only you and a handful of others understand, see yourself rocking back and forth unconsciously in an annoying manner or hear yourself speaking really, really, really quickly, v-e-r-y slowly or in a monotone voice.

 Watch other people pitch to see what gets a good reception, and what doesn't, what questions they get asked and what you can learn. Across the UK you can find plenty of pitch events, most of which you can book online on sites like Meetup or Eventbrite, so it's very easy to get a bird's-eye view of the live thing before you put yourself up for inspection.

The idea when you're pitching to funders is to get them to say 'yes', be it 'yes' to the next meeting, 'yes' to a further introduction or 'yes' to putting some money on the table and working with you. To be successful in this endeavour, you need to do all you can that's right, and eliminate as much as you can of what's not so right in the way you compose and deliver your content, your message and yourself.

Eliminating the jargon

The word *jargon* originates in the 1300s from Old French and entered the English language as 'twittering, chattering' and later as 'gibberish' – a meaning it retains to this day. Jargon is also referred to as *mumbo-jumbo* or something attributed to a specific sector, such as *legalese* or *tech speak*. The layman's definition of jargon when it comes to successful fundraising is 'I'm bored and not listening to you because you're using a bunch of words I don't understand, so I don't understand you and your proposition' – or, to put it more succinctly 'blah, blah, blah, blah, blah'. Not exactly the effect you're hoping to achieve. I'm sure you get the picture.

However, I don't want you to get the wrong idea, and think that you need to talk down to your audience and assume that they're not intelligent enough to cope with a bit of industry-specific vocabulary.

You almost always present your pitch to a diverse audience, with different backgrounds and varying levels of industry knowledge. You need to be able to communicate your proposition to the lowest common denominator on the other side of the table or the stage – and not the most well informed members of your audience.

You may have come across the acronym KISS at some stage in your professional life: Keep It Simple, Stupid – and if you want to improve your success rate in getting funding, there's no better time to invoke the rule of simplicity. If your 14-year-old nephew or your 90-year-old grandmother can't understand what you're saying, you probably want to tweak your material. If you need to overcomplicate something and load it up with a lot of jargon, you probably don't entirely understand it yourself, so you need to go back and revisit the basics.

People start to glaze over and switch off when they don't understand something, and if you're going to be successful in getting your business funded, all your materials – your business plan, your pitch deck, your investment memorandum – as well as yourself, need to be crisp, clear and concise.

You probably know someone whom you consider a bit geeky or whom you feel speaks a language all his own. You don't want to be that person when you're trying to take your business towards a successful fund raise.

Overcoming gobbledygook

There's a lot to be said for clear, simple communication, and as far back as 1979 Chrissie Maher, OBE, launched the Plain English Campaign by shredding gobbledygook content in Parliament Square, having been outraged by the lack of clear language in legal documents. She followed up with a visit to Downing Street, dressed as the Gobbledygook Monster, to deliver the first issue of the *Plain English* magazine (www.plainenglish.co.uk). Don't let her efforts be in vain. Take a leaf from her well-written magazine and manifesto, and eliminate the jargon if you want to increase your chances of success in raising funds.

Really knowing your content

As someone who has been known to forego intense preparation and wing a presentation or two, it's important to point out and reinforce the need for you to know your content well, to be fully conversant in it, and to be able to navigate your way around it with ease in case you want to refer back to a point, respond to a question or reinforce a position. During every part of the funding journey, you'll be asked questions – sometimes very pointed questions. To answer them, you need you to know your facts and have them roll off your tongue with ease.

Be thoroughly familiar with

- ✔ **Your financials:** You really need to know your stuff, and this includes your financial statements. I'm amazed at how often entrepreneurs can't answer questions on their financials when presenting to funders, or – even more of a cardinal sin – omit them entirely from the pitch deck, executive summary, investment memorandum and so on. (I talk about these documents in Chapters 5 and 6.) Your financials are the single most important bit of information in this process, so ignore them at your peril. A sure-fire way to ensure failure when you're looking to secure funding is to not talk about finance.

   Your financials includes your valuation, and you need to be prepared to confidently explain how you arrived at it and to reasonably justify your decision to go with it for your equity pitches. The valuation is very often the thing that kills a deal, so be ready to defend your position but not to fight about it.

- ✔ **Your market and the competition:** Be able to fully explain your market and acknowledge your competition, knowing how they stack up against you and what they've been up to recently. You need to present the complete market landscape – its size, characteristics, opportunities, and its predators and opportunists, who may very well be on your tail or at least attempting to catch you up.

If you're way ahead of your competitors and wrapped up warmly in a coat of protected intellectual property, making it hard for anyone to take your competitive advantage, be able to get that across, as it will earn you points on the way to 'yes'.

✔ **Relevant current events:** The day you actually present your material or attend a pitch event may be weeks or months after you prepared your material, and it's important that you not only keep the material up to date, but that you also keep yourself up to date, especially if you're in an industry where things change daily or weekly, or where regulatory changes have a significant impact on your business.

Things can happen on the day of your meeting, so be sure to watch the news, read your trade information and look out for breaking news on social media. Don't get tripped up by not being aware of some recent changes that may scupper your pitch.

It's vital that you have a hand in writing and preparing your funding documents. I've seen many business plans, financial forecasts and pitch decks that were outsourced in some way, and when the presenter, usually the business owner, was grilled on the details, he was unable to answer the questions fully, not having been involved in creating the content. Don't let this be you! Not only does it make you look unprepared, but it also sends out the signal that you don't think the funding process is that difficult – or in the worst case, important enough to warrant your time.

It goes without saying that lying when you're doing anything that concerns money is never a good idea. One could argue that telling a lie is never a good idea, but that's a whole other story. Lying, covering up or bending the truth, omitting some vital information . . . or anything along the same lines can only add to your increasing decline rate. It all comes out in the wash (or the due diligence, which I talk about in Chapter 4), so make the start of this relationship, which is built on trust, opportunity and team work, a priority from day one. If you have irregularities or one-off circumstances that you need to explain, do just that. Don't brush these issues under the carpet, hoping no funders will rip it up when they move into your house.

You want to be totally at home with your technology, so be sure to test out the actual system you'll be using – including the laptop, projector, tablet or smartphone. Stopping and starting breaks your audience's concentration and adds to your stress level.

Controlling your nerves

You often hear seasoned actors state in interviews that they still have butterflies before they go on stage, so don't be surprised if you feel a few flutters during an important meeting yourself. Successful fundraising can sometimes be the difference between make or break for your business, so you have a lot at stake. A certain amount of nervous energy can be good because it gives you a bit of an adrenaline boost and helps to focus your mind on the task at hand. However, too much of a good thing can have the opposite effect, with disastrous consequences. You need to be able to control your nerves in order to channel your nervous energy for good.

Never overlook the value of antiperspirant or baby powder to mop up some of the side effects of nerves. Feel the fear but try not to let it show or show through your clothes. If you tend to experience sweaty palms and pits during times of extreme stress, consider wearing dark clothes to conceal the evidence. It's human nature not to want to put yourself up for what you perceive to be criticism or ridicule, and most people are uncomfortable with the feeling of being judged at such a critical moment.

Different people manage and control their nerves in different ways, and you know best what works for you. Some people imagine everyone naked; some practise in the bathroom mirror; some take part in some amateur dramatics; and yet others practise meditation, get pitch coaching, go for hypnosis or drink calming herbal teas in order to stay in control.

It's important that you manage your (sometimes irrational) fears. Reframe your thoughts to focus on success and to confront your fears head-on as often as you can. (My own personal mantra is 'see it, believe it, achieve it'.) You will be uncomfortable for a while, but the more you go through the process and use your nervous energy to focus your mind, allowing your mind to catch up with your mouth, the more comfortable and relaxed you'll be, which should improve your success rate.

Warren Buffett goes to class

According to Forbes.com, the hugely successful and world-famous entrepreneurial billionaire, Warren Buffett, was 'terrified' of public speaking, to the point where, at the age of 21 and just starting out in business, he enrolled on a course in public speaking at the now renowned Dale Carnegie Institute.

In an interview for Levo League, a career site for women, Buffett went on to say 'you've got to be able to communicate in life and it's enormously important' when asked about the habits he cultivated in his 20s and 30s that he saw as the foundations for success.

Although he may be a well-known example of the need for and value of learning to control your nerves in business, in my experience, he's most definitely not alone.

Over the years, I've sat through, coached people through and judged many pitches by entrepreneurs seeking funding at various stages in their business. I've worked with people to improve their presentation skills, to drill down into their content, and sent them to other professionals to learn how to control their breathing and pacing. Some were great and in their natural element; others were less great and like the proverbial fish out of water.

A funding meeting is a two-way street, and you're assessing funders as much as they're assessing you. If you're talking to a funder who sends you into meltdown and makes you feel like you're at the Spanish Inquisition, he may not be the right fit for you, leading to an eventual 'no'. Talking to such funders is, however, very good practice, and so use it as a learning experience. (In Chapter 4, I look at the importance of choosing the right investor for you.)

Holding the audience's attention

Unless you're a trained actor, an experienced after-dinner speaker, a political orator or the former captain of your debate team, you probably have to work hard to create a compelling, lively and informative pitch that holds your audience's attention.

Getting people to pay attention, and hopefully want to take your funding proposal forward at the end of a pitch, is no mean feat. Adults have short attention spans, get bored easily, and now all of them have a handy socially accepted distraction in the form of a smartphone that they can use to amuse themselves while you talk. You have a lot to overcome if you want them to lean in, switch off their phones and listen with baited breath from your first word until your last. Getting them to relate to what you're saying and trade a little personal currency for some financial currency is not as easy as it sounds.

To help you be more successful in this challenging endeavour, make use of this checklist of things to consider, remember and include in order to hold the audience's attention:

- ✔ **Project your voice and remain upright.** Be aware of how you hold yourself, and the volume, speed and reach of your voice. This is true of a live face-to-face presentation, as well as any video presentations you make online.

  Also be aware of using irritating *thought holders,* as I call them – those pesky *ers, ums* and *ehs* that can creep into your speech, nestling alongside the *likes* and *you knows.* It's your mouth getting ahead of your brain, so go at a pace where they can live in harmony.

- ✔ **Open with a reason to make your audience stop and take notice.** It's fair to say that first impressions count and that people arrive at them pretty quickly, so you want to make yours as memorable as you can. Your first words can be a quote, a statistic or an image that creates a hush in the room, ensuring that everyone is paying attention. Starting with a really powerful or thought-provoking titbit that adds to your proposition can be very effective.

  If you're raising money for a healthcare tech business that addresses some of the issues around childhood obesity, for example, you can find some pretty jaw-dropping statistics around the UK right now, and they can definitely focus the minds of your audience.

Some people try to capture attention by showing a video, which I personally think is a mistake. Use a small clip further on if it really adds value, but funders have come to listen to you, not watch something that in essence buys you time, so think carefully before you go down that road.

✔ **Set the scene.** Tell your audience what to expect from the next few minutes so that they can follow your logic, but don't waste time telling them where the toilets are and thanking your parents for making this possible. You don't want to give them any reason to lose interest and concentration, and you only have a few precious minutes.

✔ **Tell a good story.** In Chapter 6, I look at the value of human interaction and empathy when telling your company, team or individual story in relation to the business history and positioning. You don't need to have a Shakespearean-quality tale, but try to say something that really captures attention and that your audience can relate to. You want them focused on what you're saying and not on their smartphones.

A well-placed and appropriate witty, humorous or self-deprecating remark is a powerful technique for getting your audience involved and keeping them interested. However, off-colour or offensive jokes are not. Poor delivery of a funny or sarcastic comment can easily backfire, so try your material out on an objective audience before bringing it to such an important stage.

✔ **Make each phase clear and concise.** Carry over the strategy and principles that went into your presentation material to your actual presentation. Make sure the material is easy to understand and to follow. Just as you leave plenty of white space in your written materials (including your pitch deck), pause occasionally so that your audience can reflect on your spoken words. Give people time to process your information.

✔ **Make it sharp and make it short.** You don't have a lot of time to make an impression and get your point across, so get straight to it. Make your delivery punchy, but not rushed, and stay within your allotted time slot.

✔ **Keep it flowing.** Whether it's written or spoken, you want smooth transitions in your material and delivery that flows naturally. You want to avoid awkward silences and gaps in the action as a result of technical difficulties or disjointed sections that have no obvious links to one another. Each slide should flow nicely into the next, with seamless transitions to keep you on track and your audience focused.

✔ **Let the real you shine through.** It's all too easy to assume your older, wiser, more mature persona, complete with sensible clothing and a deeper voice, when you go to pitch for something as important as money. But funders are putting their faith in you, so make sure that they can see some of the real you in your words, tone and appearance – not someone they won't recognise once their cheque is in your bank account.

✔ **Check in with your audience.** Make sure you include opportunities to check back with the audience and see if they can relate to what you're saying, even rhetorically, to ensure that they feel included and stay engaged.

✔ **Allow for real-time questions and answers as well as the possibility of a Q&A (question and answer) session at the end of your pitch.** Questions and answers at the end of a pitch can leave the audience feeling a little underwhelmed, so allowing for the possibility of both options keeps everyone involved and enables you to leave them with something memorable.

If you intended to come back to any questions that still need answering, make sure you do it and don't just ignore them. If you've run out of time, offer to answer them at the end of the session or in a one-to-one follow-up meeting.

✔ **Summarise what you just said and give a clear indication that you're wrapping up.** Avoid that awkward moment you get at a classical music concert when no one's quite sure if it's okay to clap. Making people feel stupid doesn't help your cause. Equally, most people don't remember most of what they heard ten minutes ago, so it doesn't hurt to give them a quick reminder.

✔ **Go out on a high.** Don't end with a flat phrase or trailing sentence, mumbled under your breath. 'That's all folks', or something along the same lines, is hardly likely to leave a lasting impression in people's minds. The last thing you say stays fresh in your audience's mind, so give it a bit of oomph and make it something they'll remember for a good long while.

✔ **Make sure you include a call to action.** Tell your audience what you want them to do now. If you don't ask, you won't get. Make sure they know that you want that next appointment or a meeting with their team, or whatever else you want. You won't get a commitment to fund straightaway, but you can get the next step leading up to it.

Anticipating questions

You wouldn't go for an important job interview without doing some research on the company, preparing answers for the questions you anticipate being asked and coming up with a few insightful questions to ask in return. If you really want to be given the job, you do all you can to make sure you get an offer. It's pretty much the same with funding. If you want to get the next meeting or a decision in principle, you need to be really well prepared, and part of that is anticipating questions, preparing your answers and having a few to ask in return.

Anticipating audience questions and coming up with some possible answers so you aren't caught off guard and start running off at the mouth is good advice at the best of times, but for funding situations it's essential. You'll be answering quite targeted and detail-oriented questions under pressure, and that's not easy for anyone. An additional benefit of anticipating questions and plausible answers is that it helps to ensure that you've thought things through and included all the important information in your pack before you even start the funding or pitching process.

Depending on whom you're talking to, you can be asked any number of questions. Most of the answers are covered in your presentation or pitch, but you should make sure you can answer questions around:

- ✔ **Your business:** Questions may cover:
  - The company history
  - How you chose the team
  - How much genuine traction or sales you have in the market
  - What your market looks like
  - What your unique advantages are
  - What could trip you up and make you fail

- ✔ **Your finances:** You will face quite a few questions on this subject, and some will cover:
  - Your *burn rate* – how much money you're going through each month
  - Some of your key financial ratios
  - Who else has invested or what other funding you've had
  - How much of your own money you've put in
  - When you anticipate breakeven
  - How you arrived at your valuation
  - Why you want their money
  - What you'll use it for
  - How much of a return the investor will see and when for equity, and when you can repay the money, with interest, for debt

Be clear and transparent in your answers. Be prepared for a difference in opinion and try to find the positive side to any objections whenever possible – and if there really is no common ground, then graciously agree to disagree.

Under no circumstances do you get into an argument during a pitch. You won't win, and you'll lose credibility. Remain calm and defend your position with facts and passion, but at least give the appearance of being open to suggestions. You may find that you actually learn something useful.

Setting Clear and Realistic Objectives

As part of your efforts to improve your funding success rate, it's wise to have a clear, well-planned and realistic vision for what you want to achieve, who will be involved, when you want each aspect of it to take place and what you need to make it happen. You wouldn't build a house without plans, a project management schedule, materials, people, budgets, money and a buyer; therefore, don't expect to get funding if you can't show how you're building a strong foundation, gathering the best team you can to achieve your aims and objectives in a well-thought-out time frame and getting your unique product or service to satisfied customers who make you, and your funders, a profit.

Be clear and realistic in every aspect of your communication, from your vision and mission statements to your goals and milestones, and know what you need to say to each potential funder to get him on board.

Creating your vision and mission statements helps you crystallise what you feel your business stands for, where you want to take it and what the plan looks like in practical terms. By sharing this information with your potential funders, you show them the way your business mind works, how you arrived at these statements and plans, what facts and assumptions led you there and that you've got a mid- to long-term practical plan in place to achieve them.

Composing your mission statement

I don't know about you, but when someone asks me about my company mission, I can't help thinking of a certain 1960s sci-fi television programme with an intergalactic flavour. Some people say that shows a lack of maturity, but I say I'm just a product of my media generation. Before you can take your mission statement to a galaxy far, far away (I'm mixing in a new intergalactic adventure now), you need to be able to get it out of your head and to clearly articulate it in your plan, your summary, your pitch deck, your video and face-to-face encounters.

In a few sentences at the most, your mission statement needs to:

✔ **Accurately and clearly explain what your company does or will do.** Use simple terms and focus on the company's core strengths and how you uniquely add value to the customer experience.

  Illuminate your company goals, culture, market opportunity, and ability to capitalise on your unique offering and positioning to generate a return for you, your employees and your investors.

✔ **Avoid the hype and not sound forced or unnatural.** The things that make your company stand out deserve a place in your mission statement, but steer clear of hyperbole or over-egging your uniqueness. Your mission statement shouldn't be full of empty phrases, generic terms and clichés.

✔ **Be part of the fabric of the business.** You, and all your team, should be able to recite your mission statement without reading it. If a potential funder twigs that you're just paying lip service to an admirable goal in order to impress, you'll be rumbled, adding another tick in the decline box.

✔ **Be a current, living document that you can update and amend.** Your mission statement may well change from that first day when you hit upon your passionate idea, but it should also have some longevity as it expresses the core of your business and provides the spark for the flame that ignites your team and everyone else who comes into contact with your business.

Unless you're highly skilled and experienced in business writing, you'll need to draft a few versions of your mission statement before you hit upon the final copy. Defining how you'll achieve your visionary goals means taking an in-depth look at every area of your business to decide how each will be involved in the mission, which needs thought, reflection and revision. If you have a mentor or an objective business adviser, ask him to cast a critical eye over it to help improve on both content and style. Good editing is like good deadheading – cut back hard and feed what's left, and you get a bigger, better, longer-lasting bloom as a result of all the goodness being directed to the bit that's on show.

If you're struggling to find the words to express your mission statement, by all means take inspiration from others. Just be sure that yours is written by you and about your company. There's nothing worse than a mission statement that's obviously been cobbled together from parts of other statements that have no real relevance to your business aims, objectives or abilities.

Sharing the vision

It's easy to confuse your mission statement with the vision for your company. The mission statement is like a road map for the short- to mid-term journey of your business and is based on realistic achievements that everyone can understand in practical terms and see where they fit into the plan. The mission statement is how you get to what your intentions are, as you've laid them out in your vision statement. Your *vision statement,* on the other hand, is much bigger than your company mission statement. It's what you intend to do over a period of time, and the vision statement communicates your goals to employees, the press, management teams and so on, while inspiring them to achieve your goals at the same time. Following are examples of both types:

✔ **Vision statement:** We intend to offer the fastest, cheapest broadband to every home in Britain by 2020.

✔ **Mission statement:** We'll install new networks by 2016. We'll launch new satellites by 2017. We'll connect every home and office on a region-by-region basis from 2018 to 2020.

When discussing your vision with funders, you may get good and not-so-good reactions depending on how ambitious it is for the business. You need vision because, to quote South Pole adventurer Norman Vaughan, you need to 'dream big and dare to fail'.

Steve Jobs and Apple

Apple CEO Steve Jobs had a vision of a 'computer for the rest of us' and carried that through to make Apple an icon of global business. Somewhere along the line, this vision and the man who created it came unstuck from each other. In a very public ousting Apple and its visionary CEO parted ways, resulting in lost market share.

Eventually, an older and wiser Jobs returned to the fold, was reminded of his original vision and created an amazing turnaround in the company fortunes. The rest, as they say, is history.

Your vision may take a very long time to realise and have little resemblance to what actually happens in the next two to five years. If and when your vision becomes reality, you may not recognise the company as the same business you started out with. This is a longer-term business evolution, and perfectly okay.

Great vision is often attributed to one man or woman – for example, Steve Jobs of Apple, Bill Gates of Microsoft and Ana Botín of Santander Bank. In your business, the company's vision is probably associated with you. As the founder, you're the one selling your vision to investors or funders, trying to get them to literally buy into your dream. Of course, to make this vision a reality requires the buy-in of the whole team, which includes any investors or funders along for the ride.

To increase your chances of getting a successful buy-in from potential investors or funders, do your research and find out who they are, what they're interested in, where the gaps in their portfolio are, and how they think they can help you bring your vision to market in a way that gives them a satisfactory return.

Setting goals and milestones

After you develop your vision and your mission statement, it should be easier to see your way to developing clearly outlined, integrated, time-bound and measured goals and milestones.

The actual process of setting goals and milestones forces you to be very clear about what it is you want to achieve, how these desires will be integrated into your mission statement and how they support your vision. It also forces you to set deadlines and criteria for measuring these goals, which appeals to funders who don't want to see you aimlessly squandering their money.

The most common goals you need to communicate are in the areas of finance and your market:

- ✔ Your **financial goals** relate to achieving and improving profit levels and margins, producing a return on investment and improving sales figures. You may also have a goal to raise a larger round of funding at a later date, and, depending on whom you're currently pitching to, those funders may also be interested in this round.

- ✔ Your **market goals** relate to increasing your market share and customer retention figures and are reflected in lowering the cost of sales and maximising the value in a customer relationship.

Your financial and market goals should work hand in hand, not in isolation, and you need to get that across in your presentations and pitches.

Don't set too many goals. You wind up looking like you have no focus and are trying to do too much at one time. This makes funders doubt that you can use their money wisely, hit your targets and produce a return.

In some cases, being able to achieve your ambition is limited by the amount of money you can raise, so you want everything working in your favour. Good goals should fit the vision and the mission, have enough flexibility to be adaptable when needed and be acceptable to everyone in the business as well as your funders.

Having laid out your goals, you need to show funders that you have measureable, time-framed milestones for what you will achieve and when. The milestones are stepping-stones on your path to successfully achieving your goals.

Examples of a financial milestone can be lowering operating costs by 15 per cent over the next two years or increasing your gross profit margin by 2 per cent over the next 18 months. Your market goals may be something along the lines of increasing market share by 12 per cent over the next 2 years, or getting your customer satisfaction rating up to *excellent* by the end of the year. You may actually be talking to funders who can potentially help you achieve these goals, so show them you know what they can bring to the table in addition to money.

Make sure that your company goals and milestones:

- ✔ Are written in a way that makes them easy to communicate both internally and externally, so that everyone, including funders, can easily understand them.

- ✔ Are right for your company mission and vision. They need to be universally agreed within the business so you have everyone's commitment and everyone is working towards the same end game.

- ✔ Have clearly set time limits for achieving the overall goals and all the milestones along the way. This planning gives structure and urgency to your goal setting, and shows funders that you're focused.

TRUE STORY

Goals and milestones

Some of the well-thought-out and well-paced goals I've seen set and timed to achieve are:

✔ **Café Pod:** A fantastic management team with a strong view on how coffee in pod form for coffee machines should be affordable, accessible and tasteful has gone from strength to strength. Opening its second roaster by 2014, listing in Tesco in 2015 and doubling web sales by 2016.

✔ **SubTV:** Expanding the brand from a bar-based popular music television channel aimed at the UK university student market in 2014, SubTV covered beauty, fashion and business by the third quarter of 2016, adding 8 employees to the production team and £1 million to the bottom line.

✔ Can be measured in a way that's appropriate to their topic. Financial goals may have growth percentages that are measured every month, whereas sales goals might have the raw numbers of new customers measured each year. You want to measure what matters to your business and your funders.

✔ Are realistic and achievable. Your goals need to be attainable, but also just a bit beyond your reach – commonly referred to as *stretch goals*. You don't want funders to think that you're happy to coast and not challenging yourself to go beyond your projections.

✔ Have clearly stated owners within the business who back them all the way. This also ensures that duplication of effort is kept to a minimum and someone has ultimate responsibility.

Understanding Your Investors

Investors and lenders are people just like you and me. They have feelings, they respond to stories and they have their own ideas of what a good investment looks like. You need to know what makes them tick, and why you're a good fit for their portfolio. You may want to know why, and how, they become investors in the first place. You also want to know what they've already invested in and try to find out why. Of course they're interested in a return, but they may also want to use their background and experience and be hands on in your business. An investor may have a personal reason or a cause that's close to his heart that makes him interested in certain businesses.

Find out how your potential funders like to work. Do they use intermediaries who filter proposals for them? Will they see you at a pitch day even if they don't know much about you? You want them to understand you, so it makes sense that you do the same for them.

Researching investor backgrounds and bios

In the same way that you prepare for a sales pitch, or an important job interview, it's absolutely vital that you find out all you can about your potential funders, their business successes and failures and where they've invested so far. It won't help your cause to turn up not knowing who your audience is – full stop.

In Chapter 4, I look at selecting and approaching investors that are a good fit for you and your business. Part of this is researching their backgrounds. Are they entrepreneurs who have been in your shoes, and successfully exited a business and now invest in others; or perhaps former city workers who've decided that funding SMEs is a more dynamic and exciting way to spend their free time and money? Are they seasoned professional investors who have years of experience and a large portfolio of companies already?

Use this handy checklist when researching potential funders:

- ✔ **Do your homework.** Thoroughly research and validate before deciding on which type of funding is right for you and whom to put on your funder shortlist for an approach. These relationships last for a while and they are, in some ways, even more difficult than a marriage because love won't keep you together, but contract law will.

- ✔ **Be diligent.** If you're taking on a new client or supplier and entering into a financial transaction with him, you do a fair amount of checking before you say 'yes' to giving him credit or sharing the profits from a transaction with him. Have the same degree of wariness, and pre-qualify investors in the same way. Check their financial health and their client relationship track record. Don't be blinded by the bright lights of big money and skip over the obvious checks and balances.

- ✔ **Check whether they actively invest.** Just because someone represents a fund, it doesn't mean he has any money in it by the time you come along. Some people are always willing to waste your already precious time and talk to you. You never know, he may have a friend who can invest, or he may try to persuade you to wait until he raises the next fund, but if the timing isn't right, you won't succeed.

✔ **Make the distinction between investors and lenders.** If you have no cash flow and can't repay debt, don't waste your time approaching banks or other lenders. If you're not on a high-growth trajectory and in front of investors who are right for your stage of growth, you're wasting everybody's time and slowing your funding process down. Early stage venture capital firms don't invest in the same way as early stage angel investors, for example, so know who does what. If you don't want to sell your business, don't approach investors who want to realise capital gains by selling it. (I talk about the various types of funders in Chapter 4.)

✔ **Make a list.** In the same way you'd assess job or educational opportunities, draw up an investor wish list with pros and cons on each potential funder. Include a list of things you see as *essential, desired, nice to have* or any other qualifier that's important to you. Start with 10 or 12 names, talk to 6 or 7, and as one drops out, move on to the next name on your list.

✔ **Get your timing right.** To increase your success rate with angels, venture capital firms and private equity houses, consider the time of year you make your approach and when you actually need the funds. Although it has evened out a bit over the last few years, the funding world isn't very active in the height of summer or the dead of winter.

✔ **Find out what else they can do for you.** Research each funder's network and reach. If this funder can't fund you, he may be able to help you in other ways.

Reading up on previous investments

It's important to know what an investor has previously invested in or a bank has previously funded. Check whether potential funders have gone on record to say why they've made certain investments or where they have a gap to fill.

You often hear investors talk about having a *balanced portfolio,* which means that they don't want more than one or two of a certain type of business or risk category in their portfolio. On the other hand, *niche investors* only invest in one industry sector, and if that's not yours, there's no point in contacting them.

The Internet is awash with articles, blogs, tweets, YouTube and TEDx interviews, panel discussions and debates by any number of investors and funders. You can also find articles in the trade press and national broadsheets. Investor aggregators, such as Gust (www.gust.com) and Crowdbase (www.crowdbase.com), also provide links to additional reference sites.

Chapter 8

Getting Help

After you've made the decision to ignore all your doubters, to strike out on your own, raise loads of money, create a global brand and build an incredibly talented team, you may find that, much to your surprise, your superhero status doesn't mean that you have *all* the answers to *all* the questions *all* the time. But you know what? That's perfectly okay. If you're anything like most can-do people who decide to take the entrepreneurial plunge, you're your own harshest critic, and you demand the impossible of yourself.

Help is the hardest four-letter word to use when you're used to doing everything yourself, helping others first, and putting your own needs aside, but getting ill, doing a so-so job versus a great job or, in the worst case scenario, losing it all because you were too proud to ask for help, is not a good plan. If you knew all the answers, not only would you be superhuman (and probably very annoying), but you'd also never learn anything.

Although your position can be a very lonely one at times, you absolutely don't have to do it all on your own. Whatever stage your business is at, however long you've been an entrepreneur and wherever you're located, help is at hand, and it comes in many forms.

Whether your management style is democratic, directive, collaborative or controlling, at some point you need to get some help and guidance, especially in the areas of running a business that aren't your strong points. Often, but not always, the weakest area is finance, which is especially true for the more creative amongst you. So, take advantage of the well-established, easily accessible and constantly growing business support network, both online and off.

You can find an army of advisers, mentors, consultants and sponsors out there. Every day thousands of people phone, email or meet with these services, which are often free or at a very low cost to help you get started.

 As with other business aids, the trick is not to rely on these services or to forget that ultimately you're responsible for the decisions you make. Dependency, ignorance or third-party advice is not a valid defence when things go wrong. Listen to advice, but ultimately make your own decisions.

In this chapter, I introduce you to some of the organisations you can connect with to help you get an outsider's expert view on a difficult question or concept, or to help you make some sense of the voices in your head. The people and agencies in this chapter can help you see the forest for the trees, and help you create bite-sized solutions to mountainous challenges.

Connecting with Government Services

The United Kingdom is in the grip of high growth SME (small- and medium-sized enterprise) fever – unemployment is the lowest it's been for decades, investments of all kind are up, SME exports are finally starting to pick up and British business is truly great. All of this means that all manner of government-backed, as well as privately funded, support organisations, growth schemes and business development programmes (including funding schemes) are queuing up to help you with your high-growth business. So much so, that, at times, it may be a bit difficult to navigate the support landscape, but persevere (this book helps!). Aid is there for the taking, and once you get the hang of how it works, you can transform your business.

Some of the best – and arguably, sometimes the worst – help for your business is available from government-backed services, which are often free or very good value. These services are often paid for by your taxes, so you may as well make use of them. Many of them are national in scope, but some are for specific regions, communities, age groups or sectors, so you need to read the fine print.

 A good website that gives you an overview of the support landscape is www. gov.uk/browse/business. After you see what's available, you can choose the help that's right for you and your business.

If aid or advice is offered for free, I strongly advise checking the credentials of the people giving the advice. Sometimes you get what you pay for. You need to apply the same process you'd use if you were paying for the help.

Accessing national government support

The UK government is very aware that providing support to UK SMEs helps to strengthen the broader UK economy, and also puts a positive spin on whichever party is in office at the time of strong economic growth.

The national government has been operating all sorts of one-to-one, group advice and training programmes and schemes for decades. In addition to meeting with advisers, attending workshops and taking part in exhibitions, trade missions and networking events, you may find times when actual financial support is also on offer.

Depending on the state of the economy, the government has been known to bolster non-financial support with pots of money in the form of grants, loans or co-funded equity to help fill the SME funding gaps. This money puts some much-needed cash back into the system to create jobs, boost exports and revive derelict areas.

You can expect to find government-backed support in some or all of these areas at one time or another:

- ✔ Deciding which business category is right for you
- ✔ Understanding your role and responsibilities as a director
- ✔ Determining whether you have the right skill set and personal characteristics to run a business
- ✔ Delivering business-improvement schemes and incentives
- ✔ Offering workshops and training schemes
- ✔ Locating sources of funding, including debt and equity
- ✔ Sponsoring grants, loans and equity co-funding
- ✔ Providing online and offline resources for all areas of your business

The BIS website at `www.gov.uk/government/organisations/department-for-business-innovation-skills` and the Gov.uk website at `www.gov.uk/business-finance-support-finder` are very good sources of information.

Exactly what help is on offer varies from year to year, so you need to keep checking, and a good one-stop shop to use as a launch pad is the BIS (Department for Business Innovation & Skills) website at `www.gov.uk/government/organisations/department-for-business-innovation-skills`). You can click all the different services and schemes, and go directly to the specific landing pages.

Benefitting from regional schemes

In addition to support delivered on a national level, a number of programmes are designed for and delivered in specific regions that may have distinctive or that require specialist support. These include:

- **Regional Growth Fund (RGF) (**`www.gov.uk/understanding-the-regional-growth-fund`**):** Launched in 2010, the Regional Growth Fund focuses on businesses and projects in all areas of the UK that create economic growth and sustainable employment. Investments are made alongside private sector investments. It supports businesses across all sectors and has invested £2.85 billion to help businesses grow since its inception.

- **Local Enterprise Partnerships (LEPS) (**`www.gov.uk/government/policies/local-enterprise-partnerships-leps-and-enterprise-zones`**):** The LEPS are partnerships between local authorities and businesses. They help support economic growth through enterprise partnerships and Enterprise Zones. The UK has 39 local LEPS and 24 Enterprise Zones, and these provide a mix of support, advice and training as well as some limited funding. Enterprise Zones can take advantage of tax incentives and simplified local planning regulations and business property rates, which can be of significant value to a business.

- **England – National Enterprise Network (NEN) (**`www.nationalenterprisenetwork.org`**):** A national network of enterprise support organisations, in which members offer independent advice and support on starting or growing a business. Many of these organisations also have local loan funds or grant funds targeted at local businesses, especially for those in the start-up phase. These networks can be found in over 100 locations around the country, and their website has a handy interactive map to help you find your nearest member.

- **Scotland – Scottish Enterprise (**`www.scottish-enterprise.com`**):** Scotland's main economic and innovation investment agency, Scottish Enterprise helps innovative and ambitious businesses grow. You can get help in attracting investment, developing your organisation, promoting new products and services, exporting and more. Many of the services are organised via a network of Business Gateway offices across Scotland. You can find more information at `www.bgateway.com/our-services`.

✔ **Wales – Business Wales (**www.businesswales.gov.uk**):** Business Wales provides support for people starting, running or growing a business, and includes information, advice and guidance by phone, online or face-to-face at Business Wales Centres.

Choosing Business Associations

In addition to the government-backed or subsidised business support services, you can tap into a number of commercial or semi-commercial organisations that operate on a membership model. These organisations offer information and help with a range of topics including training, lobbying, networking, purchasing and similar services tailored to a specific industry, business size or geographical group. Although they may not offer direct funding programmes, you can tap into their membership network of finance and investment consultants and advisers and get help with creating an effective funding proposition for your business.

Business support networks are ready, willing and waiting to help you be the best you can be, and to shout from the mountain tops about your success in their case studies, reports and press releases. No question is too dumb; no inquiry too trivial. As the saying goes, 'if you don't ask; you don't get'.

The next sections talk about some of the more established and well-known of these organisations.

The British Chambers of Commerce

The British Chambers of Commerce (BCC) is a membership-based organisation that caters for all shapes and sizes of business, at all stages, and in all sectors. The BCC (www.britishchambers.org.uk) is a national network of accredited chambers that are managed and developed locally, and monitored at national level to ensure they meet quality standards and deliver results to members.

The BCC currently has 92,000 members in 52 accredited UK chambers, with additional members overseas.

Business resources, trading information, training courses, export introductions and networking all come with your membership, and the offerings often are tailored to your individual needs. The BCC offers a fantastic savings on overheads to SMEs on a budget. Through its partnerships and affiliate offers, your business may save money on accommodation, print services, employment services and so on.

Through its chambers in other countries and links to UK exporting associations and expertise, the BCC is a terrific resource for SMEs that are first-time exporters, as well as for seasoned pros. The BCC can point you in the direction of the currently available export finance products, and help you successfully navigate the application process.

In addition to outbound services, the BCC also carries out surveys and consultations and produces reports on the things that really matter to business owners and managers at the coal face. The BCC is a voice for business, influencing thought leaders, opinion makers and government policy.

The Federation of Small Business (FBS)

On its website at www.fsb.org.uk, the FSB describes itself as 'the UK's largest campaigning pressure group, promoting and protecting the interests of the self employed and owners of small firms'. With hundreds of thousands of members across the UK, the FSB has been around since 1974 and offers a number of business services via its network of members for start-ups and growth businesses. Its business support services are run by experienced business owners and include business planning and environmental, legal and finance information.

One of the potentially valuable services the Federation of Small Business offers is a legal benefits package. Any business seeking funding requires a range of legal services and advice, and FSB provides access to legal advice 24 hours a day, 365 days a year.

The FSB also signposts members to sources of funding at www.fsb.org.uk/finance-for-business. It also offers advice and information on employment documentation and specially priced insurance policies for members.

Membership starts in the low hundreds of pounds, and can rise to just under £1,000, depending on the size of your organisation and your membership category.

A few more strings to your bow

Literally hundreds of organisations, associations, clubs and groups exist to help you start and grow your business. A few that may be able to meet some of your specific needs include the following:

- ✔ **Institute of Directors (IOD)** (www.iod.com)**:** The IOD refers to itself as a 'professional institute that offers a wealth of insight and inspiration', but to the user it feels like a formal club headquartered in a prestigious central London location. With satellite offices around the country and in Europe, the IOD provides terrific networking opportunities and very useful business research and information. The business library holds useful information on the financial performance of businesses in a variety of sectors, publications that explain financial ratios, margins and calculations and other information you can use when formulating your business and financial plans. It also offers members specially priced director training courses and a topical monthly business publication. It charges annual membership fees in the hundreds of pounds, as well as an election fee upon joining.

- ✔ **Prowess Women in Business** (www.charter.prowess.org.uk)**:** This organisation delivers female-friendly business advice and support through a network of members around the UK. It also hosts networking events, organises training and produces useful business guides, including a finance guide, tailored for women-led businesses. Membership is £145 per year for businesses with up to ten employees.

- ✔ **PRIME Business Club** (www.mentorsme.co.uk)**:** An offshoot of the Prince's Trust (see further along in this chapter under 'Helping Young Entrepreneurs'), PRIME provides business support, advice and guidance to entrepreneurs who are over 50 years of age, or *olderpreneurs* as they're known. It offers help in all the usual business areas, but also adds the additional information that relates to pensions and tax that affect older people. PRIME works with its clients in investment readiness, including on applications for Zopa, the online lender, and the Start-up Loan Company, the government-backed organisation that grants start-up loans to new entrepreneurs.

- ✔ **British Franchise Association (bfa)** (www.thebfa.org)**:** A voluntary self-regulatory organization for the franchise industry, the bfa offers membership on a subscription basis with a number of categories and fee levels. It aims to promote the growth of franchising in the UK, and to provide members with a code of ethical standards by which to run their business. It started from humble beginnings in 1977 and now has thousands of members, and links to international franchising groups. It has useful information on the finance options available to franchisees, and consultants and advisers within its membership.

- ✔ **Business Association of Women Entrepreneurs (BAWE)** (www.baweuk.org)**:** Run by women, BAWE is a long-standing peer group for women who want to generate revenue, grow their businesses, maximise their networking and learning opportunities and challenge the male dominated world of senior positions. Membership has tiers and starts at £80 and goes up to £250 per year.

✔ **Social Enterprise UK** (www.socialenterprise.org.uk): The trade body for businesses with a social or environmental focus, Social Enterprise UK helps with lobbying, networking, running events, training and development and research for social and environmental-minded businesses and their owners/managers. Through their networks and partnerships, you find information and events focused on raising finance for social enterprises. Membership categories and fees vary according to type and size of your organisation.

✔ **Start-ups.co.uk** (www.startups.co.uk/financial-planning): This website is a free resource site that covers many finance and funding topics for start-up and scale-up businesses. The site has articles, practical guides, hints and tips around raising finance. Topics include how to create a financial forecast, how to calculate your breakeven, VAT and your small business and so on.

Heading to Universities and Colleges

Universities and colleges around the UK offer training, funding, research, advice and support to businesses, both before and after start-up. Access is usually through any of a number of initiatives, such as:

✔ **City Lit** (www.citylit.ac.uk): Founded in 1919, City Lit is an adult education college based in Central London. It offers more than 4,000 part-time courses that cover a range of business subjects and are easily accessible and very popular. The City Lit business writing course is useful in preparing your business for finance, and is available in a couple of levels, as well as taster and fast-track versions. Check the main website and search function to find one for you, and as with most of their courses, early booking is advised. Fees vary, and there are subsidies for certain students.

✔ **Open University (OU)** (www.open.ac.uk): Founded in 1969, the Open University is a distance learning and research university offering business and subject matter courses online. The OU offers a course on considering self-employment, which covers all aspects of setting up your business, including accessing finance, at www2.open.ac.uk/students/careers/exploring-your-career-options/self-employment.

✔ **Cranfield School of Management** (www.som.cranfield.ac.uk): The Cranfield School runs the Business Growth and Development Programme, which is one of the best known and most successful programmes for motivated, ambitious owner/managers and senior managers. It's been running for over 25 years and has helped over 1,500 managers take on new skills and improve their future career and personal performances. The programme is unique in that it lets you step away from the day-to-day running of your business by attending courses over a period of weeks and then apply your newfound knowledge in your business. The cost of such an illustrious course does not come cheap, but you will almost certainly reap the benefits in knowledge, contacts and networking. You can expect to pay around £8,000 for the experience, but the course has a fund to help aspiring entrepreneurs in need of financial assistance.

✔ **London Jewellery School** (www.londonjewelleryschool.co.uk): This school runs courses ranging from one day to one year, from certificate to diploma level, all aimed at giving professionals in the jewellery trade access to high quality, practical and recognised training. Courses are offered both online and offline. In addition to training, the school has a gallery, studio space for hire and an events programme. Fees range from £99 for an online business course to £750 for a six-day business boot camp that includes financial training.

✔ **London College of Fashion, University of the Arts, London** (www.fashion.arts.ac.uk): London College of Fashion offers a number of in-house, tailored start-up business courses, such as Luxury Fashion Bag Management, Lingerie Trends and Design, Retail Design Innovation Programme and more.

Entering Incubators or Accelerators

At first glance, the terms *incubator* and *accelerator* seem to be at odds with each other. An *incubator* conjures up thoughts of slow nurturing, and an *accelerator* has a kind of 'hurry up and get it done' feeling to it, which, in terms of minimising the risk surrounding an investment, are the complete opposites. When it comes to the funds they bring to your early stage business, both types of organisations are, in fact, on the same team. Both incubator and accelerators want you to get your business idea and product or service to market as quickly as possible, and both are prepared to put some money – as well as support, advice, mentoring, networking and infrastructure – on the table to help you get there.

The most common sector to benefit from taking part in incubator or accelerator programmes is technology, but that's changing. There are now food, health and fashion counterparts in the UK. In the United States, where this model of support has been around longer, success stories such as Airbnb, a website that connects vacationers with lodging, have made incubators and accelerators very popular amongst fledgling businesses seeking finance and support for their high-growth businesses. I look more at accelerators in Chapter 11. You can also find out more by contacting UK Business Incubation (www.ukbi.co.uk) or UKSPA, the United Kingdom Science Park Association (www.ukspa.org.uk) for information on incubators.

With more than 100 incubators and accelerators across Europe, and dozens in the UK, providing a spring board for innovative businesses in need of expert advice and funding, it's important that you get the right one for your business and that you're prepared to put in the time to get the best results.

The following sections look at what you need to think about when you're entering an incubator or accelerator.

Finding the right type of incubator or accelerator

Whatever they call themselves – *incubators, accelerators, innovation hubs, hatcheries* – increasing numbers of closed-group, often niche-industry hot-houses now exist in the market, each with its own set of aims and objectives.

Some are set up by corporate venture arms of big businesses looking to find the next big thing; some by private entrepreneurs or capital groups looking to get rich quicker by investing in and nurturing new or unexploited talent and ideas. They all want to encourage new business, more jobs and more investment, so they throw their support behind fledgling ventures.

Whatever the aim, the bottom line is that entrepreneurs get funding and expert help and advice in exchange for a share in their business, and there seems to be a growing appetite for this particular brand of meal ticket.

This desire to get on board is particularly evident in innovative or technology-based businesses that have the kernel of an idea and need to develop it or that have developed the idea or product but have nowhere to turn for capital to get started. For these business owners, incubators and accelerators are an oasis in a very dry business support landscape.

Hundreds of incubators around the world graduate classes of thousands each year. Some graduates fly high when they step out of their cocoons, and others wither and die when the artificial life support is unplugged. No one's really sure how many have gone which way, but incubators certainly seem to be gaining in popularity.

Getting into an incubator or accelerator

The process of getting into an incubator or accelerator usually starts with an application that asks fairly standard questions about your business and aims. Often, you also need to submit a basic business plan, or an extended executive summary (I cover this in Chapter 3), and sometimes a video saying why you should be accepted.

It can take a while to process the applications – anywhere from a few weeks to a few months – so be sure to check the deadlines and guidelines (usually found on their websites). Take heart from the fact that usually small teams of people wade through a large number of applicants. You want them to select the best applicants, which takes time.

After you pass the initial application stage, there's an interview and a decision.

Considering the costs

Generally speaking, you find two types of incubators and accelerators: those that take an equity share in your business and those that don't. This difference is one of your most important considerations before getting on board.

Most profit-making incubators want anything from a few per cent up to 50 per cent of your business in exchange for the time and money they invest. This percentage doesn't always relate to the true valuation of your business. It is, therefore, something you need to consider very carefully.

 Not-for-profit incubators and accelerators are usually government funded and aimed at helping areas in need of regeneration. They provide space, mentoring, facilities and a good business development network. There can also be costs for business services or for rent, but these are reasonable and transparent.

Assisting Inventors and Creators

Every year more than 10,000 inspired inventors file UK patent applications to protect their intellectual property from copycats and intellectual property thieves. Getting a patent isn't guaranteed – the success rate can be as low as two per cent – and it has a very detailed, and sometimes costly, application process, so the hopeful inventors amongst you can use all the help you can get.

Some of the places you can seek help include:

- ✔ **The British Library** (www.bl.uk): Based in the Business Centre at the British Library on Euston Road, London, the library runs Inventions Advice Clinics and has an Inventor in Residence to assist with queries and provide advice and guidance to business owners and inventors. You can access this advice at any stage in your invention process, from idea to plan to prototype and beyond. The business centre also regularly offers training and workshops on financial forecasting and accessing business finance.

- ✔ **National Endowment for Science Technology and the Arts (NESTA)** (www.nesta.org.uk): NESTA is an independent charity that aims to make the UK more innovative by supporting and investing in businesses within a practical national framework. It helps businesses to bring ideas to life with the aim of improving the lives of UK citizens. NESTA has a number of useful publications on its website, including a very comprehensive guide to alternative finance at www.nesta.org. uk/publications/understanding-alternative-finance-uk-alternative-finance-industry-report-2014.

- ✔ **Innovate UK** (www.innovateuk.org): Formerly the Technology Strategy Board, Innovate UK is a government-funded body that helps businesses develop, invest in and promote technology-enabled innovative solutions and products. It offers a variety of programmes, grants, competitions and collaborations aimed at encouraging and empowering UK innovation and innovators. Working in partnership with government, research and financial institutions, Innovate UK has projects running around the country. I look at Innovate UK and its grant funding programmes in more detail in Chapter 9.

- ✔ **Institute of Patentees and Inventors** (www.invent.org.uk): A non-profit organisation, the Institute has offered support for all UK inventors since 1919. With more than 1,000 paying members, it provides advice, training and guidance on the complex issues relating to invention and innovation. The Institute covers intellectual property, design rights, manufacturing processes, funding and other information pertinent to the invention. Different membership categories exist, with annual fees of £70, plus a joining fee of £15.

If you have intellectual property to protect, see Chapter 3 for additional information.

Helping Young Entrepreneurs

Eighteen- to twenty-four-year-olds are one of the fastest growing new business categories, and as such, a number of organisations have sprung up to meet their specific needs.

- ✔ **The Prince's Trust** (www.princes-trust.org.uk): This charity was set up by the Prince of Wales in 1976 to help young people find work, set up businesses and become more able to deal with life in general. The Trust runs a range of training programmes, provides mentoring support and offers financial grants to build the confidence and motivation of disadvantaged young people. Each year, the Trust works with 50,000 young people around 80 per cent of whom move on to employment, education, training or volunteering.

- ✔ **The Bright Ideas Trust (BIT)** (www.brightideastrust.com): Founded by Tim Campbell, the first winner of *The Apprentice,* BBC edition, BIT was established to help young people aged 16 to 30, especially those from disadvantaged backgrounds, set up their own businesses. It provides business support, mentoring and funding, including Start Up Loans (SULCO) funding – in some cases in exchange for a share in the business.

- ✔ **Shell LiveWIRE** (www.shell-livewire.org): Shell LiveWIRE is a national online business advice programme supported by the multinational oil firm, Shell, to help young entrepreneurs start or accelerate their businesses. Established in 1982, the Shell LiveWIRE Programme runs an annual awards scheme with a maximum award of £10,000 and boasts a very active online community for entrepreneurs aged 16 to 30.

Part III

Exploring Your Funding Options

Comparing Debt and Equity Funding	
Debt	**Equity**
Loan = repayment	Investment = shares
Temporary use of capital	Permanent investment
Return is achieved with repaying of principal plus interest	Return is achieved with dividends, selling shares or the sale of the business

Visit www.dummies.com/extras/businessfundinguk to learn more about tax incentives for investors.

In this part . . .

- ✔ Discover what types of early stage funding are available.
- ✔ Become familiar with the variety of debt finance in the market.
- ✔ Get to grips with equity funding.
- ✔ Explore the world of alternative finance.

Chapter 9

Finding Free Money

· ·

· ·

*A*t the start of your funding journey, you probably immediately think of your bank as the first port of call. A very logical thought, as for the vast majority of people any contact with money, especially when it comes to business, goes through a bank. Your banking relationship often goes back many years. You may still bank where you opened your first savings account, it's where you put your wages, and if you're lucky enough to have a foot on the property ladder, it's where you got your mortgage. So far, so good. However, that's where the logic ends.

In all of these transactions, you're giving the bank money or pledging security in the form of property, so the risk of something going wrong from the bank's point of view is very small indeed. Your new business venture, on the other hand, is probably unproven, has yet to make any profit or perhaps even any money, and you cannot map out a clear path to being able to repay any money that the bank may choose to lend to you. In short, your business venture is chock full of all kinds of risk, in the bank's opinion. Your request for funding, rather than being music to your bank manager's ears, is setting off high-pitched piercing alarm bells, sending him scurrying double-time down the corridors of stability and risk aversion, leaving a vapour trail behind him!

Don't get me wrong. You need a bank when you start a business if for no other reason than to have a place to deposit any money you manage to raise. Plus, you need to pay the bills that inevitably come along, so stick with the relationship, but don't expect to be welcomed with open arms when it comes to asking for money. *Risk* is a dirty word in commercial banking, and at the start-up stage, you are risk with a capital *R*. I cover bank funding for all stages of your business in Chapter 12.

When the reality of the bank scenario sets in, and after sipping a herbal tea to calm your nerves, you logically turn your mind to a potential source of free money: the people who have known and nurtured you for a long time – your family and friends. After all, they like you, even love you, care about your happiness, so it must follow that they trust you to have a game-changing idea and all the skills to make it a great success. They must want to give you money to get it off the ground. Right? Nearly right.

It's probably easier to get money from family and friends than to get it from a bank, but it's by no means a dead cert (a given). Family and friends who can afford to lose money if things don't go to plan are a good source of early-stage funding, but as it's literally their own money, it's sometimes like pulling teeth to get them to sign and handover that cheque or instruct their bank to transfer the funds to your bank. It's human nature. As they stare down into the abyss that could become your bottomless money pit, imagining their good money going in after others' bad money, it's natural for them to feel a sense of panic at the moment of handing over the cash. It's your job to anticipate this, and, in exactly the same way that you'd convince a total stranger to help fund your business, you need to present a watertight case to your nearest and dearest in order to convince them that investing in your business or lending you money to get started is a good idea, with minimal risks. I look at this in more detail in Chapter 10.

This is a good time to mention the other often overlooked, but nevertheless extremely important source of free finance when it comes to gaining the financial commitment of others – you! Yes, I'll say it again: you! You are one of the most obvious sources of finance when you start or expand your business. I know, I know, you're thinking, 'Has this woman lost her mind? Doesn't she know that I'm putting my heart, my soul, my body, in fact all my time and energy into this business? Isn't that enough? How can I also be expected to put in actual hard cash?'

Like it not, you are expected to put in some of your own money. If you don't have enough faith to risk some of your own money in your new venture – have some skin in the game, so to speak – how can you expect anyone else to be a player? Investing your own money has an impact on your ability to get money out of other people. It's the idea that you're all in it together that you need to get to grips with, even though you're doing all the work and having all the sleepless nights. It may not seem fair, but, as you know, life isn't always fair.

The final frontier in your quest to find low- or no-cost funding, particularly at the early stage of your business but potentially throughout its life, is through grant and awards money, and more recently, through reward-based crowdfunding (I look at other forms of crowdfunding in Chapter 14 of this book), where products or experiences are given (instead of equity shares) in exchange for funding.

Researching and Obtaining Grants

Depending on the industry sector, stage and location of your business, a *grant* (a sum of money given to a business or an individual for a specific purpose) can be a terrific way to get some cash into your business, especially at the very early stages when cash is generally in short supply. You can also use grant monies to widen your network, boost your company profile and potentially enable your business to do some good or make a positive difference to a deprived or marginalised area of society.

Given that some of the more traditional forms of finance may be beyond your current reach, a *research grant* to develop a new product or service, or a *proof of concept grant* to prove that your product or service is viable, for example, may seem like manna from heaven in the start-up phase of your business.

Nearly every country or region has an agenda and aims that it wants to promote and develop, and using grants to encourage entrepreneurs to help them achieve their objectives is very common now. That's great news, I hear you say, and it is. However, locating the applications forms, understanding the criteria, taking the time to complete the forms, applying at the right time and understanding how to utilise the money for a commercial proposition can have you spending many precious hours working on something that may or may not give you a positive result. Be prepared to trawl through the mire of dozens of websites, racking up loads of hours and often taxing your brain to understand how you fit into the scheme, with the knowledge that you have a relatively slim chance of success. Although it's tempting to apply for free money, think long and hard before you start off down the grant road. It may well be a long and frustrating journey, with an uncertain destination.

Paying for application help

A number of professional advisers specialise in grant applications. These people charge a fee, but they take a good deal of the pain away from making grant applications.

As with other advisers, it's essential that you check the person's track record and the integrity of the service before you sign on the dotted line. Use your network, rating sites, reviews, and past clients to make sure the company is legitimate, relatively successful and good value for your money.

Beware anyone who guarantees success or refuses to explain his process. Grant funding is a highly competitive and complex arena, and no one can guarantee success.

You can stay informed about current programmes by looking at information published and available at

- ✔ The business centre in the British Library Business and IP (intellectual property) Centre in London at `www.bl.uk`. The business centre has low-cost workshops, events, free access to databases on available funding and staff to help you research and identify appropriate grants for your business. They also partner with organisations that may be able to help you identify and apply for grants.

- ✔ The Gov.uk site at `www.gov.org.uk`, covers a variety of funding options, including grants, and has a handy search function on the site, as well as links to the grants it lists.

- ✔ The website, F6S at `www.f6s.com` is another good source of information, and has some applications on its site as well. F6S is a leading portal for start-ups to find and discuss information on funding, start-up business support programmes, jobs and events. Some grant-awarding programmes use the F6S portal as an entry point to providing you with information and the initial stages of an application for funding.

Grant applications can use particular terminology and have very strict deadlines; use these tips to help make your application successful:

- ✔ Continually check the websites that provide information about your desired grants, as information, criteria, deadlines and amounts of money available can change.

- ✔ Read the full criteria and application forms before you start so you can gather the necessary information and gauge the amount of time and resources you need to complete the application on time.

- ✔ If possible, speak to the grant providers to get advice on how to complete the forms, clarify terms and get any other resource contacts that might help you.

- ✔ See whether you can speak to or email past recipients for advice, hints or tips.

- ✔ Attend free or low-cost workshops on offer at business advice centres or local further education colleges in your area or online that give you guidance on how to complete grant applications.

- ✔ Put the word out in your network that you're seeking help with applying for grants if you need extra help.

Grants and awards come and go on a regular basis. If you're serious about trying to attract some of this money, register on sites such as `www.f6s.com` — and regularly check sites that aggregate grant data, such as `www.gov.uk`, so you can receive regular newsletters, updates, changes, notices and so on. You don't want to miss out on an opportunity because you didn't know the deadline had passed.

If you're successful in your grant applications, you won't have to chase anyone to get the cash, and as grants are different from debt, you don't have to repay them. They differ from equity as well in that you don't have to provide a return to the investor. In general they're non-refundable chunks of money, doled out over a pre-determined period of time – usually linked to achieving milestones – and are offered as an incentive to entrepreneurs and businesspeople to develop something innovative or positive for the community at large. As such, a grant can provide a very welcome boost to your cash flow.

Grants aren't all good news though, as they usually have very detailed terms and conditions that you must strictly adhere to, including regular financial updates, quarterly reporting on progress, and updates on whether or not you are achieving your aims and objectives. They give with one hand and take with the other.

No one would suggest that it's not helpful to have free money – but be warned, there's no totally free lunch. Although you may not have to pay a grant back, nine times out of ten you have to abide by the organisations' specific criteria and desired outcomes, and you may need to match the amount you're awarded.

Applying for Awards

Even though it can be a time-consuming process to hunt them down and fill in the forms, applying for and winning awards can be a great source of additional cash. Winning an award – or even being shortlisted for one – often carries other benefits as part of the prize, including business support, mentoring, free work space and of course, potentially very useful publicity and networking.

Certain sectors, such as technology, biology and life sciences, green energy, long-term healthcare, education, socially minded businesses, manufacturing and certain regional businesses, have more grant funding available from both UK and EU organisations than other sectors. In fact, a number of *evergreen programmes,* awards that roll over each year, may be relevant to you and your business, even in its early stages.

Some programmes are listed in the next sections, but more can be found on the Innovate UK website at `www.innovateuk.org`. If you're serious about applying for grants and awards, visiting the site can pay dividends.

Some of the awards you can find on Innovate UK cover:

- Feasibility studies for cleaner, more efficient fuels
- The agri-tech industry

    ✔ Supply chain integration for the construction industry

    ✔ Enhancing the user experience in retail

A regular visit to the Innovate UK website is worthwhile to see what's current – and critically, when the deadlines are!

Most of these applications are complex and lengthy, so do *not* leave them until the night before. Be aware that they can put a strain on the twin resources of time and people and plan accordingly. Set strict project management timelines and deadlines if you want to have half a chance of success.

Starting off with a SMART award

One of the most well-known and high-profile awards administered by Innovate UK (www.innovateuk.org), the SMART awards – Small Firm Merit Awards for Technology – were first introduced in their original format back in 1988.

The central government launched the SMART awards before handing over responsibility to the Regional Development Agencies (RDAs) ten years later. With the demise of the RDAs a few years ago, the baton was passed to the Technology Strategy Board (TSB), which in turn became Innovate UK, and this is where the information and application process now sits.

The application process isn't generally an easy one. There are a few very important aspects to winning that you need to keep in mind, one of them being the need to match the funding with the same or similar amount. You can get these matching funds from a variety of sources – your own pocketbook, the debt or equity you raise, contributions from investors – but therein lies the rub.

Recently, a total of £75 million awarded over three years has been set aside for innovative small businesses. On average, 70 awards are given each year, broken down into three areas:

    ✔ **Proof of market:** A very early-stage award, it covers market research and intellectual property issues. It's important that you apply before you start spending money on the areas it covers, because you can't claim it back later. The maximum award size is £25,000, and it can be used to fund up to 60 per cent of the project costs over a maximum time frame of 9 months.

    ✔ **Proof of concept:** This grant can be used for carrying out feasibility studies to prove your concept has merit, for creating prototypes and for doing some testing on them. The maximum award size is £100,000 and can cover up to 60 per cent of the cost of the work over a maximum time frame of 18 months.

✔ **Development of prototype:** When you've proven there's a market and your concept is a workable one, this grant helps to further develop the prototype, create a working demonstration model and obtain further or additional intellectual property rights. The maximum at this stage is £250,000 to cover up to 35 per cent of the project costs for mid-sized firms and up to 45 per cent of the costs for a small business with a maximum time frame of 2 years.

Clearly, you need to have some funds to put into these projects at every stage, so be aware of that before you get started on the forms. You don't have any wiggle room: You will have to come up with the additional cash.

Gaining expertise with Knowledge Transfer Partnerships (KTPs)

Also found on Innovate UK are *Knowledge Transfer Partnerships* (www.ktponline.org.uk or www.innovateuk.org), which, technically speaking, are not grants but rather funding to cover up to two-thirds of the cost of a graduate associate with a particular knowledge or expertise. A small- or medium-sized enterprise (SME) can take on that associate for a specific project for a specified period of time (from six months to three years) in order to help bring the project to fruition.

Because the KTP contribution is £20,000, you really need to have a business that benefits from academic input. You also need to be able to come up with the remaining matching funds that apply to your award for the salary.

If you have an innovative idea, you can apply to work with an expert at a university or research organisation. This person can also help with the graduate recruitment. The logic behind the scheme is to help take academic know-how and apply it in a commercial environment, using the expert as the conduit between research-based and business-led organisations. Seems simple, logical and, dare I say it, laudable, but when academia collides with commerce, it can sometimes be nothing like simple, so make sure you do your research.

You can stay up to date on the latest KTPs at KTN (Knowledge Transfer Network), and also network with other businesses in your sector on www.kptonline.org.

Being Nurtured by Nesta

A very active and high-profile organisation for funding and grants is Nesta (formerly NESTA, National Endowment for Science, Technology and the Arts) at www.nesta.org.uk. Originally funded by a £250 million endowment from the UK National Lottery, Nesta is a well-known independent charity that uses the interest from a trust to meet its charitable objectives and to fund and support projects. It works primarily to enable entrepreneurs to bring exceptional innovative ideas to life by providing opportunities for grant funding, direct investment and competition or challenge prizes. Its funding programmes are supported by policy work to provide a voice for industry, research and the formation of strategic partnerships to promote innovation across a broad range of industry sectors.

Broadly speaking, Nesta funding falls into two categories: direct investment for a share in a business; and challenge prize awards with no share in the business.

With its direct investment, Nesta looks for scalable social ventures with projects that show they can make a significant social impact while still producing a return on investment. This combination isn't something you find on every business street corner, and as a result, not everyone is successful in obtaining funds. Nesta is particularly interested in businesses with projects that address major social needs and that look to create a more inclusive and accessible society, while being able to scale up and reach a wider audience.

You can see more on its investments at www.nesta.org.uk/get-funding/impact-investments.

In addition to investing directly in companies, Nesta also launched an impact investment fund for high potential, early stage social innovations through its fund management subsidiary, Nesta Investment Management. This money is invested in intermediaries that then award funds to the businesses they choose to work with in the area of social impact. Some of the better known custodians of the funds are Bridges Ventures Social Entrepreneurs Fund (www.bridgesventures.com) and the Big Issue Invest's Social Enterprise Investment Fund (www.bigissueinvest.com). These funding vehicles provide incubation, business support or corporate finance advice to innovative social ventures via a link to established organisations such as the Shaftesbury Partnership or Bethnal Green Ventures, thus extending the reach of the support and helping to ensure a successful impact is made.

The second way Nesta provides a bit of so-called free money is through challenge prizes.

Challenge prizes have a long and prestigious history in the United Kingdom, going back to the 18th century and the Longitude Prize for navigators through to the 20th century Schneider Trophy for aviators, which inspired the Spitfire, and the 21st century Ansari X-Prize, which inspires commercial ventures in space.

So the sky really is the limit when it comes to providing an incentive to find forward-thinking solutions for some of the long-term social issues of the day. As with other awards, prizes are a great way to get your hands on some cash, but also a wonderful showcase for your innovative idea or product, generating much-appreciated free publicity and raising the profile for your business.

Nesta offers a variety of challenge prize competitions with varying criteria and deadlines, so it's best to keep checking its website, but here is a sample of what you may see:

- ✔ **The European Social Innovation Competition:** €50,000 for ideas that can advance Europe's growth model.

- ✔ **The Aging Well Challenge Prize:** Funds efforts to find solutions to improve the lives of older people by reducing isolation and improving mobility.

- ✔ **Horizon 2020:** A European challenge that brings together knowledge and resources across a number of disciplines in order to find and fund breakthrough solutions in the areas of health, transport, bio-economy, creative materials and energy.

So the sky really is the limit when it comes to providing an incentive to find forward-thinking solutions for some of the long-term social issues of the day. As with other awards, prizes are a great way to get your hands on some cash, but also a wonderful showcase for your innovative idea or product, generating much-appreciated free publicity and raising the profile for your business.

Winning European awards

When you read the marketing blurb on EU funding, you'd be forgiven for thinking that it's a piece of cake . . . or tart . . . or torte to get grant funding for a worthy cross-border collaboration project. But don't be fooled by the glossy pictures of happy people having important meetings in sunny locations or the upbeat descriptions of the untold riches that await you and draw you into the lengthy application process, all the time glossing over the reality that applying for EU funding is tough, and for first timers, it can feel particularly overwhelming.

In fact, if you're a newcomer to EU funding, it's often advisable to form a consortium and seek an experienced partner to take the lead on your application. Find an experienced guide to help you navigate the choppy waters of the sea of European funding forms.

Be prepared for the red tape and bureaucracy, and strap yourself in for what can be a daunting and challenging journey on the trans-European funding express.

That said, if you manage to crack the code and are successful in obtaining EU funds, it can have a significant positive impact on your research and development (R&D) budget, and also escalate your entry to new business markets. So be aware, but don't be put off.

Horizon 2020

As I mention earlier in this chapter, Horizon 2020 (`www.ec.europa.eu`) covers some European funding awards. Open to everyone, it's the largest EU research and innovation programme ever. Horizon 2020 helps to bring about the realisation of groundbreaking discoveries and life-changing breakthroughs around societal challenges by providing some of the funding needed to take ideas and develop live products or services. It assists with job creation, adds to economic growth and safeguards Europe's position as a competitive innovator.

By connecting research and innovation, Horizon 2020 is helping to cut out some of the red tape that slows down public–private partnerships, which helps to connect innovators with networks and funders and ensure that Europe continues to produce world-class scientific results.

As of 2014, it also covers certain elements of the somewhat mysteriously named EU Seventh Framework Programme (FP7), which targets early-stage innovative companies working collaboratively on research and development with a number of other EU partners and has a current funding budget of around £54 million. The programme is set to continue until 2020.

The newly named EU Framework Programme for Research and Innovation is complemented by measures to further develop the European Research Area (ERA), thereby breaking down national barriers in order to create a genuine single market for knowledge, research and innovation. Check the website at `www.welcomeeurope.com/Horiozon 2020`.

The important things for you to know about Horizon 2020 are:

- ✔ Applications must come from a consortium of at least three partners from at least two European countries.
- ✔ Awards are granted to organisations as well as individuals.
- ✔ Successful applicants have projects that run from two to five years, with budgets of hundreds of thousands to millions of Euros.
- ✔ Typically, 50 per cent of costs are reimbursed, but the level may be as high as 75 per cent.

Part of the reason for wrapping FP7 up in Horizon 2020 seems to be to make it easier for SMEs to navigate the application process, and also to reduce the amount of time it takes to get a decision. But as with all grants, be prepared to wait patiently and keep checking the website to stay up to date on current procedures.

Eurostars

Another transnational programme that sees its second phase moved under Horizon 2020 is the publicly financed €1.2 billion Eurostars Programme (www. eurostars-eureka.eu). As with other EU-funded programmes, it's aimed at research-heavy SMEs, helping partnerships to find funding more efficiently and to get a commercial product to market in a shorter time frame.

With a 25 per cent success rate, it gives better results than some of the other EU programmes – but it wouldn't be prudent to count your chickens before they hatch. That still leaves a 75 per cent rejection rate.

Taking advantage of regional awards

Regional awards that are linked via national schemes are limited, and more often than not they take the form of a *matched loan,* in which you have to come up with the same or nearly the same amount of money as you receive, so check with your local provider to see what's on offer in your part of the country.

One of the more popular funds, which offers both match-funded loans and grants, is the Regional Growth Fund (RGF) (www.gov.uk/regional-growth-fund), set up to match-fund private sector investment that aims to create economic growth and lasting employment in a specific area of the country.

The RGF isn't about a free lunch. Most of the time it's a leg up to help unlock other funds, but it usually needs your financial input as well.

The grants are often awarded to private sector organisations looking to raise at least £1 million in order to fund a significant infrastructure project, such as a second factory or the manufacture of machinery and equipment. Household names such as Mulberry (handmade handbags) have used RGF funds to open their second factory, thereby creating jobs and adding to the economic growth of the region.

Since its launch in 2010, RGF has invested £2.85 billion to help local businesses grow and take on more staff across England. Over 100,000 jobs have already been created and a further 480,000 are expected by the mid-2020s.

You can find additional examples of successfully RGF-funded businesses at `www.greatbusiness.gov.uk/financing-growth-the-regional-growth-fund`.

Raising Money from the Crowd

If the effort to secure grant funding feels like a mammoth task, and you're unwilling to subject yourself and your team to hours of seemingly futile form filling, perhaps crowdfunding offers a more attractive alternative answer to your funding need.

Over the past few years, the business world has seen the birth and rapid growth of what appears to be a new way of raising funds, known as crowd-funding. Simply put, *crowdfunding* is an organised means for a large group of people to make mostly small individual donations to fund a business or an idea. It uses the power of the Internet to bring the two sides together. Crowdfunding replicates some of the more traditional funding activities, such as pitching for a desired amount of finance, in an online format. As finance for business goes, this new vehicle puts the entrepreneur in the driving seat, and empowers members of the public and the investor community – the crowd – to get a piece of the action as paying passengers in a number of companies. Heady stuff for both entrepreneur and investor.

However, crowdfunding as such is not an entirely new concept. In fact, a type of crowdfunding can be traced back to the 1700s, when what came to be known as *microfinance* was started by Jonathan Swift in Ireland when he set up a fund to give loans to low-income families.

Similarly, the renowned philanthropist, Dr Mohammad Yunus, established the modern version of microfinancing in 1976 when he began giving loans to women on low incomes living in Bangladesh. From these humble beginnings, more and more loans were made, and within a period of seven years, the now world-famous Grameen Bank was formed to carry on the good work. Dr Yunus and the Grameen Bank were awarded a Nobel Peace Prize in 2006.

Crowdfunding can raise funds in one of two ways:

- ✔ **Equity:** Offers some share in the business for money invested. You can also pay interest to investors and treat the funds as a loan.

- ✔ **Reward-based:** Exchanging gifts or rewards based on the amount of giving. As the entrepreneur, you set the amount and the time frame for your fundraising, determine the reward levels, and the crowd pledges money. Some sites require the campaign to be fully funded before releasing the money; others forward the funds regardless of whether you reach your goal.

So if you want vitamin-infused water for life, or a spin in a luxury electric vehicle a few times a year for the next ten years, for example, you may find a reward-based platform helps you do something useful or good, and get something useful or good for you in return.

I look at both these types of crowdfunding in Chapter 13. You can also find out more about this extremely popular topic in *Crowdsourcing For Dummies* by David Alan Grier (Wiley).

WARNING!

Although I'm talking about free money here, you may have to pay success fees that vary between four and nine per cent of the amount you raise. In addition, credit card companies and online payment services may charge up to an additional nine per cent. So the funds aren't entirely free of charge.

You can find a number of crowdfunding sites listed on the Crowdfunding Association (established 2012) website at www.ukcfa.org.uk, but the two most talked about rewards-based sites are Kickstarter and Indiegogo. (I cover each in upcoming sections.)

At the moment, both of these well-known sites operate a pledge system. People become backers and support a project with a pledge of money in order to see the project come to life. They receive a reward as a thank you instead of receiving a financial reward. The reward may be something as simple as a book or as extravagant as a walk-on part in a film, depending on how much is pledged to what project. An interesting example is that of an artist who raised funds to create a wall installation, then gave pieces of it to her backers when the exhibit ended.

Although no equity changes hands, you still need to approach reward-based crowdfunding in much the same way you would for an equity-based fund raise.

For a successful crowdfunding experience:

- Produce a well-thought-out video, delivered with enthusiasm and passion, while also ensuring that you get the facts across, as well as the reward structure.

- Tell your story effectively to get people excited about it.

- Get your timing right. From the first day of your campaign until the last day, even down to the time of day you finish, you need to time it for when people are likely to be logged on. You also need to leave enough time to get your network going and to fit the time frame within which you actually need the money.

- Make sure your perks and rewards are clearly presented and easily understood.

✔ Maximise the use of the comments section – good comments encourage more people to get involved.

✔ Create a specific link and hashtag for your campaign; they make it easier to spread the word.

Starting up with Kickstarter

Kickstarter (www.kickstarter.com) is predominantly for creative projects, be they films, games, art, design or music. It has its roots in the United States. In 2012, a UK version was launched to encourage local giving for local projects, and nearly 10 million people have pledged nearly £2 billion. The site is a resounding success, demonstrating the power of the people and the life-changing achievements that happen when people get behind each other.

In much the same way that other financially incentivised sites demand that projects reach full pledge subscription, Kickstarter is an *all-or-nothing site,* meaning that you get nothing unless your project is fully funded. You set the pledge amount, and you set the deadline, but you must then go shake the trees and make the golden fruit drop into your funding crate. To some people this seems harsh, and it does mean that you need to mobilise the power of your crowd and get people doing something versus talking about doing something for your idea, so it's a great financial firecracker.

To date, an impressive 44 per cent of projects have reached their funding goals. Creators keep 100 per cent ownership of their work, but there is a 5 per cent success fee to Kickstarter.

Moving up with Indiegogo

Founded in San Francisco in 2008, Indiegogo (www.indiegogo.com), one of the first crowdfunding sites, has a global audience. It covers the spectrum from creative ideas to start-up business ideas to charity projects.

The success rate is significantly lower than Kickstarter's, at 34 per cent. Its success fee starts at 4 per cent on a fully funded pledge, and 9 per cent on a partially funded pledge (Kickstarter doesn't offer partial funding). Indiegogo also charges up to 9 per cent on credit card and PayPal pledges, so the fees can add up. On the plus side, it refunds 5 per cent if the campaign reaches its target.

In 2014, it launched Indiegogo Life (www.life.indiegogo.com), enabling people to raise funds for life events, such as celebrations, and also for emergencies, medical expenses and so forth. Indiegogo Life is different than Indiegogo with regard to the fees it charges for the funds raised, allowing fundraisers to keep more of the money they raise.

Maximising Tax Credits

The four most dreaded letters in the English alphabet, HMRC (or Her Majesty's Revenue & Customs, if you can bear to read it in full), strike fear into the hearts of the bravest of business warriors, even those who have nothing to hide or fear. A brown envelope dropping through the door and onto the hall floor can make it seem as if a total eclipse has blocked out the bright rays of an otherwise sunny day. Years of paying tax and completing complicated tax forms, never quite sure that you got it all completely right, leave you shaking in your boots when the drab messenger of doom arrives on your usually cheery welcome mat.

Well, shut the front door and stop the presses. Help (and from the place you least expect to find it!) in the form of an R&D tax credit from HMRC may very well be on its way to you if you qualify for it and submit a successful application.

Securing R&D tax credits

To give them their proper name, Science and Technology Research and Development tax credits, more commonly referred to as R&D tax credits, have been around for over ten years. They're a UK tax incentive designed to encourage companies to invest in the R&D of innovative new products and services that help enhance the nation's competitive position as a leader in innovation. They help forward-thinking companies invest more by taking away some of the financial pain. The bonus effect is that companies can reduce their tax bill or claim payable cash credits as a proportion of their R&D expenditure.

The tax credits work by reducing the amount of profit your company is taxed on, which, in turn, lowers the amount of tax you pay. I don't want to over-simplify the process, but this may actually amount to a loss versus a pre-tax profit, which may then result in you getting some cash in exchange for sur-rendering the loss.

It's not often that you get a benefit whether you make a profit or a loss, and I don't want to imply that every application is successful, but going for a R&D tax credit is certainly worth a shot.

The amount of the credit or cash varies, depending on how much you've spent, what qualifies under the scheme, where you are in the tax year and so on, but you can recover as much as 25 per cent of qualified costs.

Although you can get the forms and file for these tax credits yourself, the currently accepted wisdom is that you're more likely to be successful and possibly get a larger return if you instruct a specialist to submit an application on your behalf. Specialists are familiar with the terminology and know how to navigate the process, saving you time and headaches, and hopefully getting you more money in your business pocket. This is one of those areas where it's best to seek advice before embarking on an application. Unless you happen to be a specialist accountant, you'll struggle.

Because the R&D tax credit is a corporate tax scheme, you can only use it once a year, and you must have completed at least one full accounting year.

Understanding entrepreneurs' tax relief

Now, I don't want to put the cart before the horse or see into the future with regards to how you may sell some shares or exit your business, but I want to have just a brief word on something you'd want to discuss with your accountant if you were going to sell some of your shares or indeed, exit the business, which is entrepreneurs' tax relief.

Set in motion in the 2008–2009 budget by MP Alastair Darling, *entrepreneurs' tax relief* was created to give business people an incentive to set up and then grow a business. The tax relief means that when an entrepreneur looks to sell some of his shares or all of the business, he pays a reduced amount of tax on the capital gains resulting from the sale.

I don't want to get into the accountancy details here – I leave that for *Understanding Business Accounting For Dummies* by Colin Barrow and John A. Tracy (Wiley) – but the relief has been extended by successive Chancellors and has a lifetime allowance associated with it for those who dip into the pot more than once. It applies to you as an individual, because you're going to have the gain. You need to have held the asset being sold for at least one year before you sell it, which is a relatively short time in the grand scheme of things, so it's a nice move on behalf of the Chancellor.

These tax schemes can be very tricky to understand and navigate. It's always best to seek professional advice in order to do it properly and to maximise your relief.

Chapter 10

Securing Early-Stage Funding

· ·

In This Chapter

▶ Getting ready for your first stage

▶ Maximising the money in your business before looking out

▶ Looking at early-stage funding options

▶ Avoiding the pitfalls when taking money from friends and family

· ·

As exciting as it is, the early stage of your business is also one of the most challenging and difficult to fund. You don't usually have the documented financial proof to validate your forecasts, patents may be pending versus approved and your valuation is more art and less science. Your potential failure rate is high, and your bank balance is low. Often you've depleted your own savings, redundancy payout or inheritance, and this causes you to turn to other sources of funding fairly early on in the game.

People often refer to both the *seed* and *post-seed stages,* when you haven't yet turned your idea into a product or a service and you're not generating any revenue, as *early stage* with regard to funding, so it's not always clear who's investing in what and at what levels. (I look at stages of funding in Chapter 2.) It gets even more confusing when a pre-revenue business gets a good deal of funding because its founders have had previous success. What's clear is that the lines have blurred since the economy, and therefore investment levels, have picked up, so as with all funding exercises, it pays to do your research and not exclude yourself from approaching both seed and early-stage investors.

The early-stage funding landscape is more complex than later stages due to the number of applicants and because it can encompass both debt and equity funding. The decisions made in these early days affect future funding rounds, especially if it's the first time you're seeking funding.

Get advice from investment-readiness or business advisors, or possibly from a mentor if you've already connected with one, on what consequences your current choices may have for the future of your business. You really need the money to take things forward before you miss your golden opportunity.

Limited though they may be, you still have a number of funding options available to you: friends, family, angel investors, venture capital funders and government-backed loan schemes. They all may seem like good options to you when you just want to go from red to green in your bank account.

Wherever your funding comes from, you have to roll up your sleeves and be prepared to get stuck in so that you can make the seeds of the money tree bear fruit. Some forms of finance are more suited to certain types of business, and your industry or sector may also have a part to play.

It goes without saying that early-stage investing carries high risks for investors. This fact is particularly important if your friends and family are getting on board. You want to make sure that they can really afford to play this high-stakes game. They're presumably investing out of love and respect for you, and you all want to keep it that way, so you have a lot to think about and a lot to discuss before letting a wet signature dry on your page.

Of course, the flip side to high risk is high reward and a better share price, which is another motivation for early-stage investors – but this glowing outcome doesn't always materialise, so temper expectations with a dose of reality.

Starting Well by Preparing Well

Before you start talking to anyone about funding your early-stage business, you need to consider several points:

- **What stage your business is in.** Are you in the pre-revenue stage? Are you gathering early revenue, but don't yet show a profit? Is your business still just an idea?

- **How much money you need.** Know what you need it for and what you're offering in return.

- **What type of funding you need and want.** Do you want equity from a crowdfunding platform, or an early-stage investment fund or an individual business angel investor? Would you like your family members to lend you money or to sell them a share in your business?

- **Who is a likely funder.** Get a good list together based on research, advisor input and talking to people to narrow down a target list of likely funders for your business and your stage. Find out what funders are active in the areas you need and in your social and business networks. You want to make sure you exhaust every connection, link and introduction so that you feel you've done all you can to achieve your goal.

✔ **Who may be able to invest in future rounds, if that's applicable to your business.** Although it may seem early days, you should always have one eye on your future funding needs and consider what impact earlier funding rounds may have on later rounds. For example, equity crowdfunding your chocolate bar business can be a great way to get money and new customers in, but if you plan to raise larger amounts of equity to build a chocolate factory later on, your future investors may not be happy with hundreds of crowdfunded investors already on board. Research the funding journey of companies similar to yours and see what paths they chose.

✔ **Who is happy to have other investors or funders on board at the same time.** Some investors only want other sophisticated investors in the game, some don't want your business to carry any debt while they're providing funds and others have different restrictions.

✔ **Where your business is based.** Some early-stage funders prefer to invest or were created to invest in certain geographical areas of the UK. If you have active investors, they may also prefer to invest in businesses on their own doorstep so they can keep a closer eye on and a more active hand in them.

✔ **Your sector or industry and who is investing in this area.** You're looking to see who's interested in what your business does, and who can bring some extra value. Investors sometimes have a very narrow focus, choosing to specialise in one business area, and aren't interested in a mixed portfolio; others want diversity in the type of business they invest in, but stick with only one stage, like an SEIS (Seed Enterprise Investment Scheme) fund.

You need to find out who's doing what, what their criteria and application processes are and if they actually have money to invest. Otherwise, you'll waste a lot of time and wind up feeling very frustrated and very behind in your planning.

On the subject of time, remember that this whole process can take many weeks, if not months, so plan accordingly – and prepare to be distracted from actually running your business.

If your industry has its own professional bodies, take a look at upcoming events, professional networks and seminars that they may be putting on that deal with early-stage investing.

Getting and staying organised

It may seem like a pointless administrative task to you, but it's a vital process in fundraising: keeping track of all the research, emails, contacts, responses, calls, meetings and the rest. Essentially, you need to create a mini contact relationship management system (CRM), because believe me, after you've collected up hundreds of business cards, looked at dozens of websites, followed up tens of introductions, sent an untold number of emails, called to hound for an appointment and been held at the gate by countless gatekeepers, you'll forget who said what to whom, when, where and why, and you'll wind up confused and start resending information to people who already struggle to get through their inbox.

A simple Excel spreadsheet is good enough. Don't make the mistake of storing it all in your head or on pieces of paper, napkins, backs of envelopes and so on. The information is too vital to lose or forget, and you need to look and be in control and up to date.

Use this checklist to keep your information under control:

✔ Create a spreadsheet that works for you and that includes all the possible headings for how you can contact funders.

✔ Update it after every interaction, whether it's an email, a call, meeting or whatever, and note what actually took place – and what happens next. For example, 'executive summary sent after call and agreed to follow up in two days', with diary alerts set for future actions.

✔ Make columns to keep track of reasons you were turned down and changes you made as a result, so you make sure you're listening to feedback and constructive criticism. You don't want to hawk the same old lame proposition around to a larger investor community. To paraphrase a well-known saying, 'If it's broke, then fix it'.

✔ Set a time in your diary to update your spreadsheet and review it each week, or more often if it's very active, and stick to it the same way you'd turn up for a team meeting.

Getting Money into Your Business without Looking Outside

In this book, you discover a lot about funding your business using external investors, lenders or other funding providers at different stages of your business. What's also worth taking a look at are the ways you may be able to fund your business by keeping more of your own money and revenue in it. You can find ways of boosting your financial position with money that has no strings attached to it, before or while you're looking for larger funding amounts. Not to be sneezed at, these tactics can stop you from giving too much of your business away in the form of equity to investors, and they can also put you in a better position when it comes to showing potential funders that you know what you're doing when it comes to managing your business finances.

Some self-funding methods to investigate are:

✔ **Taking deposits and pre-payments:** If you're setting up something like a training business or consultancy, you can probably get some money into your business without spending too much by taking deposits and prepayments before you've written a course or done a scoping meeting with a client.

✔ **Stretching your payment terms:** If you're launching a business that sells a product and you know your suppliers well, you can try to ride the wave of an unspoken interest-free loan by taking advantage of 30-, 60- or 90-day credit terms. Generous payment terms become a way of funding your early days or your expansion days when cash flow is tight and you're in danger of not being able to keep up with demand – commonly known as *overtrading*.

✔ **Winning competitions or being awarded grants:** You may be eligible for and awarded a grant or win a competition that gives you a much-needed funding boost with few or no strings attached (refer to Chapter 9 for more on competitions and grants). This money can help to get you on track for your next stage of growth and your next round of funding.

At the time of writing, I have six clients who've been in this position in the past two months, not to mention many others who've gone before them. Some of them also received free mentoring, office space, marketing help and introductions to investors, as well as attendance at events with some pretty serious global movers and shakers.

3-D holographic advert company Kino Mo took advantage of a great opportunity to get a cash prize and some marketing help, memberships and other goodies when it entered Pitch to Rich (www.virginmedia business.co.uk) in 2015, and found itself on the winning side of none other than Richard Branson. 2015 was the second year of the competition, and Branson was looking for innovative business ideas and energised entrepreneurs at the start-up and growth stages of their business. The competition took place online and winners were chosen by the public and a panel of celebrity business people.

Competitions are great, and you may reap some pretty useful rewards, but they're also usually very time-consuming, so think it through before you get started on that application. Ask yourself how much of your time will be taken up in something that may have a low chance of success, and make sure that you have that time to spare.

✔ **Reward- or donation-based crowdfunding:** You may be able to raise funds via a reward-based crowdfunding campaign, avoiding the need to give up shares in your business. (I explore crowdfunding in more detail in Chapter 9.) You bring in funding and simultaneously get market exposure in your target market, which is extremely helpful for future sales revenue and market penetration.

✔ **Receiving a personal loan:** If you're just starting out and exploring the debt side of funding, you're unlikely to get a loan for your business from a high street bank, but you may be eligible for a personal loan using a government-backed scheme that has lower interest rates–for example, the Start Up Loan Company (SULCO), which I talk about Chapter 12.

✔ **Thinking outside the box:** You may do what a friend of mine did years ago, and fund your business using cash prizes won on television game shows! A step closer to better odds than buying a lottery ticket, but a massively creative bit of thinking and a long shot, nonetheless.

✔ **Accessing additional personal finance:** Although it's still external debt, you can maximise your personal debt options, making the investment from you more significant before you approach the external market.

Be very careful and get qualified advice before making the choice to fund your business start-up with personal debt. You may live to regret it. If you choose to max out your credit cards or seek finance from your credit union, for example, you need to be sure you're not putting yourself into scalding hot water. All your personal funding options still have repayment dates and amounts, and you shouldn't ignore these facts. If you can't repay it, don't borrow it.

✔ **Releasing cash from property:** You may be fortunate enough to have some equity in your property or an additional property that you can sell to release some cash for your business.

Think very hard before you put your home on the line in this way. Seek professional advice and do not enter this decision lightly. If your family winds up with no place to live, fixing that will take all your attention and energy, leaving you no time for your new business.

Before applying for any personal debt to put towards your early-stage business, get professional advice to make sure you can afford it and that it won't have any lasting or significant negative impact on your credit profile or your living situation. The Financial Conduct Authority (FCA) (www.fca.org.uk) is a good place to start when looking for a qualified advisor.

✔ **Releasing cash from your pension:** Under changes in the pension laws, as of April 2015, you may be able to free up some of the money in your pension fund to start your new adventure. As people are living longer and looking at second or third careers, the real impact on national and personal budgets is not yet known. Once again, it's critical that you make sure you can afford this and do it properly, as this money is meant to be your nest egg. You can find information at www.pensions.gov.uk.

Exploring External Sources of Early-Stage Funding

After you've explored or exhausted your personal funding options and the options within your business, you can look at the variety of early-stage funding options outside your business. More funding sources pop up every month, and include:

- ✔ **Accelerators and incubators:** Seed (incubators) early-stage (accelerators) funding and support organisations that typically take a share in your business, provide support, mentoring and office space.

- ✔ **Seed funds:** Investor finance for your business at its pre-trading stage.

- ✔ **Early-stage angels:** Wealthy individuals or networked investors who typically invest at the early stages of your business in return for shares.

- ✔ **Venture capitalists (VCs):** A firm of investors that manages and invests a fund of money, typically during growth stages.

- ✔ **Crowdfunding:** Platform-based debt, equity or reward funding that sees many people each investing in or lending a small amount in your business.

- ✔ **Corporate venture funds:** The investment of corporate venture capital funds into external start-ups.

Joining an accelerator or an incubator

You may be lucky enough to be accepted into an early-stage accelerator or incubator, which I look at in more detail in Chapter 8. In these systems, funds are injected into your business alongside mentoring, commercial introductions and office space, most often in exchange for a share in the business. Getting this attention early can help your chances in the next round of fundraising.

The percentage of your business you part with varies from 0 to 2 per cent with some incubators to roughly 7 to 8 per cent with some accelerators, which may take percentages in stages, based on milestones.

Growing from seed funds

You can seek out funds set up specifically for very early, pre-trading stages of a business, known as *seed rounds*.

Seed money may include some *ring-fenced funds,* funds designated for a specific use, by early-stage VCs, complicating what is already quite a fluid landscape.

In recent years, the term *seed* has become a bit elastic in its usage. I've seen it as low as those first few tens of thousands of pounds, all the way up to half a million, which is one big seed! (See Seedcamp at www.seedcamp.com for a seed fund attached to an accelerator.)

Seed rounds can come from family and friends, but they can also come from specific seed funds set up to fund between £50,000 and £150,000. The funds may come with mentoring and accelerator benefits as well. VC firms have seed funds, equity crowdfunding has a seed focus, and you may find specific SEIS tax-incentive-based funds, like the Ascension fund (www.ascensionfund.com), which is an early-stage investment fund specialising in the technology, media and telecoms industries. It acts as the funding vehicle and only funds SEIS-eligible companies in their early stages.

You may receive funding from both sophisticated and less sophisticated investors who take advantage of the tax-efficient SEIS scheme. SEIS investors come from all ends of the investor spectrum and can include equity platforms and early-stage individual or networked angels, such as those I look at in Chapter 13. Early-stage angels often are prepared to put their money into a business so long as it has additional funding and some traction in its market (which proves that the idea has legs). The need for earnings and co-investment is more prevalent in the tech sector, where the barriers to entry can be relatively low, and there's a lot of free help and advice around to help give your business lift off and put you in front of mentors, panellists, and speakers who may also be early-stage investors.

If you have a technology-related business, you may be eligible for research and development tax credits (find information on these in Chapter 9), which help put money back into your business or limit your losses.

Praising early-stage angels

Angel investors, individual or networked investors with high net worth, used to come in a little later in the process but are rapidly moving into the seed space. In the UK, you can find over 18,000 active angel investors; in the US, the number has grown to over 300,000 in the past two years. This trend is likely to continue as networks like Gust and Angel List make it easier for you to approach angels directly, widening your option pool.

Interesting early-stage venture capitalists (VCs)

If you're familiar with the equity investing food chain, you may think that your early stage is too early for a venture capital firm to be interested in, and a few years ago, you would have been right.

Not that I'm saying VCs are falling over themselves on their way to invest in your early-stage business, but buoyed by the boom in lucrative tech businesses, some VC firms have taken the bold step of getting in early so as to be in position for future funding rounds if they think your company is a winner. In fact, global investment by VCs in London-based companies hit a record £455 million during the first quarter of 2015.

A number of VC firms now have funds set aside specifically for seed rounds. The more active and familiar in the UK include:

- ✔ **Passion Capital** (www.passioncapital.com): An early-stage tech investor

- ✔ **Balderton Capital** (www.balderton.com): Early-stage investors with a tech focus who are also very active in the US

- ✔ **Index Ventures** (http://indexventures.com): A global venture capital firm which focuses on the technology and life science sectors

- ✔ **Dawn Capital** (http://dawncapital.com): A venture capital fund focused on the enterprise software and financial technology sectors

- ✔ **Accel Partners** (www.accel.com): A traditional VC with a 30-year history of investing at different stages

As I often say, it's never too early to start a dialogue with a VC. The more forward thinking amongst them invest time and skills at the very early stage of your business, growing and nurturing the relationships they believe are a good fit and offer a good return. They can often take a collaborative approach, sitting alongside other investors, like angels, or a mass of crowdfunders. However, sometimes VCs compete with each other for the same business, which can have the effect of driving your company valuation beyond your original intention. I discuss how to prepare and approach VCs in more detail in Chapter 13.

As you would with all investors, challenge VCs and make sure that they're a good fit for you and your business. Ask them how they will help your business grow and eventually exit – trade sale, management buyout, for example – in addition to putting money in. Ask them how quickly they can execute a deal, and what matters more to them – top-line revenue growth (most likely) or getting a good return from their overall portfolio of investments.

Raising funds through crowdfunding

Depending on your industry, *crowdfunding*, or raising small amounts of money from a large number of people usually through an online platform, can be a good place to source early-stage funding. (I talk about crowdfunding in more detail in Chapter 14.)

An increasing number of start-ups are now launched through crowdfunding platforms, where they can raise equity and gain market exposure. According to Massolution, a research and advisory firm that specialises in crowdsourcing solutions for social enterprises, global crowdfunding experienced unprecedented growth in 2014, expanding by 167 per cent to reach £10.8 billion raised, up from £4 billion in 2013. This is set to increase to £23 billion in 2015, surpassing VCs (which average roughly £20 billion per year). That said, many VCs see the value in crowdfunding and are happy to collaborate – they're willing to invest alongside others in the crowd (while indulging in a little healthy competition).

Although crowdfunding grows in popularity for funding early-stage business, be aware that it's not an overnight process. You need to do a lot of public relations to nudge your circle of potential investors to invest via the platform so that you can spark the flame that fuels the funding fire.

Venturing into corporate venture funds

Also becoming increasingly popular at the early stages of funding is the corporate venture fund. Large companies are increasingly investing their own funds in seed rounds of early-stage businesses for a variety of reasons:

- ✔ Finding test beds for new products and services
- ✔ Looking for companies that fill a gap in an area that benefits their strategic objectives
- ✔ Taking an innovative company off the market to gain a competitive advantage

Companies as diverse as Microsoft, Unilever, Santander Bank and John Lewis all have venture funds investing in seed rounds and farther up the funding chain, so it pays to see who's investing in your industry.

Accepting Money from Friends, Family and Fools

One source of funding very close to home, and therefore often the elephant in the room, is from your friends, family and the odd acquaintance that gets pulled in. You may hear this last category referred to as *fools* in funding circles, as they're seen as a bit softer of heart and less knowledgeable about the finer details of investing and may make a few more mistakes than the professional investors. If you exhaust all your other options and you still need to find the money, you wind up asking those closest to you to break open their piggy banks, raid their savings accounts, dust off and liquidate their share portfolios and dig deep down behind the sofa cushions before emptying every proverbial pocket they have to help you realise your dream.

Friends and family rounds of fundraising can sometimes be the easiest ones you ever do because you're essentially preaching to the converted. They can also be some of the most difficult, because those near and dear may not be easily parted from their money. Not that your inner circle is full of fools, but it's their money, so they're not always quick to write the cheque out.

Assuming that you've shared your plans to start or grow your business with those closest to you, they're aware of your need to find some funding to get this party started. Indeed, some of them may hear the sound of the drum before it reaches them and beat a retreat by fleeing the country or setting their phones to automatic voicemail in order to sidestep a potentially uncomfortable conversation. However, most of them will want to help in whatever way they can. Remember that no one wants to feel compelled to help, and frankly, most of them shouldn't invest because they don't really know what they're getting into and can't afford to lose their life savings if you don't deliver the goods. It's up to you to make them feel that they're going along willingly and also to help them tread carefully and within their means.

Those closest to you see you through rose-tinted spectacles, wanting the best outcome. They may not have the vision or the experience to spot the faults and cracks in your business plan. They still remember the blue ribbon you brought home three years running in the county amateur under-12s summer bank holiday weekend horse show, everyone basking in the glory of your gold. Their objectivity goes out the window, in most cases, and they may not challenge you to check and double-check your assumptions and projections before launching at full pelt. On the other hand, you may come from a family with a history of running a business who can empathise with your situation and may be able to add value as well as funding.

Start by drawing up a list of likely investors in your circle, and then arrange some informal meetings to feel them out on the idea. If they seem interested, get them to sign a non-disclosure agreement, or an NDA, like everyone else does, and once that's done, you can send them your business plan.

Make a list of who's in your circle of friends:

- ✔ Accountants
- ✔ Lawyers
- ✔ Other professional services employees who may have maxed out their taxable contributions and are looking for another way to lessen the capital gains tax blow
- ✔ Local businessmen who understand your business and have some money to invest
- ✔ Local high-profile celebrities or names who know you and can add some value
- ✔ Relatives both near and far

Some accountants club together and form syndicates that invest in early-stage businesses, so it's always worth asking your own accountant, or those in your circle, if she's looking for good investments. You may uncover some new blood in the early-stage investment pool, especially in places like London where it can feel like everyone is pitching to the same people.

Your business plan needs to give every investor the details on the business you're looking to fund, and family and friends are no exception. Tell them how much equity you're prepared to give away if they're making an equity investment or how little interest you want to pay on debt, if they're making a loan.

This is also a good time to let them know how much or how little you want them to be involved in the actual business. If you're considering an SEIS investment, you don't want very much involvement. But, if you think they can genuinely add value in an active way, and you're comfortable with that, you can start to lay it out here. I advise keeping friends and family out of the day-to-day running of a business if you want to keep relations cordial. If it's an investor you're after and not a partner, you need to make that crystal clear.

Be prepared for questions, as you would be when pitching to any investor. You can perhaps deal with some of these on the phone, but follow up in an email to make sure that everyone hears and understands the same thing. If they're not professional investors or people who work in or on the fringes of the sector, they'll need time to digest it all. Do all you can to make sure they understand fully, or it will only come back to haunt you later on. If you're a start-up, you are by definition high risk, so give them some space to process, think and perhaps change their minds.

Eventually, you'll get to a formal meeting with them and their advisors, who may be lawyers, accountants or financial directors, for example, to discuss the vehicle for investing.

Avoiding potential pitfalls

I don't know about you, but I come from a large southern Mediterranean family, and we love a good argument, or a very loud conversation, as we prefer to call it, especially if it comes with the added bonus of the potential to hold a grudge. One of the best ways to ensure a family feud is to involve your family in matters of money. Just like oil and water, this can be a tricky combination to mix without a spoonful of sugar and a little bit of vinegar thrown in to help blend it and keep it smooth and palatable.

Statistically, anywhere up to 90 per cent of new start-ups fail. Not that I want to put any negative thoughts in your head, but it's something you need to keep in the back of your mind when asking your nearest and dearest to invest. They need to be made aware of all possible outcomes, and you all need to be comfortable with this.

If you base the arrangement on treating them fairly with either a percentage of equity or a reasonable interest rate, making sure their needs are aligned with your business needs; observe the same rules of full disclosure and governance, not cutting corners on putting together robust internal procedures; and use a strong board (as you do with the rest of the world), you're going a long way to avoiding any long term unpleasantries or broken branches in your family tree. Going through this process can also be a good way to check in your own mind how well you think you've planned and tried to mitigate risks and encourage success. If you're prepared to risk years of uncomfortable family functions, you want to be sure you've done all you can to make your business a success.

You also need to think about the way the potential fallout affects you. If you see your business going down the pan, would you still keep going because you have family or friends' money tied up, and you want to keep trying for them instead of doing the logical thing and bowing out? Fear and guilt are great motivators in certain circumstances, but think carefully before they become the drivers in your business.

If you have co-founders or a management team with shares, they may not appreciate your desire to be loyal. In much the same way you err on the side of caution to prevent a disaster in your business, your need to succeed at all costs where family and friends are concerned may cause you to take even bigger risks, grasping at straws in a desperate bid to make the thing work and give them a return on their investment.

Some useful tips and guidelines when getting investment from friends, family and those close to you:

- ✔ Always get something in writing and use a qualified solicitor to draw up the paperwork.

- ✔ Make sure investors know that they may lose their money as well as make a profit and that they're okay with this.

- ✔ Be sure to explain any limitations in terms of their involvement, avoiding the need for uncomfortable conversations later on. You'd be surprised at how everyone suddenly becomes an expert when she's invested or loaned your business some money.

- ✔ Make sure the whole family is aware of the arrangement, especially if by so doing you can avoid additional friction because you eliminate any surprises.

- ✔ Take advantage of the current tax incentive schemes, such as SEIS, whenever appropriate.

- ✔ Resist the temptation to give your new funders a job or a role in the business unless they are really the right people for the jobs. No one wants dead weight around the place.

- ✔ Be very strict with yourself as regards sticking to these rules, and don't suddenly start acting strangely around these people. If you do all you can to keep it strictly business, you'll have no reason to feel indebted to those nearest and dearest to you.

Understanding the impact on future rounds

The relief that comes from knowing that your friends and family have your back and are there to give you the financial leg up you need at a critical point in time is immense. All your sleepless nights fade into the background like a distant memory once you have the funds to tide you over until working capital or your next funding round come to the rescue. It may help you to raise some more seed or early-stage money by having someone else on board, as it gives others the confidence to jump in, or it may make you play safe, ultimately lowering the value of your company in the market.

You need to consider, however, another potential downside to this type of funding, in the way it can impact future rounds or completing a funding round later on. What seems like someone throwing you a lifeline while you're drowning in a sea of uncertainty may be the thing that stops you from getting a more sophisticated investor, or *smart money,* on board. Unrelated investors sometimes don't want to have to deal with your Aunt Nellie or Mr Miggins next door, who put in what they consider *dumb money,* or money invested by small, private investors with little or no investing or business experience.

Family investors who dominate a board create a different dynamic to having sophisticated investors on board. Often the next-round investor will want to buy them out or restructure their place on the board so that she can reset the tone, sharpen the governance, and prepare your business for a high-growth future.

The other purely financial reason for wanting to clear the family out is that early, family investors may have the option to buy into later open rounds at a lower price, impacting on the exit value for all investors – higher for family; lower for new investors – which will not go down well.

From your family investor's point of view, as the number of shares increase and their value is diluted, your cousin can wind up holding more of something that is less valuable than it was when she first invested, so she may get a bit miffed.

Early-stage family and friends investing is a much-debated topic, particularly with the seemingly unstoppable rise of crowdfunding, which has changed the face of investing and added to the blurring of the lines between who is investing at what stage.

After you've raised the initial money and as you start looking at a first proper round of £750,000 and above, you may find a few doors slamming in your face. You may be unable to raise follow-on funding from sophisticated investors – you're *orphaned,* as the trade calls it.

Inexperienced investors often lack the expertise, network and experience necessary to add value in follow-on rounds, which more professional investors have as a matter of course, and therefore impact the way in which some investors see the next round.

On the other hand, as Goncalo de Vasconcelos, one of the founders of the very successful investor-led platform, Syndicate Room, said, 'Having friends in early rounds is perfectly normal and doesn't have to have any negative impact on any round. The secret is to get good legal advice and to keep it simple. What I observe over and over again when it has a detrimental effect in follow-on rounds is when the early agreements are complex and as a result, put later investors off due to the legal complexity of the deal'.

The best advice is to keep the deal structure simple if family is involved, and to make sure that they understand the possibility of their shares being diluted or worth less money in the future, making it easier for the professional investors to manage them in later rounds.

Getting it in writing

Whether it's equity or debt, it goes without saying that you need to get it in writing. Don't make agreements over the phone or over the buffet table at a family wedding, and then not get them in writing before you go forward.

You feel the weight of the world is lifted from your shoulders when people you know come to your rescue, and your investors feel good that they've been able to help a friend or a relative in need. But it's madness to accept these offers of help without attaching some strings to them in order to safeguard your relationship and ensure that the money stays in the business for as long as you need it there. Taking money from friends, family and other folks if you don't have a formal arrangement with them is foolhardy. A formal agreement avoids that earth-shattering phone call out of the blue when Aunt Maggie says she needs the money back as soon as possible, and you're stuck between the rock and hard place of family relations being ruined forever or somehow scraping together the money she now wants back.

You can realise a variety of tax benefits for both equity and debt, and it benefits both the investor and your business as the investee to have these professionally drawn up and witnessed.

For equity, you can access tax incentives using the Seed Enterprise Investment Scheme (SEIS, which I look at in Chapter 13). I discuss tax benefits for debt in the next section.

Paying back loans versus giving away shares

If you really can't bear the thought of giving any equity away, and you're lucky enough to know people, a bank, or an alternative funder who'll lend you the money you need, it's important to get the agreement in writing. It's also important to do the same for any director's loans – yours or other director's – so it can be seen in the company's financial documents and repaid at an appropriate time. Discuss this with your accountant so you get it right from the start.

If you decide to go with the option of accepting a loan from friends or family, treat it exactly the same way you'd treat a loan from a stranger. You both need to seek professional advice in the areas you need it and create a formal, written, legally binding agreement.

If you can, keep the agreement simple and avoid complicated deals and structures common with more sophisticated lenders. You want to do right by this group and keep it fair and as simple as possible, especially if they've never done anything like this before. More experienced folks – any bankers, accountants or lawyers in your closest circles – may be more familiar and more confident with the process.

One of the more common advantages in borrowing from family and friends is that you usually get a better rate of interest, and you can negotiate some flexibility with regard to payment schedules, payment holidays and deferred or delayed repayments. The flexibility helps to ease your cash flow, and gives you some breathing space if you come upon hard times or a bump in your business road.

Be aware that tax implications exist that go with a loan for both you and the lender. For your business, you'll be able to deduct the interest from your taxable profit; the lender must declare the interest received from you as taxable income, and so she needs to be made aware of this from the start.

As you'd do with equity investing, set out the terms of the loan in a legal document and keep very good records of all the repayments made.

A variation on a straightforward loan from friends and family is the option of having what's known as a *convertible loan note,* which is a loan that converts to equity at a future date or on the achievement of a certain milestone. That date or milestone is often before the next round of funding. You can cap this type of investor to a percentage of equity that you're comfortable with, like 10 per cent, and perhaps offer some other incentives that apply to them before the next round as a reward. Again, make sure you get professional advice from a qualified source – and that everyone understands it – before you agree to anything.

Don't treat taking money from family and friends like taking candy from a baby. Whether it's equity or debt, this decision and process comes with a warning label. It's a serious legal matter that also comes heavily laden with responsibility and a feeling of wanting to do right by those who've placed their faith and funds in you.

Your investors agree to stick by you through thick and thin, and you both sign up for all sorts of legal rights and wrongs. Enter the agreement with careful consideration, honesty, respect and integrity, backed up with transparency in all your dealings, and you'll go a long way to preserving a business and personal relationship that will endure long after your business has been sold, failed, or the agreement has expired.

Very often this group of people give you this money out of a genuine desire to help or out of love, and even though you discuss the possibility of loss and failure, it won't be something they really consider until it's staring them in the face. If the worst happens, you want to do all you can to soften the blow for both of you because you're talking about real people with real money and real emotions.

Chapter 11

Securing Accelerator Finance

· ·

· ·

Most people agree that the word *accelerator* has a positive meaning. In a business sense, the word gives you an almost tangible sense of your business putting its proverbial pedal to the metal and taking off like a rocket-powered race car, speeding over the finish line to success. I imagine that the people behind many of the most well known UK accelerators would be happy with that effect.

This chapter covers the ins and outs of accelerators and how to make the most of them.

Comparing Accelerators and Incubators

Before I dive deep into the potential benefits of receiving accelerator finance, it's useful to make a distinction between incubators and accelerators. These terms are often used interchangeably, and although you can get funding from both, incubators tend to be advantageous in the idea or pre-start stage of your business, whereas an accelerator guides you as you transition from pre-start to start-up phase and then speed your growth using funding, education, learning, mentoring and showcasing.

In a nutshell, an *accelerator* provides services to support your business, often in return for equity, as your business begins to scale and grow. *Incubators* focus on very early-stage, small companies that may have an idea that needs developing into more of a business.

Most incubators are for purely commercial start-ups, providing very early-stage support for an idea that will morph into a business in the not-too-distant future. Others offer support – often securing public funding – to companies focused on the science and technology or higher education sectors, where high-cost, long-term research is required.

An incubator may focus on growing or *hot housing,* helping your seed of a business idea take root in your seed stage. An incubator helps get your idea to a product or service in the market. Equity is usually taken but often funding is *in kind* – office space, mentoring, training, showcasing and so on, and the amount of equity taken is small.

If you're in an incubator, your place in the market is not fully clarified, and chances are that by the time you leave the safety of the cosseted incubator space, your business will be unrecognisable from what it was when you entered.

Typically, an accelerator assists you for around 10 to 15 weeks. Although many accelerators are aimed at tech firms – be they medical, educational, financial technology or otherwise – you can now find some non-tech ones, such as for food and beverages, with more beginning to pop up around the UK.

Accelerators can provide a supportive, safe place to prove your idea has legs and develop your strategy in a meaningful way. They usually have a fantastic network of contacts and a pretty impressive group of experienced, relevant mentors who can help to thrust your business forward and keep you on track and accountable.

Accelerators are focused on the point at which you scale up your growth. You're at the stage just before a venture capitalist (VC) may show interest – VCs are in the wings waiting to see evidence of scalable growth – and many accelerators make introductions to these funders at the end of their support process.

The wider world of funding views businesses in accelerators in one of two ways:

- ✔ You're sizzling hot because the competition to be selected is super fierce.
- ✔ You're too early to be of interest to anyone who's making serious investments and of no interest at this point.

The people running the accelerator need to do all they can to combat the latter point of view. By making a small investment in your business, an accelerator acts as the touchpaper to ignite your rapid growth in exchange for a single-digit equity share, paving the way for eventually getting you in front of willing and able next-round investors.

Exchanging Equity for Support

Accelerators provide support in a variety of guises from training to showcasing. They're also a proving ground for what they hope will be the next colossal success. The aim of an accelerator is to invest early and get in on the ground floor of the next big thing.

Accelerators offer different options for how much equity you're willing to give up in exchange for funds and support. Arrangements may be something like a 3 per cent interest in your business in return for access to all the accelerator's services, but no lump sum of funds; or 7 per cent for access to all the services and an additional lump sum of money on top. Some offer straight money for shares and others offer a combination with what's known as *convertible debt,* which, in simple terms, sees debt offered to you turning into shares at a later date. The range is broad.

In the UK, accelerators come in all shapes and sizes, but some of the more recognisable names are shown in Table 11-1.

 When selecting an accelerator and choosing to accept funding from it, make sure that you choose the right accelerator for your business and that you're satisfied that your business is getting value for money in return for the equity you're giving up.

Considering the true cost

Although it may not seem like it at the time, funding from an accelerator can be some of the most expensive money you receive. Getting support, a certain amount of office space, say £10,000, an accounting and payroll package and some broadband – some components of a typical package – in exchange for 7 or 10 per cent of your company's market value may wind up seeing you give away a value of ten times that amount if your business grows well and outperforms expectations. So, an accelerator can be a very expensive way to purchase some very basic services.

It's absolutely true that you get rid of some of your worries, sleepless nights and feelings of isolation and confusion as well. However, remember that although an accelerator may ignite your growth, it won't continue to fan the flames of growth if you're not receiving follow-on funding after you leave the nest.

Table 11-1 A Selection of UK Accelerators

Accelerator (URL)	Specialty	Location	Programme Length	Investment/Equity
Accelerator Academy (www.acceleratoracademy.com)	Digital	London	12 weeks	£600 flat fee; refunded if your company raises funds within 3 months
Bethnal Green Ventures (www.bethnalgreenventures.com)	Tech	London	3 months	£15,000 for 6%
Collider (www.collider.io)	Advertising and marketing	London	4 months	£50,000 for 11% with charges and a pyramid system for proven success
Emerge Education (www.emerge.education)	Education	London	3 months	£15,000 for 3–8%
Goldman Sachs 10,000 Small Businesses (www.goldmansachs.com or www.ucl.ac.uk/advances-programmes)	Scalable business	London and Yorkshire - operating through universities	6 months	None
Idea Alive (www.ideaalive.co.uk)	Digital	Manchester/ Liverpool	10 weeks	Charge of 1% of amount raised or £5,000 (whichever is greater)
Ignite 100 (www.ignite100.com)	Software	Newcastle-upon-Tyne	14 weeks	£18,000 for 6–9%
Level 39 (www.level39.co)	Finance, cyber-security, retail	London	Works on a membership basis	Depending on membership
Oxygen Accelerator (www.oxygenaccelerator.com)	Tech	Birmingham	13 weeks	£18,000 for 8%
Seedcamp (www.seedcamp.com)	Tech	London (UK office)	3 months	Up to $250,000 for up to 10%
Startupbootcamp (www.startupbootcamp.org)	Global scaling	London (UK office)	3 months	Several variable offers
Tech Stars (www.techstars.com/london-program)	Tech	London	3 weeks	$118,000 for 7–10%
Wayra (www.wayra.co.uk)	Tech	London (UK office)	6–12 months	£40,000 in services for 7–10%

You need to make a value-for-money decision. Typically, you won't have a lot of capital at the point that you're considering an accelerator, so it looks like a good deal. But, if you hit or surpass your growth targets, and your business is flying high and worth a million pounds, and you've given 10 per cent equity to the accelerator, essentially you've paid £100,000 for that £10,000 of support.

Office space and broadband don't drive growth. It's a seductive package on offer, but you need to be sure it makes financial sense for you and your business before you sign on the dotted line.

Helping to accelerate your commercial growth

Every accelerator has its own take on how to help connect you to commercial opportunities, but they all have some similarities in *pitch days* and *demo days,* when you present your business and funding proposition to either potential customers or investors with a view to helping you accelerate your commercial growth.

Some, like Accenture, may have mentors like the employees of Goldman Sachs, where you can meet potential direct clients or collaborators via the mentor network. Others, like Startupbootcamp FinTech, have showcase and demo days, where a curated group of companies can meet directly with financial service providers, funders and other businesses in the supply chain in order to strike up a deal. Pretty much all of them have mentors and trainers who will share their contacts directly with you as a mentee, making a personal introduction to get the ball rolling.

Critical to getting a foot on the commercial ladder is the quality of your pitch, so as most programmes wind down, the emphasis is on perfecting your pitch. Your hours of preparing and practising your pitch culminate in some kind of event day, no matter which accelerator you're on. Oxygen Accelerator, which says it works with 'continent-shifting ideas', ends its programme with a demo day, as do Startupbootcamp FinTech, Techstars and many others. These demo days are closed-room, invitation-only events where you have the opportunity to give full answers to investors who are chosen for their potential interest in your venture.

Advising you on perfect pitching

Help with pitching may be a bit patchy in other parts of the country, but you find no shortage of pitch-training opportunities in London and the major UK cities, which are now being billed as the Northern Powerhouse. Therefore, pitch training and advising in an accelerator needs to be pretty good – and then some – in order to make it worth your time and equity.

Support in this key area of raising funds and securing commercial contracts needs to be specific to your sector and not readily or widely available to everyone and his uncle. It also needs to tell it like it is, in a no-holds-barred kind of way, providing constructive criticism and the benefit of hindsight and years of insider knowledge, skills and wisdom to help you improve and impress in the quickest possible time.

This kind of small group or one-on-one pitch practice should be aimed at helping you create interest and excitement around your business. You want to be positioned in front of primed investors who want what you have to offer. You need to create a knock-out pitch deck and presentation that gives you the best shot at getting your next round of funds in the shortest possible time frame. (I talk about perfecting your pitch in Chapter 6.)

Providing introductions to funders

One of the main reasons for joining an accelerator is to secure introductions to future funders.

Accelerators have the contacts and relationships required in order to have the ear of the investment community – poised and ready to put their hands in their pockets to fund what you have to offer. Accelerators help you jump what may otherwise be a high hurdle and provide you with a safe space to do it in.

Your chosen accelerator acts as a filter or a screening process for investors, curating a list of top-notch opportunities for when you're ready to bring your product or service to the market, find a willing customer to buy it and start on your path to success.

The more selective the accelerator, the more sizzling the companies it selects. Accelerators are looking for companies that will set the phones alight and start a feeding frenzy amongst the best VC firms.

To get a sense of what the investment opportunities may be for your business, it pays to do your homework. Look into who got funded and by which investors, and check out whether the funders are still actively investing and if they're doing so in your market. You want to make sure that they're not passive investors, hanging around doing a bit of research but not intending to take it any further.

Checking the Benefits

The funding you receive from an accelerator is obviously important, but it's far less useful without the additional benefits that accompany the money and help propel your business forward. Getting you in front of investors, connecting you to commercial opportunities and giving your business a much higher profile in the marketplace are all incredibly valuable benefits of taking part in these programmes.

Although you find slight variations in what they provide, a typical offer from an accelerator in the current marketplace includes:

✔ A crash course in business development to start you off.

✔ A tie-in with business providers, giving you discounts on core services including legal and accountancy.

✔ Workspace and access to accelerator staff.

✔ Introductions to key investors at home and abroad. Some accelerators run scheduled trips to offices in other cities and other countries for each programme.

✔ Inclusion in exclusive, invitation-only audiences and also to broader networking events, where you can expose your business to other clients of the accelerator, build connections and create further commercial and peer networks.

✔ Mentoring services that give you regular sessions with specialists and industry experts.

✔ A full schedule of seminars and lectures to extend your knowledge.

The accelerator may or may not offer a certain amount of money as well.

When you're considering joining an accelerator, research what's on offer in each of the areas on this list, making sure that you're satisfied that you're going to get good value from them all in exchange for transferring some of your equity. Consider what the market value of the services offered adds up to and whether your business needs all of them. Then do your own maths on the value of these services to your company in comparison to the percentage you're giving up now and, more vitally, how that percentage may look in the future. Research and calculate before making any kind of decision.

You're selected by an accelerator because its directors think your business will grow and is worth the risk. When you hit your growth targets, you want to be sure in your own mind that it was all worthwhile and that you got good value from all the services of the accelerator in exchange for giving something up. Look beyond the initial flattery at being asked to be part of it, and look into the true value of what you're getting.

Mentoring on hand

An analysis of top New York City tech firms found that those with founders who were mentored by industry experts outperform those who were not. While many start-ups can flail for months trying to secure capital, an appropriate mentor can steer you through the wilderness because he's been there and done that. Returns on start-ups engaged in a mentoring scheme include more significant acquisitions, investor traction and a greater internal scale of employees.

But not just any mentor will do. You need a mentor that performs at the level you aspire for your company to meet. Consistent contact with your mentor is vital and the time you spend together should always be precious. For additional information on making the most of your mentors, see Chapter 16.

One of the great things about mentoring in an accelerator is that it's much more structured than your run-of-the-mill mentoring. Your accelerator mentor forces you to set realistic milestones that the investors have a vested interest in you achieving. They've put some money in and now they need to get you into shape to go out and get more money to protect and grow their investment – they want you to succeed. They operate a lean system, and so money is tightly controlled and every element of the programme, including mentoring, needs to contribute to funding success.

Mentors are usually highly experienced, well known and highly regarded in their own industry areas, and if they're investors, they've successfully exited businesses in the past.

Over the weeks of the programme – usually about 12 – you meet with your industry-specific mentors for around 5 to 12 hours. This takes on a variety of formats – some meetings are on a one-to-one basis, some are small group meetings with other participants and mentors and some are with business contacts outside of the programme.

Mentoring through an accelerator is more intensive and hands on, from both ends, than a normal mentoring relationship. Accelerator mentors offer guidance on everything from strategy to financial detail. These accelerator programmes are often referred to as *boot camps,* harking back to the military term describing the first 12 weeks of training when you join the services. Straightaway you know this isn't going to be a holiday camp or a bunch of people sitting around patting each other on the back over a bottle of wine.

In addition to the structure and discipline, your mentor will focus on leadership skills. This can be difficult to master for a new business owner, and especially for a first-time entrepreneur. But you need to lead your team and inspire trust in your staff, investors and clients, which is no small thing.

By the end of the programme, mentors drive start-ups towards a tipping point – you either raise additional investment quickly or you fail. There's nothing loose or wishy-washy about this mentoring. Learn fast; fail or succeed fast.

This mentoring style is becoming a benchmark that potential funders for the next round look at. Knowing you've been through the process and have been mentored and advised takes away some of the risk associated with competitors who didn't make the accelerator grade. One place that the hard work of both you and your mentor is evident is in the demo day events, which take place at the end of the accelerator programme. They've now become famous – or infamous – for their pitches showcasing the results of good mentoring.

The whole accelerator process is also a great opportunity for peer-to-peer mentoring. Peer support and the camaraderie of the participants means that they often help and learn from each other and share funding contacts along the way.

To determine whether the mentoring of a start-up boot camp is appropriate to your business, do your own value assessment using the following questions:

- ✔ Is similar mentoring available in the marketplace to the same level?
- ✔ Are the mentors a good match to the needs of your business?
- ✔ Are the mentors on the leading edge in terms of their experience, contacts and working knowledge of trends in the market?
- ✔ Can you meet them to check that before buying in?

Benefitting from past experience

The people who set the accelerators up are usually serial entrepreneurs who've successfully exited companies themselves. They want to spot the next big things, but also want to give back or pay forward into the next generation of the UK business community.

Accelerator boards are a well-connected group, with enviable networks, and often have the ear of people in commerce, government and finance; therefore, they have genuine influence and reach, which you benefit from as a participant in the programme.

It's much more common now for corporations to sponsor accelerator firms, and many offer employees as mentors. This model of Goliath helping David may seem strange, but a mentor gets to keep his finger on the pulse of current industry trends, which he can bring to the attention of his powers that be. Mentors also get the chance to give something back, and perhaps even be part of the opportunity that follows when a business they sponsor takes off for the stratosphere.

A sampling of corporate accelerators

Many corporate accelerators provide in-depth help to the businesses they mentor. Some of the biggest programmes include the following:

✔ A version of an accelerator that started in America and has been going for a number of years is the Goldman Sachs 10,000 Small Businesses programme, which has a strong focus on developing scalable business models with the companies in its cohorts. The programme offers its employees' time along with workshops, seminars, networking, mentoring and meet-the-buyer events. Goldman Sachs also mentors the Accenture Accelerator and has been known to have invested in a participant who had a technology solution it could use in the development of a new commercial product it was bringing to market, so it has a number or contact points to share its skills and expertise in creating commercial opportunities. In that instance, Goldman Sachs got the technology and the small business got to see what's really necessary for working with a large, heavily regulated business, as well as the money and opportunity it needed to

get its technology to market with the help of a prestigious global brand.

✔ Techstars, a London- and New York-based accelerator sponsored by Barclays, offers access to many of its top team. The 13-week programme has a financial tech focus (although not exclusively), and offers access to Barclays's data and technology, world-class mentoring and training by industry experts. It also provides introductions to Barclays's networks, office space and a pitch opportunity at its prestigious demo day. Investment comes to you from Techstars, and one of the key benefits is learning how to work with and successfully navigate large firms like Barclays.

✔ Collider, a London-based marketing and advertising accelerator, is sponsored by Unilever, and several of its top people mentor. In 2015, Unilever Foundry launched the Foundry 50 at Cannes. This initiative puts start-ups right in front of industry professionals at one of its biggest annual events. And 10 of these 50 start-ups came directly from Collider.

Introducing you to commercial opportunities

By the time you complete an accelerator, you hopefully have a product or a service ready for someone to buy and investors who want to put some money up to back you. You also have a network of mentors, funders and trainers, other mentees and service providers who are ready, willing and able to make introductions, share leads, open up their personal and professional networks or bring you into their portfolio group with a view to accelerating your commercial growth.

The very fact that you were accepted onto and completed the accelerator programme is a big tick in the commercial box, but it's not enough on its own to get a contract or a deal signed and executed. It's your calling card, but you'll still fare better with the introduction ahead of your arrival.

If you receive funding from an early-stage venture capitalist group, for example, and become part of a stable of companies, it's in the group's best interest to make you as commercially successful and profitable as possible. It's the same for the accelerator if it also has a share in your business because the better you do, the better the return on its investments.

Case studies of success

Evaluating the success of an accelerator can be measured in a number of ways, including knowledge from training, better informed entrepreneurs, successful introductions to lucrative commercial deals and, of course, funds raised by participants. You can also look at the value a company achieved when sold, but some of these accelerators are too new to have plentiful exit data.

A few shining examples of making the most of an accelerator include the following:

✔ **Airbnb:** The hottest accelerator success story of the moment is the online home-swapping network. In late 2014, the company was valued at $13 billion, just six years after it was founded in 2008. The concept was founded by American roommates, Brian Chesky and Joe Gebbia. To help fund the original site (`airbedandbreakfast. com`), the duo designed special edition election-themed breakfast cereal, Obamo O's and Cap'n McCains. In two months, 800 boxes were sold at $40 each. This quirky move caught the attention of US accelerator funding giant Y Combinator. From here its rapid growth continued and, at the time of writing, it seems unstoppable.

✔ **Dropbox:** This online file-sharing tool is a classic accelerator breakthrough story. Created by MIT students Drew Houston and Arash Ferdowsi, Dropbox was one of the first companies to prove, on a grand scale, that accelerators work. Another Y Combinator alumni, within three years of launch, Dropbox had 50 million registered users. And the next year it doubled this. Having recently partnered with Microsoft to integrate Dropbox with Office applications on iOS, Dropbox continues to grow.

✔ **Transferwise:** This has disrupted the international money transfer market by offering a system with very low charges, utilising a peer-to-peer network of local people to make local payments. A graduate of the Seedcamp Accelerator in 2012, Transferwise received seed funding of $1.3 million from a consortium including Index Ventures and individual investors, such as Max Levchin (co-founder of PayPal) and David Yu (former CEO of Betfair). It's gone on to raise money from the likes of Richard Branson and Peter Thiel, and as of January 2015 had raised $91 million in funding.

Choosing and Being Chosen

Accelerators are open to all businesses at the right stage and in the right sector, but make no mistake, the competition is stiff, and the process is an arduous one.

You'll be screened in or out on answers to both fact and opinion about your business, its competitive landscape and why your team is right for the job of taking your early stage business to future success for you and your investors.

Then you'll be questioned, observed, put on the spot and tested to see how you defend your position, react to the possibility of change and whether you have the skills to work as part of a class or groups of participants all seeking investment and success.

The majority of applicants are not chosen: as few as 1 per cent and as much as 5 per cent of applicants are chosen to be part of an accelerator programme. However, the contacts, exposure and experience to perform under scrutiny that you gain just from applying can be very worthwhile.

Applying to an accelerator

Every accelerator has its own application process, and as most accelerators accept a maximum of just 5 per cent of applicants, it's good to review the application process thoroughly, prepare well in advance and try to speak to someone who's been through it before, so that you are well-informed.

Apply early, as accelerators get hundreds of applications, and it takes time to read them all. The sooner an accelerator sees your information, the earlier it can do research on you get to know your business better.

You're asked a series of questions, which is usually done online on your chosen accelerator's website or via a nominated site like F6S (www.f6s.com) that filters out the really unsuitable candidates. The questions will be about your business product or service and may include:

- ✔ What is the problem you've identified and the solution your business offers?
- ✔ What stage is your business at?
- ✔ What customers do you already have?
- ✔ Do you have any revenue yet?

✔ What are the characteristics of your marketplace?

✔ Who are your competitors?

✔ What makes your business unique?

✔ Who is on your team?

✔ Have you raised any funding so far?

✔ How do you see the future of your business?

If the accelerator likes what it sees, you'll be asked along for an interview with the partners running the programme and possibly with a mentor. This is also your time to ask your questions and to ask if you can meet a current participant on the programme to get an entrepreneur's point of view.

At this point in the process, most accelerators whittle the applicant numbers down to perhaps double the final number of businesses they will accept and invite you along to a selection day, so they can make their final choice. *Selection days* are usually one or two days when you take part in simulations, role plays, question-and-answer sessions and informal conversations. You meet industry experts, mentors, investors and accelerator partners who test and observe you to see if you have the commitment, open-mindedness, work ethic and quality of team it takes to be chosen, as well as to see whether you fit in with the rest of the participants, or *cohort,* and the accelerator team. For most accelerators this is enough to choose the final, successful participants.

Checking before you commit

If you want to see whether your business may benefit from taking part in an accelerator, check out the track record of some that have been running for at least a year. By that time the *graduates,* or companies who were on the programme, should've had enough time to show a visible impact as a result of taking part. It's in everyone's interest to help you accelerate your commercial growth, and it's a good idea to have a look at some of the success stories from different accelerators – but also check out some of the also-rans to see why they weren't as successful before you make your choice.

When choosing an accelerator, look for companies that you feel match yours as closely as possible in style or business model, technology and so on so that you're comparing like for like.

If you can, get in touch with some of the previous participants and get a first-hand opinion as to whether or not they benefitted from the programme, the mentors, the networking and the cash injection. Did they benefit from being part of this elite community and did they think it was good value for money?

Choose an accelerator that can genuinely move your business towards growth and investment by taking a small amount of equity from your business in exchange for services. Make sure that you know the value and quality of the services the accelerator provides before signing up to the deal. It's very easy to give away too much in exchange for a small amount of money, only to have to buy that share back later at a much higher price; therefore, do your homework thoroughly before you make your final decision. Refer to Table 11-1 for information on some of the most prominent accelerators.

Chapter 12

Considering Debt and Other Bank Funding

A t some time or another, you've probably been in debt – from buying a car, a house, a new kitchen, a holiday or a handbag – or student loans, which is many people's first encounter with debt. Most everyday debt takes the form of a personal loan, or a hire purchase agreement with set interest rates, payment dates and an agreed term or length of the lending agreement.

Extending this experience to your business probably feels somewhat familiar and therefore less threatening or frightening than other forms of finance.

In this chapter, I cover the basics about debt itself and guide you through the range of debt funding available to business owners like yourself.

Explaining Debt Basics

Debt, which means something owed, comes in many forms and flavours, and can be quite useful – even necessary – during the life of your business. Broadly speaking, you have three key business reasons to use debt:

▸ **To fund working capital needs:** To cover a temporary shortfall in cash as you experience rapid business growth.

▸ **To purchase an asset:** To fund a new piece of kit or equipment as your business upgrades to streamline its manufacturing process, creating more sales at a better margin.

✔ **To finance overseas trade:** To take on a lucrative contract that means you need to increase your production levels and use an overseas supplier, so some form of export finance debt is required on a temporary basis.

Typically, debt has five main components, and all debt has some combination of the five:

✔ **Capital or principal:** The amount you borrow before interest.

✔ **Interest rate:** The percentage you pay to the lender – essentially, the cost of the loan.

✔ **Time or duration:** The amount of time you have to repay the loan.

✔ **Security:** The asset(s) you proffer as an indication of your ability to meet the cost of the loan.

✔ **Fixed charges:** Usually the administrative costs associated with the debt that may include things like lender application fees.

The three main categories of debt are:

✔ **Secured:** The loan is made against the value of an asset that you own, which no one else has any financial right over. This asset, which may be equipment, premises, vehicles or shares, can be sold if you need to pay the debt back.

For larger loans, a bank often requires the loan to be secured against an asset, such as a business property and/or requires a personal guarantee, such as a residential home from a company director, in order to help ensure that the bank gets repaid. Freeholds or properties with longer leases are the most valuable asset you can use for security, and the loan amount is linked to their value. In some instances, you can limit the scope and duration of personal guarantees – for example when set against a business achieving certain amounts of turnover, or linked to a time period for review to determine whether the guarantee is still required.

✔ **Unsecured:** The loan is made with no assets available to provide as security for repayment. Getting an unsecured loan means that you have no plan B other than repaying the capital and *freezing* the interest payments – or putting them on hold – for a while.

Because there's nothing to back up an unsecured loan if the business can't make the repayments, these loans have higher rates of interest and are usually for smaller amounts than secured loans.

✔ **Guaranteed:** The loan is backed by an asset base, such as earnings ability, that a lender can make a claim on to repay the debt if the business can't.

The following list explains the common forms of debt roughly in order from most restrictive to least:

- **Loan:** Money that's borrowed and paid back with interest. You can take out a loan from a bank, an online platform lender, a specialist lender such as an asset lender or from friends and family. Loans vary in length from two to ten years with two to five years being an average for a business loan. They also vary in interest rate, which depends on your credit history, the economy, and the risk profile the lender tolerates. I've seen loans as low as 3 per cent and as high as 20 per cent, for example, but loans are made on a case-by-case basis.

  Loans have what are known as *covenants* that cover things like interest rates and the loan-to-value amount in a commercial mortgage.

- **Overdraft:** A pre-approved temporary bank debt, with interest, that creates a shortfall or deficit in your current account. An overdraft activates when you spend more than you have in your bank account. As money comes into your account, your overdraft is reduced. You pay a higher-than-normal interest rate on overdraft amounts.

- **Asset finance:** Money that's borrowed, with interest, in order to purchase an asset, such as equipment. These arrangements are usually longer in term than a simple bank loan and secured by the asset being purchased.

- **Invoice finance:** A way for your business to borrow money based on the unpaid amount due from customers on outstanding invoices. Banks as well as specialist invoice financiers provide funds so that you can get money into your business immediately and repay the loan when the customer pays the invoice. Fees are charged and are either fixed or variable depending on the financier. You can use invoice finance on a case-by-case basis or for all your yearly invoices, depending on your needs and the invoice financier's terms.

- **Commercial mortgage:** A mortgage loan, with interest and a set term, secured by property and used to acquire, refinance or develop commercial property.

- **Trade finance:** Debt that usually refers to import-export purchases or sales, and can be for payment facilities to help an overseas buyer with payment, money held to provide a guarantee for payment, deposit payments and so on. Banks or specialist trade finance companies can advance you the money, with interest charges, and you repay it at an agreed later date.

- **Peer-to-peer lending:** A system in which unrelated individuals loan money. Borrowers (your business) and lenders use a non-bank intermediary, such as a platform lender, to facilitate the transaction. Administration fees and interest are charged. Some peer-to-peer platforms set the rate of interest, while others operate an auction method, allowing lenders to bid to lend at a certain rate of interest. As with all debt, generally speaking, the better your credit history and ability to repay the debt, the lower the rate of interest you pay.

Each type of debt services a different type of need, and you may have several types at the same time. It's entirely possible to have an overdraft at the same time as you use asset finance, for example, or to have a commercial mortgage and use invoice finance, as long as your business doesn't take on too much debt for it to be able to service every month. What's important is that you use the right product or service for the right length of time and at a price your business can afford.

Typically, businesses go to these sources to fund debt:

✔ **Banks:** Whether they're the national banks, smaller high street banks or the newer challenger banks, banks offer overdrafts, term loans, asset finance and invoice finance.

✔ **Peer-to-peer and other platforms:** Peer-to-peer lending platforms facilitate transactions between unrelated lenders and borrowers.

✔ **Private debt:** Money that you borrow from friends or family. You should still have a formal agreement for terms of interest and repayment. Usually, you pay less interest on private debt and have more flexibility in the agreed date for repayment.

✔ **Bonds:** Debt products issued by a company, either directly or via one of the financial intermediary platforms, that are longer than 1 year in duration (and can be as long as 30 years). Bonds are issued by the company wanting to raise the funds, which then owes the people who buy a bond a debt and some interest, but not all the interest paid. The two common types of business bonds are

• **Zero coupon bonds** have no regular interest payments.

• **Convertible bonds** include the option for the bond holder to convert the debt to equity share in a company at a later date.

Bond issuers are obliged to pay the lenders, or bondholders, interest on the bond amount, known as a *coupon,* and, as with a regular loan, repay the principal at a later date.

Realising that debt isn't always a bad thing

Debt has many connotations, evoking different feelings depending on how it factors in your life:

✔ Being **debt-free** usually creates a sense of relief because it means that you've paid off your loans, enabling you to make financial decisions based on desire rather than need.

✔ **Bad debt** has a very negative connotation, because it means your business is unexpectedly out of pocket.

✔ Being in a **debt trap** makes you feel like you've no way out of a bad situation, and you feel helpless to make it better.

However thinking of debt makes you feel, at some point or other your business will probably need to take some on.

Having debt in your business is not a bad thing. However, managing debt badly, paying over the odds for it or failing to meet the repayment terms and finding yourself in default is. These failures are not the fault of the debt, but of the way you manage it. If you understand how you can make debt work for your business, you have a valuable funding tool.

Table 12-1 shows some pros and cons about taking on debt.

Table 12-1	Good and Not-So-Good Aspects of Debt
Good Things	**Not-So-Great Things**
Usually very straightforward. Repayments are agreed in advance so you can budget and plan going forward and minimise the impact on your cash flow.	A loan or an overdraft can be called in to be paid in full at any time if you're unable to meet the terms, or your account shows signs that your business is in trouble.
In the UK at the moment, government-backed schemes make loans available to business owners who don't have assets to pledge as security.	If you exceed your overdraft limit without authorisation, you're charged a penalty.
The interest on a loan is often much lower than on an overdraft, so a loan can save you money if you need the money for a long period of time.	If you repay a loan before its due date, you may be charged early redemption or early repayment fees, so check the small print.
If your need is short term and temporary, an overdraft can be a quick solution to your problem.	Lenders always look at both your business and personal credit histories, which may result in a decline or a higher rate of interest if you've had problems in the past.

(continued)

Table 12-1 (continued)

Good Things	Not-So-Great Things
With a debt facility, like an overdraft, you only pay interest on what you use, so you have the peace of mind of being able to draw down on the funds and only pay for what you use.	In most cases, a loan for your business requires a personal guarantee from you as well as some security in case you can't meet the repayments.
Your business can claim tax relief on interest payments.	Regular repayments can be tricky if your business has variable amounts of income and cash in the bank.
Repayment terms and interest rates come in all shapes and sizes, and chances are you'll be able to find one that works for your business.	Some types of debt are more expensive than others, and you may not be able to refinance to a cheaper interest rate if your business circumstances change, putting a strain on your cash flow.

Getting ready to be scrutinised

If you're thinking of getting a business loan from a bank, it's bit like selling to a customer: When you see a customer you want to sign up, you do all you can to persuade her that you offer a deal that's good for her. When you're working out how to get a small business loan, you're effectively selling your idea of the loan to the bank manager. It's your job to persuade the bank that it's in the bank's best interests to lend you the money.

To help you win them over, have your paperwork well prepared and also have your financial history and management skills in good working order and as blemish-free as possible.

Lenders apply what they know as CAMPARI – it's nothing to do with the drink – to potential borrowers:

- ✔ **C is for character.** This means your background and experience and evidence of good financial management skills. Lenders want to see that you have a good business track record and a history of conducting your business affairs with integrity.

- ✔ **A is for ability.** What is the ability of the business to repay the loan? Are you likely to be profitable, and have enough working capital to repay the debt? Are you able to prudently manage the finances of your business to ensure repayment?

- ✔ **M is for margin.** How much money is the bank going to make from the business loan? Does the risk-return ratio stack up for them?

✔ **P is for purpose.** Be prepared to explain in detail why you want to borrow the money. For example, you expanding or are you plugging a cash hole; is it for equipment or for a temporary stock purchase, for example. The bank wants to know that you've thought it through, and that you have a logical and genuine need.

The bank representative may comment on your purpose in general terms, and question your reasoning, but you know much more about your business than she does, so just ready your defence. Equally, the lender knows about her loans, so be guided by her on what form of finance may be best for your purpose.

✔ **A is for amount.** How much do you need? Do your forecasts show that you've established the correct amount, allowing a slight margin for error? Are you being realistic or are you asking for the exact amount you need without thinking ahead a bit or allowing for a bit of overspend?

✔ **R is for repayment.** How long do you need the money for? Can you afford the repayments? Do you have a history of successfully repaying similar amounts? Can you personally cover the amount if the business can't?

✔ **I is for insurance.** The bank may ask if security is available to cover the amount of the debt. It may also ask you to consider taking out insurance cover to bump it up if you can't offer the full amount of personal security.

Borrowing from a Bank

In the UK, traditionally you borrowed money from what came to be known as *high street banks* – the main, large retail banks that have a presence in every high street. High street banks take deposits from customers and then lend a certain amount of the deposited amount out, with an interest charge on top of it, to make profit.

Banks lend money, or *capital,* with an interest charge in order to make money. They judge your business's ability to repay the loan and decide whether or not to agree to lend and at what rate of interest.

If you've been out of touch for the past few years, you may not be aware that high street banks have been receiving a bit of a bashing for all the trouble they found themselves in after 2008 and the global financial crisis. As a result, many businesses that need funding still find it nigh on impossible to get a bank to lend them any money. The criteria and restrictions are now much tighter, and the banks' appetite for risk is now very low. Gone are the days when money was relatively easy to get hold of and you could confidently approach your bank when you needed a financial hand.

For some top-rated business customers, banks remain a good source of debt funding. However, in 2014, bank lending to small- and medium-sized enterprises (SMEs) was down by £400 million according to a professional services firm, BDO International, report. A number of reasons exist for this, ranging from the banks tightening up on lending criteria to businesses not even trying to apply for bank debt and alternative funders entering the market to take some of the custom from the banks. So, a bank is a far from reliable funding solution for most entrepreneurs.

Recent years have seen the emergence of more and more *challenger banks* in the UK. These are usually smaller banks set up to challenge the more established national brands by offering superior service, more competitive deals or a combination of both. These banks are often based online, are without a branch network and are very appealing to a younger generation of business customer that prefers a quick and easy smartphone transaction to a lengthy branch visit. Some challenger banks buck the trend, like Metro Bank, which has a growing number of stores its customers can visit, but others, like Atom and Starling Bank, as well as First Direct (an offshoot of HSBC Bank), are mainly based online.

These digitally focused challengers are trying to take on the big four in the UK – Barclays, Lloyds, HSBC and RBS (Royal Bank of Scotland) – and shake up the industry in favour of the customer, but it's early days.

Some industry experts see challenger banks as validation of the shambles that the UK government, aided by the banking industry itself, has made of the banking industry. Others see them as a brave new world that will take the place of the big four and bring about some much-needed competition. It's too early to say how much of an impact they have on business lending, but they are definitely an option you shouldn't discount when shopping around for debt.

Getting started with a term loan

A *term loan,* or a commercial loan that's for a set period of time and repaid over that time frame, usually in regular instalments, is probably the most familiar form of business borrowing from your bank. A term loan is a pretty standard commercial loan, often used to fund a major investment in your business or to make a specific acquisition.

They vary in their length of time, but most loan terms are between one and ten years, with five being the average duration. A term loan usually has a fixed interest rate, but may instead have a rate that's linked to the Bank of England base rate, with a certain percentage of interest added to it that changes as the base rate changes. Payments are usually monthly, but can also be quarterly if that suits your cash flow better and your bank agrees.

A term loan is often the best option for an established SME, provided you have a stable going concern and you're able to make the monthly repayments from working capital. These loans work well for investing in equipment or premises and for purchasing assets that you'll reap the benefit from over a long period of time, such as databases or, in some cases, purchasing the assets of another business.

You may be fortunate enough to be offered a *capital repayment holiday,* during which time you're only paying the interest and deferring the capital part of the payment until you get more money coming in to your business.

So far, so good, but I can see you asking, 'Where's the catch?' Well, strictly speaking, not a catch, but a condition of term loans is that they usually require some collateral or security – the application process is now much more rigorous than it was in days gone by.

If you need to fund equipment or premises, look into and compare the cost of other options, such as leasing versus purchasing outright. You may need to pay an upfront deposit and monthly leasing payments, but regular maintenance and upgrades may be part of the deal, which saves money and hassle in the long run.

To borrow money, you need to submit quite a bit of documentation, which is great to have but time-consuming to produce, so before you give yourself a monumental task, make sure it makes sense for your current needs. The documentation can include any or all of the following:

- ✔ Up-to-date business plan.
- ✔ Executive summary (maximum two pages).
- ✔ Pitch deck or presentation.
- ✔ Trading accounts (up to three years if you've been trading).
- ✔ Management accounts (make sure they use up-to-the-minute numbers).
- ✔ Latest VAT returns, if you're registered.
- ✔ Financial projections for up to three years, including cash flow forecasts.

    The projections should show that you can repay the debt out of working capital. Be sure to include profit and loss forecasts and balance sheet projections with an accompanying list of assumptions as to how you arrived at the figures. You may also need a sensitivity analysis illustrating the impact of sales dropping by 10 or 20 per cent in a year. (For more on sensitivity analyses, head to Chapter 5.)

- ✔ Business and personal bank statements.
- ✔ List of aged debtors and creditors.
- ✔ ALIE (statement of Assets, Liabilities, Income and Expenses).
- ✔ Any supporting material, including signed contracts, intentions to purchase and agreed orders.

I talk about most of the business documents you need in Chapter 3, your business plan in Chapter 5 and the pitch deck in Chapter 6.

You can look for a term loan from any lender. You're not restricted to your current bank, which may think you have enough debt for their risk appetite at the moment and turn you down. Not all banks are created equal, and some lean towards the consumer versus the business customer. You can appeal a decision if you get rejected, and you can also shop around to get the best deal.

The level of financial strength required to be successful in securing a term loan varies slightly from bank to bank, and is linked to its level of risk and exposure. Do your research into what a bank's loan portfolio looks like, and sound out your bank manager before you make a formal approach. She will look at how you manage your account and what else you're doing with the bank, so it's best to keep a clean sheet and to develop as much of a working relationship as you can with your bank so you're not a total stranger when the time comes to apply for a loan.

If you're a member of a professional association or organisation that's negotiated preferential rates for its members, it's a good idea to dust off the membership terms and conditions and see if you can save yourself some stress and some money at the same time.

Keep these five Cs in mind when applying for a term loan:

- ✔ **Character:** Look at the way you've managed your account and your business – you can be sure the bank will!

- ✔ **Creditworthiness:** Consider the amount of debt or exposure you're already carrying. Makes sure that you can afford to take on more debt, and also that you've got a credit rating that will make a bank say 'yes'.

- ✔ **Collateral or security:** Contrary to popular opinion, banks don't want to become the new owners of your assets, but they do want to know that some of them can be turned into liquid cash if they're required to repay the loan.

- ✔ **Covenants:** Loans often have clauses that prohibit you from taking on other debt without a consultation and a justification. Be sure to ask and to check the small print.

- ✔ **Confidence:** Lenders need to be confident in your abilities and in your plan, forecasts and assumptions.

All loans have a cost for setting the loan up, penalties for late payment, often penalties for early repayment and an impact on your credit file for breaching the terms of the loan agreement.

Going with government schemes – Enterprise Finance Guarantee Scheme

You can access a term loan from a bank via the Enterprise Finance Guarantee Scheme, which used to be called the Small Firms Loan Guarantee Scheme. The scheme offers loans to businesses that have been turned down by other commercial lenders for reasons other than the financial health of the business, and whose owners don't have any property or other assets to put up as security for a loan (or possibly any significant trading track record). The bulk of the risk is covered by a government guarantee and the rest is covered by the bank that makes the loan.

The Scheme has been in existence under one name or another since 1981, and a number of high street banks are approved to do the lending. Over 20,000 businesses have been funded to date, to the tune of just over £2 billion in loans, so it's a very active scheme. You can find more information at www.gov.uk/understanding-the-enterprise-finance-guarantee.

Some specifics of Enterprise Finance Guarantee Scheme loans:

- Loan amounts range from £1,000 to £1.2 million.

- Qualifying companies have a turnover of under £25 million.

- Repayment terms are from three months to ten years in duration or term.

- The government guarantees 75 per cent of the loan.

Enterprise Finance Guarantee Scheme loans are very useful to companies constrained by contractual obligations that make them unattractive for products such as invoice factoring or discounting (see the upcoming section, 'Exploring debtor finance' for more).

Trying SULCO for start-up loans

Another government-funded national loan scheme overseen by the British Business Bank, SULCO provides start-up loans to entrepreneurs between the ages of 18 and 30. Loans can be up to £25,000 with a current interest rate of 6 per cent, and an average loan size of £6,000, which is expected to rise in the near future. The loans are meant to provide capital to help younger business owners get their businesses off the ground.

SULCO loans are made to the business owner and not the business. Be aware of this fact when considering this option.

The application requires a business plan, including financial forecasts. If you're awarded a loan, you're also offered workshops, mentors and ongoing advice and assistance to help ensure that you're well informed and given the best possible chance of succeeding. SULCO also tries to arrange specially negotiated discounts for useful products and services, such as software, so check the website at www.startuploans.co.uk on a regular basis for your eligibility for such discounts.

Taking out a commercial mortgage

Like your personal mortgage, *commercial mortgages* have a fixed term, a capital element and a fixed or variable interest rate over a fixed repayment schedule, but they're granted to purchase business or commercial, not residential, property.

You can get a commercial mortgage from banks, building societies and specialist lenders. Generally, the maximum loan amount is up to 70 or 75 per cent of the value of the property, so it's tighter than it would be for your residential mortgage.

Interest can be fixed term or variable, which changes with the market rates; if you're lucky, you can ask for a little payment holiday on the capital portion of the mortgage, and pay only the interest for that time.

Using personal debt

You can fund some of your business growth or start-up needs by using personal debt and, in effect, making a loan to your business with the money you borrow.

If you haven't been able to secure commercial lending, getting a personal loan is an option, but not one I suggest lightly or as a first choice. Personally, I don't like mixing business with personal debt, but that's just one woman's opinion. If you ask ten other people, you'll probably get a mixed response for and against personal borrowing. Ultimately, it comes down to the level of risk and pressure you're comfortable with.

When you're personally liable for repaying the debt, this puts extra pressure on you to make sure the business can pay you so that you can repay the loan. Taking out a personal loan obviously has an impact on your personal credit rating and borrowing ability.

You don't get the extra help a SULCO loan offers (see the preceding section) with a straightforward personal loan from your bank or from friends and family, so you need to consider the downside of such borrowing should you find yourself unable to meet your repayments.

Another even less desirable way of using personal debt to fund your business is by using credit cards and/or cash advances on your cards. As tempting as it is to use zero per cent interest offers or credit card cheques to get a cash advance, these offers often have quite steep arrangement fees and interest rates if you take longer than the interest-free period to repay the money. Check the fine print carefully and be pretty sure that you'll be able to repay the full amount due before any of the other charges kick in. It can wind up being very costly and can also be a slippery slope to mounting debt if you let it run on.

Evaluating long-term versus short-term funding

This list talks about the type of funding best in certain circumstances:

- **Bank loans versus overdrafts:** Years ago, when I first started working in a bank, I remember one of the trainers saying 'long-term need, long-term debt; short-term need, short-term debt'. Short-term debt that's used for long-term needs just ends up becoming a very expensive inappropriate term loan, and short-term debt that's used for long-term needs ends up becoming a very expensive plaster over a wound that won't heal quickly. Overdrafts are for short-term needs, whereas loans are more suited to long-term funding needs.

- **Loans:** Loans are used when you need funding over a period of time, which can be longer than year. A term loan of two to five years might be suitable if you're borrowing for something specific, such as an inventory purchase that you know you'll repay within a month or so. A short-term loan offers cheaper interest rates than an overdraft does, and you can see a clear repayment date.

- **Securing an overdraft:** You're probably familiar with overdrafts on personal accounts, if only because you turned it down when your bank offered it. Business overdrafts are useful when your funding need is short-term in nature and happens rarely, or it's short-term in nature and happens regularly throughout the year because that's the nature of your business cycle. If your business has fluctuating working capital needs or regular peaks and troughs, an overdraft can be just the help you need.

Overdrafts are arranged with the bank you have your business account with. You have to complete an application form and pay a fee, starting at around £100, and rising depending on the amount of the facility. Interest rates are pretty steep when you dip into the facility, so be aware of the real cost to your business. In most cases, overdrafts are payable on demand if you default on any of the rules for using them. If you need to use the facility, once it's been approved you can dip in and out as required.

Completing an application doesn't mean that getting the overdraft is a done deal – the criteria have been tightened significantly since 2008. At the moment, banks are making it harder to get an overdraft facility for your business account. In recent years, banks have had stricter regulations imposed on them with regard to overdraft facilities, and they must carry out a much more rigorous application process before granting you a business overdraft.

Check the Money website at `www.money. co.uk/loans/business-loans.htm` for comparison information.

Approaching Niche Lenders

Since the cataclysmic economic events of 2008 and the further tightening of the lending criteria in 2014, it's become increasingly difficult to secure high street lending for your business. This, in turn, has given a new lease of life to the somewhat underrated niche lending market, which has been traditionally misunderstood and under-utilised, and is now becoming much more common as a debt funding option.

Niche lenders specialise in one market segment and devise a product or a suite of products unique to that market. These lenders are different to high street lenders in substance, criteria, terms and cost.

Often accessed by borrowers who can't meet the exacting standards of a high street bank due to some blemish on their financial scorecard or a lack of security to back a loan, niche lending is now used by many firms that may need a more lenient assessment of their ability to sustain current income growth and affordability of a loan, or require a much shorter time frame to use the money. In return, you agree to accept a higher rate of interest or harsher terms if you default.

You can find a rich variety of niche financing out there at the moment, and I look at several in the next sections.

Finding an asset finance firm

Asset finance is using loans to enable you to obtain a variety of items for your business, from the furniture to the ovens for baking your tasty, low-calorie muffins or the van you use to get them from your kitchens to the shops that stock them. It's a form of finance that helps you purchase those elusive items you need in order to make your plans a reality, and in a shorter time frame than if you had to wait until you had all the money upfront. If you wait, you may miss your window of opportunity, so it's better to see if you can get it financed, or financed in part, and take advantage of that open window of opportunity before it becomes a closed door.

With asset finance, the loans are secured against the asset being financed, so the need for additional security is minimal. You know that the funding is in place for the duration of the agreement. You may want to refinance as you go along if you want to upgrade to a better model of van or a more ergonomically designed set of office chairs, because you still have the asset that can be sold if you look like you're going to default on the loan.

Asset finance can provide you with the full cost of the asset you want to purchase upfront; an even more cash-flow-friendly option is _asset finance leasing,_ which transfers the right to the asset to you for the length of an agreed lease on it, and you pay for it over time instead of all at once.

Asset finance leasing is a form of asset finance that's just the ticket when you need to acquire a _fixed asset_ (something that lasts beyond a few months), such as a machine, vehicle, or some other piece of equipment, but you don't necessarily need to own it outright or go out and pay for it all at once.

If you need to buy a coffee-roasting machine that will eventually lead to fantastic sales and employment for a team of people, but the purchase puts undue strain on your cash flow if you need to get it from Italy to you in the UK, lease finance is an attractive option. You've probably come across it in relation to cars or fleet vehicles, which are often leased for larger sales teams who cover large territories.

If you satisfy the usual lending criteria, finance for leasing fixed assets instead of buying them outright should be offered to you. Lease financing can usually be arranged quickly, which is a major benefit.

The asset is owned by the _lessor,_ or the company offering the lease finance, but you often have the opportunity to purchase the asset at the end of the lease. Interest is charged and you need to look at the cost of this money in the same way as you look at other forms of debt.

As an option that does away with the need for an upfront payment or an outright payment of a large amount, lease finance is a good way to ease the strain on your cash flow and avoiding taking money for a longer term asset out of your shorter term working capital money or financing its purchase using a short-term funding product, like an overdraft facility.

Exploring debtor finance

Debtor finance is an umbrella term used to describe finance and the process of helping to fund a business using its _accounts receivable,_ or money owed to it by customers, as collateral for advancing the business money. If your business has low working capital in the bank or gets into cash-flow problems because of lengthy payment terms to customers, debtor finance can be a good source of funds and assistance. Two of the most common forms of this finance are invoice factoring and invoice discounting.

Invoice factoring

Although it's not a loan, _invoice factoring_ is a form of finance that may be offered by a subsidiary of a bank or niche funders, such as the platform funders Market Invoice (www.marketinvoice.com) or Platform Black (www.platformblack.com). I look at alternative finance and cover invoice factoring in more detail in Chapter 14.

Factoring helps you to release money that's tied up in unpaid invoices into your business, and helps you manage your receivables, saving you time and money while improving your cash flow.

An invoice-factoring provider takes control of your invoices to customers and takes on the job of making sure those invoices get paid. The factoring provider advances you the amount due, minus certain fees, if they're happy with the quality of the invoices and have confidence the invoices will be paid.

Factoring agents charge you, and so you need to make sure that you account for those costs in your pricing margins. Some factoring services want you to sign up for a long-term working relationship that covers all your invoices and that you can end only when all your outstanding invoices have been satisfied. As with any financial decision, consider what's best for you and your business before signing an agreement.

A cost-effective alternative to a long-term arrangement is something like Market Invoice (www.marketinvoice.com), an online marketplace that allows you to auction off your invoices to a community of investors, either on a one-off basis or on a longer-term arrangement. In using such a platform, you receive payment straightaway and the investor, or purchaser of your invoice, receives a profit when the payment from your customer comes in.

Invoice discounting

Similar to invoice factoring, with *invoice discounting* (which enables you to sell your invoices in a similar way to invoice factoring, but with discounting), you retain control over the administration of your sales ledger and outstanding invoices – so you still have to make sure that the invoices get paid. Like factoring agents, invoice discounters want to know that the quality of your sales ledger is high, and the systems and procedures you use to support it are robust, or they won't take you on as a client.

Invoice discounting can also be used for overseas invoices.

Addressing the need for temporary finance

At any point in your business journey, you may find yourself with the need to secure some temporary finance. You may need a cash advance to use for working capital, a short-term loan to get you to a trade show to make that big overseas sale or funding to cover some daily expenses while you wait for your research and development rebate cheque to arrive. Whatever the reason, your bank may not be the right place to look for this kind of temporary finance, especially if you have no security to put up against it. In order to meet this demand from businesses, a number of online funders have sprung up offering different products, prices and propositions. A few of the better publicised among them are:

- **Ezbob (www.ezbob.com):** Ezbob has been very active in providing short-term unsecured business loans since 2012. Ezbob is an automated online lending platform you borrow directly from. You get an instant online decision after you upload the essential documents to the platform and enter the amount you want to borrow and for how long.

  To be eligible, your business needs to be turning over at least £10,000 per annum, and have been registered in the UK for at least 12 months. You also need to have a valid business debit card, business bank statements, and a VAT return if you're VAT registered, as well as being a director or owner of your business. Shareholders in Ezbob include the government-backed Angel CoFund.

- **Iwoca (www.iwoca.co.uk):** Iwoca offers instant working capital and provides flexible credit to SMEs. It uses advanced technology to calculate your risk profile and predict your future financial health based on your trading data, using thousands of data points to give you a quick answer for your working capital need.

- **Just Cashflow (www.just-cashflow.com):** Just Cashflow is one of a bunch offering a *revolving credit facility,* which isn't a traditional loan in that there's no repayment date, as such, but interest does accrue and is paid on a weekly basis. It's a flexible solution, providing facilities from £10,000 to £500,000 based on your cash flow patterns and credit history, with varying rates of interest based on your credit profile.

- **Liberis (www.liberis.co.uk):** Liberis offers flexible finance, known as a merchant or business cash advance, paid back from your future card terminal transactions and based on the historical amount of your card receipts. The funder purchases a fixed percentage of your future credit and debit card transactions at a discounted price, and advances the cash into your bank account, usually within ten working days. You repay on a schedule, which could be daily, paying a percentage on each transaction amount.

Looking at Peer-to-Peer Lending

Over the past four or five years, a major innovation in lending has come from what is known as *peer-to-peer lenders,* which are online platforms that act as intermediaries between unrelated borrowers and lenders. In fact, peer-to-peer lending started in earnest about ten years ago with personal debt platforms, but with the decline in high street lending to businesses, it's really come of age.

Peer-to-peer lending (P2PL) occurs when individuals or institutions lend money to other individuals, or in this case, businesses, via an online platform, in return for interest and capital payments. Lenders bid for an interest rate that they'd like to lend at, and borrowers then accept a loan at the lowest acceptable rate. This system essentially counters the traditional bank model, in which a person deposits money and then you borrow it. Borrowers have the opportunity to get a lower rate of interest than they can in the traditional marketplace (often 10 per cent or less) with a faster decision, and lenders have the chance to use their spare cash to get a better return on it than plonking it in a low-interest-paying savings account or something similar.

The platform facilitates the matching of different lenders to different borrowers, creating and using a network of peers. The platform also allows for your network to lend to your business using a clearly defined and structured method, taking some of the hassle out of having them lend to you directly.

Although peer-to-peer lending started out with a much smaller loan size than a traditional bank would consider, which encouraged both lenders and borrowers to get on board, this is changing. Loan sizes are getting more significant, now up to £1,000,000 in some cases, and even higher for commercial property lending.

P2PL is a direct alternative to bank loans and is usually quicker to arrange. Both secured and unsecured loans are available, with investors bidding to lend you the money and set the interest rates. Lenders usually require a trading track record and complete financials and financial information, so they're not going to be an option for every business. Credit checks are carried out in the same way that they would be for a financial institution, and underwriters are part of the decision-making process, again the same way they'd be for a bank.

The platform carries out all the checks on the borrower, weeding out any unsuitable candidates, and facilitates the payment flow when the loan has been agreed and signed off. The platforms make their money either by taking a one-off fee for being a facilitator or an ongoing fee to lenders to help facilitate the servicing of the loan. They have much lower overheads than a high street bank, so usually offer more competitive fees all round. Everybody wins.

Platforms have pretty strict criteria on which they lend and are regulated by the Financial Conduct Authority (FCA) in order to protect both the borrower's and the lender's rights.

Identifying key P2PL players

The most well known platform for businesses is Funding Circle, and for personal loans, Zopa, both of which have recently created mutually beneficial referral partnerships with Santander Bank and Metro Bank, respectively.

✔ **Funding Circle** (www.fundingcircle.com) is currently the second largest lender, having lent £1 billion (£701,388,960 in the UK) to 8,000 SMEs in the UK and US as of April 2015. It has over 40,000 lenders, which include individuals, the UK government, local councils and a university. Funding Circle offers business loans from £5,000 – £1 million (£3 million for commercial property).

✔ **Ratesetter** (www.ratesetter.com), which was established in 2010, offers business loans up to £500,000 in the UK and in Australia. It now has a provision against bad debt to protect lenders, and has over 23,000 lenders and over 113,000 borrowers.

✔ **Zopa** (www.zopa.com) was the first platform set up in 2005, and is currently the largest UK P2PL with over 500,000 customers. It was the first to give loans to the clients of PRIME, the Prince's Trust business-advice service for people over 50 years of age, and it set the scene for all that have followed.

Other peer-to-peer platforms include Market Invoice and Assetz Capital, which I cover in Chapter 14.

The P2PL marketplace is in constant flux, with new entrants arriving on a monthly basis, so you need to stay abreast of all the changes and how they can affect your business lending needs. It's a time of great upheaval in commercial lending, and definitely a case of watch this space if you want to be well informed and well prepared to take advantage of what's on offer.

Applying for micro lending

In addition to bank and platform lending, a number of community development finance initiatives and institutions provide micro finance loans to businesses that can't get finance elsewhere. Perhaps your trading history or your financial forecasts don't satisfy a bank lender; if so, micro loans offer a more flexible alternative.

Microlenders are a source of ethical finance, so they're selective about what they invest in. There are local members around the country to help with a loan to get your business started or to grow.

Microlenders have funded thousands of businesses, and you can see some of their success stories and find out more about members near you on the community finance membership website at www.findingfinance.org.uk.

Combining Debt and Equity

You can get external finance into your business in two ways – debt or equity. Sometimes the two collide, overlap or follow up from each other, and on the odd occasion they can also appear in the same financial product, such as mezzanine debt or venture debt.

Exploring hybrid lending: Debt funds

As the need for and flexibility in debt finance grows, a number of seemingly esoteric debt products are stepping out of the shadows and into the light that surrounds high-growth SMEs who don't want to give away increasing amounts of their hard-earned equity. One area that has been popular in the US and languishing a bit in Europe, but is now seeing a bit of a renaissance in the UK due to tighter lending restrictions post 2008, is debt funds.

Debt funds provide an alternative source of funding that's more bespoke in nature than bank loans, and usually involves debt with some form of *equity warrant* – the right to purchase a certain number of shares at a given price and a given time. This warrant adds an element of equity to the transaction, at the end of the loan period, thus making it a bit of a hybrid offering. What it doesn't do is provide working capital finance, so it's not replacing banks completely.

Typical amounts provided by debt funds are £500,000 to £5 million, but an average range is £500,000 to £1.5 million.

I recently had clients looking to avoid getting another round of equity investment to fund further growth in equipment, stock and a web upgrade, but they had a very good trading record with blue-chip customers in the global food industry. Debt funds, or *venture debt* as it's sometimes known, was a good alternative option for them in case they were unable to secure traditional bank finance due to the severe strain their expansion plans would put on working capital – the way in which the bank would look to be repaid.

Debt funds are a good option for event-based growth, where the risk may be a bit higher and where a bank may otherwise shy away, and where the company looking to borrow the money doesn't want to dilute its equity in any meaningful way.

As debt funds have the flexibility to tailor their offering to an individual company's needs, they may provide debt at a senior level, which is the first level of your company's liabilities and means that these people get paid first, ahead of your other creditors. The funding may be secured by some form of collateral in the form of a *lien,* which gives the lender the right to keep the collateral until you repay the loan on an asset, and include an option or a warrant for some equity shares at the end of the facility period.

Debt funds tend to be a bit more expensive than bank debt, but they fill a particular need when a company has few alternatives, so it's a case of biting the bullet if you can service the loan and living with the rest of the lender's demands.

They're becoming better known in the UK as the menu of funding sources expands, but you don't have a long track record to assess this complicated funding structure as yet, so it's one to watch and consider very carefully.

A good example of a private debt funder is BMS Finance (www.bms-finance.com). It's part of the GLI Finance family of companies, and was established in 2003 after directors saw a gap in the market, particularly around companies heavy on intellectual property and customer relationships but light on revenue.

BMS Finance provides a bespoke debt finance package that meets the needs of early-stage businesses that are just short of being profitable. These companies typically have strong management teams and a proven business model that shows they can grow and scale the business but are either still burning through a lot of cash or are too much of a risk to a high street lender.

Although BMS started with technology clients, it now has a mixed portfolio and sees demand from other sectors.

Exploring mezzanine debt

Not many lenders offer *mezzanine finance,* a flexible debt product that's tailored to the profile of your individual company as a borrower. It's typically used to finance growth in your business once it's been funded by equity and for situations when you don't want to take on any more investors.

As finance goes, it combines the features of debt and equity in one new product. It's debt funding that has some of the characteristics of equity, and it ranks below debt provided by bankers in the debt hierarchy.

As debt capital, unusually, it gives the lender the right to convert to an equity share in the business if the loan isn't paid in full and on time. It's usually used when the funding need is at least £500,000 and neither pure debt nor pure equity fits the bill. It's typically used for product development, new infrastructure equipment needs and mergers and acquisitions.

There doesn't appear to be one right or wrong way to package mezzanine debt, but what all forms of it seem to have in common is:

- **Cash coupon,** which is the interest on the advance, paid periodically over the course of the facility.

- **Payment in kind,** usually an additional interest payment added to the capital, which is paid only at the maturity of the loan.

- **Warrants, or a share of the profits,** that result from the growth of the company if the loan isn't repaid in full and on time.

Mezzanine providers charge a higher rate of interest than a standard high street bank loan, as they're unlikely to recover the debt if your business goes bust.

One well-known provider of mezzanine finance is Santander Bank, which launched its Breakthrough Programme in March 2012. One of the key components of the programme is the Growth Capital Fund, which provides debt finance for companies that are well along in their growth phase.

Growth capital means that your business can avoid diluting, or watering down, your equity position further but still fund your aggressive growth plans, which may include:

- Investing in new technology

- Investing in new equipment

- Taking on senior, more expensive members of staff

- Expanding your business overseas

Santander Growth Capital provides:

- Mezzanine loans of £500,000 to £5 million, which can be used alongside other senior debt you already have

- Repayment terms of two to five years.

- Interest rates that are split and paid at different times, with some interest rolled up into the principal repayment amount later on.

- Capital that's repaid at the end of the term (so two to five years) unless it's refinanced.

Vital Ingredient, the healthy food chain, grew from 11 to 20 outlets in one year after receiving a £2.75 million funding package from Santander Growth Capital, creating 15 jobs per unit and boosting revenue from £5 million to a projected £12 million in one year.

Funding through venture debt

Breaking it down to its simplest terms, *venture debt,* or *venture lending,* provides working capital to early stage companies that have had funding from venture capital (VC) firms and now need a financial injection in order to hit the next milestone and improve the company's valuation for its next round of equity funding.

No longer really a result of not having enough VC money to go around, which is when venture debt came into its own a few years back, it's now more a case of venture debt providing an attractive alternative to equity because it decreases the amount of money that needs to be invested into a company in follow-on rounds, and can help to generate better returns on exit due to less equity dilution.

Though the use of debt financing to fund company growth is an accepted strategy in many businesses, VC and debt have not always made for good bedfellows.

Even though there's now much more VC money swishing about, and the level of funding for each round and the timing of funding for each round is shorter than it was ten years ago, there's still a need to keep an eye on the amount of money an early-stage company is going through before it turns a profit from the VC point of view. You also want to watch how much of your company gets given away in an effort to give it enough runway to reach its high growth destination and tip over into profit.

Venture debt can be a good solution for both the investors and the investees, as it buys time between equity rounds and preserves current equity stakes.

It should be said that although it's a flexible solution, venture debt can also be an expensive solution, and it's not the right solution for every company. Struggling to repay the debt can put a serious strain on a youngish business's cash position.

Debt finance can raise a few objections with new investors in the next funding round, who may not take too kindly to some of their money being used to pay it off. However, for start-ups, the valuation proposition is generally more important than this objection because if the debt can bring a higher valuation, it would seem to be a worthwhile strategy. For more mature companies, where the pool of investors gets smaller as you reach higher funding rounds, venture debt can be a good solution as it offers an alternative source of capital at a lower cost.

So, what's in it for the lenders? In return for the loan, the venture lenders receive principal and interest payments, as per a normal loan, together with warrants, and sometimes, depending upon the contract, the right to invest in a future round.

Possible uses for venture debt include:

✔ To purchase equipment which can be a venture debt or a venture leasing product, similar to other lease finance I discuss earlier in this chapter.

✔ Working capital for operational growth needs.

✔ As a *bridging loan* – a short-term, secured loan when you want more flexibility whilst arranging longer-term debt or equity funding.

✔ To cover accounts receivable or a line of credit that can be drawn down if needed to cover monies due in from customers. This assumes your business has quite a large sales volume at this point, so payment delays have a significant impact on daily operations.

✔ As a pre-IPO (initial public offering) loan. If your business is looking to go for an IPO, a venture debt loan is similar to mezzanine debt (see 'Exploring mezzanine debt' earlier in the chapter) and would be slightly larger in size, reaching maturity after one or two years.

Chapter 13

Understanding Equity Funding

. . . .

In This Chapter

▶ Exploring the difference between debt and equity

▶ Taking flight with business angels

▶ Embarking on a funding adventure with venture capitalists

▶ Sampling the delights of larger equity finance options

▶ Reminding yourself why tax efficiency matters to you and to investors

. . . .

*G*one are the dark days of the recession of the 1990s, when getting equity investment was a mystical process, more a function of who you knew than who you could find an equitable match with. Gone are the days when you had to have the right personal contacts and connections to even get a whiff of an investor, or you encountered advisors or mentors who didn't have a clue what you were talking about. Gone are the days when you had no options. We've come a long way towards creating easier access to readily available and clearly understandable forms of equity finance as a form of business funding for small- and medium-sized enterprises (SMEs), and we're still going further.

Equity funding is a way of financing your business by selling shares to investors who put up money, or *capital,* in return for a stake in your business. There are no guarantees that they will make a good return on this investment, and they're aware of this going in. In addition to buying a stake in your business, equity investors usually bring much needed and valuable resources to your business (such as their skills, experience and contacts) and can really help you with your evolving strategy.

Despite some high-profile cases in the business press and a plethora of free or low-cost seminars and workshops on how equity funding works, according to the Business Finance Guide 2014 (published by the British Business Bank and the ICAEW, Institute of Chartered Accountants in England and Wales), only about 5 per cent of SMEs are tapping into this rich vein of funding. There appears to be a lack of genuine understanding and awareness where equity finance is concerned, and it's in everyone's best interest if I can help put that right.

Investors whose interests, goals and objectives are In line with yours, and who are prepared to hand over cash in exchange for shares in your business may be just what your business needs in order to secure its long-term growth and success. If they get in early and stay on to invest in later years, that's a bonus.

One round of funding very often has an impact on the next, so it's vital that you don't look at funding in isolation. Spend some time thinking about your future funding needs before you accept any current funding solutions.

In this chapter, I cover the three most talked about areas of equity investment – angels, crowdfunding and venture capital – along with the less common private equity and corporate venture funds.

Understanding Equity and Debt

Before you delve deep into equity funding, I give you a little refresher on debt and an overview of the difference between the two. When investors put money into your business in exchange for shares, that's an *equity transaction*. Investors don't expect a return in the normal course of you running your business as a lender would. Investors recover their investments when they sell their shareholdings to other investors, or when the assets of your business are liquidated and proceeds distributed among the shareholders. Table 13-1 highlights these differences:

Table 13-1	Comparing Debt and Equity Funding
Debt	**Equity**
Loan = repayment	Investment = shares
Temporary use of capital	Permanent investment
Return is achieved with repaying of principal plus interest	Return is achieved with dividends, selling shares or the sale of the business

Raising equity finance is a costly business, in terms of both time and money, so be prepared for whichever format you choose to be expensive in more ways than one. Some of the costs you may encounter are:

✔ Anything from three to nine months of senior management's time in order to find, negotiate and close an investment deal.

✔ Travel time and costs. Investors may not be only in the UK. You may find investors in India, Monaco, the US and elsewhere.

✔ Professional fees may be incurred when you turn to advisors on sources of funding, a reasonable company valuation, possible structures of deals and guidance on how to choose from the options available.

✔ Investors may require you to secure or strengthen your intellectual property (IP) rights, staff contracts, product licenses and so forth, before agreeing the final structure of the deal.

✔ Investors may require detailed financial data and verification of contracts and supplier arrangements before finalising a deal. This may require you to engage higher level accountancy services for higher fees.

✔ Taking on equity means entering into a complex legal agreement between your business and the investor and substantial fees in legal advice and documentation.

Raising equity opens your business up to intense scrutiny. You may be a little uncomfortable with the amount and level of detail in the information you have to share. Raising equity also means giving up some control, and you have to be comfortable with this aspect before you begin the process.

Pitching to Angels

Equity comes in a variety of forms, and one of the most popular comes to you in the shape of *business angels,* who are very wealthy individuals or groups of individuals that band together as formal networks or syndicates, and invest their personal capital in early-stage businesses.

One of the earliest providers of equity funding in your business, this growing army of celestial currency providers are now part of the fabric of the richly woven tapestry of your high-growth business's cloak.

Now, business angels don't walk around wearing wings and bask in the soft light of a halo, but when you really need them, it can feel like they were sent from above to help.

Looking at what makes an angel

Angels see the potential growth in your business and get on board relatively early, or they join up with their peers to keep feeding the meter as your business grows.

The term *angel investor* allegedly originates from Broadway in New York City, where struggling theatre companies were rescued by wealthy individuals who invested in their productions and saved the day. Many years later, in 1978, William Wetzel, the founder of the Center for Venture Research, completed a pioneering study on how entrepreneurs raised seed capital in the US. He began using the term *angel* to describe the investors that supported fledgling businesses.

Angel investors are often retired or exited entrepreneurs themselves, or executives who want to stay connected to the buzz of new or high-growth ventures. They want a financial return but also want to use their knowledge, expertise and network to help businesses realise their goals and ambitions. They generally want to continue to feel a valued part of the business community, adding to their contacts and learning about new industries while helping or mentoring business owners who still need to understand the tried-and-tested rules of running a successful enterprise. They can invest in one or a number of businesses.

Angels offer a source of valuable advice and experience and can act as a sounding board and a voice of reason for you and your management team.

Encountering angels

You encounter your angels in a variety of ways – business contacts or networks, accelerator programmes, online directories, seminars and workshops, or through a fund or a platform.

According to the UK Business Angel Association (UKBAA), the UK currently has over 18,000 active angels, acting as individuals or as networked or syndicated angel groups. Groups sometimes take the lead on an angel investment and share deal flow and opportunities, as well as the due diligence process, with other angels, enabling them to make larger investments and manage the deals on portals or a platform, like Gust or the UKBAA.

The early angels, such as the now well-known Angels Den, were pioneers in bringing angel investing to the wider SME market. I can recall sitting with the founder of Angels Den, the colourful and outspoken Bill Morrow, when I was working as a freelance business advisor wanting to understand how this newfangled, low-cost, online platform, with its structured application forms and pool of potential angel investors, could be of use to my clients who were seeking non-debt finance. Angels Den now boasts a very successful portfolio of investments, so he was definitely on to something!

Pitching to angels

When pitching to angels, give your business the best shot at raising the funds you need by using these tips:

- ✔ Start your research early to identify angels with the right fit, experience and gaps in their portfolios, and begin networking and creating relationships as soon as possible. Be aware that the whole process takes quite a long time, and factor that into your forecasts.

- ✔ Prepare your documentation well and have a great business plan, executive summary and investment memorandum. Be sure to have all your paperwork in order, up to date and close to hand. (I cover your documentation in detail in Chapters 5 and 6.)

✔ Lock down any intellectual property you need to secure by pursuing patents, copyrights and other documentation. (I talk about IP issues in depth in Chapter 3.)

✔ Create a show-stopping pitch deck (discussed in Chapter 6), practise your physical pitch until you know it inside out and backwards, and be sure to include financial forecasts, your company valuation, the amount of investment you're seeking, how you'll use it, what's in it for the investor and when you plan to exit.

✔ Do all you can to make your business an attractive, tax-efficient investment for them.

Before you head out to your meeting with your potential angel investors, use the following checklist to be sure you're completely prepared:

✔ Clearly identify your proposition and investment opportunity – what's the problem you've identified and what's your solution.

✔ Be able to show how it makes money – what's the model.

✔ Tell the investors what the size of your market is and how you're going to penetrate it.

✔ Outline your competitive edge and advantage, including any intellectual property rights.

✔ Wow them with your management team.

✔ Hit them with the numbers. You'll need financial projections, complete with ratios and milestones, and a time frame that makes sense with regard to the investment.

✔ State your valuation (which I talk about in the next section), but don't defend it to the death at the expense of getting funded.

✔ Show them why you can achieve your growth plans – or even better, surpass them.

✔ Be clear about how much money you're looking to raise and what it's going to be used for.

✔ Be able to articulate how your potential exit strategy will see them achieve their desired returns.

Tapping into angel investor syndicates

You may have been part of a lottery syndicate or know the term from business stories. A *syndicate* is essentially people banding together to put money into something as a group. A syndicate increases the amount available to invest while spreading the risk – and reward – among the group. Angel investor syndicates are pretty similar and are very much part of the everyday furniture when it comes to funding businesses.

Some syndicates are created by the angels themselves, and others meet through associations and trade bodies, such as the UKBAA, which is highly regarded in the sector. Members can choose to create a syndicate and invest alongside each other, perhaps with a lead investor, and as of 2015, can use the members' platform to coordinate and track their activity and progress.

Angels, like other funders, are taking advantage of the surge in online platforms and register as individuals or indeed, as a group, forming a syndicate of angel investors.

Angel syndicates provide an easily accessible link between you, as a seeker of funding, and them, as providers of funding, often on an efficient platform that provides a window into the opportunities for all members of the syndicate.

The syndicate also shoulders the burden of due diligence for the group, which adds to its attraction for investors.

One of the best known syndicate groups is Syndicate Room (www.syndicateroom.com), which is an investor-led equity platform that allows less sophisticated investors to invest alongside more experienced investors but on the same equitable terms. It's a good example of how syndicate funding works for both the investors and the investees. Check out the nearby sidebar 'The story of Syndicate Room' for more information.

The story of Syndicate Room

Syndicate Room was co-funded by Goncalo de Vasconcelos, who had been working with Cambridge-based business angels when he identified a problem with the way valuations were being dictated by companies at the expense of inexperienced investors. His vision was to create a platform that let the more inexperienced investor invest alongside the wiser, more seasoned investor, with investments starting from £1,000. Inexperienced investors could essentially piggyback on the experience of others while investing on the same economic terms. Its lead investors are among some of the country's most active and well-known investors, such as John Milner, an entrepreneur turned angel investor.

Since 2013, Syndicate Room has grown to almost £40 million invested in more than 50 companies, and recently raised some of its own investment (£1.2 million) in 24 hours. Their own raise was a powerful indication of its popularity, success and perceived integrity. I was in the audience when Syndicate Room announced the opportunity, and the atmosphere was nothing short of electric.

Syndicate Room was the first to equity crowdfund a Hollywood movie, and the first to crowdfund an *IPO*, or initial public offering, of a company's shares on a public stock exchange, Eighty per cent of the companies listed on the platform have reached their targets, and all except one of them are still trading.

Goncalo de Vasconcelos, co-founder of Syndicate Room, offers advice for entrepreneurs looking to raise funds using a syndicate:

- ✔ **Know your stuff.** This means you need to know your numbers (both actuals and forecasts), your technology, your customers, your market, your management team . . . know everything. You don't know what investors are going to ask, so you need to be prepared for any question they may throw at you.

- ✔ **Think about your audience and understand what makes them tick.** Is it your business's technology, scalability or the potential financial return that will interest possible investors most?

- ✔ **Know which investors you're looking for.** The right investors will guide and support you as well as offer helpful introductions that will make you a very successful entrepreneur.

- ✔ **Be very clear what your business does and make sure you can articulate your vision for its future.** Know how much money you'll need to achieve this vision and the amount of equity you're prepared to give up, and be ready to explain where it's going to take your business.

- ✔ **Bring your pitch to life and make it interesting.** Investors like a good story and you'll increase your chances of securing funding.

- ✔ **Be ready for negative feedback and take it in a constructive way.** Some investors may not invest at first, but if you listen to their feedback and address their concerns you may well find that they end up investing in your business at a later stage.

Excellent advice for all types of fundraising, and straight from the feet on the street.

Syndicate Room funds cancer-finding tool

In December 2014, Lightpoint Medical raised £1 million on Syndicate Room to bring its two main products, LightPath and EnLight, to the EU and US markets. The products address the greatest challenge in cancer surgery – there's no straightforward way to find cancer. Lightpoint's groundbreaking technology identifies cancer in real time during surgery and helps surgeons remove it accurately, reducing the need for repeat operations.

The funding round was led by Oxford Technology Management, which specialises in making and managing investments in start-up and early-stage technology-based businesses with high growth prospects. Since receiving funding, Lightpoint has begun clinical trials in London and successfully imaged prostate cancer. The company's management and commercial teams have grown, and both products remain on schedule for launch.

Arriving at a Valuation

In any discussion on raising funds, you encounter the somewhat sticky question of arriving at a valuation for your business. The method you choose may take a top-down or a bottom-up view, but all methods take into account the additional money you may need to raise along the way in the future and a certain amount of *dilution,* or adding more shareholders which reduces everybody's proportion of the shareholding. Eventually, you arrive at what looks like an acceptable number before money is invested.

When people talk about the valuation process, they're often referring to the textbook formulas that look at things like complicated discounted cash flows, asset valuations, or transactions comparisons that masters of business administration (MBAs) and corporate finance people learn in detail.

I strongly advise that you seek professional advice to do your valuation. Unless you're a corporate finance professional, you need to find someone who understands business numbers. Not using a professional is a bit like me trying to wire my own flat – no guarantees of success and a good chance of a dangerous failure. Valuation is an imperfect exercise, and it involves objective and subjective assessments with regard to risk, your marketplace, the team, and your achievements or potential for achievement, mixed with experience and a reading on which way your sector wind is blowing. Get the right person for the job.

Valuation has been described as finance meets science meets art meets alchemy. Your quest is to take the raw materials of your business and combine them with that unquantifiable ingredient that turns them to gold – and a golden valuation.

I imagine that all equity investors are sick of being asked about how to value your business to ensure that it gets funded. They usually reply along the lines of, 'Well, that depends . . . '. And, having done it for my own business, I have to admit that's true.

So if it depends, just what does it depend on, this elusive valuation formula? Well, the key issues are recent valuations of similar businesses in your sector, changing assessments of the opportunities ahead of you, the general availability of money and the mood of the times. The investment climate may sweep some investors – especially the less experienced – up in a wave of funding frenzy, not wanting to miss out.

Valuation in *Dragons' Den* – A case in point

On a recent episode of the very popular BBC TV series *Dragons' Den*, a hopeful was seeking £1 million investment into his business that he'd valued at £20 million. That valuation made Peter Jones, the captain of industry (whom I have the privilege of knowing from his work with young entrepreneurs), say to the potential investee, 'I'm very angry about your valuation' . . . or words to that effect. As anyone who's ever watched the show knows, very often the deal goes sour because the investors don't think the valuation is realistic.

To his credit, the hapless victim defended his position, saying that old valuation models are out of step for modern technology businesses. I have to admit that some part of me agreed with his assessment of what's going on in pockets of the market, and especially technology – but I also agreed with the dragons. I regularly ask myself whether the market is heading for a valuation bubble in tech firms, and wonder if it may be better for entrepreneurs to focus on creating an actual business with solid foundations instead of aspiring to be the next billion-dollar valuation owner.

Equally impressive was how this entrepreneur understood that he was *selling* shares in his business to enable him to realise his dreams – not giving them away – thus creating a sense of loss (which many entrepreneurs forget at some point or other). He knew this was a negotiation – perhaps a bit prematurely on his part – and that he had some say over the outcome. Tricky that one, because it should be give and take, but it's key to know what to give and take on, and when in the funding discussion to do it. (However, straight off the bat when you're still an unknown quantity is probably not the best time!)

The components that make up your valuation are debated and discussed, but some of the most often used are:

- The valuation of recent companies in your same or similar space, and how they fared when exiting

- Whether, in the eyes of investors, your sector is sizzling, like financial technology (referred to as *fintech*) is at the moment, or not, which could depress your valuation, particularly in your start-up phase when you haven't got much of a track record

- Your management team appears to be red hot, and may include someone who's led a previous successful exit or two

- The availability of money in the equity investor marketplace

- The involvement of investors who know your sector well and can see the potential of your business against the backdrop of industry and trend knowledge

- The willingness of an investor to pay more than the perceived market rate because he understands the opportunity and your enthusiasm to achieve it, while desiring a certain return on his investment

✔ Roughly how many rounds of investment you'll need until exit and what's the likely impact on the value of investor's shares

✔ The need for an investor to not be left out or miss the funding boat when activity levels are high

✔ Gut instinct

There is no one source or method for valuation, but a couple of useful links to help you understand the mechanics of the process are www.drisk.it and www.bizequity.com.

Pre-money valuation is the amount you value your business at before investment; *post-money valuation* is the amount you value your business at after you receive investment.

Keep an open mind when deciding on your company valuation because it could be the thing that scuppers your equity fundraising plans somewhere along your growth journey. You don't want to pitch it too low and undervalue your business, but you also don't want to go in so high and so fixed in your position that you walk away with nothing. It's a sales and negotiation process, not a stand-off.

Approaching High Net Worth Individuals

You frequently need a bit more than you and your small army of loved ones can muster up to keep fanning the flame of early growth.

One potential source of additional external funding can come in the form of a high net worth individual with deep pockets. Such investors have a number of motivations for investing. They may want to add to their growing portfolio of investments in high-growth businesses generating nice returns, or they may already be involved in a similar or complementary business and see a growth opportunity for you. They may also want to reduce a capital gains tax payment, or just do something interesting with their money in a tax-efficient way. Investing in your business may work out for both of you!

You may come across some of these individuals at events, seminars and in online groups, like those on LinkedIn and Meetup. Your accountant (or a friend's accountant) or lawyer may know people in their circles. You'll have to do a bit of networking and to snare one of these useful financial animals.

Finding a high net worth individual to invest in your business comes with both advantages and drawbacks:

✔ Pros:

- Come to the rescue at the exact time you need them to help fund growth

- May have industry knowledge

- May help up-skill the management team

- May bring commercial introductions

✔ Cons:

- May want a larger stake in your business than you'd like to sell

- May cause problems with your current shareholders

Using Crowdfunding

Crowdfunding is a means of raising finance by harnessing the power and the funds of a large number of people who each put in a small amount of money. Crowdfunding comes in several flavours, including *equity crowdfunding,* in which investors take a share in your business, and *debt-based crowdfunding,* in which lenders get some interest on their loans. This chapter looks at equity-based crowdfunding, but for full information on this type of alternative finance, head to Chapter 14.

In some ways, these ever-expanding new kids on the funding block present a threat to the less agile, more risk-averse venture capital funders. Crowdfunding platforms have much lower transaction costs than traditional venture capitalists (VCs). Granted, the additional number of investors changes the risk profile, making future rounds of funding less appealing to VCs, but crowdfunding is going to steal some of venture capital's market share.

Equity crowdfunding alone was responsible for over £28 million in funded deals in 2014, representing just under 20 per cent of all visible equity deals funded that year, and up significantly from 2 per cent in 2011.

Crowdfunding often offers a lower cost but is always a more democratic option for both investors and SMEs seeking funding. Democracy doesn't mean that the guiding investment principles of due diligence and a sound business growth proposition go out the window. Far from it. The industry players are very aware of the need to make the process as transparent and risk free as possible, while still providing a good return for investors and a good deal for investees. They're hoping for a long run, and it would appear doing their best to reward their supporters and prove their detractors wrong, and ensure that they stick around for the foreseeable future and beyond.

Although each equity-based crowdfunding organisation has its own peculiarities, what is common to all of them is that:

- ✔ They spend quite a bit of time working with you to prepare your business before you go onto the platforms in order to give you the best chance of success.

- ✔ They do a lot of promotion to attract investors or lenders to the website.

- ✔ They handle the mechanics of the introductions to funders.

- ✔ They keep an eye on what happens after the funds have been received.

Head to Chapter 14 for more on crowdfunding platforms and how to access them.

Don't be fooled by the simplicity of this funding model. Obtaining equity investment using crowdfunding is not an overnight event, and you still have investment risk for both parties. Depending on how much work you've done on your business, your business plan, your financial forecasts and gathering your part of the investor crowd, it can take 20 to 60 hours of preparation, and up to three months to raise the funds – if you're even successful. So, it's not something you do when you have just two weeks to raise the money to develop your website!

Regulation and the FCA (Financial Conduct Authority)

Some people believe that the regulators haven't really woken up to the scale of crowdfunding and to how fast it's growing. They worry that when the first thing goes wrong on a crowdfunding platform, regulators will overreact and pull down the shutters on large parts of the marketplace, preventing ordinary people from being able to invest. Regulators exist to protect the public and to prevent trouble, while still allowing enough flexibility to ensure that innovation is keeping pace with marketplace demands.

Currently the regulators still have their hands full with the aftermath of some of the big bank scandals, so perhaps they'll start paying much closer attention to crowdfunding in the years to come – but for the moment, crowdfunding comes under the banner of the FCA (however,

the thresholds and standards for the sector are still being clarified).

The UK is known for taking an open-minded stance and a 'sit back and watch' approach to new developments in financial technology. Regulators don't want to shove legislation down the throats of fledging industries and choke them before they have time to grow. The government is also acutely aware of its duty to protect the public's interests.

This is an evolving process, and you monitor progress too, regularly checking for updates on the FCA website (www.fca.org.uk) and any other reputable financial news and information sources, such as the *Financial Times* website at www.ft.com.

TRUE STORY

CrowdBnk – A crowdfunding hybrid

CrowdBnk is an equity and debt crowdfunding platform offering investors the opportunity to invest in exciting, well-vetted, early stage and established businesses.

Not surprisingly, it has a pretty tough assessment process and makes all businesses on its platform go through a rigorous CrowdBnk Bootcamp programme. CrowdBnk offers a high level of professional support to both investors and businesses, and (as if it needs any additional incentive to help you get it right) it also becomes a shareholder in every business that it successfully funds on the platform. To date, it has funded 20 businesses, to the amount of £16 million.

According to one of its founders, Ayan Mitra, the idea for CrowdBnk came about in New York in 2009. Kickstarter had just been launched, and he'd participated in some of its deals. At the same time, he was helping a start-up raise capital using traditional means, and finding it a bit of an uphill battle, with the company nearly going out of business. In doing his research, Ayan discovered that every year 25,000 companies fail to find finance at their terms, and as yet, there was no platform available to make it easier for these businesses. That's where the idea for CrowdBnk was born.

CrowdBnk operates an Internet platform that provides an easy way for investors to learn about your business and make their decision to invest. The platform provides them with all the information they need to make a decision, including your investment memorandum (refer to Chapters 4 and 6), interviews with your CEO and pitch videos showcasing the business. It also runs a number of investor events,

which give investors the chance to meet you in person. Finally, it organises one-to-one sessions with your CEO should an investor want to meet in a more personal setting.

For a recent debt raise for a Hampshire-based vineyard, Hambledon, CrowdBnk investors were able to invest in the English Fizz Mini Bond and get a return of 8 per cent per annum. The English Fizz Mini Bond stood out in the market because it was secured on the assets of the Hambledon business, and was convertible into equity at the end of the five-year term. Over 65 investors poured into the fund raise over a two-month period.

Breezie is a service aimed at the millions of people who struggle to use the Internet, primarily those over the age of 65. It solves this problem through a unique combination of software, services and the latest breakthroughs in tablet design. The service includes an online facility for the family/support person to manage and personalise the Breezie: setting up accounts, adjusting security, adding apps and contacts and so on. The company needed to raise £252,000 for further development and for additional marketing. It chose to crowdfund on CrowdBnk in order to access a wider base of high net worth individuals and professional investors, and to widen its customer base while raising funds. Breezie actually raised £600,768 over 80 days, via 22 investors who shared 33.75 per cent of the equity. Both Breezie and CrowdBnk worked very hard to promote the opportunity, with Breezie activating its own crowd to bring in 60 per cent of the money raised.

Getting the Timing Right for Venture Capital Funding

You've emptied your bank account, altered your friends and family relationships forever, borrowed and paid back your debt, been touched by an angel or been part of the crowd . . . now it's time for your business to sample the delights on offer from a venture capitalist (VC).

The upturn in the economy and the boom in areas such as fintech and medtech (financial and medical technologies, respectively) have collided to create a renewed sense of optimism and a belief in innovation as the answer to all investment prayers.

Accelerator graduates and other companies who have adopted a low-overhead, light-governance approach are burning less money and attracting more interest from traditionally later stage investors at an earlier stage, so you need to be aware of a few things when you enter the realm of the venture capital investor:

✔ At some point, you will fail when trying to raise venture capital, and even if you do raise funds and get extra help and advice, this isn't a guarantee that your business will flourish and succeed.

✔ VCs allow for a number of companies in their portfolio to fail, some to do okay, some to do well, and one or two to do very well. They may not necessarily become super rich from investing in you, and equally you may not become super rich; you need to understand that from the outset.

✔ Venture capital funds run in ten-year cycles for investors, but your business will be expected to make a return on its investment in three to seven years (with five as the average). VCs spread their risk and timing throughout their portfolio, and often make follow-on investments in the business's next funding round throughout the fund's life cycle.

✔ Venture capital firms look for high-growth, fast-growing businesses that aren't dependent on the founder still being there in three, five or seven years. If an investee is looking at an IPO in seven or eight years, it may provide the VC's exit.

✔ You can't fire your VC, so choose wisely. (I give you tips for choosing the right investor for you and your business in Chapter 4.) Doing your research and your due diligence can go out the window in the excitement of the fundraising process; don't let that happen.

✔ Each fund has its own focus and each partner within a firm has a specialisation. All funds have a reward structure that goes beyond the arrangement with the investee company.

Look at your venture capital firm as another member of the team from the outset. Your vision, mission statement and goals need to align with theirs – or actually theirs with yours – so you're all on the same page and working towards the same business and financial success. The venture capital firm will have a seat on your board, and the last thing you want is internal disagreements. You're like a singing artist and his management, except that you'll probably have a longer relationship with your VC.

Venture capital provides the funding to accelerate your success, but you may crash and burn before you get to the finish line. If you become a casualty of this funding war, be proud of your battle scars, learn from the experience, and come back in another guise as someone who knows the score and, as a result, is still attractive to funders. Whatever mistakes you made, you certainly won't make them twice, and as an educated consumer of venture capital funds, you side-step a lot of the usual learning and are attractive to funders who know that you understand the game. Work hard, work smart and keep your relationships alive. VCs invest largely in you and your potential, and if you performed well even though the business failed, you're still in a good place.

On the roller-coaster ride of equity funding, this phase of growth sits somewhere in the middle, and again, as it is in life, the middle bit can often be the most complicated, the busiest, the most demanding and the scariest part of any journey. If you've got a rapidly growing business – with a great team, amazing and unique products or services that are making money for your current investors, and the opportunity to achieve global scale in the future – you potentially have what It takes to sell shares to the public on the open markets. In other words, you're ready for venture capital.

You can seek VC funding at any part of your expansion stage of business. Keep in mind that investors are looking for consistently high levels of growth, a scalable product or service and a business that's refined its systems and mechanics to the point where it's eliminated most operating risks. Investors want to see that you're hitting, or nearly hitting, every milestone you face along the way.

Of course, you start seeking potential VCs long before you reach this stage, because you need to start your preparations early. Work your networks to build relationships, make sure that your business documentation and procedures are in tip-top condition, and be able to withstand the intense scrutiny of the microscope to ensure funding success.

Increasingly, and potentially somewhat frustratingly for you, the lines between angels and early-stage venture capital are blurring. What should be a good thing – more available capital in the marketplace – can sometimes make it more confusing as to who's funding what and at what stage, which makes your job a little harder.

Depending on your industry, your rate of growth and your potential for scalable expansion, you may be talking to angels and early-stage VCs at the same time, with each of them coming from a slightly different angle and approach.

The UK doesn't have as many early-stage venture capital funds as in the US, for example, so some venture capital funds take a punt on what they think will be a good later stage investment, and get in early – usually with the pledge for additional later funding set against milestones that trigger the release of the next bit of funding. Whatever the stage, they bring the same new network of contacts, expertise, experience and tighter governance to your business, so be ready for life as you know it to change radically.

Moving On to Private Equity

As you get nearer to exiting the roller-coaster ride of funding, private equity funding becomes an option for your high-growth, solidly established business poised for significant expansion (possibly including overseas expansion).

In the same way as other forms of equity, you're exchanging money from investors for a share in your business – but for me, this is equity funding with a capital *E* because the amounts are much higher, the process is much more expensive, the control you hand over is much greater, the corporate governance is far stricter and the pool of funders is much smaller.

Private equity (PE) firms raise their funds via institutional investors, such as pension funds and insurance companies, and invest them, usually along with borrowed money and maybe some venture capital or funding from ultra-high net worth individuals.

By this time in your business journey, most, if not all, of your early investors have cashed in and left the ride; your angels have probably left the building too, and your VCs are ready for a good return for the price of their entry ticket. It may be the perfect time for a private equity firm to bring strategic, financial and operational assistance for roughly five to seven years before selling shares in your business on an open stock exchange and taking their leave.

PE funders roll up their sleeves and get their hands dirty, bringing their skills, experience and contacts to bear in a positive way on the businesses they invest in. They sometimes fund management buy-outs or management buy-ins, which I discuss in Chapter 17, but these are at the low end of their funding scale. A more typical investment would see them start at £10 million and go upwards to the hundreds of millions – dizzying heights as far as equity investing is concerned.

Although equity investments continue to increase, especially at the seed and early-growth stages, many business never get to the PE stage. For those that do, it can take years before they look for £10–20 million upwards. However, depending on your industry and your growth potential, you may wind up being approached by a PE house sooner than expected if it has identified your business as established and scalable and can see areas where it can make it run more efficiently.

It's never too early to start creating funding relationships: it's always good to listen and learn, even if you don't need the funding yet. Relationships on the PE side take longer to percolate, so it's best to start early.

To determine whether you're a candidate for PE funding, ask whether your business is:

- ✔ Well-established and showing significant, predictable growth year on year

- ✔ *Scalable,* meaning it's capable of significant, and sometimes global, growth in sales, employee numbers, offices, manufacturing facilities, training for staff and so on

- ✔ Able to go global

- ✔ Low risk and potentially high reward or return

- ✔ Looking for a large amount of money

A good place to look further information is www.bvca.co.uk/ PrivateEquityExplained/FAQsinPrivateEquity.aspx.

Exploring Corporate Venturing

A great idea is a beautiful thing. An idea that can be turned into a business that can feed and clothe you and possibly make you very wealthy . . . now that's a fantastic thing. Bridging that gap between your great idea and seeing it in the market can sometimes take you on a very difficult journey. Being a resourceful entrepreneur, you're determined to leave no stone unturned in your quest to raise finance, so don't overlook the increasingly prevalent and popular option of corporate venture capital (CVC) funds.

A newish lifeline to your fledging company, CVC funds offer money, resources and contacts.

Be aware that CVC funds come with strings attached, so do your homework and go in with both eyes wide open and both feet planted firmly on the ground.

CVC funds are a special form of venture capital, usually set aside to make equity investments in high-growth, high-potential, privately owned businesses. Not a completely new form of venture funding, the current crop of CVC investors make an effort to have a separate venture team, but one that's actively integrated into the overall strategic and business aims of the corporation, helping to ensure that more successful and long-lasting investments are made and everyone is on the same team.

Large corporates invest in companies for financial reasons, as a form of accelerated or extended research and development, or as a way to take out some of the upcoming competition in the marketplace before its competitors do the same. Unlike typical venture capital investments, which typically have one end game – financial return on investment – CVC can have more than one aim for the investor.

CVC funds offer a great way to get your early stage venture funded, and also to give you the kudos that comes with being selected by and attached to a large corporate with respect in the market. It gives you access to large research and development facilities, and often to the historical data of the investor, allowing you to put your product or service through its paces in a safe environment.

If you're in a regulated industry, the connection can help you navigate the requirements more swiftly and successfully.

You have access to a network of experienced managers, mentors and innovators, from which you can drink up knowledge and learn from the experiences of others while being guided on your path to growth. Large corporates have contacts and networks that you'd take years to develop alone, and accessing the opportunities these present may see your business rocket into the growth stratosphere.

When pitching for CVC funds:

- ✔ Point out what's in it for the corporation. Although it's investing in your business, it's all about them, darling.

- ✔ Know how you fit into the corporation's strategy.

- ✔ Don't wait until you're running out of money to ask for the funding. Desperation is a colour that looks bad on everyone.

- ✔ Look to the CVC fund's customers for support, wherever and however possible, and try to get the people on the ground, as well as the folks at the top, interested in your business.

A number of successful CVC partnerships currently exist in the market – far too many to talk about here. They have pros and cons, and long-term implications for your business, so although they look enticing at first glance, you need to investigate the detail. Make sure that you're not boxing your business into a corner, putting limitations on your eventual exit or walking into the unthinkable situation whereby you could end up out of business if you don't fit neatly beneath the corporate wing you're sheltering under.

If you're unsure whether a large corporation in your sector has a programme, be bold and ask what they have on offer. More and more CVC funds are popping up in tech, food and beverage, consumer goods, media and so on, so it doesn't hurt to ask.

Advantages of CVC funding include:

- ✔ **Strategic investing:** CVC funds offer so much more than the money. A corporate investor who wants you as part of its strategy opens global doors, contacts and business relationships, helping your brand to punch well above its weight.

- ✔ **Access to technology:** If the investment is part of the CVC fund's innovation agenda, you get access to some pretty amazing and valuable technology and tech teams to accelerate the development of your company's products or services.

- ✔ **Human resources:** Having the investment of a large corporate also gives you access to some of its brightest minds, working with you to achieve your goals in much less time while you benefit from years of knowledge and experience.

Disadvantages of CVC funding include:

- ✔ **Strategic fit:** Make sure that you're key to the funder's strategic aims, and not just something that it wants to dabble in or, in the worst case, shut down in order to keep competition out of the market.

- ✔ **Control:** Read the small print in your agreements to see how much control over your activities and company direction the CVC funder has, especially where it relates to your eventual sale or other joint ventures, and so on.

- ✔ **Impact on other investors:** If a mammoth company is involved, it may put smaller investors off or, even worse, send them running in the direction of your competitors.

- ✔ **Speed:** You may be quick and agile as a start-up or early-stage business, but the corporate giant you're talking to is most likely slower and more lumbering in its speed and the manner in which it moves. This can be very frustrating, and it can slow you down to the point of inertia.

Knowing the Equity Tax and Legal Framework

Since the 1990s, the UK Treasury has extended a helping hand to both businesses and investors in the form of a number of tax-efficient schemes aimed at encouraging investment in *unlisted companies,* companies not on the stock exchange but with shares available for the general public to purchase. Born out of the lack of readily available funding to SMEs in the 1980s, tax incentives were the practical manifestation aimed at helping businesses access capital in order to grow.

Fast forward to the early 1990's and the announcement of the EIS (Enterprise Investment Scheme), which set the tax efficiency stall out and spawned a new generation of investors.

The EIS continues in an updated format, and has been joined by a younger sibling, the SEIS (Seed Enterprise Investment Scheme), which your business and your investors can be part of in your early stage of growth. These two schemes are actively used by equity investors, from individuals to angel networks to early stage VCs.

Such tax incentive schemes have helped make the UK an attractive place to set up shop – especially for technology businesses – and have tempted North American and European businesses to our shores.

These schemes are best explained by your accountant, and you should check out the HMRC (Her Majesty's Revenue & Customs) website (`www.hmrc.gov.org.uk`) for updates and information because this isn't an area for mistakes, minor or major, and it can be difficult to grasp the ins and outs unless you have an accountancy background.

Understanding the Seed Enterprise Investment Scheme

The SEIS, or Seed Enterprise Investment Scheme, comes into action at the time of new company shares being issued. Both the company receiving the investment and the investors making the investment must be approved by HMRC before they can transact.

Individual investors and angels seeking tax-efficient ways of investing, are usually active in this space. Investments are made either by individuals or groups using special group investment vehicles, known as special purpose vehicles, or SPVs. An SPV has a nominee structure in which the entrepreneur can have multiple investors, but everyone is wrapped up in one agreement, so the business owner deals with one nominated spokesperson of the group.

SEIS has a number of criteria that you need to abide by, and the key elements are:

✔ SEIS-approved companies can receive a maximum of £150,000 of investment under the scheme.

- ✔ Your company must have fewer than 25 full-time equivalent employees.

- ✔ Your company must have less than £200,000 worth of assets before you apply.

- ✔ Your company can't have had any funds from EIS or a *Venture Capital Trust (VCT),* an investment vehicle that enables private equity firms to invest in small, growing companies.

- ✔ Your company must have started trading within the past two years to qualify for SEIS and must not be listed on any stock exchange.

Numbers play a large role in SEIS; some key facts and figures are:

- ✔ SEIS incentivises investors to invest in your early stage company, by providing 50 per cent income tax relief on investments up to £100,000 per year, so an investor get £5,000 off his tax bill for investing £10,000.

- ✔ You're limited to raising a maximum of £150,000 under SEIS.

  Once you've spent 70 per cent of your SEIS raise, you may be eligible for EIS, so it may not be the end of the road.

- ✔ SEIS and EIS investors pay no capital gains tax on the final disposal of their shares so long as your company remains a qualifying SEIS or EIS company for three years. That's an amazing windfall if you turn out to be the next big thing!

Making the most of the Enterprise Investment Scheme

The EIS is one way HMRC lends a helping hand to businesses. The EIS provides investors with incentives to invest in a range of tax reliefs set against making investments in smaller, higher risk, unlisted companies like yours.

The EIS has been a bit of a game-changer for SMEs. What was a novel experience seven or eight years ago is now a pretty common occurrence for SMEs and their investors. You're seeking investment and prepared to sell some shares in your business. The EIS makes it that much easier for an investor to want to part with his money, giving the added bonus of the tax relief whether they win, lose or draw in terms of your business performance.

Important restrictions exist with regard to how your investor is connected to your business, and you need to know about these ahead of time. A business angel, for example, who's a director but receives no remuneration, is okay as an investor; your fellow remunerated director or employee is not okay. Anyone holding a controlling share in your business is not eligible, either. There's always something in the small print – get yourself up to speed before you waste your time.

As both the EIS and SEIS are more complex than they first appear and have certain limitations and exclusions, as well as an order of steps to follow, you'd be wise to seek professional advice and have an accountant sort out the paperwork. You don't want to disqualify your company by making a schoolchild error.

You can find information and guidance on www.hmrc.gov.org.uk.

EIS has a number of criteria that you must be aware of, and some of the key point are:

- Companies can receive a maximum of £5 million in one year from all the schemes – EIS, SEIS and VCT.
- Investors can invest up to £1 million per person.
- Your company must have fewer than 250 full-time equivalent employees.
- Your company must have less than £15 million of assets.

In order for your investors to claim their tax relief, you need to file an EIS3 form, so add that to your to-do list. In fact, the whole EIS/SEIS process is fraught with places for you to put a foot wrong, from your investors unknowingly disqualifying themselves to you not following the due process when issuing shares; therefore, it's wise to get an accountant to process the forms.

In order to illustrate some real-life examples, check out the crowdfunding site Crowdcube at www.crowdcube.com.

Becoming Familiar with Term Sheets

When you accept venture capital investment, you enter into a partnership of sorts between your business and the venture capital investor. In order to document what you've decided is fair and acceptable and what the agreed valuation is, you set out to create a written agreement.

The document that sets out what you've agreed is called a _term sheet,_ or to give it its proper name, _heads of terms._ Term sheets aren't legally binding, but they're helpful because they set out the terms upon which the investment is offered. A term sheet serves as a template for the more detailed legal documents that follow after you agree the terms and close the deal, and the investors actually purchase the shares in your business. They're usually used by venture capital firms, but also angel investors, and contain the _headline,_ or principal terms of the deal on the table, which can be negotiated and eventually agreed without the need to get down to the minute details if agreeing the broader, more general terms of the agreement isn't going well. Having a terms sheet saves you both time and money.

A term sheet contains a lot of important and technical information, and depending on what funding round you're in, you may never have seen anything like it. Take legal advice and make sure that you completely understand what you're signing before you sign it.

No two term sheets are exactly alike, but most of them have three sections: funding, corporate governance and liquidation. Some of the sections common to many term sheets include:

- ✔ Investment type – shares or convertible debt, for example
- ✔ Valuation
- ✔ Liquidation preference – who gets paid first when the company is sold or when assets need to be sold, for example
- ✔ Voting rights – who controls the company

Term sheets are the domain of lawyers, so make sure that you've set some budget aside for them, but if you want to see a good example of a plain talking, simple English term sheet then look no further than the download which can be found on www.passioncapital.com offered by the hugely experienced investor and UK government adviser Eileen Burbidge of Passion Capital. I also posted one at www.dummies.com/extras/businessfundinguk.

Chapter 14

Considering Alternative Finance

· ·

· ·

The strength of the UK's economic recovery after the financial crisis of 2008 has seen high-growth small- and medium-sized enterprises (SMEs) on the increase, virtually flooding the funding market with deal flow of all colours, shapes and sizes.

Whereas, in years gone by, investors would pick over the same old pile of propositions looking for the proverbial needle in the haystack, investors and funders now shop around for opportunities and are much more choosy – knowing that not every business can deliver the returns they're looking for.

In recent years, banks have been hesitant to lend or have been short of funds (or sometimes both), and like the phoenix from the ashes of the funding cauldron, a brave new industry that includes alternative platforms and crowdfunding has risen – an industry that meets the needs of finance-hungry entrepreneurs, the exacting standards of the modern investor and the great British public's desire to put its hard-earned cash to even harder work. These ingredients create a high-octane cocktail in an industry that's been calling out to be shaken *and* stirred – and everyone's jockeying for a position at the bar.

Fortunately for all parties concerned, you can now consider many other sources of finance if high street lenders and investors are hesitating to back your plan and ideas. Entrepreneurs have become very creative at finding new ways to source the finance they need and not taking 'no' for an answer for something that matters so much to them.

In this chapter, I take a look at some of the forms alternative finance takes, the criteria for successful applications, the cost implications to you and your business and the conduits for tapping into this rich vein of funding.

Recognising the Rise of Alternative Funding

When it comes to lending, many entrepreneurs have found banks slow, hesitant and expensive. Because of this, and a new wave in accessible technology solutions, a different and great wave of innovation is underway in the financial services sector.

The expansion of funding sources

The boom in alternative, or non-bank, finance has been pronounced. Newer forms of borrowing – like crowdfunding – have now joined the mainstream marketplace alongside longer-standing specialist services like invoice financing and bonds, which are taking on new forms to reach their target audiences. New products and funders keep entering the market, to provide fresh options in the space between banks and investors.

Although alternative finance as a new form of funding has been around for a little over ten years, its recent growth and popularity mean that mainstream finance needs to move over and make room for this newish kid on the block; it looks like she's here to stay. It's an exciting time to be looking for – or offering – funding.

In the UK in 2014, £1 billion of support was provided by alternative products and services to over 7,000 small businesses. The number of these new funding knights able to come to your financial rescue is expanding to fill the gap left by the banking sector cutting its lending to entrepreneurs – which was down by £400 million in the same year – and they're here to stay. This groundswell of growth is expected to continue with an estimated £4.4 billion of alternative finance projected to be delivered in 2015 alone.

The industry spans the length and breadth of the kingdom, but the biggest uptake is in London and the South-East, with no real clear contender for the number two position.

However, it's not all plain sailing for alternative funders, and some entrepreneurs remain unconvinced. According to the UK Alternative Finance Industry Report, 2014, the 60 percent or so of SMEs that haven't tried alternative finance remain sceptical and say they're 'unlikely' to access this form of funding any time soon.

Where do entrepreneurs look for finance?

BMG Market Research surveyed 1,000 SMEs for the British Business Bank during August and September 2014 to find out the source of their funding. The results were:

- ✔ Credit cards: 93 per cent
- ✔ Leasing/hire purchase: 85 per cent
- ✔ Government/local authority grants: 67 per cent
- ✔ Venture capitalists: 55 per cent

- ✔ Asset finance: 53 per cent
- ✔ Business angels: 36 per cent
- ✔ Peer-to-peer lending: 35 per cent
- ✔ Crowdfunding: 32 per cent
- ✔ Export/import finance: 31 per cent
- ✔ Mezzanine finance: 15 per cent

The 2014 British Business Bank SME finance report revealed (in an analysis of the sources of finance used by 1,000 entrepreneurs in the UK) that more than a third were now using peer-to-peer lending products of the kind provided by Crowdcube, Funding Circle, Zopa and others. That number is guaranteed to rise. One day very soon, alternative forms of funding will no longer be alternative, but finding their rightful place in the mainstream.

Many entrepreneurs are unfamiliar with non-bank products. As a result, these resources are underused and provide only a tiny percentage of the credit currently accessed by businesses. That's changing month by month, however, and business start-ups and growth would be at a far lower level without them. Check out the nearby sidebar 'Where do entrepreneurs look for finance?' for a snapshot of where SMEs have been seeking their funding.

As always, there may be a devil or two in the details. Be sure to understand exactly how these forms of finance work, what they cost, how to make successful applications and what impact they'll have on the cash flow, financial profile and balance sheet of your business (as you would with any deal agreed with an investor or facility agreed with a bank).

Checklist for considering alternative finance

When your business is growing and you've been turned away by traditional funders, alternative finance can be a great solution. The number and type of alternative funders is growing, so you really need to keep up to date and find out which alternative is best suited to your funding needs. Keep in mind the following checklist:

✔ Consider the stage your business is in – you can get alternative funding from seed to scaling up to becoming established. See who fits the bill for your stage. (I cover the stages of a business in Chapter 2.)

✔ Make sure that you know what matters to you and your business. You can find a financial solution whether it's debt or equity, long- or short-term funding, a single funder or a whole group. The trick is to know what fulfils your financial needs but also sits well with your future funding rounds.

✔ New entrants constantly enter this market, so make sure that you do your homework and don't miss out. Some funders are for assets; some are for working capital; some are for invoice finance – do your own due diligence.

✔ Get any advice you require before you fill in one number on any form and definitely before you press Send on your online application form.

Freeing Up Money in Unpaid Invoices

Many years ago, when I was advising small and micro businesses, I became aware of the fact that large businesses or organisations took a very relaxed approach towards the payment terms they agreed with their suppliers, be they small or large. Because small businesses wanted the kudos of being stocked at or associated with these large, sometimes prestigious, outlets, they'd bite the bullet and take the hit on getting a timely payment into their struggling enterprise. Many of them virtually crippled their cash flow and working capital position, and sometimes literally starved themselves of the lifeblood of their business and their actual selves in the process. Many meals were skipped and many of their suppliers went hungry, too. Over the years, successive governments and small business lobbying groups have done a good deal to change this, and there are fines and penalties for late payment, but the reality is you can still wait 60, 90 or 120 days to get paid.

If money is coming in too slowly, consider invoice financing. In simple terms, *invoice financing* is a scheme in which someone advances you money, using your unpaid invoices as security for the advance. In effect, you're selling your invoices on to someone who gives you a percentage of the value of the invoice upfront.

The buyer may take ownership of the invoice and responsibility for collecting the money due, a process usually known as *factoring*. As the money the invoice service advances is secured by the invoice, the buyer will check the financial standing of the invoicee before lending and want to know that you have successfully provided goods and services of the kind involved, thus reducing the risk of the invoice being disputed.

Invoice financing is a great way of getting cash due to your business into your hands quickly. You get the cash you need without waiting up to 120 days for money to come in, which eases the strain on your cash flow.

Invoice financing is not a new option. This alternative to traditional bank support has been around for a long while, and many businesses use it or consider using it at some point. Previously, it was hard to get without a trading track record; it was always a long term thing; and it was very expensive, squeezing already tight margins. So, in practical terms, it was difficult for smaller businesses to access, but that's changed now.

Like any financial service, invoice finance comes at a price. If you're planning to use a product like this, shop around, research the costs involved and make sure your margins are high enough to cover the fees. This is particularly important if you're considering an invoice financing arrangement due to unexpected cash flow difficulties rather than as part of your long-term business plan.

Some providers ask you to consider signing a long-term contract, locking you into their fee structure whether you use the facility or not. This practice is dying out, and many providers now offer a flexible facility that can be used for a one-off invoice, or over a longer period of time without high ongoing costs. Do your homework and get the service and product that's right for your business.

Going through the process

If you engage an invoice financier, the process goes something like this:

1. **The financier buys the debt owed to you by a customer the financier has confidence will pay.**

2. **The financier provides 80 per cent or more of the money due to you straight away.**

3. **The financier collects the money owed in one of two ways:**

   • **Factoring agents** collect the full amount directly from your customer.

   • **Invoice discounters** have you collect the money from your customer. (More on this in Chapter 12.)

4. **The invoice financier takes a fee and passes the balance on to you.**

For example, you're owed £80,000 by a reputable customer. You sell the invoice to an invoice financier for £68,000 (85 per cent). The financier collects £80,000 from your customer and pays you the remaining £12,000, minus its fee and interest, when it receives the money.

Use this check to determine whether invoice financing is a good option for you:

- ✔ Are you waiting for payments from reliable customers?
- ✔ Can you accommodate the fees and interest charged by the invoice finance company into your cash flow?
- ✔ Do you want a service that's more flexible than a bank loan?
- ✔ If it takes two to three weeks to set up, is it still helpful?

If your answers are 'yes', invoice financing may be right for your business.

Finding an invoice financier

You can obtain this service from a bank, which usually has a separate invoice finance company, but a bank is usually more expensive and also more restrictive in its terms and conditions than an invoice finance service. The greatest variety and flexibility of prices and deals is to be found elsewhere in the specialist providers' alternative landscape.

A web search may throw up scores of providers – some sector specific, some more supportive towards small businesses and start-ups. Use a comparison site like Funding Options at www.fundingoptions.com, which aggregates and compares information on a wide variety of funders or www.compare invoicefinance.com, which compares offers from banks and specialist invoice finance providers, to make a shortlist. When you're making your choice, check the details of the process, and the flexibility, fees and interest payments involved and compare at least four or five providers before making a decision.

Invoice financing has gone digital. MarketInvoice is the first peer-to-peer business online platform, providing finance specifically against invoices. During its first four years, it loaned more than £40 million. Check it out at www.marketinvoice.com.

Table 14-1 shows some active invoice lenders, how much they provide to whom and how to apply:

Table 14-1	Comparing Select Invoice Financers			
Provider (URL)	**Services**	**Amount**	**Criteria**	**How to Apply**
GapCap (www.gapcap.co.uk)	Selective, or single (versus all your invoices in one year) invoice finance and supply-chain finance	Up to 85% of invoice value with no set upper limit	SME with an *invoice to creditworthy*, or financially robust, business	Online, but you can speak to a team member face-to-face
MarketInvoice (www.marketinvoice.com)	Peer-to-peer lending provider that allows investors to buy your invoices and advance you the cash	Flexible – no upper limit on the amount of the invoice, but the amount of the advance varies	UK or Irish based business trading for at least 6 months with revenue of £100,000 minimum that sells products or services and gets paid on clear terms	Online; upload your invoice to be sold and receive funds within one working day
Platform Black (www.platformblack.com)	Immediate cash advance for each invoice you register to trade via an auction, or on a fixed price, on their platform.	No restrictions if you qualify; you determine the percentage of the invoice you want advanced	Registered UK businesses, trading for a minimum of 2 years; exceptions can be made on a case-by-case basis	Online

Trying Trade Finance

Trade finance is another form of funding that provides working capital for the gaps in the delivery, purchase and sale of goods and services, be they domestic or international transactions. *Trade finance* may involve debt financing for manufacturing or distributing your products, finance to advance you payments based on invoices to your overseas suppliers or finance to help you reassure overseas sellers that you have the funds to pay for products you import. It's finance that's offered by banks as well as specialist trade finance firms, and, like invoice financing, may be offered by some specialist financiers.

Whether it's stretching out payment terms, buying yourself some discounts or boxing clever and getting your customers to fill your coffers before you give over the treasure, you can use the money hidden in your business or tied up with suppliers and customers to fund some growth at any stage of your business.

Equally, if you're in the expansion stage of your business having conquered the UK market and being ready to plant a Union Jack on top of a foreign summit, for example, you may find that export finance products and services such as buyer credit facilities or export working capital funding, which I cover in 'Making use of export support finance' a bit later, are the perfect partner in your quest for world domination.

Or it may be that you have a business that usually requires large, upfront outlays of cash for equipment or facilities, in which case *asset finance solutions,* which take the asset you're purchasing as security for the debt, may be just the ticket. Whether you lease or purchase assets, you can find finance products that ease the strain, and they're becoming more popular with SMEs and more accessible with the advent of online funding platforms.

Using suppliers and customers

Possibly not the first thing that comes to your mind, but suppliers and customers can be useful sources of funding that requires no external input, particularly at the start of your business and during times of significant growth activity. Getting money in upfront – or stretching out payment due dates – adds to your positive cash flow balance and decreases your reliance on external forms of funding, like factoring or short-term loans.

The prices and deals you secure with suppliers are often a major factor in the success of your business and the smooth running of your cash flow. Before setting out to raise funds to cover your working capital costs, it's worth looking into this often overlooked alternative funding source and trying to renegotiate the terms and costs of your existing customer and supplier relationships. Agreeing improved credit terms, discounts and return agreements with both groups can reduce your funding needs.

Reconfiguring your supply chain to reduce the working capital tied up in your business or your need to raise funds is an obvious way to transform the financial challenges you're dealing with. You can try several tacks:

> ✔ **Discuss buying on credit or on better credit terms.** Whenever possible, look to push your payment dates to 90 days or more, lengthening your payment terms and retaining cash to drive growth in your business for longer. If you can do this, it's the equivalent of getting a short-term, interest-free loan without the paperwork.

The longer you work with a supplier, the more likely you are to succeed in getting good terms. If you don't get a better deal or offer, review your supply chain and get quotes from other potential suppliers. Switch to them, or use the fact that you have an alternative as leverage in your discussions.

Your business needs to have a good credit history and rating to pull this off as most suppliers will check these before granting you a longer grace period.

The flipside approach is to offer to pay your suppliers before the usual due date if they'll give you a discount for early payment.

✔ **Buy on consignment or on a sell-or-return basis.** By taking this approach, you don't have to lay out any money up front. You pay when you sell the goods and return any that you don't use. Large department stores often buy from smaller suppliers this way, passing the pressure to the supplier, and keeping more cash to develop their own business.

✔ **Use your customers.** Ask regulars, well-resourced clients and new customers to pay deposits or to pay in advance so the revenues strengthen your cash flow before you produce or sell your goods or services. If you provide a service that's unique or distinctive, or one that satisfies a legal requirement for a client, getting paid upfront isn't too difficult to pull off. If you develop a reputation for being the best at what you do, you can more easily negotiate upfront payments.

Making use of export support finance

You may never need to use funding to help you with exports, but if selling into other countries is part of your growth plan, then you'll come across the government-backed UK Trade and Industry business support programmes (www.gov.uk/government/organisations/uk-trade-investment), which help you with the steps and practicalities of exporting, and UK Export Finance, which helps with finance solutions to the steps in exporting.

Exports are a major priority for the government, so it helps by providing advice, guidance, intelligence and contacts in your target country and offering specialist financial products from UK Export Finance. In effect, this organisation acts as the UK's export credit agency. It helps you to export goods and services by providing a variety of credit facilities, guarantees and insurance policies that take some of the risk out of trading overseas. It can also lend money to your overseas buyers, if they meet lending criteria, which helps your customers to pay you more quickly, which has a welcome effect on your cash flow.

As a UK exporter, you can apply for loans, lines of credit, guarantees and insurance policies in a number of ways from UK Export Finance. Visit its website at www.ukexportfinance.gov.uk and make an appointment with a UK Export Finance Advisor to make sure that you get accurate advice and a full understanding of what's on offer and what the implications are for your business.

UK Export Finance can help with a number of financial solutions, including:

- ✔ Bond insurance policies
- ✔ Buyer credit facilities
- ✔ Debt conversion schemes
- ✔ Direct lending facilities
- ✔ Export working capital schemes
- ✔ Insurance cover
- ✔ Letter of credit guarantee schemes
- ✔ Supplier credit financing facilities

Is export assistance right for you? Answer these questions to find out:

- ✔ Do you have the prospect of significant overseas sales?
- ✔ Is your credit need directly related to export opportunities?
- ✔ Would your deals and revenues be more secure with these arrangements?

If your answer to any of these questions is 'yes', get acquainted with the services of UK Export Finance.

Accessing Asset-Based Finance

Your company may have physical assets that you can use to secure loans to purchase those or other physical assets. This is most likely to be the case if you own plant and machinery, stock or property. *Asset-based finance* is a specialist form of finance that provides term loans and working capital solutions secured by the equipment, machinery, inventory, accounts receivable or premises being financed.

Like other areas of alternative finance, asset-based finance is expanding fast as the risks to lenders are minimal and the impact on the day-to-day operation of a business is small. The cost in terms of interest is also often lower than other forms of funding, so if you have creditworthy assets this may be an opportunity to pursue.

Asset financiers

- ✔ Lend against the physical assets they take a charge against.
- ✔ Provide sums based on the value attributed to the assets.
- ✔ Lift their charge against the asset when repayment is complete.

There was a time when asset-based lending was seen as somewhat of a desperate measure, risking the firm's crown jewels in exchange for cold, hard cash. That's no longer the case as most businesses prefer a leaner, more agile business model, throwing off the shackles of owning expensive goods and assets that can't easily be converted to ready cash, and preferring more liquidity to outright ownership of physical assets. Most reputable asset-based financiers operating in the UK are members of the Asset Based Finance Association at www.abfa.org.uk.

Asset-based financing includes:

- ✔ **Financing possessions:** The funding provider buys the asset on your behalf, and you pay an initial deposit upfront. The remaining balance, plus interest, is then repaid over an agreed period of time. During the time you're paying it off, the financier retains the ownership and title of the asset, and you are, for all intents and purposes, hiring it from her. Once you make your final payment, the ownership passes to you.

- ✔ **Leasing:** A contract is created between your business and the asset provider, making the asset available to your business to use for a set period of time in exchange for an agreed payment. One obvious plus is that you don't have to find all the cash at once to enable you to get the asset – the machine, the van or whatever – and start using it. Secondly, you may be able to get upgrades during the period of the agreement and may be able to buy the asset outright for a nominal amount at the end of the leasing term.

Is asset-based finance right for you?

- ✔ Does your firm own property, a plant, equipment or stock?
- ✔ Is the resale value of the assets in proportion to your funding need?
- ✔ Are you ready for the risk that the loss of these assets would pose to your business?

If your answers are 'yes', asset-based financing may be a way to fund your next steps.

Going Online to Platform Funders

Platforms are online services, used both by financial intermediaries on behalf of their clients and directly by consumers to view and administer their investment portfolios. A business platform therefore allows lenders, investors and entrepreneurs to collaborate and process data and relationships in an efficient and transparent way.

Astonishing developments in technology and the increasingly pervasive aspect of the Internet and smartphones has ushered in an era of unprecedented growth in the online alternative finance industry. Some see platform and app-enabled funding as the industrial revolution of finance, creating a greater awareness of new and exciting finance options, and a surge in business lending and investing, aiming to satisfy the seemingly insatiable finance needs of SMEs for working capital, growth funding, overseas expansion and the financing of business assets.

The Internet certainly provides a common meeting ground for investors and lenders looking for somewhere to invest their money for a good return, and businesses like yours looking for a welcoming online portal that offers an introduction to those who have money and want to part with it.

Online platforms are particularly useful to companies at the smaller end of the SME classification. In the past, small businesses may have been overlooked or excluded by traditional funders, but they now have access to a diverse and plentiful source of appropriately sized funding options.

The platforms are jostling for position, carving out niche markets and coming up with increasingly innovative ways to enable successful transactions. Funding has come a long way from the nerve-racking face-to-face meeting with your local bank manager (or the more shady bail-out transacted down a metaphorical dark alley when a business owner found herself at a funding impasse).

I don't want to give you the impression that platforms have created a veritable free-for-all when it comes to funding. On the contrary, most platforms operate strict controls and criteria, meaning that some businesses are still excluded from raising funds. And, given the debacle leading up to the financial crash of 2008, perhaps that's not such a bad thing. After all, platforms are profit-making businesses, and if they don't protect their assets – their investors, lenders and borrowers or investees – they won't be around for long and they won't make much money.

For most platforms, you need to show a good trading track record, complete with financials and forecasts that put everyone at ease. Many businesses turned down by a traditional lender approach a platform, but many of them get turned down by the platforms for some of the same reasons.

Perhaps not surprisingly, sole traders don't fare as well as more established businesses, and it's entirely possible that some of those excluded from business funding will look to a platform for personal funding – which can then be ploughed into the business. Exact numbers are unavailable right now, but it's apparent that more and more entrepreneurial sole traders are using online platforms to access funding.

Both loan and equity-based crowdfunding platforms are regulated by the FCA (Financial Conduct Authority; www.fca.org), which helps protect investors. Peer-to-peer (P2P) lenders have to adhere to strict guidelines around capital, money and disclosure requirements. Investment-based platforms, both debt and equity, also fall under this umbrella.

The UK excels in platform funding, and recent changes in US law have opened up and widened the pool of potential US investors. You can also find significant European platforms, like the French Wiseed, which is a well-known, active crowdfunding platform along the lines of the UK's Crowdcube, and, as in the UK, this market is set to continue to grow.

Bank versus non-bank finance

Although platforms pose a very real threat to mainstream banking organisations, a number of banks have gone for a collaborative versus a competitive approach, and you can now see Santander Bank and Funding Circle in alliance, and Metro Bank and Zopa tying up on the personal side.

There's a logical and natural referral mechanism at work here. More one-time odd couples may tie the knot and become collaborators rather than competitors as banks continue to refer their rejected or unsuitable business clients to other providers. In 2016, banks will be able to online information portals, such as Funding Options (www.fundingoptions.com), and others of a similar ilk, to make sure that SME customers get the right finance at the right time.

Debt and equity online platforms

Online platforms come in both debt and equity guises, but they're often lumped together and referred to as the peer-to-peer marketplace (P2PL), so make sure that you know what you're looking at when you're shopping around. The chaos of alternative lending has been likened to the Wild West, but I'd say it's now settling down to be a progressive, law-abiding town, where you can grow your business and rest a bit easier at night.

A few types of platforms are:

- **Invoice financing platforms:** Lenders buy your invoices at a discounted price and then sell them back to you for a profit. (Refer to 'Freeing Up Money in Unpaid Invoices' earlier in this chapter.)

- **P2PL platforms:** The principle here is the same as traditional lending in that lenders offer your business money in return for you repaying the capital plus interest – the platform takes the place of the sweaty-palm-inducing meeting with bank managers. (Discover more in the next section, 'Online peer-to-peer platforms'.)

- **Crowdfunding platforms for debt and equity:** For debt, lenders purchase some form of a security, normally a bond, in return for capital and interest repayments. For equity, investors purchase shares in early stage growth businesses, expecting to see business growth in the form of a good return on their capital and healthy dividend pay-outs.

- **Crowdfunding platforms for rewards:** Individuals pledge money in return for some form of product, service or activity reward.

I talk about crowdfunding in the upcoming section, 'Crowdfunding platforms'.

Precise data on usage of funds and the overall impact on the businesses funded isn't readily available at this point, and the available data is open to speculation and interpretation. So, check your sources carefully and weigh the information. This lack of information is especially true for equity-based platforms; it's too early to see if the returns are as good as expected.

Online peer-to-peer platforms

In the last few years, P2PL has become a fast-growing and vital source of finance for new and growing businesses. Many business owners, who had been turned down or given the run-around in the traditional funding markets, turned to their peers to raise funding for expansion, working capital needs and, to a lesser extent, asset purchase. Many used the funds to grow both turnover and profit, and although some businesses may have received funding elsewhere, their owners were game enough to try this new flexible form of funding. Lenders are primarily looking for a better return than they can get elsewhere, so it's a perfect synergy between the two sides of a very valuable coin for the continued growth of the UK economy as a whole.

P2PL portals

- Are intermediaries between lenders and borrowers
- Manage their transactions online

✔ Carry out credit checks and due diligence on applicants

✔ Enable lenders to choose from clients seeking loans

✔ Provide a wider range of cheap unsecured loans than banks

More than £200 million is lent to businesses every 12 months through these lending platforms in the UK, and that figure has been doubling each year. In fact, the recent boom in online P2PL loans has been so successful that high street banks, corporate finance providers, pension funds and even government departments have also become lenders, getting on the platform bandwagon.

Britain is by far the best place in Europe to raise money in this way, with the sector growing at a rapid rate. In fact, the scale of P2PL in Europe is set to grow beyond €7,000 million in 2015 according to the latest research from the University of Cambridge Business School.

From your perspective, one of the main attractions of P2PL loans is that they're usually unsecured. Property or luxury assets are not generally required as collateral for the loan, making it easier for you to apply if you're not asset rich. Despite this lack of security, the sites are regulated – which should be important to you.

Another positive for you is that P2PL portals make lenders compete to secure borrowers, which has the advantage of pushing interest rates down. The interest rate for the loan is determined by lenders competing in a reverse auction, within parameters set by due diligence on your borrower's ability to repay the loan.

Some P2PL portals are well established, while others are new on the financial block. They tend to have lower overheads than traditional banking institutions, so they have fewer costs to pass on to customers. Table 14-2 shows selected P2P platforms, their unique selling point (USP), when they started, where they are and who they loan to and how:

Table 14-2	Select Peer-to-Peer Lenders		
Platform (URL)	*Unique Selling Point*	*Target Borrower*	*Lending Model*
Assetz Capital (www.assetzcapital.co.uk)	Active in matching peers	Business	Auction
Funding Circle (www.fundingcircle.com)	Government backed as well as individual lenders	Business	Auction
Funding Knight (www.fundingknight.com)	Flexibility on funding options	Business	Auction

(continued)

Table 14-2 *(continued)*

Platform (URL)	Unique Selling Point	Target Borrower	Lending Model
Market Invoice (www.marketinvoice.com)	Funds often advanced within 24 hours	Business	Auction
Ratesetter (www.ratesetter.com)	Customers set their own rates	Individuals	Market
Thin Cats (www.thincats.com)	Businesses vetted by sponsors	Business	Auction

Faster, easy to use, transparent transactions and, sometimes, better terms mean that these online lending platforms are fast becoming the first choice of small businesses looking to secure credit. As Stuart Law, chief executive of Assetz Capital, told the Financial Times in June 2015, 'In terms of business lending, you ain't seen nothing yet'.

Many lending platforms are members of the Peer2Peer Finance Association, which profiles their variety at www.p2pfa.info/p2pfa-members. You can also find a useful comparison page at www.p2pmoney.co.uk/companies.htm.

Is a P2PL right for you? Ask yourself whether you want a loan that's

- ✔ Fast and easy to secure
- ✔ Cheaper and more flexible than a bank loan
- ✔ Managed online
- ✔ Available in a month

Last in the alphabet, first of P2P lenders: Zopa

Zopa, the very first P2P consumer lending company, has been running for over a decade. During that time it has delivered loans with a total value of more than £500 million. It's the largest player in the booming new marketplace for loans.

Funding Circle has been around since 2010 and it has developed a strong reputation for delivering loans to small businesses. Other portals that have proven their worth include Ratesetter and

Lending Works, and the P2P invoice finance platform MarketInvoice. The UK currently has 16 P2P platforms for business loans in the UK, with the total set to carry on rising.

Since 2012, the UK government (in the form of the British Business Bank) has been making public money available to small businesses in the form of loans through Funding Circle, so you have plenty of people enabling and willing this industry on.

If your answers are mostly 'yes' – and why wouldn't they be? – then P2PL is probably worth checking out.

Crowdfunding platforms

Keeping it simple, *crowdfunding* is a means of raising finance by harnessing the power and the funds of a large number of people who each put in a small amount of money in return for some kind of reward – either a financial stake in your business (equity) or some form of product or service. Most investors are looking for a strong return on their money, and most businesses are looking for seed capital or working capital as well as contacts and networks to tap into.

Crowdfunding isn't a new funding phenomenon. In fact, it has a long and varied history, appearing in different guises throughout time, but with the advent of modern technology, it's never been as popular and accessible as it is now. This format really took root in 2012–13, with significant uptake since its formation.

Crowdfunding typically follows one of the following formats:

- **Crowdsourcing:** Using the reward-based method of raising funds (refer to Chapter 9 for more on this), businesses offer incentives in kind, discounts and restricted offers from their business instead of equity shares.

- **Debt-based crowdfunding:** Peer-to-peer platforms assess and score applicants seeking debt, and provide information to potential lenders who buy a debt security in return for interest and capital repayments. (Refer to Chapter 12 for more on peer-to-peer funding options.)

- **Equity-based crowdfunding:** Popular with early-stage businesses, but also for the more established business, an investment is made in return for a share in your business. (I explain this type in Chapter 13.)

- **Property crowdfunding:** This involves people buying shares in a property. It's sometimes, but not often, used in business.

For your early-stage business, crowdfunding may be the answer to your prayers. For example, if your drinks business needs money and some more thirsty customers, crowdfunding can help you kill two birds with one stone; if you're a theatrical impresario in need of cash for your latest film or play, giving someone a ticket to help you write your meal ticket may be just the ticket for your venture. For your more established business that needs to attract a different market, raising awareness as well as income through crowdfunding can offer a solution.

People, and increasingly institutions, pool their money to get behind an idea or a business venture and invest. You may get the support of 10 people or 3,000 people, which offers a boost to your marketing efforts, and you find different sites for different types of crowdfunding. Crowdfunding attracts members of the public as well as angels and investor networks, further blurring the lines when it comes to equity investing in particular.

Crowdfunding is hugely transformational in the world of business funding because it reduces the cost of a transaction and gives people access to funding opportunities that weren't there before.

Crowdfunding is a good place to channel anyone in your circle of friends and family who want to invest, particularly as you need to bring some of the crowd to get the momentum going.

As you consider equity crowdfunding, keep in mind how the process generally works:

1. **After you identify the best platform for your business, go online and upload some information on your business, following the guidance and prompts on the site.**

2. **Your proposal is reviewed to see if you meet the criteria and can go forward.**

3. **Based on feedback from the platform, you do further work on your funding application content.**

   You submit information, including financials and a pitch deck, to the site where it will be checked and due diligence carried out.

4. **You upload your pitch video, customer testimonials and other relevant – or required – materials and are given a specific amount of time in which to raise a specific amount of money.**

   Your marketing and public relations, or PR, machine kicks into action! Both you and the site launch into a comprehensive PR, social media, event- and direct-marketing campaign aimed at attracting investors to your offer. (Check Chapter 6 for information on producing your pitch video.)

5. **You track your progress on the site, monitor what works and what doesn't and watch the funds go up and the clock tick down.**

6. **Hopefully, you're successful and you raise the specified amount – or more – in the given time frame.**

   The money goes into a separate account for safekeeping.

Many crowdfunding sites are conducted on an *all or nothing basis,* meaning that you have to raise your full amount or return, as in not keep, the amount you raised.

Fees are charged, and they vary in percentage points as well as stages. You may have upfront fees, a percentage of the money raised, and a future percentage linked to the rising share value over time.

A few housekeeping pointers to help you navigate crowdfunding sites – they

- ✔ Ask you to prepare video appeals, incentivised offers and background information.

- ✔ Require you to build a PR campaign to drive potential donors or investors to your offer.

- ✔ Usually take a percentage of the sum raised.

- ✔ Sometimes require you to raise all your target amount and to forfeit funds if you don't raise the full target amount.

Table 14-3 lists some crowdfunding sites good for early-stage business projects.

Table 14-3	Select Crowdfunders			
Platform (URL)	*Date Established*	*Fees to Company*	*Criteria*	*How It Works*
CrowdBnk (www.crowdbnk.com)	Summer 2013	Success fee of 5% of funds raised; 2–3% of funds raised through card transactions; 1% of funds raised as legal fees, capped at £10,000	Dependent on unique selling point, proof of concept, scalability, team, network, tax status, funding amount	Projects listed for up to 90 days
Crowdcube (www.crowdcube.com)	Feb 2011	When you reach target, success fee of 6.5%; administration fee of £1,250; corporate services fee of £1,250	Registered UK company; residents over the age of 18; have business plan and financial forecasts to upload	Submit and instantly publish pitches online with 30 days to reach funding target
Seedrs (www.seedrs.com)	July 2012	7.5% of funds raised	EU residents over the age of 18; process subject to UK law; funding up to £150,000	You create a campaign to run over 60 days; Seedrs promotes it

(continued)

Table 14-3 *(continued)*

Platform (URL)	Date Established	Fees to Company	Criteria	How It Works
Syndicate Room (www.syndicateroom.com)	Sept 2013	Flat fee on all funds raised through the platform, which includes set up of administration and nominee structure; a one-off legal and compliance fee	Minimum equity funding of £150,000; 25% of equity sought already committed to site	Pitch online with consultation of an existing lead investor
VentureFounders (www.startupcrowdfunding.com/platforms/venturefounders)	Aug 2013	6% on funds raised; 3% mentoring fee for 3 years of support plus fixed-sum one-off legal fee	Subjective selection criteria applied to UK businesses seeking to raise £150,000 – £2 million	In-person meeting followed by interactive Q&A with investors throughout a 90-day campaign

You can find a complete list of crowdfunding sites in a directory that's produced by Nesta, at www.nesta.org.uk/crowdfunding. and also at the UK Crowdfunding Association website at www.ukcfa.org.uk.

Is crowdfunding right for you? Answer these questions to find out:

✔ Would customers pay in advance for your product or service?

✔ Can you offer incentives?

✔ Do you have good communication skills for video or presentations?

✔ Can you drive people towards your offer through marketing and partnership activity?

✔ Does the three months or more that this requires fit in with your plans?

If your answers are 'yes', crowdfunding donations may be a way for you to fund a new product or service.

Reward-based crowdfunding

The best and cheapest money comes from your customers. Thousands of businesses each year make incentivised offers on crowdfunding sites. You can offer goods and services and special deals in return for contributions. It's an increasingly popular way to raise small sums of working capital for your new businesses or to develop new products for your going concern.

Gyms use donation sites to offer reduced-cost memberships to fundraise for new equipment. Product developers offer discounts on advance orders. Musicians raise cash for equipment by offering free tickets and a chance to meet the band. You essentially get your customers to help with your funding campaign.

For service businesses, consulting companies, and small manufacturers and creative companies, this is a particularly useful way to secure funds during the start-up phase because it involves low outgoings and payments before work commences, and the campaign helps to build a customer base.

Equity-based crowdfunding

Some crowdfunding sites help you to raise funds in exchange for equity. I talk about this format in Chapter 13. Investors put their money into your business in exchange for receiving a share in it, and you open up your market to a new audience, as well as hopefully receiving a fresh injection of contacts and some guidance from your new investors.

According to Nesta's 2014 Understanding Alternative Finance report, it takes, on average, 125 investors to fund an equity deal. I personally know clients who wound up with 486 investors, which has an impact on your next round of funding, for better or for worse. If your next round is early-stage venture capital, for example, be aware that venture capitalists (VCs) may not want to deal with the aftermath of a crowdfunding campaign, cleaning up or clearing out those hundreds of people. Do your homework before you post your campaign.

Some platforms use a *special purpose vehicle,* which is a separate legal entity formed to house all the shareholdings with one single representative, for aggregating investors. Seedrs is one example.

As with reward-based sites, you'll be expected to produce a pitch video and to mount a fairly aggressive public relations or PR campaign, so take into consideration the amount of time, money and effort this involves.

Looking at Differences in Digital Funding

In 2014, the Financial Conduct Authority (FCA) defined its stance for 'lend to save' (also known as P2P lenders), putting strict systems in place to protect all parties. The online equity-based crowdfunders also fall under the FCA's guidelines, helping to protect consumers using such platforms. FCA guidelines also protect some of the digital lending platforms that don't ask for security, are funding aggregators – so not direct lenders – or that are lenders them-selves and fall under FCA rules.

Considering the risks

As with any platform, it pays to do your homework and know what the busi-ness model is, who you're actually borrowing the money from, what the pen-alties for late payment are and what the real cost of the money is.

You have no guarantee that your business will get approval to receive fund-ing, so it's best not to be too cocky and to think that it's a done deal, espe-cially if you're going for a lower amount (say £50,000), which may be done entirely on the platform and not require any human interaction, and so pro-vide no opportunity for you to plead your case.

If you have tight time frames and are relying on this money, you may want to consider seeking advice from a professional who helps in the preparation of these online applications, helping you to get it right the first time.

Loan funding agreements, be they large or small, all have some things in common, and one is small print. Be sure you read it so you know what you're signing. What happens if you default on the loan? What are you promising? What's the repayment schedule? What happens to the debt if you leave the business or you exit the business in a trade sale? Ask all the same things you'd ask if you went into a bank to get a loan. You can easily forget to find out basic information if you're doing an online application.

Living with the higher costs

In exchange for a potentially ten-minute decision on your loan, you may be paying a higher percentage of interest than you'd have to elsewhere. You may be making repayments every day, or every week or every month.

It's very easy to ignore these important things when you're desperate for the money.

Once you have the money, assuming you're lucky enough to get it, keep in mind what you borrowed it for in the first place. You had a need and a gap, so don't go spending it frivolously or all at once, and make any necessary changes in your business to strengthen your financial position. If you blow it all at once, you still need to pay it back – your liability doesn't go away overnight.

Table 14-4 shows some major players in the digital lending field, the services they provide, how much money they offer and the requirements they demand.

Table 14-4	Key Unsecured Digital Lenders		
Provider (URL)	_Services_	_Amount_	_Criteria_
Boost Capital (www. boostcapital. co.uk)	Small business loan programme for business owners predominantly in the service indus-try; funds received within 5 days	£3,000 to £500,000	Trading for at least 9 months; Positive daily bank balance; Acceptable credit; No excessive tax liens, open judgements or bankruptcies
Ezbob (www. ezbob.com)	Financing through a web portal for small to medium businesses in as little as 10 minutes	Up to £120,000	Over 18-years-old; UK-registered com-pany; Valid business debit card; Application submitted by director/ owner/partner; Minimum annual turnover of £10,000; 12 months registered as a UK business
Funding Circle (www. fundingcircle. com)	Government-backed lending alongside thou-sands of private individuals and institutions within about a week	£5,000 to £1 million	Annual turnover of at least £50,000; At least 2 years of filed accounts; For limited companies, non-limited companies, LLPs, sole traders or partnerships

(continued)

Table 14-4 *(continued)*

Provider (URL)	Services	Amount	Criteria
Funding Knight (www.funding knight.com)	Matches investors and selected British businesses via an online platform, alongside thousands of private individuals and institutions	£25,000 to £1 million	Trading for 2 years with at least 1 year of filed accounts including P&L and balance sheet; 12-month cash-flow forecast; Schedule of all other loans; Copies of last 3 bank statements; Statements of assets & liabilities
TradeRiver Finance (www.trade riverfinance. com)	Releasing working capital to businesses	Typical limit of £100,000	Business registered in UK; At least two years trading history; Creditworthy; Revenue exceeds £500,000
UKBond Network (www.ukbond network.com)	Delivering bespoke financing options over a term of between 1 and 3 years via a unique bond auction platform	£0.5 million to £4 million	No minimum trading period; No minimum asset cover; No minimum revenues; Security preferred but personal guarantees not necessary; Issuers can be private as well as listed companies

Considering Bonds

In recent years, the SME marketplace has seen increasing activity in the area of bonds. Although not mainstream in terms of volume, a *bond* is a form of loan in which investors agree to lend a certain sum to a business for a fixed period of time, specifying a fixed annual return. The return is analogous to interest, and is known as the *coupon*. At the end of the fixed period, bond holders expect repayment of the initial amount they put up. It's like a complicated IOU in some ways. It can be a great way to raise funds for your high-growth business if you're reasonably sure you can deliver on your aggressive growth forecasts.

Well-established businesses with strong growth prospects have the opportunity to raise funds for expansion through this route. Medium-size businesses increasingly find that bonds offer the opportunity to raise affordable funds for long-term growth an attractive prospect. For example, businesses such as the restaurant chain Leon and the green energy company Ecotricity funded their expansion with bonds.

Large bonds with a value of many millions of pounds are issued by large institutional investors. Small businesses can secure retail bonds from £1,000 to many hundreds of thousands of pounds from individual investors, savers and fund managers. Bonds can also be self-issued. You issue the bonds and offer them for sale to individuals, customers or the community, sometimes using platforms. Self-issue bonds are driven by you.

Funding with bonds sometimes resembles crowdfunding, and it can be used in crowdfunding campaigns. Crowdcube issues non-saleable mini bonds, for example, and Hotel Chocolat used this route to approach the members of its Tasting Club, offering £2,000 and £4,000 bonds, with the coupon or dividend paid as chocolate.

Bond financiers

✔ Assess your growth prospects and ability to repay

✔ Lend against an agreement specifying coupon/dividend payments and a redemption date

✔ Can sell on their bond to others

Is bond finance right for you? If your answers are 'yes' to the following questions, bond financing may be a suitable way to fund your next steps:

✔ Is your business set for predictable strong growth based on this funding?

✔ Are you in a market and of a scale that would interest bond financiers of scale?

✔ Is a bond a better option for you or your potential backers than equity?

Action planning for alternative finance

If you're going for online P2P, it may take a month to get your funds, so you need to become your own project manager and do the following tasks:

- ✔ Audit providers and select the best.
- ✔ Prepare the financial and business information required.
- ✔ Submit the opportunity online.

Receiving crowdfunding donations can take three months or more. You need to take care of the following before you make your appeal:

- ✔ Identify and price incentive offers that you can afford.
- ✔ Prepare a phased marketing campaign that will drive large numbers towards these offers.
- ✔ Prepare your case, video and presentation materials for the platform.
- ✔ Have some donors on standby ready to make the donations on day one and at later points, giving the appeal momentum.
- ✔ Make your appeal online.

It can take a month to arrange for invoice financing. Preparation steps include:

- ✔ Audit providers and select the best.
- ✔ Identify the customer(s) whose invoice(s) qualify.
- ✔ Prepare the financial and business information required.

Asset-based funds can take a month or more to come in. Before you start, do the following:

- ✔ Estimate the current resale value of each physical asset.
- ✔ Audit providers and select the best.
- ✔ Prepare the financial and business information required.
- ✔ Negotiate agreements.

Bond funding may take five months or more; to prepare, you should:

- ✔ Investigate the market of potential buyers.
- ✔ Draft the financial parameters, coupon payment and value of the bond you're seeking.
- ✔ Obtain specialist help.
- ✔ Prepare the bond issue campaign.

Export support can take a few months to get to your coffers and requires you to:

- ✔ Review the products available through UK Export Finance.
- ✔ Meet with an adviser.
- ✔ Select the products and services you're eligible for and that you require.
- ✔ Identify the usual lead-in times required to secure them.
- ✔ Discuss the supporting business and financial information required in each case.
- ✔ Produce the evidence required.

If you're able to renegotiate terms with your suppliers and customers, it can take two to three months to have an impact on your cash flow. To prepare, do the following:

- ✔ Model the impact of the desired changes on your cash flow.
- ✔ Review your supply chain and identify other potential suppliers.
- ✔ Secure new quotes from existing and potential suppliers.
- ✔ Close the deal on a new supplier cost profile.
- ✔ Review your customer base and pricing schedules.
- ✔ Introduce targeted pricing changes.

Part IV
Going for Growth

Business Name
Business Address
Suburb
Template from www.BusinessTemplates.biz

Profit & Loss Statement

for the period 1 January 2009 to 31 December 2009		
Income		
Sales	$120,200.00	
Services	$55,000.00	
Other Income	$2,520.00	
Total Income		$177,720.00
Expenses		
Accounting	$2,500.00	
Advertising	$7,500.00	
Assets-Small	$100.00	
Bank Charges	$962.40	
Depreciation	$2,385.00	
Electricity	$2,994.90	
Hire of Equipment	$4,200.00	
Insurance	$1,221.00	
Interest	$2,401.66	
Motor Vehicle	$1,203.50	
Office Supplies	$962.11	
Postage & Printing	$725.00	
Rent	$15,610.00	
Repairs & Maintenance	$1,082.00	
Stationery	$660.00	
Subscriptions	$3,690.00	
Telephone	$2,165.00	
Training/Seminars	$2,200.00	
Wages & Oncosts	$65,000.00	
Total Expenses		$117,562.57

Visit www.dummies.com/extras/businessfundinguk to learn more about the pros and cons of exiting with a trade sale.

In this part . . .

- ✔ Get a handle on how to measure growth performance and become a lean, mean, investment-friendly business machine.

- ✔ Understand how using external expertise can help your business grow.

- ✔ Investigate the obvious and not-so-obvious strategies for growth.

Chapter 15

Measuring Performance

· ·

In This Chapter

▶ Checking key performance indicators (KPIs)

▶ Using your financial data to measure performance

▶ Keeping an eye on risk

▶ Using your reputation and position in the market

· ·

I'm not certain that all business pundits would agree on the identity of the genius who spoke the often-quoted words, 'What gets measured gets managed', but it's usually attributed to the world-famous business guru, Peter Drucker. It's also usually only quoted in part, and, as Simon Caulkin of *The Observer* points out, that misquote is often a dangerous thing, as it can lead to measuring for the wrong motives or reasons.

The full quote is: 'What gets measured gets managed – even when it's pointless to measure and manage it, and even if it harms the purpose of the organisation to do so'. Heed the warning when it comes to measuring the performance of your business because what you measure is what you pay attention to and what drives behaviour in your organisation.

Everyone on your team needs to be singing from the same hymn sheet, and you need all team behaviour to be in line with the vision and goals of the organisation. If everyone's at odds, you end up with an unhelpful situation with different weights and priorities being given to different measures and a lack of cohesion within your organisation.

When you look at measuring performance – regularly reviewing all areas of your business against a set of measurable performance indicators – you need to make adjustments and revisions as you go along to be sure that what you're measuring provides a meaningful barometer for your business. You need to know how your business stacks up in today's dynamic business environment, as your goal and ambitions are put to the test by your customers, your peers, your competitors and the economic environment. Regular reviews, and measuring what matters, help to give you the edge.

Ask yourself where your business is now, where it's meant to be going, and how you're going to get it there, then start to break down the things that matter – and that you can measure – in the key areas of finance, operations, marketing, human resources and technology.

You can be sure that potential funders will be looking at your business to see if you have processes and procedures in place for measuring key performance indicators. They want to know that their money won't go into a black hole with no system of checks and balances for the amounts and uses you ultimately choose.

They also want to know that all areas of the business are being monitored and measured in a transparent and easily understood manner, to ensure the money's being put to good use and for a good return and that you're compliant where necessary – meeting health and safety or financial safeguards, for example – and recording your company's decisions in a form that can be verified at some future point, if need be.

Like yourself, funders are also looking at your business now, and at its future potential, and they want to be sure you have a good idea of how you'll get from A to B and how to fine-tune the steps on that journey along the way.

Keeping Up with Key Performance Indicators (KPIs)

Before looking at the individual business areas that can be measured when assessing performance, step back and take a broader view of what needs to be measured and monitored. You can then use this broad view to set up key performance indictors that you can link to your measurements.

Key performance indictors, or *KPIs,* are tools that your organisation uses to define, measure and monitor performance over a defined period of time. They're designed to help you achieve the overall strategic and operational goals of your business. As such, they're pivotal to the success of your organisation – they provide a target to aim for, allowing you to measure how much above or below target you actually are.

As with any journey, if you don't know your desired destination, you waste a lot of time, take winding roads that lead nowhere, arrive later than you planned and you may even arrive at a completely different destination than you'd intended. Your KPIs set out a road map with measured milestones that help you get to an agreed destination.

Choosing what to measure

To get started, you need to decide what to measure, how frequently to measure it and what processes work best to get an accurate indication of how your business is performing.

Small-and medium-sized enterprises (SMEs) come in all shapes and sizes, and the things that matter to each of them may vary, but some indicators or measurements apply to all businesses and these need to be defined and agreed at the outset.

No matter what industry or stage of business you're in, you need to focus on the key drivers that matter to your business and can give you an indication of overall success when you add all the parts together to make a whole.

Measure the drivers relevant to your individual circumstances and business objectives. Review your own business drivers and come up with a customised list of performance measures unique to your business. Some common drivers are:

- Billing hours (the number of hours spent on work that you can bill a client for versus administration)
- Call handling times
- Customer service levels
- Man hours on a fixed price contract
- PR (public relations) column inches
- Production cost per unit of items that you sell
- Profitability ratios
- Sales figures
- Staff turnover

You may want to look at manufacturing time, resources needed, number of clients developed and fees. There's no right or wrong or better or worse. What matters is that you measure what actually enables you to improve the performance of your business, because that's what matters to funders.

Your KPIs need to meet a number of key criteria:

- **Be linked as closely as possible to the overall goals and ambitions for your business:** Make your goals challenging but achievable, and be specific so that they're easier to measure. For example, increasing market share is a laudable goal, but hard to achieve in any meaningful way if you don't assign a percentage to it.

- **Cover areas of performance in your business that you're able to influence and control:** If you're in a highly regulated business, there's no point in measuring anything that's already being monitored, apart from maybe the cost of compliance, because you can't change it.

- **Be measured with an easily understood metric or scorecard so that everyone agrees on the value of what you're measuring:** If it's around technology, for example, be able to measure research and development spending, or the time it takes to develop a new product before it starts generating income.

- **Use an agreed-upon method for collecting and analysing the data you collect:** You need to be able to quantify the assessment of your performance in a simple numbers and standard rating system, eliminating as much of the subjective element as possible. Everyone sees things differently and you can't get a critical mass indicator if you have lots of different criteria and opinions.

Have no more than three or four KPIs per area of your business. If you have too many KPIs, the measurements become unwieldy and you can get lost in the statistics.

Measuring with SMART targets

The targets you aim for and measure with KPIs need to be SMART – specific, measurable, achievable, realistic and time-bound.

Using KPIs ensures that your targets meet the first two criteria, as all KPIs should by definition be specific and measurable.

Make sure that your goals are:

- **Specific:** Don't leave your goals open-ended or fluffy. Attribute specific numbers, dates and so on in order to make sure they're crystal clear. For example, 'Increase sales' is too unfocused. 'Increase sales by 20 per cent by year-end' is clearer, and also measurable.

- **Measurable:** Set a benchmark and then decide exactly how much higher you intend to aim.

- **Achievable:** Ambitious targets motivate and inspire your employees, but they have to be realistic or they become quite the opposite, and you risk demotivating your team. Look at your recent performance to get a sense of what's feasible.

- **Realistic:** Setting realistic targets means being fair on the people who have to reach them. Make sure that you only ask for performance improvements in areas that your staff can actually influence.

- **Time-bound:** Progress towards a goal is more rapid if employees have a clear sense of the deadlines against which their progress will be assessed.

Creating a KPI dashboard

Putting your KPIs together in an easily understood document is known as creating a *management dashboard*. Typically, this is done in a software package that enables you to integrate data from all parts of your business, and perhaps from individual managers' reports, and interpret it before putting it into useful reports, spreadsheets, graphic representations and so on. This software enables you to have an overview of individual areas of performance, and individual employee performance, as well as the collective whole, and to share this information in a format that is easy to use and easy to understand. As with a car or a plane dashboard, this arrangement enables you to get an overview of all the key indicators at any given time, and to respond when you see an indicator (cash!) plummeting on the dashboard. You are the pilot in control of steering your craft to a successful landing.

In addition to measuring the things that matter to your own business, standard performance measures apply to all businesses and need to be included in your KPI dashboard. These include:

- ✔ Financial performance measures, such as your ability to pay your company debts over time, how much working capital you have readily available to meet daily needs, how quickly your invoices get paid and how slowly you pay your suppliers, as well as how well each pound invested generates a return for investors in your business.

- ✔ Quality standards, such as national and international kitemarks or certifications, like ISO 9000 quality management systems.

- ✔ Customer-centric measures, such as customer retention figures, the lifetime value of a customer relationship and customer acquisition rates.

- ✔ Employee or staff-focused measures, such as how often staff leave and need to be replaced and how much it costs to hire and train new employees in relation to how long it takes them to become productive and add value to your company bottom line.

- ✔ Competitor measures, such as trade reports, Internet rankings, annual reports, business publications and websites. These help you to benchmark your business against others in your industry by comparing your KPIs like-for-like against your competition.

Some argue that profitability is the main measure of the performance of your business, but although this indicator is extremely important, it's one of many that work in combination and allow your business to trade profitably while continuing to grow. Success across a number of key measures helps to cement your position in the market from the perspective of your peers, your employees and the funding community.

Working together, these indicators also provide you with an ongoing, real-time early-warning system in case a dip in your performance goes unnoticed until you run your annual reports, by which time it can be more difficult to recover from potential danger.

Understanding why you measure performance

The real purpose of measuring your company performance is to drive improvements in future performance and make sure you're not damaging the company as you grow.

You want your company performance to ensure that your business provides a good return for investors and offers an attractive proposition to the wider market if you decide to go public, or to your next-round investor.

Measuring your KPIs helps you do this in two ways:

- ✔ **KPIs help you spot a potential problem a mile away and head it off at the pass.** This shows prudent management skills on your part and is a powerful tool when it comes to showing investors or the market the level of maturity in your business and your team.

  The converse to this indicator is that it helps you also spot an opportunity off in the distance, which gives you a head start on your competitors, can potentially increase your market share and revenues and, again, makes you a more attractive investment as a growth business.

- ✔ **Measuring your KPIs helps to make your employees more productive, more focused and more aligned with your strategic goals.** This inevitably improves your profitability and helps you to look strong in your market.

Assigning responsibility and resources

After you identify the targets you believe will deliver the strategic growth you're aiming for, assign clear responsibility for who's delivering on each of them.

It's fine for your top-level strategic objectives to be abstract and business-wide, but your KPIs need to be concrete and clearly owned by a department or individual.

Hitting your targets is unlikely to be a cost-free process, so be ready to make the necessary resources available when needed. Also, undertake regular reviews to keep momentum and motivation levels up, and to make changes if the progress made isn't as expected.

Using Your Financials

Your financials form an important part of your road map to success, and are particularly important for your growing business, as they guide you and remind you of what's important. They alert you to incoming danger and help you find a solution to head it off at the pass. They challenge your assumptions and your thinking. They help you measure your success – or lack of it. They let you know if your strategy, implementation and execution are all aligned and contributing to the bottom line.

After you get funding, you may banish your financial documents to the bottom drawer of a filing cabinet, locking them safely away where they're destined never to see the light of day – until your next funding round is upon you. Now, you can tell from my tone that this bottom-drawer syndrome is nothing new, and it's by no means unique to you. But take my advice to break with SME tradition and regularly update your financials.

It's much easier to manage for growth if you really understand and drill down into the detail of your financials. Use them to see what's working financially for your business, where you may be able to fund expansion and where something may require extra attention.

Your financials are extremely important to your investors or funders because they provide the numbers to assess your profitability, growth and shareholder value. Be prepared to stand by them, to defend them and to produce updates in a timely manner and on a regular basis.

When measuring financial performance, most growing businesses focus on profitability, but consider the importance of cash flow with regard to daily survival and growing income as an indication of growing market share and an improving return on capital employed in the business. In fact, it's good practice to keep a close watch on all financial indicators in your business so that you don't miss lurking dangers.

Get a handle on how to measure your financial performance using commonly accepted and universally understood ratios and calculations, some of which I explore in this chapter. You can also find much more information in *Understanding Business Accounting For Dummies* by Colin Barrow and John A. Tracy (Wiley).

Monitor your KPIs and analyse them on a regular basis. This provides you with the information you need to monitor cash flow, profitable sales and overheads.

Updating your profit and loss to measure performance

Profit and loss statements (P&Ls) that show your business income, expenses and what's leftover are necessary and integral elements of any business plan, along with your cash flow forecast and balance sheet. They forecast key information that investors look for and represent a reference point against actual data, which you can update as it emerges.

By making you focus on forecasting and documenting your expected revenues and costs, the process of creating a P&L enables you to produce a report detailing the likely trading performance for the year ahead, which is critical information for funders. Investors want to see that you're hitting your income targets and that your business has healthy margins. A P&L also gives you data that you can use to create comparisons with as you get additional actual figures to update, so you can take quick action to remedy a problem situation or head it off at the pass.

If you're an established business, P&L data is easier to arrive at as you can use past performance data as a reference point. If you're just starting out and lack a trading history, the process is a bit more difficult, but also makes it more valuable to you and to your funders, as you both need some references to know whether your new business is on track.

Some of the key performance indicators from your P&Ls – and any business's P&Ls – include:

- ✔ **Gross profit margin:** How much money you made after subtracting the direct costs of sales.

- ✔ **Net profit margin:** A narrow measure of profits that takes all costs, not just direct ones, into account. All overheads, as well as interest and tax payments, are included in this profit calculation.

- ✔ **Operating margin:** This sits between the gross and net profit margin. Overheads are taken into account, but interest and tax payments are not. For this reason, it is also known as the EBIT (earnings before interest and taxes) margin.

- ✔ **Return on capital employed:** This calculates your net profit as a percentage of the total capital employed in a business. This allows you to see how well the money invested in your business is performing.

Figure 15-1 shows what a good P&L looks like.

Business Name
Business Address
Suburb
Template from www.BusinessTemplates.biz

Profit & Loss Statement

for the period 1 January 2009 to 31 December 2009		
Income		
Sales	$120,200.00	
Services	$55,000.00	
Other Income	$2,520.00	
Total Income		$177,720.00
Expenses		
Accounting	$2,500.00	
Advertising	$7,500.00	
Assets-Small	$100.00	
Bank Charges	$962.40	
Depreciation	$2,385.00	
Electricity	$2,994.90	
Hire of Equipment	$4,200.00	
Insurance	$1,221.00	
Interest	$2,401.66	
Motor Vehicle	$1,203.50	
Office Supplies	$962.11	
Postage & Printing	$725.00	
Rent	$15,610.00	
Repairs & Maintenance	$1,082.00	
Stationery	$660.00	
Subscriptions	$3,690.00	
Telephone	$2,165.00	
Training/Seminars	$2,200.00	
Wages & Oncosts	$65,000.00	
Total Expenses		$117,562.57

Figure 15-1:
A sample
P&L.

Keeping your cash flow current

Notice the word 'flow' in the title: The essence of your *cash flow* forecast is to chart, monitor and plan the flow of cash in and out of your business. If updated regularly and correctly, it's a fantastic tool for measuring the ongoing performance of your business.

Some of the KPIs you can measure with regard to cash flow are:

- **Credit control:** Be strict about adhering to your payment terms, so you don't end up giving your clients a free loan and putting your own business in jeopardy. If payment terms are 30 days, that doesn't mean 60, 90 or 120 days.

  Find the balance between being firm about collecting your money on time and damaging your commercial relationships. Initiate strict payment terms from day one with any new clients.

- **Credit terms:** Be very strict about the terms you offer to customers, choosing payment terms that they can adhere to, and that are good for you. For example, 30 days payment is clear, and it gives them one month to pay, and you one month to wait. Also try to get paid before you deliver by using a *pro forma invoice,* which is an estimate of what the goods or services can cost, and is paid before the product or service is seen, with any necessary price reconciliation done later on.

  Of course, you want the exact opposite where you're concerned, and you want to maximise your credit terms, making your cash flow work better for you.

- **Invoicing:** This may sound very obvious, but I'm always amazed at businesses that invoice one day per month. Why wait? Spread it throughout the month; this staggers your incoming payments too.

- **Tax and value-added tax (VAT):** Use your cash flow documents to forecast tax and VAT payments, and hive off a certain amount each month into a separate bank account so you don't get caught short.

Used properly, a cash flow document lets you – and your funders see ahead so that you can be proactive and plan, instead of reactive and scrambling around in the dark to find a way forward.

Keeping enough cash in the business is crucial to giving you the breathing space to run your growing business, so your cash flow document is one of the most useful tools in your financial toolbox for predicting when you may run into trouble. It gives you a warning signal and acts as a trigger to take offensive action.

Knowing your month-on-month financial position is not only good financial management, but it also enables you to make sure that you have enough money to cover your monthly outgoings; to be able to amend or manipulate credit terms; to apply ahead of time for an overdraft facility; and to avoid nasty tax or VAT surprises.

Cash flow figures are especially useful when raising funds, but are equally valuable as a warning sign when you're heading for a negative cash position. In some instances, cash flow can give you an indication of some of the ways out of an impending hole.

Expansion or significant growth levels can eat up cash faster than your profit is able to replace it, and if you're on a high-growth, high-return trajectory, you have a good chance of burning through cash at an alarming rate. Investors can see and understand this and look to you to manage and control it; lenders will panic and look to you to get it under control so that they can get their money back.

Financial documents are like interlocking parts of a very serious puzzle. They're all connected to each other and need to be seen together, not in isolation, to give you a realistic view of what you're tracking and measuring.

Picturing the present with your balance sheet

A *balance sheet* is a financial statement that represents a snapshot of your business's financial position on one day in time. It gives a funder an idea of:

- ✔ How solvent your business is by showing your current assets and current liabilities. Your balance sheet gives an indication of your company's efficient running by illustrating its ability to pay its current liabilities, like debt and accounts payable, using current assets, such as cash in the bank, inventory or accounts receivable.

- ✔ How liquid your assets are. This shows how much of your assets are in the form of cash or assets that can be easily converted to cash, like stocks and shares, and how much is tied up in inventory or equipment that takes longer to turn into cash

- ✔ How your business is being financed – with debt or equity investments from shareholders.

- ✔ How much capital is being used to get a good return. This looks at capital invested by shareholders, the value of any fixed assets, cash at hand or in the bank, current accounts receivable and current inventory you hold, minus current liabilities to illustrate how your business uses long-term and current assets over a specific period of time in order to generate a good return. Investors are keen to get a sense of what kind of return their capital might make if they invest.

A balance sheet lists a business's assets from most to least liquid and its liabilities, including debts, mortgages and expenses. The difference between the total assets and the total liabilities leaves you with a business's *equity,* which is what an investor uses to help evaluate your business.

Your balance sheet shows the relationship between assets and liabilities in your business. Do they net out or have you got more liabilities than assets? How much money does your business owe in the short and longer term? These are important performance measurements to an investor or funder.

Some commonly used and universally understood ratios you use to assess the financial performance of your growing business include:

✔ **Liquidity ratios:** These show how able you are to meet your short-term financial obligations.

Some liquidity ratios are:

- **Current ratio:** Current assets divided by current liabilities. This assesses whether you have sufficient assets to cover your liabilities. A ratio of two shows you have twice as many current assets as current liabilities.

- **Quick, or acid-test, ratio:** Current assets – excluding stock – divided by current liabilities. A ratio of one shows that liquidity levels are high – an indication of solid financial health.

✔ **Solvency ratios:** These tell you how much exposure you have to long-term debt and how likely it is that you can sustain that amount of debt over time.

An example of a solvency ratio is *gearing,* which is arrived at by dividing all your loans and bank overdrafts by equity. The higher the gearing, the more vulnerable the company is to increasing interest rates. Most lenders refuse further finance when gearing exceeds 50 per cent.

✔ **Efficiency ratios:** These give an indication of how tightly you're running your ship and include:

- **Debtors' turnover:** The average of credit sales divided by the average level of debtors. This shows how long it takes to collect payments. A low ratio may mean payment terms need tightening up.

- **Creditors' turnover:** The average cost of sales divided by the average amount of credit that is taken from suppliers. This shows how long your business takes to pay suppliers. Suppliers may withdraw credit if you regularly pay late.

- **Stock turnover:** The average cost of sales divided by the average value of stock. This ratio indicates how long you hold stock before selling. A lower stock turnover may mean lower profits.

✔ **Profitability ratios:** These indicate how well you're using the capital in your business. Calculate your profitability ratios as follows:

- Divide net profit before tax by the total value of capital employed to see how good your return on the capital used in your business is. This can then be compared with what the same amount of money (loans and shares) would have earned on deposit or in the stock market.

- You can also use the *net profit ratio* to evaluate your profitability. Divide the net profit before tax by the total value of net sales (sales less returns) to see how good your net profit is. This can then be compared with the same ratio in other periods or with the ratio of competitors.

  The net profit ratio is one of the ratios used to determine whether a business is making progress.

Mitigating Risk

As a business owner, you face a number of risks and challenges to your business performance on a daily basis. Some of these risks are within your control to a certain extent, but others aren't. Managing and mitigating risk is part and parcel of being at the head of a growing business, so you need to accept it as part of your business life.

Any business that's had external investment as part of its growth journey has an extra dimension of risk to consider. You know that shareholders expect a return as a reward for the risk they've taken by investing in your business. What's more, they usually want higher than average returns, which means you have to take some risks in order to achieve the desired end game. The way your business performs and how you measure this performance is linked to the risks you take in order to achieve a better than average performance for you, your team and your shareholders.

Whatever stage of growth you're at and however you got there, you have ways to manage, eliminate, tolerate or minimise risk and to mitigate its impact on your growing business.

Being aware of risk is the first step towards managing it. Once you know it should be on your radar, you're more likely to be able to identify risk areas that you need to manage and that you can turn into rewards. You'll be tested and judged on your performance in managing risk, whether it's your financial risks, people risks, broader economic risks, or the risks around the way you're perceived and positioned within your market. This will test your skill, tenacity and courage as a manager, a motivator and the person leading the charge to becoming a highly profitable, highly valued company in your industry.

Tracking revenue growth levels

Entrepreneurs, and especially new entrepreneurs, see rising revenue figures as the main indicator of growth. However, although revenue is important, you need to look at it along with other performance indicators and view all your indicators as a whole as you attempt to strike a balance between the factors needed for aggressive growth and those needed to manage risk.

You want the best out of both worlds – terrific revenue generation with a reduction in risk and a balanced performance measurement system.

Comparing staffing levels and activity

As sure as day follows night, as your business grows, so will the number of people you employ. Their performance and impact are part of what you measure and track when measuring the overall performance of your business. Investors and funders do the same thing, so you need to keep on top of how your staff are performing and have formal systems in place for setting targets and measuring success.

You don't necessarily need complicated processes and programmes to have an effective means of measuring staff impact on performance. You can follow a number of well-worn paths with simple structures that you can embed in your company culture as you continue to grow, which will be easily understood by the outside world and investors alike. They include:

- **Meetings and appraisals:** Both informal and formal meetings and appraisals provide very immediate, direct and easily understood and compared ways of monitoring and encouraging the progress of individual employees. Not only do they provide a forum for frank and open feedback and exchanges, but they also form the basis for creating employee development plans, targets for the year ahead and agreed methods for measuring success, achievements and rewards.

  You can use these opportunities to encourage a positive, productive attitude in your growing team, and you may even unearth a gem of an idea or discover the early stage of a problem that has yet to fester and infect your business.

- **Regular staff meetings:** Not only are they useful for keeping staff up-to-date on all the activity in your business, but they can also provide an early warning of concerns or fears that may otherwise take some time to come to the attention of you and your management team.

- **Employee performance measured in relation to contributions to the bottom line:** Looking at employee performance from a financial perspective can be a very valuable, and sometimes very sobering, management tool. You can use a number of methods to measure this, but some of the most common are sales output or revenue contribution per employee and/or the resulting profit per employee.

You can also look at ways in which team members are able to cut costs and make other internal savings, allowing you to add to the bottom line. This can be easier when you can track units of widgets or sales per person, but the theory can be applied to any industry and *useful or productive hours* can be substituted for *widgets* in the services industries.

As you grow, investors need to see that you're in control and managing the efficiency and productivity of the people in your business, which isn't always easy for the first-time entrepreneur or the super-busy entrepreneur.

Retaining staff

One of the things that can damage your performance and the way your company is perceived in the marketplace is a high level of staff turnover. It's a sign to the market that you're doing something wrong, either in the way you interview and hire or the way you treat your staff, which won't have a positive impact on the value of your business.

The other, more apparent, impact of staff leaving is that it costs a lot of money to recruit, train and embed employees, so each time you need to replace an employee, it affects your bottom line.

Another key factor to consider when staff leave is the preservation of intellectual property, sensitive and confidential data and continuing client relationships. If any of these are compromised, it can have a devastating effect on your growing business.

When it comes to staff retention, prevention is better than cure. So, create a good working environment with incentives and opportunities and a very clear way to measure staff input and reward. Keep all team members productive, profitable, engaged and enjoying themselves.

Use these tips to get staffing right in the first place:

- Hire the right people for the right role at the right time – on your first attempt. Seek advice and help from mentors or other professionals to get an objective eye on your hiring process.

- Provide opportunities for employees to develop new skills that they can use to further develop your business.

- Make sure that the whole team is aware of and on board with your vision, and that they feel empowered and part of making it a reality.

- Provide continuous feedback and make sure you consult team members at all levels of position and in all areas of the business, not just the senior management in one or two areas.

✔ Reward achievement and commitment.

✔ Create an enjoyable team environment.

Assessing Your Performance in Your Market

As you look at measuring the performance of your growing business and setting your KPIs – while reviewing your plans and revisiting your market in relation to your strategic overview – it's a good time to pause and compare your original or current assessment of opportunities with what's out there at the moment. It's a great opportunity for you to evaluate the impact of certain forces at work in your sector, certain competitors active in your marketplace, how you cope and compare with these influences and what effect this has on your performance.

Some aspects to consider as you look at your position in the market are:

✔ Significant or sudden changes in your market

✔ New products or emerging services that may pose a threat

✔ Changes in your customers' needs or the way they access products and services within your market

✔ External factors such as economic shifts, technological changes or threats from overseas competitors

Measuring your business performance against others: Benchmarking

A useful tool for assessing your performance in the market is looking at how you compare to your competition. Investors are very interested in how you rank within your market.

By comparing yourself with other businesses, you get a better understanding of your own business – where you excel, where you're weak and what you can do to improve. You can also check how individual departments within your business compare to each other.

Who to benchmark yourself against

Compare your business against others in the same sector, although not necessarily the same size. You may have a competitor that's smaller but very disruptive and can take on the bigger fish in your pond. Or you may have very aggressive growth targets that you want to achieve in a fairly short space of time, so you may look to compare your business with a more established market leader. What's important is that you take into account your market position and your business objectives to determine the exact comparisons you want to make.

What to benchmark

Aim to benchmark the same performance measures you use for your KPIs – you identified these as the key performance drivers for success in your business. (See 'Keeping Up with Key Performance Indicators KPIs' earlier in this chapter.)

How to benchmark

If you're on top of your growing business, you have all the facts and figures you need for your own business, so you just need to find as much information as you can on your competitors or others in your market.

Some suggestions for finding this information are:

- ✔ Trade organisations, professional associations or government departments for your sector
- ✔ Commercial reports on your market, which you can subscribe to or may be available online or at a library

Measuring against other businesses: Conducting a competitor analysis

As a growing business, you have a much better idea of who your real competitors are and how they stack up against you than you did when you first started out. Early on, doing market research and competitor analyses may seem like an extravagant waste of time and money, but as you look at the changing face and value of your business and have to report on a regular basis to funders (who want to know how you compare in your marketplace), you can see the benefits of having this information to hand and up-to-date.

The type of competitor information that's useful to you depends on the type of business you are and the market you're operating in. Look at your competitors to determine:

- ✔ What they offer and how it compares to what you offer.
- ✔ How they price their products – low margin, high volume? High margin, low volume?
- ✔ What their customer profile and numbers look like compared with yours.

 ✔ What their competitive advantages and disadvantages are compared with yours.

 ✔ The opportunities available for you to enter the market with a new product or service that may weaken their position.

The SWOT analysis I talk about in Chapter 3 is a good basis for a competitor analysis.

Enhancing and Measuring Your Value in the Marketplace

Your financial performance is clearly an indicator of success, measuring both historical and future performance with your financial statements and the returns that your company provides to investors along your whole funding journey. But you also need to cement your position in the market, securing your customer base and staying one step ahead of your competition. The outside world sees your business through the lens of pubic relations (PR), benchmarking and economic performance, but your value goes much deeper than that. It touches on the values that you set out in your business plan, and the way that your team creates the right environment for the growth that ultimately benefits them, you and your investors.

Considering the way others see you: Measurement and your customers

Strong brand loyalty and customer awareness are intangible assets that add to your company's value in terms of goodwill, so they're important to the top and bottom lines of your business.

When you start your business, your marketing plan includes your target market, how you'll acquire customers, which segment they fall into and how you'll make customer service a priority. In many cases, that's the last time you consider the value in giving good customer service until you start losing customers, and your sales and profits are negatively impacted. You may fail to translate your lofty customer service goals into things that you can measure, so you lose the sense of how to measure their impact on your performance.

You spend a lot of time and money acquiring customers. In order to keep customers, you have to spend even more time and money. It costs three-to-seven times as much to get a new customer as it does to retain an old one. Your company performance can suffer as a result of overlooking customer retention.

Install measurements for customer retention and service from the start of your business and continue to measure this KPI as you grow. You can look at the quality of customer service or the length of time to recruit customers and how long you retain them. Equally important is how you perform with regard to customer service and what feedback you get.

After you get a new customer, you don't want to lose him because the cost of having to replace him over and over again means that you never get to a profitable sale. You want to focus on not just acquiring a customer but also retaining a customer, because this focus helps to make your business more profitable. Therefore, measure not only how long it takes and how much it costs to win a customer but your retention and repeat business figures as well.

Sometimes you find 100 new clients, but only 20 of them stay with you and become profitable. Finding more like those 20 is a valuable exercise.

Investors are interested in how much it costs to acquire a customer and how long it takes you to *amortise*, or spread out, the cost until that customer becomes profitable. The longer a customer stays with you, the longer you have to spread the cost of acquiring him. He usually also spends more over time and refers other customers to you.

A customer who knows you well doesn't usually need as much hand-holding as a new customer, so he's more profitable to you.

Customer feedback is essential to measuring your company performance. Remind yourself what you know about your customers at regular intervals. Ask them if they're getting what they need from your business and how you can improve on the product, service or experience for them. Look for as many ways of capturing customer feedback as possible, including:

- ✓ **Sales data:** What your customers choose to buy (or not to buy) provides the clearest indication of how they see your value add. A good CRM (customer relationship management) system can provide a useful tool for gathering customer data and also a clear and uniform method for analysing this data so that you can use it to improve performance.

- ✓ **Complaints:** Most customers just go somewhere else rather than complain, so this feedback gives you valuable information about your performance.

- ✓ **Customer reviews:** A useful and often very powerful tool, customer reviews are a great source of information as to how your business is performing.

When you lose a customer, one of your competitors likely gains one.

When reviewing your business's performance, assess your customer base and market positioning as a key part of the process. Update your marketing plan at least as often as your business plan.

Assessing the quality of your management

Most of the measures of company performance have an outward focus: looking at how customers see you, how shareholders view the return on their investment and how the market perceives your performance in relation to brand image and positioning. Valid though these measures may be, one of the key areas for investors when it comes to company performance is the management team.

It's the management team's responsibility to make sure that excellent performance is a result of the decisions and processes they set in motion, so it's only right that they should be assessed when considering the increasing value of the business, both internally and externally.

If new investors are involved, it's very likely that they'll take up board and non-executive director roles in your business, which enables them to keep a watchful eye over the whole management team. As part of your new corporate governance mandate, these advisors let you know when you've done something well and also when you've coloured outside the lines and need to be reined in.

Getting a helping hand

Depending on the experience of your team and the stage of your business, you may find it helpful to bring in some external experts to strengthen the team and give them the skills they need to take them to the next level of management. This can include:

- Employing skilled consultants in areas where you have no time or opportunity to develop in-house skills
- Appointing an experienced non-executive director who can provide a regular, impartial assessment of how you're doing, where you can improve and how you can gain from adding to or subtracting members from the team

Creating an impression with your brand image

Your *brand* goes beyond a customer association with a product or a service and encompasses what you stand for, your reputation in the marketplace, your company values and your company style. It's a part of everything you put into the public domain – your logo, your website, your imagery and the way you interact with your customer base.

Building a brand takes a good deal of time, money and attention. A brand is something that has a value for your business in real time financial terms. In addition, a strong brand has value when you and your investors exit your business.

Building your brand is worth trying to get right. You then need to monitor its impact on your company finances, market positioning and customer engagement, which all impact your brand value and your profit margins.

Strong brands have clear patterns of association. Weaker brands are less clearly defined. Brand image can be combined with sales performance and brand awareness to help you measure and understand the key brand associations that drive sales.

Is one smartphone really better than another? Does one soft drink really taste better than its competitors? Brands connect with their customers on a much deeper level than a phone call or a taste, and in doing so, they create brand loyalty, which in turn drives sales and, hopefully, profitability. Your brand stands for something that a customer identifies with, and that in turn, creates a value that you can measure and monitor.

Producing a stimulating annual report

You may think of an annual report as a beautifully printed, professionally bound coffee-table book in a business's reception area and as something a world away from the current worries of your day. But after you receive investment funds and have shareholders, or if you're considering a public offering for your business, you need to produce a document for general distribution that gives an indication of how your business is performing, where you're spending your – and their – money and what your plans for the future look like.

An annual report can tell the market what direction your sales are heading; how you're funding your growth or bailing your business out with debt or equity; how you're coping with the economy at large; and whether you have business and financial prowess or need some more practice. Investors know how to read these reports and they'll be able to see where you are, where you've been and where you're going and decide if they agree.

Try to make your annual report stimulating and a reflection of your company values and strategic aims. It should be a celebration of all things good from the past and present, an explanation of things that may not have quite gone to plan, and an upbeat message as to what the year ahead has in store. It shouldn't be a never-ending series of charts, figures, random photos and tiny, dense text. Avoid the stock photos and stock phrases that see your reader dozing off and wishing they'd opted for the 20-year-old copy of *Country Life*.

In addition to including key information, pay attention to layout and the amount of white space on the page. The human eye absorbs only 10 per cent of what it sees on a page, and the human brain retains even less, so leave plenty of white space and break up the paragraphs into bite-size, easily read and understood chunks of information.

Make sure employee photos are up-to-date and don't resemble passport photos or mug shots. They need to convey the image you want your company to get across and be a true representation of the team. Put your best foot forward, and make sure the shoe fits the current foot and not one from your school yearbook (unless you're a 16-year-old entrepreneur!).

For a look at some companies that have created some very good annual reports, head to www.forbes.com and search for '5 Brands That Nailed Their Annual Reports'.

Maximising public relations opportunities

In the movie *Field of Dreams,* Kevin Costner's character receives some whispered advice that encourages him to build his baseball field of dreams. The tagline is, 'If you build it, they will come'. Only in movies are you allowed to remain in a dreamlike state and have your dreams come to life. If you're a business looking to measure your performance with PR, then wakey! wakey! You need to persuade, cajole, and at the very least let potential customers know you're there, or they most assuredly will not come.

The column inches or centimetres of coverage your business generates is an indication of how the market sees you. It also allows you to tell the market what you want it to hear. This in itself is not an indicator of true performance, but used wisely you can maximise PR opportunities to raise your company profile and highlight your position as the founder for some performance-enhancing opportunities.

To maximise your PR return, you also want to makes sure you're getting value for money from your public relations activities.

The key is that 'What gets measured gets managed' (turn to the beginning of this chapter for more on the origins of this quote), so use these points to help you measure your PR effectiveness:

✔ Set and agree clear and measurable campaign goals up front.

✔ Agree the campaign success criteria and the base or benchmark you're measuring from.

✔ Agree on methodology. How will you evaluate? Is it easy to use, clear, repeatable and consistent?

✔ Agree the focus. What are you evaluating (quantity and quality) and across which platforms (broadcast, radio, print, online, social media)?

✔ Agree frequency of measurement – and how and when to report back.

✔ Set a budget.

✔ Focus on commercial outcomes. Measure the effect on outcomes rather than outputs. Make sure you answer the question: What are the proven business benefits to the organisation?

Chapter 16

Getting a Mentor

In This Chapter

▶ Maintaining a relationship with a mentor

▶ Finding and selecting a mentor

▶ Reaching out to your business network

▶ Tapping into business support schemes

*T*he concept of mentoring is by no means a new idea. In fact, its roots go back to Ancient Greece in Homer's *Odyssey* when Odysseus began his famous *odyssey,* or long journey, to find his men after war, leaving his infant son in the care of a companion called Mentor, thus creating the counselling relationship we know today as mentoring. Mentoring comes in many forms – parent to child, coach to player, teacher to student, manager to employee and so on – but the gist of it is that of a more experienced person helping a less experienced person to logic things out and achieve her goals.

Although it may be new to you as the owner of a small- or medium-sized business, mentoring has been around for ages in bigger businesses. In very large firms with tens or hundreds of thousands of employees, the mentoring process is part of an employee's professional and personal development, and happens at very junior to very senior levels. In companies where learning and development go hand in hand with leadership development, the mentoring process helps ambitious Annies rise through the ranks and offers shy Saras guidance and support in navigating their career development journeys.

The growth in organisations that supply mentors as part of business support services, along with online mentoring services that seem to be part of every business publication, magazine and newsletter, means that you can find plenty of mentors, both paid and unpaid, offering their services to the stressed, confused or inexperienced entrepreneur. In addition to these mere mortal mentors, you can also find a number of very well-known entrepreneurs who run or have exited from successful companies and now offer the less experienced the benefit of their substantial and high-profile experience.

In this chapter, I take you through the process of understanding the role and responsibilities of the mentor/mentee relationship. I discuss strategies to help you maximise your relationship with a mentor, and I signpost you to resources that can help you find appropriate and effective mentors.

Looking at the Mentor/Mentee Relationship

You may think of mentoring for what I'd term the softer business skills, like marketing or anything to do with taking on staff, talent development, team building and the like, but don't overlook it as an extremely useful source of ideas, inspiration and direction when you're looking to raise funds.

Funding your business may be a completely new experience. If you've raised funds before, you know it can be a somewhat confusing, occasionally scary and always very time-consuming exercise, so any help in the form of an experienced mentor should be sought after and welcomed.

A mentor can help in a variety of areas:

- ✔ Help you locate useful resources.
- ✔ See the things that you may otherwise overlook.
- ✔ Provide a safe place to practise your pitch. (I talk about developing your pitch in Chapter 6.)
- ✔ Give you an opportunity to learn from someone else's mistakes and experience.
- ✔ Share useful contacts in the financial world and help open doors that might otherwise be firmly wedged shut when you approach without an introduction. Your mentor may even be a potential investor!

A mentor questions and probes while gently steering you on a journey of self-discovery. A mentor helps supplement your knowledge as you discover more and draw on your own decision-making skills. A mentor is not there to judge you, so you're free to be yourself when discussing your fundraising. You don't need to pretend that you're more knowledgeable than you really are, that you're completely comfortable with all the financial terms, formulae and ratios or even that you're in total command of all your facts, figures and forecasts. Of course, you need to be able to speak intelligently about all these things when it comes time to approach funders, and a mentor can help you gain that knowledge.

A mentor with a social conscience

One of the UK's best-known mentors is Paul Lindlay, founder of the award-winning, health-conscious children's food brand, Ella's Kitchen. He sold Ella's Kitchen for £66 million in 2013. Paul is frequently seen travelling around the country offering advice and guidance to entrepreneurs in need of inspiration; sometimes offering personal mentoring to a lucky few.

For Paul, it's important that a brand has, and stays true to, a social purpose as well as a business purpose and uses commercial ambition to help tackle social challenges.

Mentors are willing to guide you, and they can lead you to discover the solutions to your problems, or perhaps even figure out exactly what the problem is! It sounds crazy, but you won't always be able to see the forest for the trees to easily identify what the precise problem is. A mentor can help you develop your strategy even before you start plugging the numbers into spreadsheets, which can save you a lot of time later on and give you a clear direction in the finance area of your business. Mentors have their own experiences, but also the experience that comes from mentoring other companies like yours, so they provide a fantastic overview that you couldn't possibly get on your own.

Mentors are everywhere, and come in all shapes and sizes. The trick is finding the right mentor for you and for your business. When you're looking for a mentor, use this checklist:

- ✔ Ask yourself where you are in your business and managerial development and why you think you need a mentor.

- ✔ Be clear about what skills and resources you're lacking and what you want to have in a mentor. Create a clear picture of what you want your mentor to help you with, so that mentor candidates understand why you're approaching them and can evaluate their ability to help.

- ✔ Do your research. Look at who has successfully reached your desired destination or milestone, bearing in mind that she may not be in the same industry or indeed the same city or country.

- ✔ Get out there and meet people! Work your networks to increase your chances of meeting likely mentors and to get introductions.

Mentoring only works if you work with it. Sending one email, making one phone call or attending one event, with no follow up or regularity is not the recipe for mentoring success. As with all business relationships, you have to work on it, review it and monitor it in order to ensure that it's really helping you achieve your goals.

Mentoring and the gender gap

In recent years, mentoring for entrepreneurs and within small- and medium-sized enterprises, or SMEs, has really taken off, and is now a firm fixture in running your own business. It must be pointed out, however, that the uptake of mentoring services is higher for men than it is for women.

A 2015 Citi AM article cites the results of a poll that found 43 per cent of women felt uncomfortable networking with someone they didn't know, versus 33 per cent for men.

Since 2012 government-sponsored services have attempted to address this imbalance and get more women to take part in business networking opportunities.

According to *The Next Women Business Magazine,* 'If women started businesses at the same rate as men, it is estimated that there would be an additional 150,000 extra start-ups each year in the UK'. So, although I'm not one to beat the gender drum, there's clearly an argument for more women finding a mentor.

When you're in a mentoring relationship, keep it healthy and balanced with these tips:

- ✔ Make sure you have some give in what can become a very take-oriented relationship. You may not be able to offer your mentor much of anything in the way of compensation, but things like introductions to non-executive positions, speaking engagements and additional clients may be very much appreciated by your mentor. Nobody likes a totally selfish person, so find something you can do for your mentor.

  Having a mentor is a bonus, not a right. Demanding someone's time because you think you deserve it is not usually well received.

- ✔ To make your mentor feel she's really helping, it's wise to take up some of her suggestions or the ideas you create together. Mentors are generally very busy people and don't want to think they're wasting their time giving advice that's never taken.

- ✔ Close the virtuous mentoring circle and give back to your business community by finding someone to mentor yourself. The concept of what goes around comes around is valid. Best to keep the karmic circle going!

Finding a Mentor through a Trade Association

The UK boasts hundreds of trade associations, and you can find one for pretty much any profession – bookmaker, plumber, upholsterer, IT professional, gas fitter, glazier, hairdresser, crowdfunder, marketer – the list goes on and on. Use a reputable search engine or visit your library research department to find a veritable treasure chest of trade associations to connect with, join and fully exploit to your benefit.

Trade associations are at the heart of what matters in their industries, and represent the voice and the views of their members, both at the grassroots and up to the highest levels of government. Membership represents a badge of quality assurance, which you can place on your marketing materials once you're a member, letting others know you abide by certain standards, and possibly giving you an edge when a prospect is looking for a new supplier.

Although you may never have attended an event or known of their existence, trade associations are not a new thing. In fact, the concept has been around since the Roman Empire. Trade associations evolved into something akin to what exists today in 16th century England when individual industry guilds provided training, rules for wages and working hours and protection of the rights of both the merchants and the individual artisans. Their position was further cemented during the Industrial Revolution, and like most things making a positive difference to working life, they remain part of the modern-day landscape.

Taking advantage of peer networking and support

Trade associations can be extremely useful for finding mentors, and like you and your business, they come in all shapes and sizes. With specific knowledge of your business sector, a trade association offers a unique opportunity to find support from a fellow member who may have been exactly where you are. An association member may already have gone through the agony and the ecstasy of getting funding, and lived to tell the tale that can now give you the very valuable benefit of hindsight.

Associations can also provide a mentor who is very well connected in your industry. Such a mentor can open otherwise closed doors and smooth the way with a well-placed recommendation or endorsement for you, your business and your team. This personal contact can significantly enhance your entry to new markets and potentially your bottom line.

Trade associations can be great hunting grounds for potential board members, advisors and, dare I say it, even investors, all of which can improve your chances of success when making any funding applications.

Increasing opportunities for new business

In addition to a being a good place to source a mentor, a trade association also offers financial benefits, specialist or legal advice, training and development opportunities and strength in numbers. The result of bringing all this weight to bear can be seen in significant discounts or preferential rates on goods and services, the offer of speaking opportunities at events that are otherwise difficult to secure, excellent networking opportunities and influence over policy, technical changes and in other areas that matter to the association's membership. On potentially costly items like insurance, vehicles, employment advice and training, the savings from being part of an association can be significant, and far outweigh the cost of annual membership.

Associations are often well placed to offer specialist advice, particularly of a technical, legal and commercial nature – advice not usually available to small- and medium-sized enterprises (SMEs). A trade association may have access to sensitive information, details of impending changes that affect your industry and a pile of statistical analysis that may be just what you need to complete your business plan or funding documentation. They can also make your voice heard in specific research and *vox pop* (voice of the people) projects such as a survey on accessing bank finance that you'd otherwise struggle to take part in, but that can have an impact on your business. By being a member, you're able to be involved first-hand and influence policy and working conditions.

Not to be overlooked or forgotten, the conference and events calendars of trade associations provide fantastic opportunities to develop new business deals, meet potential mentors, start new business relationships and learn a thing or two before heading off to the mandatory dinner/dance to let your hair down.

Contacting Your Extended Network

As a youngster I was a member of the Scouts (Brownies and the Girl Guides). Once a year, we were forced to sell boxes of cookies (biscuits) for charity. We found this extremely exciting – we got to experience the thrill of collecting real money, which was ours to guard for a fleeting moment, but more importantly, we got to eat the product! What we also got to do was make a very long list of friends, friends of friends, extended family members, teachers, clergy, local shopkeepers and so on, because in order to sell the highest number of boxes and win a prize, we had to rely – heavily – on tapping into our extended networks.

You may not be hawking mint-chocolate chip biscuits, but somewhere in your extended network you may just find the perfect mentor, guide and advisor for you and your business. The connection can come from anywhere – through Aunt Shirley's oldest son or your printer's sister-in-law – so draw up that list of contacts in your immediate network and turn it into an even larger contact list of your extended network.

Be aware that sometimes the most helpful people are right on your doorstep or in your next immediate vertical relationship – people in the contact list of your relatives, or in the lists of contact you have in similar management roles, but different industries. Contacts may come from your personal circle, business organisations, school, college or university classes, those who share your hobbies or pastimes, people you meet volunteering or groups you join online.

You can keep adding to your contact list, but it's important to take stock of what you already have in your inventory that can help take your business to the next level. Save yourself time, effort and frustration by not trying to create an extended network from scratch.

Use a contact management system to organise potential mentors exactly as you would for any business contacts. Scraps of paper and business cards are easily damaged or lost, and they can't tell you what you discussed or agreed to.

Tapping into local, national and international business networks

You'll know you've gone too far in tapping your extended network when people stop taking your calls and avoid making eye contact with you at functions and events. Before you bleed the well of well meaning well-wishers dry, have a look at other ways to extend your network by joining local, national and international networks. These come in both online and offline varieties. (It's also worth a look at *Business Networking For Dummies* by Stefan Thomas, published by Wiley, which is packed full of useful information, tips and resources.)

Networking organisations can be a great place to find a mentor, advisor, investors and potential customers and business partners. The format, cost and location vary, but the aim is the same – to connect you with other useful professionals.

You can find contact details from a variety of sources:

- ✔ Use social media, such as Facebook, LinkedIn, Twitter and Meetup.
- ✔ Go online to find blogs, forums, online directories, business information and support websites.
- ✔ Try your local chamber of commerce, events and business show listings, libraries, places of worship, accountancy firms, further education (FE) college notice boards, newsletters, hubs, clubs, accelerators and incubators.

Check Chapter 8 for additional resources on finding contacts.

Don't discount national and international organisations thinking you won't be able to access them. Very often these organisations have local chapters that target the business needs of a specific geographical area, industry group, gender or ethnic group. By getting in touch with the larger organisation, you can connect with business people who live and work in your locale.

The technology, food and creative sectors are particularly active in national and international groups. These broad-based groups can be a godsend for rural industries that may not have time or opportunity for face-to-face interaction.

You can find hundreds of networking organisations in the UK and further afield, and far too many to list here, but some of the more widespread and well known can be found in the following list. You're pretty certain to find one that has a chapter near you, but if not, why not start one yourself!

- ✔ **BNI** (www.bni.co.uk): BNI is a well-established business networking referral organisation with a global reach. It has over 13,000 members in the UK and Ireland, with hundreds of thousands of referrals every year. BNI is great if you're a morning person as it tends to hold meetings over breakfast, or as they call it, 'the most important meal of the day'.

- ✔ **The Business Network** (www.business-network.co.uk): Established in the UK over 20 years ago, The Business Network attracts senior decision makers to its monthly lunchtime events. It provides a business-focused format for building close working links and establishing an invaluable support network of business contacts.

- ✔ **Meetup** (www.meetup.com): According to its website, 'Meetup is the world's largest network of local groups'. It's very easy for anyone to organise a local group or join one of the thousands already set up. More than 9,000 groups get together in local communities each day, each one with the goal of improving themselves or their communities.

- ✔ **Prowess** (www.prowess.org.uk): Prowess provides business information to female-led businesses. Its website offers a wide range of women's business networks across the UK. All of those listed have regular local meetings and click-through links on the site.

- ✔ **Enterprising Women** (www.enterprising-women.org/business-support/mentoring): Enterprising Women aims to help women achieve business success by empowering, connecting, training and inspiring them. Mentors are offered free of charge to members, and members are from all parts of the UK, at all stages in business and from a variety of sectors and backgrounds.

✔ **Women 1st Mentoring Programme** (`http://women1st.co.uk`): Women 1st is passionate about transforming the gender balance on boards in the tourism and visitor economy sector (hospitality, passenger transport, travel, tourism and retail), and supporting women who aspire to senior leadership roles to fulfil their career ambitions. Mentors in senior roles are available at no cost to members.

Networking is different from *selling,* and you will have more success at networking if you listen and exchange information and don't try to sell during an event. Make your contacts and follow up later.

Engaging with international business networks

Unless you travel a lot for business, own a Lear jet or hire a yacht, international networks function predominantly online and frequently make use of social media and technology in order to be effective.

You can thank Britain's own Tim Berners-Lee for the birth of the worldwide web, as we lay people know it. As the name implies, the web covers the world, so you can create, develop your business and engage with like-minded people all round the globe, 24 hours a day, 7 days a week, 365 days a year.

Taking part in online discussion groups

Developing your international business network can take many forms, but the most common and overarching is by taking part in online discussions that have international participants.

You can find online groups and discussion forums for most business questions and points of view.

It's not wise to take in part in loads of groups at once, emailing or contacting people at random, because a scatter-gun approach rarely pays dividends and makes you look like you lack focus or any kind of filter.

If you join forums looking for potential mentors or advisors, research them very carefully. Spend a few months as a light-touch participant. Make sure the forum is genuine and professional enough for you to start reaching out. You can see who may be a useful contact and a good fit for you as a mentor, and you can message or connect via the site or on other familiar business networking sites, such as LinkedIn.

The most commonly used network for business is LinkedIn, which has the facility for you to create or join a niche group, which raises your profile but also enables you to ask questions, connect with people in your industry or those who have a similar functional role and gain useful information and contacts. Members who accept your invitation or who you may want to approach for advice or mentoring can respond via LinkedIn, enhancing the security of your information and correspondence.

Other countries have different sites, and some that you may want to consider are:

- ✔ **Viadeo** (www.viadeo.com) and **Xing** (www.xing.com) are similar to LinkedIn but with a European focus. Not very well known in the English-speaking world, Viadeo has more than 35 million members and is the market leader in Italy, Spain and, of course, France. The company recently made significant acquisitions in India and, more strategically, China. Xing has similar aims but is headquartered in Hamburg, Germany.

- ✔ **GeeksOnaPlane** (www.geeksonaplane.com) is part of the well-known group 500 Startups. You can learn about high-growth technology markets worldwide via this site that unites geeks and explores cross-border opportunities. You can even request an invite to join the group on international travels.

Don't forget the old standbys that are present in many countries and have become an integral part of how and with whom you do business. Facebook, Google Groups for Business and Twitter can be extremely helpful in the right hands when used appropriately. They allow you to take initial contact to a deeper level, to see what other people say about your contacts and to pace yourself when creating business relationships.

Participating in online webinars and conferences

Used in conjunction with discussion groups and forums or on their own, online webinars and conferences can be a good way to learn about and interact with potential mentors and industry professionals. They take place every day in all parts of the world. Usually a biography or resume of the speaker is published online ahead of the event, giving you useful information and also serving as a starting point from which to do additional research on a potential mentor.

If you're considering a mentoring request, stay online for the question-and-answer session. It can be well worth it.

Joining your alumni organisation

You may prefer to bury higher education or past employment experiences deep in your memory vault, shunning reunions or requests for donations of money and time, but alumni groups can be fertile hunting grounds for a potential mentor. After all, you share common experiences and a mutual frame of reference, albeit for a specific point in time, and even the worst work or study experiences have some redeeming features, if only to teach you never to repeat them. Added to this is the fact that most people don't remember who they journeyed alongside but are too embarrassed to admit to it, so odds are no one will remember why you turn a whiter shade of pale when you think of days gone by.

Some of my own alumni groups include illustrious members such as real estate mogul and politician Donald Trump, Vernon Hill of Metrobank, fashion designer Tory Burch and John Legend, the wonderful R&B musician. They also include a veritable army of lawyers, accountants, bankers and physicians – all of whom can come in mighty handy in certain situations. Mine is also a very international crowd, with thousands of members in the UK, and this makes for great social events where we strengthen our bonds under the shared-experience banner. When you take a closer look, members of your alumni groups may surprise you!

Alumni organisations spring forth from a variety of sources, but educational and corporate groups are usually the largest and most active, as well as the easiest to stay in touch with, either online or off.

Alumni associations exist to strengthen the ties between past graduates, the communities they live and work in, and the organisation that set them up. They are often national or international in reach, and organised into chapters by city, region or country. Groups organise social events, talks, travel, and usually publish a magazine or newsletter. Alumni groups also sponsor forums, blogs and paid adverts. If you're very lucky, your group is a member of an affiliate organisation, instantly multiplying your chances of finding a willing sounding board, an older and wiser point of view or an objective pair of eyes for your business; rich pickings, indeed.

Open to all ages and walks of life, they can be particularly useful to recent alumna in search of advice, connections and mentoring from older, more experienced members of the groups. These groups provide a good support system for newbies and a place to develop new business relationships with people with similar backgrounds.

In addition to educational alumni organisations, you can also find corporate alumni associations made up of former employees of a business who stay in touch on a regular basis. In many ways, these are very similar to the educational groups, forming online groups on sites such as LinkedIn and having a closed-group newsletter or even a printed publication. Most have a main company group across all divisions, as well as focused subgroups for different divisions or functional areas.

These associations are growing in popularity and becoming an important part of a personal business network. They provide commercial opportunities, job boards, training and development information, networking and, of course, mentoring opportunities.

Check with your previous employers to see if they have groups you can join or search company names online.

Engaging with a Business Support Scheme

For many years, the UK has had a variety of free or low-cost business support schemes. These schemes offer practical advice to start-up and growth businesses on a variety of topics, including business planning methods and skills, accessing and raising finance, mentoring and taking a business to an international audience.

In Chapter 8, I cover some of the ways you can engage with business support schemes in a more general way, and it's always worth contacting your local business support agency to see what mentoring support is on offer.

Some of these schemes are free of cost, while others serve as an introduction agency to consultants and advisors who also offering mentoring for a fee. MentorsMe (www.mentorsme.org) and the Institute of Enterprise and Entrepreneurs (www.ioee.uk) both have free mentoring services, networking events and an online newsletter.

It's worth checking what's available in your area for face-to-face mentoring sessions, but also what's provided by national programmes that you may be able to utilise through conference call providers such as Skype or Powwownow. These virtual mentoring sessions can sometimes be more effective than face-to-face meetings as there are no distractions, no travel time and flexibility in terms of scheduling. You can even do them in your pyjamas, but I advise choosing an appropriate camera angle!

Signing up with local enterprise agencies

Most local enterprise agencies are members of the National Federation of Enterprise Agencies (NFEA) (www.nfea.com), trading as the National Enterprise Network. The NFEA claims to have conducted hundreds of thousands of advice sessions, reaching tens of thousands of established companies, and the same again in pre-start businesses. In other words, there's no shortage of opportunities to get help, advice and guidance from your local enterprise agency at every stage of your business.

NFEA members represent all types of agencies working to support business men and women, connecting them with opportunities, giving them new skills and generally helping to make a positive contribution to UK economy.

It's universally accepted that business owners who seek support to set up or grow their businesses are more likely to survive and thrive than those who don't. So it's worth a phone call, a web search or a half-hour appointment to see if these enterprise warriors can help you win the business success battle.

Looking at other support agencies and organisations

In addition to the NFEA members, you can find a number of regularly recurring regional, national, age- or sector-specific mentoring schemes and agencies. Here are a few of the more active:

- ✔ **ERDF (European Regional Development Fund) programmes (**www. gov.uk/guidance/applying-for-erdf-funding**):** These business advice and mentoring programmes are free to join. They're funded by the European Union and delivered on the ground by a variety of organisations, such as enterprise agencies, local authorities and private businesses. The amount of support is usually capped, and the funding goes in cycles, so it's best to keep checking online.

  Some of these schemes are for specific areas, and some are for specific industry types, but they all tend to be for companies of under £40 million in turnover, up to 250 employees and already trading for at least six months.

  Mentoring features in every programme in addition to group training and one-on-one support. They can be great for networking, finding new business opportunities and getting some time with an experienced mentor.

- ✔ **IOEE (Institute of Enterprise and Entrepreneurs) (**www.ioee.uk**):** Members of the small firms enterprise development initiative (SFEDI) are accredited by IOEE and are experienced business people who have been trained by Get Mentoring (www.getmentoring.org), a government-funded initiative set up to encourage business mentoring across the UK. They're not business advisers, but they're usually up to date with business knowledge and contacts, and they're committed to giving at least one hour a month to mentoring business owners and managers who are serious about growth.

> ✔ **PRIME (Prince's Trust for Mature Entrepreneurs)** (`www.mentorsme.co.uk/organisations/The-Princes-Initiative`): In addition to offering business advice and training to the older entrepreneur, PRIME also offers mentoring from business professionals who can relate to the challenges and fears of the more mature business owner. Whether you're a first-timer or a serial entrepreneur, going into business later in life can be very daunting and being mentored by someone who really knows how you feel goes a long way to building your confidence and skill set.

I talk about the pros and cons of applying to accelerators from a financial perspective in Chapter 8. If your application is successful, you can benefit from access to industry experts for one-on-one mentoring after you're accepted and enrolled.

Taking part in online support groups

National and international peer-to-peer support groups abound online. They cover anything from how to get the best out of your employees to figuring out how the new regulations for your industry affect your business.

E-mentoring, or shared learning online, from people just like you who've been there, done it and bought the T-shirt can be a fantastic way to get straightforward, easily understood mentoring born out of another entrepreneur's personal experience. It also provides you with the opportunity to share your pearls of wisdom with the wider business community.

Self-formed groups are often the result of someone's frustration at not finding a useful answer to a nagging problem or needing a place to vent and share. These groups can be a good source of very practical solutions and a virtual shoulder to cry on. However, they can also be full of unstructured, unfiltered and unqualified information and opinions, so choose wisely, Grasshopper. Check out the reviews and dip your toe in the water before diving in at the deep end of an online session.

Chapter 17

Exploring Strategies for Growth

. . . .

In This Chapter

▶ Working within the new normal after accepting investment

▶ Exploring growing organically and by acquisition

▶ Using debt to expand

▶ Going public

▶ Preparing for your exit

. . . .

*G*etting your business up and running and funded in the early stages is pretty hard work, and keeping that momentum going so that you achieve your growth goals and milestones is even harder work. If you've taken on equity, you have more people involved in your business, all demanding your time and business information on a regular basis.

When the economy is good, your growth seems easier, and all forms of finance are generally more plentiful and easier to acquire. When times are tough, your business skills and prudent financial management will be tested.

If you venture beyond the UK borders, you'll face additional challenges to both your finances and your business processes and procedures, which test you in ways you've yet to imagine.

As you grow your market share and expand your team, be mindful of what you ultimately want to achieve, be that selling shares in your company on the stock exchange, merging it with another business, having your senior management team buy you out or selling to a big industry player, leaving you to put your feet up and take a well-earned break.

In this chapter, I explore some of the options for growth funding, the challenges of having investors on board, and the potential exits for your business.

Dealing with Financiers Post-Investment

When you come down from the natural high that's associated with procuring investment and knowing that you'll be able to get started on creating the business of your dreams, you may experience a bit of a bump as you return to Earth and your feet touch the ground again when it slowly dawns on you that you're no longer the only owner of your business.

Instead of having the luxury of gradually getting used to your new working conditions post money, you're given a new set of rules on day one – you go from fairly free and easy to much more structured and formal. The new *shareholder agreements,* which set out shareholder rights and obligations, and *articles of association,* which set out the purpose of your company, as well as the duties and responsibilities of company directors, are filed at Companies House. You formalise the paperwork to finalise the transition of power, and a few new directors are staring you in the face.

Keep in mind that your new partners/advisors/directors are well meaning, well intentioned and have both your and their best interests at heart. So trust the process and make a mental note to be better prepared when it happens again in the next round of funding.

Sharing your business

When I asked Alex Stephany of Just Park (which has Index Ventures and 3,000 other investors via Crowdcube as shareholders) about his attitude towards sharing the business, he replied with a measured, logical answer, and with no ego whatsoever: 'It's what's best for the business'. I suggest taking a leaf out of his book, accepting what you've done and getting on with making it the best decision you could make for the future of your business.

With other people having a stake in your business, you can expect more rigorous reporting and compliance procedures than you may be used to. As with most things in life, some of it will be acceptable and easy enough, but some of it will be very new to you, take time to learn and won't always be something you want to be told to do. It's not all smooth sailing, and there will be times when sharing ownership will test your patience, your skills and your professionalism.

As the entrepreneur at the helm of this newly funded company, you need to take on some new skills and tasks pretty quickly:

✔ **Establish procedures for good investor relations.** A good deal of your time will now be spent on regularly scheduled board meetings and reporting to active as well as less active investors. At the same time, you're working to move the company forward in line with the vision and strategy agreed between you and your investors in the run up to investing.

✔ **Accommodate a new board structure and directorships.** Your team may have been you and one other person or you and a few others; you now need to deal with a board, non-executive directors and a new structure.

✔ **Accept input and involvement from your non-executive and investor directors.** Although everyone shares and supports the vision for the business, the level of influence you once had shifts away from you to create a new dynamic. Decisions that don't go your way are a real possibility. This is particularly evident if things don't go to plan and company performance is below what is expected, which has a direct impact on investors' returns. Not surprisingly, they'll want to have more of a say in how the ship gets back on course. If additional funds are required to get it back on track, then they'll be even more involved.

Remember to consider your mechanisms and readiness to deal with board and investor conflicts.

It's never too early to start planning for future funding. Think about whether your current funders will consider future investment rounds. If you're going to look to other funders in the future, think about how this will sit with your current lot and how to deal with that situation.

Bringing a valuable resource to the business

After funds, one of the most important things an investor brings to your business is a contingent of experienced, business savvy, well-connected and ambitious individuals who want to see your business flourish and grow. They can take on a variety of roles, but the most common are as:

✔ Chairman of the board

✔ Board members

✔ Non-executive directors

New shareholders may also be involved in appointing a financial director, if you don't already have one.

By taking on these roles, not only are investors able to keep a close eye on their investment, but they also show their commitment to your business and its growth. They often have the experience to make a smooth transition to this new regime, while simultaneously inspiring your team and motivating you to get on with hitting the milestones agreed in the aggressive growth you mapped out together. Their visibility is a help to you and your team and adds to your chances of success.

Your new advisors can also keep you on the straight and narrow with regard to increased governance and reporting requirements. Board meetings often take place once a month, and you'll spend a lot of your time on preparing paperwork and reports for these meetings. New board members or directors can provide you with guidance and templates to get you started, and help with the smooth running of the meetings and their resulting actions.

Recording and keeping information on the discussions and results of board meetings is crucial to your next round of funding, as future investors will want to see this documentation as part of their due diligence.

Technically, *corporate governance* is the system by which companies are directed and controlled. The purpose of corporate governance, according to the ICAEW (Institute of Chartered Accountants in England and Wales) is to help bring about effective but prudent management that can deliver the long-term success of your business. The board of your company is responsible for ensuring that your company is behaving responsibly and prudently, and so your board plays a role in your corporate governance. Your shareholders get involved in governance by appointing directors to make sure that it happens – to the best of their knowledge.

You can find information on the responsibilities of all directors and documentation for board meetings either on the Companies House website at www.companieshouse.com or the Institute of Directors website at www.iod.com, where information and training is available for members.

The role of the board

Generally, your board applies a guiding hand to the running of the company, making sure that you, as the founder and CEO, along with the rest of your team, are performing well, and that the business is performing in line with its agreed articles of association and the goals and objectives set out with the investment. The board members have many and varied responsibilities and functions, among which are the following:

- ✔ Ensure that the business operates within the law and with the right level of governance.

- ✔ Make sure that the company's financial position is solid and operates as an active company with good financial checks and balances, and is able to meet short-term liabilities.

- ✔ Make sure that all contracts, salary agreements, and shareholder agreements and plans are legal.

- ✔ Chair the board meetings, ensuring that they run smoothly and efficiently.

- ✔ Report to shareholders on a regular basis.

- ✔ Assist with the next round of fundraising and additional finance needs, as appropriate and when required. The board should anticipate funding needs.

The role of non-executive directors

A *non-executive director* is someone who's involved in strategic, planning or policy issues in your business. This director has a seat on the board, but is not part of the executive team, so he's not involved in making day-to-day decisions.

The roles of non-executive directors are varied and diverse, as are their backgrounds and skills, but they all contribute in a positive way to the growth of your business and your team. They can contribute in a variety of ways:

- ✔ Bring an extensive and valuable network and book of contacts.

- ✔ Bring a fresh pair of eyes and a different perspective. Directors aren't always experienced in your particular industry, but they're definitely experienced businesspeople.

- ✔ Bring a skill you may be light in or lacking – legal, human resource, some form of marketing or sales, for example.

- ✔ Act as a sounding board and learning platform for you and your senior team. They've been there, done it and bought the T-shirt, and they know how you're feeling.

Investor directors can fall into the category of non-executive directors, but, as they're part of the fund or have been nominated by the fund, they're not independent and so they have investor interest closest to their hearts and minds. When the going gets tough, you may wish they'd get going, but they won't. Work out how to manage them and expect them to put the investors' interests first.

Funding with debt

Businesses whose need for growth funding isn't great and whose current team, give or take a couple of new additions, is capable of implementing a growth plan that calls for non-equity arrangements, have the option of debt funding, which brings its own post-funding rules and requirements. (For more on debt funding, turn to Chapter 12.)

What can safely be said about both lenders and investors is that neither of them wants any surprises after they've given you the money. If you have any nasties on your radar, best to tell them sooner rather than later and deal with the consequences head on.

When it comes to debt, or lenders, make sure that you have a plan to pay off the loan, and make sure that you never go over your limits on any of the debt facilities or products you've agreed without getting approval first. Any red flags or warning signs about the way you manage their money can work against you.

Repayments are likely to be made by direct debit, and you will probably have some restrictions or covenants that you'll have to adhere to. For example, you may have to keep a certain amount of money in your account at all times. If you fail to meet these requirements, it will be evident in your account balance. If you've taken on debt to fund your expansion and growth, the lender will be monitoring your activity closely, making sure that you stick to your limits and you use the money for the purpose stated in your application. A lender keeps a constant eye on your account and can see when it's going south as quickly as you can.

Like equity investors, lenders want to see your monthly management accounts and a three-month rolling cash flow forecast, along with some assumptions and explanations. The following list is a good guide for what you'll need to keep updated:

- Profit and loss (P&L) statement
- Cash flow forecasts
- Timing differences of money coming in (if you have accruals and work in progress)
- Balance sheet

I discuss P&Ls, cash flow forecasts and balance sheets in Chapter 15.

Always explain variances between forecasts and actuals as soon as possible, and produce accounts within one week of the month ending.

Investing in future rounds

Any company that has received investment, and is serious about generating a far better than average return for its investors and founders, knows the need to sustain a meaningful rate of growth and to plan for the next round of funding sooner rather than later.

The board will be thinking of this well ahead of the time that funding is required, because as you and they will know from experience, this fundraising thing takes a lot of time!

On the plus side, the increase in corporate governance, reporting and monitoring means that you'll have a regularly updated and well-laid-out professional system for regularly updating your financial information and documents, including cash flow forecasts, so you'll see the next round funding need on the horizon and not have to flap about getting all the paperwork in order at the last minute.

The very fact that you've gone out to raise investment indicates that you're on a high-growth trajectory, so it's inevitable that you'll need additional funds in the not-too-distant future.

A valuable by-product of having fresh blood pumped into the board and non-executive director roster is that these new members have plenty of collective experience at updating, revising and refining business strategies and plans. They can help ensure that your documents are updated at regular intervals and in a format that's both meaningful for internal discussions and acceptable for external funding approaches at the appropriate time. You'll thank them for all the nagging and nudging when you realise how much time and effort they really save and how much value they add.

They also come in handy when it comes to updating your company valuation, which you need to do before going for the next round of funding. What used to be down to you to figure out is now a much slicker operation that brings all the contacts, knowledge and networks of your current investors to bear. For this next round, your information will be tighter, the level of content will be more sophisticated and the presentation will be more professional, with you being led and guided by someone chosen by the board to help prepare and cast an eye over the materials. It's a bit like going from adolescence to adulthood in business terms.

Your new team won't be totally altruistic. Your new investors, directors and board members may be looking to protect their rights with regard to future rounds as agreed in your terms, so keep that in mind – particularly when deciding on the new valuation.

Expanding Organically or via Acquisition

When I ran my second business, I was a victim of my own success, and grew from a one-room office to a large floor of offices within a couple of years. I also grew from a few members of staff to quite a few more, and one of them, who was crucial to my business, lost both her parents in a few short months and decided to move abroad. To say that this was a testing time for me, and for my wonderful but long-suffering husband, is an understatement.

Faced with a commercial fork in the road, I had to make a decision on how to go forward with my growth plans. I had to decide whether to hire additional staff and move into larger leased premises, which meant borrowing money at fairly high rates to fund the expansion, and continue to steadily grow my successful training business, or to instead save a few years of blood, sweat and tears and acquire a competitor to gain more-or-less instant growth. It took me a few months, but I decided on acquisition. I'd done my research and identified a competitor ripe for acquisition. It had repeat business, a steady income stream, owned a whole building and had some very experienced staff. I'd also spoken to a friend who worked in investment banking, and I was confident that he would help me arrange the finance. Yippee! Of course, before I could complete the transaction, the business I had hoped to acquire had a change of heart, and I instead had three offers to buy my business. In the end, I went for the sale.

My story illustrates the dilemma of organic expansion versus growth by acquisition – a situation many entrepreneurs find themselves in at one time or another. Indeed, you may be standing at that crossroad one day, too. Many successful businesses look to acquisition as a way to grow quickly, to eliminate some of the competition, and to position themselves for their next round of funding or their public listing.

Another very good example of friendly acquisition is Wahanda, the free appointment booking system for the beauty and spa industries. I attended a beauty trade event, and had the pleasure of meeting Lopo Champalimaud, one of the founders of Wahanda, and formerly part of the lastminute. com team. Earlier in the day, on Twitter, I'd seen that Wahanda had just announced the acquisition of a Dutch firm, which I wanted to discuss with him. Before I could ask my question, I discovered that Wahanda had gone from 100 employees in 2014 to 400 in 2015 by acquiring six companies along the way, and I began to understand its plans for becoming the biggest and best online site in the world for booking beauty and wellbeing experiences – and that more acquisitions would surely follow. Although the funding roster changed, by all accounts it was an amicable affair.

Both growth options have their pluses and minuses, and bring a different dimension to your organisation. Table 17-1 shows some of the pros and cons.

Table 17-1	Comparing Methods of Growth
Organic Growth	*Growth by Acquisition*
May not be fast enough to satisfy the needs of your new investors.	Can be a much quicker route to growth as you acquire instant market share, distribution channels, products and services, and intellectual property (IP), plus the good reputation of the brand you're acquiring.
Can be seen as a safer option because you avoid the risks associated with acquiring another business and any undiscovered problems or issues. No due diligence is 100 per cent foolproof – and there's none of the fall-out you get when trying to merge company cultures, financials and legalities.	You sometimes get more than you bargained for and uncover a few skeletons in the closet once the ink has dried, which you're stuck with. In some cases, you can acquire the assets of a company without acquiring all the liabilities, but this requires specialist advice and negotiation.
Usually much slower and therefore not as steep a growth trajectory over a five-year period.	Dealing with the casualties of acquisition can be costly, time-consuming and unpleasant. You have the inevitable cost cutting, personnel streamlining, and areas of cultural mismatch that need ironing out, and this can present an expensive distraction.

Organic Growth	Growth by Acquisition
It can wind up being costly because you have to find, train and retain staff, continually fund new product or service development and keep sourcing new clients and keeping them engaged.	

Like most things, you may find that there's much more to growing your business than just throwing more money at your current model or finding a chunk of money to go out and buy someone else's business. Each option has its obstacles and challenges, and both can pay handsome dividends if done well and at the right time.

As a strategy for growth, expansion organically or by acquisition definitely adds value to a shareholder's income and capital, and equips your business with a more sustainable income stream, a stronger and wider customer base as well as additional products and services.

Expanding overseas

The recent explosion in funding growth in technology-based businesses, many of which are now starting to look to the US, Africa, Continental Europe and elsewhere for their expansion, means it's worth mentioning the option of overseas expansion. If your domestic market is fairly saturated, international expansion and acquisition can be a great way to develop a *lateral market* – an entirely new market for an existing product or service line that you've made slight modifications to. However, overseas expansion has its own special quirks.

Overseas expansion carries an additional risk in the potential for cultural clashes, which is something to be very aware of. Consider cross-cultural issues carefully before you start down this road.

The cost associated with setting up an office abroad is generally much higher than it is in the UK. Do your research and talk to others who've gone before you for some firsthand knowledge and experiences. Along the same lines, employing people overseas can be a costly matter, so again, do your homework.

It may be possible to get a facilitator in the country you're targeting to help you identify and navigate around opportunities, and this is particularly useful if you're not fluent in the target destination language or haven't worked there before. Local knowledge and language skills are paramount. I look at a formal agent arrangement in the upcoming section 'Forming alliances', and this may be a less risky way to establish a foothold in an overseas market.

A free or low-cost resource closer to home is UKTI (UK Trade and Industry) (www.ukti.gov), where you can find help, guidance, support and advice for taking your product or business abroad.

Seeking additional growth funding

Funding comes in many shapes and sizes, and a good chunk of it, whether it's debt, equity or alternative funding, can be used to fund growth. The trick is getting the right type of funding at the right time and on the right terms, in order to achieve additional growth without crippling the organisation.

You can grow your business in a number of ways by using effective marketing, good sales techniques, profitable partnerships and joint ventures, clever promotion and innovative ideas and designs. Coupled with a great team and well-managed cash flow, you can successfully grow your business over time – inevitably, of course, hitting peaks and troughs along the way.

Whatever route you choose to go down, and however you choose to fund it, some commonalities apply:

✔ **You need a current business plan.** Keep your plan as up-to-date as possible, especially if you're reasonably sure you'll be going for additional funding in the not-too-distant future. Stopping to update your plan while your growing business is in mid-flow puts a great strain on your time and places great stress upon you.

Hopefully your figures show that you're hitting your targets and milestones and that you can either support the new debt you may take on or continue to be on target to reach the return your investors are expecting to see. You want to avoid dipping too low, especially if you've been equity funded, or you can find your valuation dipping lower into a down round, which makes it harder for you to raise additional funds and also makes your current investors play harder ball with you.

✔ **Your valuation needs to be up-to-date.** As part of updating your business plan, look at updating your company valuation as well so that you know what you're going to market with for the next round. Whether it's straight equity, debt that has an equity provision at the end of the lending period or term debt, you need to update your valuation. Your aim is to increase your valuation without too much dilution of shares, which can be a bit tricky (as I discuss in Chapter 13).

✔ **You should nominate a lead for fundraising.** The fundraising process takes time, so consider asking a board member to assist you and take the lead on this, leaving you free to run the business.

✔ **You have to be clear about where existing investors stand.** Some investors may have pre-emptive rights to invest in the new round and avoid diluting their shareholding further, choosing to follow their money. They usually have a ceiling amount that they want to invest, which may not be all the money you need, so you need to look elsewhere. Equally, you may be looking for a fresh new lead investor with your fresh new valuation, and although your other investors may be okay with this, your new investor may not be so happy if he gets blocked by the old team. You need to be clear about where everybody stands at the start and the end of the process.

✔ **You need to prepare if you're taking on new investors.** New investors or funders can bring fresh blood, perspectives and, importantly, contacts, but they need educating. This process can be time-consuming, so make sure all your board papers, company procedures and policies information, and anything else that's useful, is kept up-to-date.

New investors probably also want a seat on your board, so think ahead to how big that will make your board. Bigger may be too big to handle efficiently, and wind up being counterproductive, making it harder to get things done.

Looking at Debt Rounds and Reasons

Depending on the type of business you have and the amount of money you need, debt can be a good option for growth funding.

For example, if you had equity funding initially, and your company outsources the manufacturing of chocolate drinks, you may be better off with straightforward debt to cover your stock purchases, some staffing and a bit of online marketing.

If you're thinking about taking on more equity, but you don't want to dilute your current shareholding arrangements, and you don't need a huge amount of money, you may prefer to look at *convertible debt,* which is debt that converts to equity at some later point in time.

Equally, if you're equity funded and need at least another million, but don't want to dilute your shareholding any further, you may consider *venture debt,* an arrangement in which some of the debt converts to equity at a certain time. With its quasi debt-equity products, venture debt may be just the ticket.

The chapters in Part III go through the variety of funding options available to you.

Equity rounds, reasons and investors – A typical growth journey

If equity is the right way for you to go, you need to consider many things besides the money, but your growth journey may look something like this:

✔ **Seed round:** You're figuring out your product or service, finding your market and building your customer base. You may take on a few employees, launch a new or revamped product and start to ramp up the numbers in your user base.

- **Typical amount:** £100,000 to £1 million.

- **Typical investors:** Angels, high net worth individuals and private individuals.

✔ **Series A:** You're starting to scale the business and testing and tweaking the business model to get it right for your market. This may include scaling distribution channels, expanding your locations and proving your business model works.

- **Typical amount:** Anywhere from £1 to £10 million. In recent years, this round has become larger and earlier, blurring the lines between seed and series A funding.

- **Typical investors:** Early stage VCs, possibly co-invested with angels who invested in your earlier round.

✔ **Series B:** You're starting to scale your growth, and usually – but not always – have good traction in the market and a proven business model that can stand up to adversity and scrutiny. You may need to take on staff, start exploring overseas opportunities to widen your customer base or make some small acquisitions.

- **Typical amount:** Anywhere from £5 million to tens of millions.

- **Typical investors:** VCs – may be led by early-stage VCs or some of your series A investors, with additional investment from later stage VCs.

✔ **Series C:** To fund further accelerated growth – provide the additional capital needed to scale your business – you may go international for your funding by making an acquisition or by capturing more of your profit-making market at speed.

- **Typical amount:** Tens to hundreds of millions.

- **Typical investors:** VCs from earlier rounds, but can also be new private equity funds, hedge funds or other institutional funds (which can again change the level of control you have in your business and intensify your reporting and corporate governance).

Obtaining funding to make an acquisition

I cover a number of ways to fund an acquisition with either debt or equity in this chapter, but you can find plenty of additional, more creative options to consider as well, which I cover in the next sections. Although the options I present are by no means exhaustive, they provide a good starting point.

Personal funds and borrowing

If you have any left, your own savings or personal finances are an option. Equally, you can borrow from friends and family – an option I discuss in Chapter 10. You can also consider personal loans, and, as I talk about in Chapter 12, some government-backed schemes can help you in this area, too.

As you contemplate personal funding, consider these options:

- **Don't go it alone.** No one said you have to do everything on your own, so you may find a partner to join in and make the acquisition with you. Again, this is like a marriage, so be sure you get all the terms and conditions locked down before you say 'yes'. Your new partner may bring funding or take a *sweat equity stake,* putting in time in return for a piece of the action in the new business.

- **Spread the payments.** If you're a good negotiator and have a willing participant on the other side of the table, try to structure the acquisition deal in staged payments, keeping the old owner on board for a while to help make a smooth and profitable transition.

- **Take out a business loan.** You can access a number of sources for this money, as I discuss in Chapter 12. Maybe the acquisition target has some assets that you can borrow against. Get creative.

- **Seek additional equity.** You can approach angels or high net worth individuals who know you and your track record and may also want to get involved post-purchase.

Forming alliances

Forming a strategic alliance can be a great way to grow your business and take it to a new level of unprecedented growth. It can also be fraught with difficulties: if it's not set up and managed properly, it can bring your business to its knees. You've heard the saying that two heads are better than one, but that's not true if they're constantly knocking into each other and giving you both a professional headache.

You can form successful alliances for your growing business in a number of ways, and they include:

- **Partnership:** Your business and another commercial entity form a contractual or less formal working relationship with clear parameters, in which you both share risks and responsibilities as well as rewards.

You each may bring certain skills or abilities to the partnership that complement each other well, and you both appear instantly larger and more substantial as businesses.

✔ **Joint venture:** You and another business agree to create a new business entity for a finite period of time. You both contribute equally in assets and share equally in revenue gained, as well as expenses.

✔ **Licensing or using an overseas agent:** In a licensing agreement, you give another business the right to produce your product or deliver your service in a specific territory for a specific period of time, displaying your branding, trademark and so on. An agent represents your business in other territories, and may or may not also be licensed by you to sell.

Successful alliances can provide:

✔ A larger pool of resources to fish in and supplement to those in your growing business

✔ A new set of skills and a new team of capable people to share your managerial load and bring a fresh perspective

✔ More hands to make lighter work – a whole new set of skilled employees to share the work and double your joint productivity

✔ Possible introductions to new markets, both here and abroad

✔ A sharing of any risk associated with trying new ideas and opportunities

In order to give your alliance a fighting chance, consider some of these basic guidelines:

✔ Be very clear about what it is that you're trying to achieve with regards to growth. Set clear, measureable targets, assign responsibility and consider writing a joint business plan for this new working relationship.

✔ Seek complementary opportunities to join in with, and be clear about the value you both bring to the table. Make sure that any differences have an outlet for success and aren't going to set you up for failure.

✔ Establish formal working guidelines, systems and procedures as soon as possible, in the same way you would with any co-working relationship. Make sure that you do this in the spirit of collaboration and not control.

✔ Manage your key external and internal relationships, and make sure that all your internal relationships understand what the goals are and where they fit into this new equation.

Considering a Public Listing

If you've explored and exploited all the other options for growth, and you're ready to take a very grown-up plunge, you may consider taking your company public, or applying to list your shares on a public stock exchange. An *IPO (initial public offering)* offers your shares for sale to larger and institutional investors and sometimes also to the general public. It's a seismic shift in the way your company operates, so it's not a decision to be taken lightly.

You may consider a public share offering for a number of reasons, which include:

✔ Financing your future growth

✔ Improving your balance sheet

✔ Opening up your investor base

✔ Creating an incentive scheme for employees using share option plans

✔ Providing an opportunity for current shareholders with restricted shares to convert them to more liquid shares, which are more readily converted to cash

✔ Raising funds to make an acquisition

Whatever the reason, if you've identified this as a milestone in your company journey and you're ready to raise equity funds in this way, prepare yourself for a lot of internal introspection into how well your company is really run – as well as for a very lengthy and expensive process. You may decide to abort the IPO if it looks like the timing is off or something in the market happens to affect your listing, and you won't recoup the funds you spent preparing.

The decision to float your shares on the open market needs to be based in reality. The quality of your management team, a realistic assessment of how your business is performing, what the prospects for the future are and if it's the right time in the growth stage of your business to press *go* all need to be taken into account before you start the process.

Conventional wisdom says that a business that's achieved a certain amount of annual revenue, say £100 million, and has consistently been profitable is ready to withstand the process of an IPO with a valuation that's high enough to be able to sell shares to a variety of investors without diluting its equity into an unrecognisable position in the process.

However, consider the following checklist to see whether your business ticks all the right IPO boxes:

✔ Do you have a strong, predictable and consistent revenue stream that your business can sustain, and an ability to take that income to an even higher plateau after the IPO?

✔ Can you stare yourself in the mirror and, hand on heart, know that you've cleaned up any area where you may have a chink in your corporate armour – like being overly dependent on one very large customer, or having some bit of kit that will soon become obsolete (the consequences of which will rain down on you after you go public)?

If you answer 'yes' to these questions, you may just conclude that you're ready for an IPO.

The UK has two main exchanges for trading stocks:

- ✔ **London Stock Exchange (LSE):** Founded in 1801, the LSE is located in the City of London and is the third-largest stock exchange in the world (when measured by market capitalisation). The LSE allows larger companies to access capital, increase their profile and obtain a market valuation, thus taking them on the full IPO journey. Your business must have been trading for at least three years, and depending on the listing, different rules apply to different percentages of shares.

  Although it has more stringent requirements, the High Growth Segment gives your company the opportunity to fund its growth while preparing for an official listing. The main exchange has deeper pools of capital, more sophisticated benchmarking systems and higher media and investment profile than AIM.

- ✔ **AIM (formerly the Alternative Investment Market):** AIM is based in London and is the LSE's international market for smaller companies, allowing them to float shares with a more flexible regulatory system than the one applicable to the main market. A wide range of smaller businesses, including early stage, venture capital-backed, as well as more established companies, join AIM seeking access to growth capital for expansion.

  AIM is the most successful growth market in the world. Since its launch in 1995, over 3,000 companies from across the globe have chosen to join it.

Preparing for an IPO

Getting an IPO right and getting the timing right is a tricky process. You can help yourself by engaging in a bit of beating the bushes, or investor relations activity, and drumming up some interest even before you make the announcement. As time-consuming as this is, your IPO roadshow serves as a litmus test, helping you gauge investor opinion as to whether or not you'll get a good reception. It's also your opportunity to interact with journalists, suppliers and customers and analysts, so make sure that you've got your strategy clear and you've planned your activities.

Another method you can use for dipping your toe in the water is the *grey market analysis,* in which investors can trade shares in your company before its official IPO day, giving you an indication as to interest and also whether you've got the valuation right. This worked well for the Royal Mail and Twitter: both saw their opening day share values either very near or higher than the reading taken in the grey market; both had strong management teams and good growth strategies, and investors could see a good yield ahead.

As you consider a public listing, make sure that you can tick off every item in this checklist:

✔ Your company financial performance is impressive and consistent and shows a healthy balance sheet.

✔ You can articulate how your business is governed and what financial controls are in place.

✔ Your potential growth path is clear. You have a plan to cover the risks and how you'll mitigate them, and your plans look realistically impressive.

✔ You have a detailed business plan covering everything from your corporate strategy to your market overview, including your growth aims and objectives.

✔ You're able to explain what you're planning to do with the new funds that result from the offering.

✔ You and your team can explain and defend your business plan to investors, the press and analysts.

The LSE has teamed up with Imperial College in London to provide training that helps to prepare you and your business for a public listing. Not a bad idea, especially if you've never done this before, so have a look at its website, www.londonstockexchange.com, for more details.

Although it may seem like a public offering is the only option to aim for and also the most desirable option for all concerned, that's far from the truth. An IPO isn't something to be entered into lightly. It's an extremely costly, time-consuming and stressful process, and one that few SMEs enter into each year in the UK.

Timing your IPO

If, after much soul searching and intensive research, you decide to take your company public, you need to consider the timing of the offering as well as the time it takes to take your business public, and plan accordingly. Not only can the process be very long, but it's a huge distraction to the day-to-day running of the business, which can be costly in other ways.

To take your company to IPO is a lengthy process that starts long before it shows up in the business dailies. In truth, an IPO starts years before you start the actual process of listing on an exchange, and then it requires months of extensive and specialised professional advice, often seeing you nominate an adviser, a lawyer and an accountant, as well as a public relations (PR) firm for drumming up interest and organising roadshows, to make sure you're doing it right.

Successful IPOs

Not every IPO is smooth sailing, but the two companies here were ultimately successful:

✔ Aldermore Bank got its successful IPO at the second time of asking. It had to put the process on hold due to a downturn in the stock market earlier on. Share price rose immediately after the bank was listed on the stock exchange, and it had a good outcome to what must have been an expensive process.

✔ Sophos, a UK technology company, had a very successful IPO on the London Stock Exchange in 2015, raising £352 million with a £1 billion company valuation.

Your company procedures and policies, and its corporate governance, will need to hold up under the microscope and cost of extensive due diligence, which leaves no stone unturned before going to market, and ensures that no negative surprises that can scupper or delay a successful listing.

Components to consider for an IPO:

✔ **Size:** For years, conventional wisdom said that unless your business was going for a good number of years and turning over more than £100 million a year for AIM, and £250 million for the larger exchanges, it wasn't worth going for an IPO. More recent business wisdom changed this view somewhat, and companies are considering IPO with lower revenue targets but convincing growth targets.

✔ **Timing:** IPOs are best timed to coincide with strong investor interest. Like most things where investors are concerned, the most active times are spring to early summer and the autumn months of September to December. August tends to see everyone off somewhere else, and the Christmas period sees a drop in activity while everyone is wrapping up the year-end and focused on festivities. However, this isn't set in stone, and a lot can happen between the times you make it known that you're considering an IPO and when you actually go public. The economy can be a cruel mistress and luck may not be on your side.

Listings on an exchange can take two to three years to plan. Your company's ability to keep hold of all its significant contracts and continue to pump out positive financial results in the run up to a listing can change with the passing of time, and investors don't like to see this just before reaching down to put their hands in their pockets.

✔ **Valuation:** By going down the IPO route, you're effectively saying that you need to raise a certain amount of cash that you think the business is worth. Investors may not necessarily agree with you. In the tech or scientific world, for example, value is often linked to patents and intellectual property versus lots of cash rolling in on a continual basis, and this can affect the way that investors view the valuation.

Valuations look to future cash flows, which can be difficult to predict accurately.

Considering Your Exit Options

An IPO is by no means your only option for exiting your high-growth business. In fact, in the UK, it's the option least chosen, even though there's been a larger uptake in the last year or so. So, you're best to explore and acquaint yourself with what else is on offer. The following sections discuss other options to consider.

Agreeing to ongoing commitments

Selling your business can give you a great sense of accomplishment, the opportunity to write the next chapter of your life, and, of course, some cash in the bank and some shares in your portfolio.

But, as I know all too well, selling your business doesn't end your involvement. So, before you stop setting your alarm and start heading for the beach, remember that in most cases the seller warrants, or guarantees, that the key facts of the sale are true and provides assurances or indemnities in case of any contract breach that may occur after the ink has dried.

Most sales include a year of *earn-out,* or a period of time that you work in the new business in order to provide continuity and your institutional memory. Often, you continue to work in the new firm for one or two years to ensure a smooth handover and continuity of income. Your final payment, earned at the end of the transition period, may be dependent on hitting set targets within that time frame.

If targets are linked to profit, it's a matter of accounting procedures; if they're linked to turnover, be very sure that you have clearly outlined processes for determining who's responsible for bringing that money in. Turnover is a much more subjective measurement than profit, and, if possible, to be avoided when linked to earn-out.

If you're lucky enough to receive full payment for your business in one lump sum, you at least have that peace of mind. More often than not, however, payments are staggered or phased, so if you want your money, you have to stay engaged. Earn-out can become burn out if you're not careful.

Lastly, most agreements have a *non-compete clause* prohibiting you from participating in a competing business for a specified amount of time. You're definitely expected to respect all confidentiality and your duty of care.

Selling your business: A trade sale

A *trade sale,* or selling to another business already in your sector or wanting to get into your sector, is the most common form of exit for you and for your investors. Timing and planning are key, but if you're the solution to someone else's problem, as I have experienced myself, or you fill in the final piece to another company's jigsaw by giving it instant access to a missing market, you may find that a trade sale is just the ticket for you and your investors.

Often, you know who may be a good trade buyer for your business because you're active in the market and aware of the company's activity – or gaps in their activity. For example, if you're an educational technology business, perhaps developing new educational technology that comes with a patent or patent pending, you may be seen as a relatively inexpensive acquisition for research and development for a large educational resource company. Many trade acquisitions consist of ideas or assets that complement existing operations, so it's best to keep your ear to the ground and your eyes open to opportunities.

Also popular is the use of a specialist broker who makes introductions on behalf of both buyers and sellers for fees that can also cover assisting you with your selling documentation. As with all advisers, it's your responsibility to check them out thoroughly and to be satisfied with their terms and conditions before signing on the dotted line.

Whichever way you decide to enact your trade sale, settle yourself in for a rough ride. You have to fight your corner hard if you're going to get the best deal for you. It's not in the buyer's interest to give you any more than he can get away with. Know your value, get some reinforcements in to do some of your negotiating and be prepared to fight – metaphorically speaking.

With any trade sale, it pays you to look at the areas where you can have some direct influence and those where you can't.

Areas you can have some direct influence over include:

- ✔ Succession planning
- ✔ Robust procedures, controls and monitoring
- ✔ Customer base, with no heavy reliance on one customer or segment
- ✔ Range of products and services, so that if one area suffers it doesn't bring the business down
- ✔ A great reputation in the market that can withstand any changes at the top
- ✔ A great internal culture – a happy, thriving workforce is more likely to stay put

Areas you can't have direct influence over include:

✔ **The market:** You alone can't influence the market, unless you happen to be Bill Gates or Warren Buffett. Seek professional advice and closely follow your market when looking at the timing of your exit. Be aware that something may happen that's out of your control and can have a negative – or positive – impact on your exit plans, and you'll just have to live with it.

✔ **Customer reaction:** Your customers' reactions to your exit may signal a mini stampede due to doubts about their relationship with the business as it goes forward. Do all you can to make sure that the business isn't dependent on your being there, and hope that after an initial adjustment period, everything will even out. Whatever action you take to mitigate it, be prepared for a little bit of backlash from your existing customers.

Merging with another business

Despite the fact that merging may feel like it's the same as being acquired by another business, differences do exist, and they include:

✔ Two firms literally become one – two separate entities cease to exist. In an acquisition, the business being acquired typically stays the same legal and accounting entity.

✔ A merger requires some specialist accounting and legal work to be done to combine the two entities correctly.

✔ Although the two businesses are merging into one, the truth is that – more often than not – one has seniority over the other, having been more significant before the merger.

The decision-making process has to combine two sets of needs and desires, sometimes pulling in opposite directions to varying degrees. Some of the areas that may be affected include:

✔ **Staffing:** Who stays and who goes, and who gets moved sideways

✔ **Location:** Where to locate the new entity

✔ **Property/assets:** How to dispose of the property and other assets of one of the businesses

✔ **Management:** What the new management structure will look like

✔ **Company culture:** How to blend the two companies' cultures

All of these are very sensitive and sometimes highly political decisions, and none of them is straightforward to make or communicate.

Management buyouts and management buy-ins

At some point in your business life, you may decide that you've had enough – and that although you can still get around under your own steam, you'd like to exit your business but not hand it over to your erstwhile competitors or leave it to languish and wither on the vine. If it's a family business, perhaps the next generation has no interest. If it's been a tough time economically, maybe you're on a slippery slope to receivership, and you see a part of the wreck that can be salvaged. It may be that you see the writing on the wall and you want to get out before the going gets really tough. Or perhaps it's just a part of your business that you're thinking of parting with because it's not pulling its weight and is a drain on the rest of the company, and you can't – or don't want to – raise more money to bail it out.

Whatever the reason, while you're contemplating your best move, some of your team may also be thinking that it's time for you to put your feet up or that they can do your job better. They may start the ball rolling before you've warmed up and left the bench, initiating what's known as a *management buyout,* or an MBO.

On the other hand, you may be approached by an external management team that wants to buy in to your business – which can provide you with a fresh injection of capital and a team that still has energy to burn. That can also be a difficult emotional time for you as a business owner. This new arrangement may usurp some of your power and also put the fright into your employees, which you'll need to manage.

Management buyout (MBO)

Depending on your relationship with your team and your funders, your management team may approach you to float the idea of a buyout of your company whether you think you're ready to leave or not. They may even engage an advisory firm, making it an altogether more formal process. If your managers are looking at an MBO, they obviously think they can steer the ship better than you can, and they're probably also looking for a way to keep their jobs and preserve the business.

The management team generally think that anything you can do, it can do better. But it may be bamboozled by the financial rigours that the new funders demand and overwhelmed by the task of keeping the business on target for the aggressive growth it promised to the private equity house, bank or venture capital firm. If the new team has overpromised and the figures don't stack up, everyone gets jittery. In fact, it's in everyone's interest, including whoever stumps up the money, for you to hang around, mopping up any messes and providing continuity, continued financial performance and confidence for staff, customers and funders.

Equally, the management team's funders may not necessarily be experienced in your marketplace or that familiar with the management team, but they need both the business and the team to perform if they're going to realise a stellar return on their investment. This is often why they put a member of their own tribe on the board.

If funders have put up their money looking to get a great return and the business starts to go south, it will demand the patience and foresight of a saintly funding team to stop the rot quickly, make sure to keep the people who oil the gears in position and to take swift action to get the new management back on course. Equity funders tend not to be in it for the do-gooding, so they'll be demanding, even if they're aware of the need to put performance before profit in the early days.

The basics of an MBO are as follows:

- ✔ The existing management team buys into your business.

- ✔ The management team needs to stump up some of the cost of the MBO, possibly using debt while it waits for venture capital or private equity funding to come through.

- ✔ It may keep your company's longevity going.

- ✔ The management team is knowledgeable about the business and can therefore make small, more immediate changes, thus creating instant impact.

- ✔ As part of the deal, the management team can be given an incentive to maximise returns.

MBOs are popular with private equity investors because the risk is relatively low, the return is within a three-to-four-year time frame and the new managers have some skin in the game.

Management buy-in (MBI)

In contrast to your current team buying into your company, an MBI, or *management buy-in,* occurs when an external management team buys into your business. Your own management team may not have the skills or the desire to carry out an MBO but outsiders may. The purchase is usually funded by venture capital or private equity plus some of the new management team's own money, which often involves personally guaranteed debt due to the need for speed when raising the cash. (The due diligence process for venture capital or private equity money can cause cumbersome delays.)

Although you may feel fraught with emotion at having someone come in and set up camp on your turf, and your staff may feel jittery about keeping their jobs, an MBI may be a good exit solution and should at least be considered.

In an MBI:

- ✔ You sell to a new management team.
- ✔ It normally has the backing of a private equity or venture capital firm.
- ✔ The new management team usually brings some of its own funds as well as external funding.
- ✔ Your position is at risk, because the new management team may decide that you're part of the old problem and not necessarily part of the new solution.

Exiting from angel or venture investors

In the same way that you exit your business – or quasi-exit your business if you stay on in one way or another – your investors want to exit your business at some point as well. As with their other investments, they want to reap their capital gains rewards and recycle their money by investing in new deals.

Investment funds have varying life cycles and durations, and some can be as long as eight to ten years, but they typically exit your business in four to five years, moving slowly out of all their current investments in years six through ten of the fund life cycle. Angels often hold for up to five years, but everyone looks to exit the investment at some point. This is perfectly natural and may pave the way for your next round of investment, but you need to be aware of a few things as you go through this uncoupling.

Depending on what you negotiate and agree to in your term sheet when you raise your funds, investors have certain rights that you need to remember when you look to exit. Be sure that you're comfortable with them before you sign off on the term sheet, because it's too late if you change your mind later on.

Usually referred to as *drag and tag rights,* the most common carryover rights look something like this:

- ✔ **Drag** or **drag along rights** essentially mean a majority shareholder can force a minority shareholder to join in on the sale of the company. The majority owner doing the dragging must ensure that the minority shareholders have the same price, terms and conditions as any other seller. So in essence, the majority shareholder is protected and the others have to follow suit.

- ✔ **Tag** or **tag along rights** protect the minority shareholder, enabling him to tag along and be included in any negotiations around the sale of company shares and giving him the right to follow along with the sale of the majority stakeholder shares.

Part V

The Part of Tens

In this part . . .

- ✔ Avoid some of the most common mistakes new business founders make.

- ✔ Learn the key terms you need before you get started.

- ✔ Know what funders think, but don't necessarily say.

- ✔ Get yourself into pole position to win the funding race.

Chapter 18

Ten (Plus One) Pitfalls to Avoid

In This Chapter
▶ Strengthening your knowledge base
▶ Staying on top of financial information
▶ Attracting investment with a realistic proposition

*I*f the most recent economic downturn has taught us anything, it's that no business is immune to financial difficulty, decline and disaster. Surely no one expected giants like major investment banks to fall, alongside thousands of one-man bands, micro businesses and SMEs (small- and medium-sized enterprises) that were caught up in the aftershock of an economic earthquake on an unprecedented scale. But fall they did, and the bigger they were, the harder they fell.

Hundreds of thousands of small businesses close each year, many of them early on in their trading lives. You no doubt make an effort to learn from your failures, but it's always better to avoid them in the first place, especially if they're liable to wipe you out entirely.

This chapter covers the key problem areas to steer clear of in order to avoid financial disaster.

Knowing Too Little

As the founder, owner, director and general person in charge, the buck stops with you. For that reason alone you need to make sure that you have a minimal understanding of all the business areas in your enterprise. Your role as captain of the ship will take you into uncharted waters if you've never had to draft a marketing strategy, coach a new employee through a difficult transaction or negotiate an overdraft with the bank. On any given day, your skills and expertise will be tested in a variety of ways, and you won't want to be found wanting.

As your business grows and develops, you will be repeatedly called upon to be the commercial equivalent of a jack-of-all-trades, whilst never forgetting that you are still the master of one – steering the ship safely through dangerous waters and arriving at your destination with minimal casualties and ahead of schedule.

In my experience, it is absolutely imperative that you and your team have defined roles and responsibilities, and avoid the trap of duplicating efforts and wasting time because 'we're a start-up'. Poppycock. If you start as you mean to go on, you may fall off the wagon every once in a while, but you will be a better leader of a more efficient organisation in the long run.

Being Complacent about Your Knowlege

Even though it may seem like a waste of time or an additional expense at a time when you can least afford it, taking courses that help you brush up or learn skills you need to run your new business is well worth the investment in time and money. The knowledge gained will pay dividends in understanding, confidence and contacts.

Training comes in all sizes and formats these days, so finding the course you need at a reasonable cost and in convenient format can be done. You can find a course for yourself or your employees via the advice and support channels I talk about in Chapter 8 and through websites such as:

- ✔ **learndirect (**www.learndirect.com**):** As the UK's largest provider of training and employment services with a network of 400 delivery locations, learndirect offers flexible distance learning and online courses, as well as part- and full-time classroom courses throughout the UK. Millions have already successfully used the service for formal qualifications in things like maths and English, vocational qualifications, finding or applying to be an apprentice, and short online courses in anything from software to Swahili. For a business looking to sharpen its competitive edge, be it an SME or a blue-chip market leader, check the business section of the learndirect website for specific focused courses.

- ✔ **Open University Business School (**www.open.ac.uk/business-school**):** I mention the Open University in Chapter 8, and it has a specific Business School that offers management and professional development courses mostly online and accessible all over the world. Courses include an accredited MBA (master of business administration) programme and other accredited business courses suitable for all learners, no matter your stage or skill level.

✔ **Udemy** (www.udemy.com/21-golden-rules-for-entrepreneurs):
Udemy offers down-to-earth, practical and free courses to entrepreneurs.
One such course is 21 Critical Lessons for Entrepreneurs, which offers
real-world insight into running and funding your business with lessons
and skills that are easily applied to your business.

Being Overly Optimistic about Your Market

By nature of the fact that you've decided to turn your back on the world of
paid employment, throw caution to the wind and take your chances walking the high wire of business without a safety net, it's safe to say that you're
an optimist.

This much-admired characteristic is essential as you'll need to face and
overcome many challenges, hurdles and obstacles – self-made or laid before
you – all the while holding true to your belief that you have *the* solution to
the problem and that you can make a successful, scalable business out of
it. You may have enough belief to move mountains, but you cannot – and
should not – project your optimism onto the market at large.

The one thing you can't afford is to be overly optimistic about the market
or your potential market. Just because you and a bunch of your mates think
your product is the next best thing, and you've tested it with a few focus
groups, don't fall into the trap of thinking that you'll attract a significant
market share and race ahead while your competitors are snoozing. Always do
plenty of well-documented market research and testing.

At the same time, don't assume that anyone who doesn't share your vision
can be made to come round to your point of view. Getting people on board
is a lengthy process that requires time and a good deal of money, and it may
not produce the desired result in the end.

If the rest of the market doesn't share your view that your product or
service is the next big thing or if investors aren't ready to get on board,
you may be heading for disaster. In addition, you almost certainly won't
be able to convince a funder to say 'yes'. If you decide to go ahead without
solid market research, risking house and home, you're likely to end up in
financial hardship.

Underestimating Funding Time

Like so many things in life, raising funds for your business always takes longer than you think, and you always need the money three months before you start looking for it. It's human nature to put off asking for money until the last minute. But, it's bad planning to underestimate the amount of time it takes, and this is especially true for equity and crowdfunding. (I talk about these in Chapter 13.) It can also be an expensive exercise, certainly costly in your time as well as money, so you keep putting it off, until boom! You win the contract and can't buy the stock; you find the perfect location, but can't pay the deposit or kit it out and so on.

A good rule is to allow at least six months to raise funds and expect it to take up a good amount of your time and at least five figures of your precious money in valuation, negotiation, legal and success fees. (I look at the timing of fundraising in Chapter 13.)

Using your cash flow forecast as a guide, work out a timeline for your fundraising effort and assign tasks, people and costs at certain dates in order to plan time, money and physical resources and not lose track of any of the key steps in the process.

Investing Too Little at the Start

Your desire to start your own business may grow out of a hobby, a redundancy or a belief that you can do it better than the place you work at, so suffice it to say that not a lot of planning or resource goes into setting up.

Despite the fact that this type of illogic flies in the face of all common sense, trust me; you're not alone. Don't feel you need to pretend otherwise, because this is more common than you think. The realisation of a problem often comes to light when you hit your first cash buffer and realise you need help to fix it.

Being a lean, mean machine is one thing, but shoestring financial planning usually leads to not having enough money in the business to take you from lift-off to the first milestone. Inevitably, panic sets in. Combine this with a desire to have the best-looking office in the best part of town with the best website and the best team in place – all of which cost money, of course – and you can wind up losing your competitive edge before you even get to market.

Something you can do that goes a long way to eliminating this potential failure is a simple cash-flow forecast (which I cover in more detail in Chapter 3). It tells you how much you need to get started, when that investment starts to generate income within the business, and when you're likely to need a top up.

Forgetting How You Generate Profit

Find yourself a quiet space where no one can hear you, and repeat after me: 'Revenue does not equal profit'. Now, say it again, write it down somewhere you will be reminded of it – often – and never forget it! *Profit* is what's left in the business after you allow for the cost of making or providing a service and all the overheads or expenses you need to run your business. Profit is not revenue or sales income.

Don't get me wrong, escalating sales figures will – and should – make you feel successful, but don't be blinded by the bright lights of rising income figures. You can have all the sales income in the world, but if you don't get the selling price right and lowest price on the cost to get your product or service out the door while keeping the running costs as low as possible, you will never make a profit.

When you hear, 'revenue is vanity and cash sanity', it means having actual cash in the bank after all the costs have been deducted is how you keep your head. I go one step further and remind you of the one of the ratios I look at in Chapter 20, gross profit margin. This margin is a key indicator of profitability in a business. You can research typical gross profit margins for your industry online.

Essentially, *gross profit* is sales income minus the costs associated with making your product or delivering your service. It doesn't take into account any of the other expenses in the business that you have more control over, such as rent or phone.

If your gross profit margin is right for your industry, you're in a good position to succeed; if your margin is too low, then you can never make a profit. In that case, look at the cost of goods/labour and the pricing of your product or service and make some adjustments.

Overvaluing Your Business

You may have seen television shows like BBC's *Dragon's Den* or the US version, *Shark Tank,* in which hopeful entrepreneurs get shot down at the last minute due to excessive business valuations. If you overvalue your business, it's safe to say investors won't give you any money. This is especially true in the early stage of a business when it's difficult to arrive at a valuation using traditional methods that require some financial history. Early investors must rely on comparable companies in the same sector and stage and the potential value at exit, using their experience and know-how.

Do your homework with regard to valuations and exits of similar companies in your sector so that you appear knowledgeable and aware when courting early investors. Be able to point out why your business is better at plugging the gaps than others, and give investors confidence in a good return.

Although valuation is a bit of science mixed and art, peppered with gut feeling, experience and market forces, you can use a number of methods for arriving at a valuation. Chapter 15 contains some hints and tips for maximising your chances of presenting an acceptable valuation to an investor.

Early traction in the market helps to give investors a guide as to the likely performance of your business. Add to this the experience of your team, whether you are past the prototype stage and have some early sales, the menacing presence of other hungry investors (only if this is genuinely true) and you can create an appetite for a deal a hungry investor doesn't want to miss out on.

Ignoring Accounting

Many entrepreneurs see accounting as a necessary evil and something done off-site by worker bees in the back-office hives of accountancy offices. Some business owners give attention to their accountants just once a year in order to file an annual return and keep HMRC (Her Majesty's Revenue & Customs) at bay.

Although I have a certain amount of sympathy for you here, not wishing to ignore the fact that your hard-earned profits are taxed, I also want you to heed the warning that you ignore accounting at your peril. In the worst case, your first accounts can wind up being your only and last accounts, or at the very least require a good deal of expensive rescue work.

Ignoring your accountant is dangerous and also a missed opportunity to learn a new skill, take advantage of potentially valuable tax breaks, gain control over your business finances and, dare I say it, even learn to enjoy the logical puzzle that is accounting for SMEs.

Understanding your accounts and looking at them regularly, at least on a monthly basis and more frequently when things are difficult or large purchases need to be made, helps you see where you can free up money being tied up in other ways, suppliers you can negotiate better terms with, interest rates and payment plans that may no longer be the best offer in town and so forth. If you're VAT registered, you can use your accounts and accounting software to project forward and illustrate your potential liability or refund, helping you plan better and avoid nasty surprises. Your accounts, when properly formatted and regularly updated, also show you your margins, including the all-important gross profit margin, which can be tracked and any problems highlighted early on.

In accounting terms, ignorance is not a valid defence. Your accountant may prepare the documents, but you sign them as a person in authority and are ultimately responsible for their accuracy.

If you, like thousands of other entrepreneurs, most notably Richard Branson, have the added challenge of dyslexia or dyspraxia, which makes reading spreadsheets more of a bugbear, check out the variety of helpful hardware and software solutions to help make your life a bit easier. Voice recognition software and different coloured filters for computer screens are just a couple of examples of what's available. Contact the associations or organizations for your particular condition to discover what practical solutions they can provide.

Forgetting Working Capital

Most business owners, be they novices or old hands, can work out how much finance or investment they need for the things that are obvious and easy to put a price on: IT (information technology) equipment, rent deposits, patent applications, training, legal costs, vehicles and so on. Depending on your industry and what stage your business is in, you finance these costs in a variety of ways.

You may think that you've thought of everything when it comes to putting money into your business, but frequently entrepreneurs or business owners forget about the money needed for *working capital,* money that comes into the business from day-to-day trading used to pay for things like salaries and recurring monthly bills. The timing of when this money comes into the business coffers can put considerable financial strain on a business, and indeed, has been known to bring a business to its knees. If this money is from customers who owe you for goods and services, for example, and they are 30, 60 or 90 days late with their payments, you can imagine the impact on running your business and the need to look elsewhere – often your own pocket – to fund the gap.

Few new businesses are profitable from day one, and it usually takes a while to get to the *break-even point* where you're not yet profit making and equally not losing money but just about to tip over into profit. It's vitally important that you start with enough money to cover this period of time, which typically lasts from three to six months.

Working capital needs are different for different types of industries and sectors, and you need to know the flash points for your own business and plan accordingly. For example, retailers don't usually have a problem with cash because money comes in instantly from customers at the tills or online. Retailers, however, often need to keep a hefty inventory and forking out for the products in advance can cause working capital problems, especially if they have any seasonality to their range, such as Christmas or beach products. Seasonal sales cause huge peaks and troughs in a business's cash position and produce scary moments when revenues are low during the off-season. Inventory planning and projections are critical for these businesses.

Manufacturers may wait many months before the raw materials and labour they pay for upfront or in 30 days become finished products, shipped and paid for by the end-user. It doesn't matter if you're making high-end dresses or injection-moulded industrial pipes, the timing can be the same. In these types of businesses, if your sales suddenly skyrocket and orders are coming in thick and fast, you run the risk of running out of money to keep making your products, known as *over-trading*. If you don't have enough working capital or can't get hold of some form of working capital finance quickly enough, your success will be your downfall. Bittersweet, I think you'd agree.

Choosing the Wrong Team

Although you're at the helm of your business, steering a course to success, carefully navigating icebergs, battling fast moving currents and harnessing the power of winds of change, no man (or woman) is an island, and the quality of the team you surround yourself with plays an important role in the success of your business.

I spent years in the recruitment industry and developed a sixth sense when it came to a good hire, along with a standard set of 14 probing questions that made candidates unwittingly disclose their weaknesses and highlight their strengths. Most business owners don't have the luxury of this kind of experience and tend to make some pretty basic errors when forming a team. One typical mistake is working with people who are just like you. Of course you want to spend time with people you like and who are like you – we all do – but in a business environment, complementary – not identical – skill sets are what matter. Experience and expertise should matter more than getting along well and being friends.

It's helpful to enlist the aid of outsiders when interviewing or searching for staff. They can be business people, recruitment agencies, advisors or mentors, and not necessarily in your industry or sector. (Chapter 16 provides some useful resources for external help.)

In addition to the skill set, you need to define the role and be crystal clear about the expectations for every member of the team. Leaving your employees to figure out their responsibilities on their own only leads to disappointment, ill feeling and additional costs as you replace them for under-performance.

Assuming Investors Read Your Plan

Having put a lot of hard work and effort into writing what you hope to be an investment-winning business plan, it's not surprising that you assume potential investors read it from cover to cover and made detailed notes in the margins. I hate to disappoint you, but most investors don't delve into your painstakingly written and carefully laid-out plan unless they like what they read in the executive summary and want to find out more before they physically meet you. Don't take it personally, but do take it on board and make your executive summary leave them wanting more.

Typically, investors receive more than 100 business plans a week, and they're notorious for having short attention spans – a lethal combination as far as you're concerned. Knowing this, you can understand why they don't have the time or inclination to trawl through thousands of pages a week, and you should adjust your offering accordingly.

Whatever round of investment or type of funding you need, it's important that you think like an investor or a lender in order to ensure your plan gets read and acted upon. Investors want to maximise their potential return on an investment while minimising their exposure to risk, so make sure that comes across in your opening summary.

Chapter 19

Ten Things Funders Don't Tell You

In This Chapter

▶ Looking at the tips and tricks of the funding trade

▶ Highlighting tests, targets and how your business tallies up

▶ Helping you improve your business credit profile

*H*aving good relationships with funders is vital to maximising the positive aspects of taking on investment or loans. However, funders are businesspeople, not friends, and as such they usually remain loyal to their organisations more so than their clients or customers, so set your expectation levels accordingly. It's very easy to forget that you're involved in a financial transaction with varying levels of goodwill and support thrown in, and to fall into a false sense of security, believing that their focus is entirely on your best interests. This just isn't the case.

Maintaining and promoting transparency as far as possible in your relationships with funders is a good thing, but be aware that funders don't tell you everything that goes on in front of and behind the scenes – in the same way that you don't tell your valued customers the warts-and-all stories associated with their customer accounts. In this chapter, I look at ten key things that funders may not share with you.

They Allow the Computer to Make Decisions

You may be familiar with the catchphrase from a well-known British comedy show, delivered in a very dry, lifeless voice, when the customer in the travel agency is rejected for his chosen destination: 'Computer says "no".' You may have heard this same phrase at your bank's offices. You're in good company, because on average, only one to two out of every ten debt deals get funded using the computer unaided by human intervention.

In the case of equity, if you apply via a platform, the initial online screening process may reject you before you even get to the more complicated forms.

The objective scoring system shows no mercy and takes no prisoners. If you don't meet the stringent criteria, you get filtered out at the first hurdle, theoretically saving time and money for all concerned.

With the increasing number of online funders, computer-assessed funding decisions are a hotly debated topic. Not long ago, I took part in a roundtable discussion with international lenders debating the role of human versus machine in making lending decisions. In other words, at what point is a human being with reason and experience needed to take over from a machine that uses algorithms? We all agreed that up to £50,000 a machine – a computer – is good enough for a final decision; beyond that, the decision needs a human touch. This is not a view universally shared by all high street lenders or popular funding platforms, but it's a signal to you to find out all you can about the potential funder's scoring criteria, and to then do all you can to get your profile shipshape before you make any funding applications.

They Work to Internal Bank Targets

Most businesses have internal targets, be they sales targets, customer acquisition targets, targets to minimise loss and so on. Funders are no different, and also have internal targets for the amount of money to get out the door and which business sectors and types they want to be in receipt of their funds, as well as targets to minimise defaults or write-offs.

Human nature being what it is, if someone has targets, as sure as the sun rises in the east, he works to meet those targets. So, if a funder has reached his target in a particular area, your perfectly fundable proposition still won't get funding.

 Banks set internal limits to minimise risk and exposure, and funds have a finite amount of money aimed at a fixed number of investments, usually spread across a number of sectors. Ask questions to see if it's worth your time to pursue a funder at any given time.

They Can Refer You to Other Funders

To be perfectly honest, it's not the duty or responsibility of a lender or investor to refer you on to another funder, but this may change on the debt side. Currently, some voluntary arrangements are in place for funders to refer you on via selected platforms, such as Funding Options (www.fundingoptions.com), where you can see a selection of funders. It's unclear whether this will become mandatory.

Some of the more forward-thinking early adopters of a referral scheme include Santander Bank referring to Funding Circle and Metro Bank referring to the online lender Zopa. By referring out companies they can't help, funders give those companies a chance to get funded elsewhere and also create a channel for finding additional bank customers – a win-win situation.

Equity funders have no need to point you in another direction, but they sometimes do if they're working in partnership or in a referral arrangement with other investors. You can see whether they're in a partnership by looking at their websites and searching online, but you'll probably rarely find out if they're getting a referral commission from other investors. A good example of a partnership is the current London Co-Investment Fund (LCIF), which covers both debt and equity and matches a fund provided by the Mayor's Office to funds from a number of other funders, such as Wellington Partners, Balderton Capital and Crowdcube. The LCIF is set to run until April 2016, and you can find more information at www.lcif.org.

The need for additional transparency and options stems largely from the decline in traditional lending to small- and medium-sized enterprises (SMEs), and the need to keep feeding economic growth now that the most recent recession is coming to an end.

So the moral of the story is to always ask if the lender that's not funding you can refer you to someone else. The funder can only say 'no', and you may be pleasantly surprised.

They Ban Certain High-Risk Sectors

High risk is largely something that occurs in banks in relation to lending and isn't really an equity issue. Although you and I may have an opinion on what constitutes a high-risk sector, banks may take a different view. And, a bank may well make its views known to internal staff and to any business or financial advisors who introduce clients or prospects to a bank.

Industries such as professional services are normally seen as safer, due to their low overheads and limited exposure, whereas a new bistro is seen as high risk because so many food outlets go out of business in their first year. Businesses with high upfront costs leave banks exposed to changes in the economy.

Banks don't want to put businesses they view as high risk off using their other services and products, so they don't make a big song and dance about the sectors they see as high risk.

Risk can shift from one sector to another and from one bank to another, depending on how much lending the bank has already done in a certain sector. If a bank feels it's made enough loans in an industry and has enough financial risk exposure in an area, it may decide internally to put a hold on lending to that area.

They Use Ratios to Test Your Application

As with most things financial, banks use a number of ratios in order to arrive at some opinions about your business and compare it to others in your field.

Ratios can be particularly useful during times of business growth, as the raw numbers change but the ratios always represent the same point of comparison.

Simply put, a *ratio* is a number expressed as a proportion of another number. Funders use three or four ratios to measure a company's financial health:

- **Gross profit margin:** This calculation shows the proportion of money left over from revenue after subtracting the direct cost of generating that revenue: Gross profit margin = revenue – the cost of goods/revenue. The gross profit margin is an indicator of a company's ability to price its products and services correctly, pay just enough to sell them and still have enough money left over to cover the operating expenses and build for the future. I look at this in more detail in Chapter 20.

- **Operating profit margin:** This calculation illustrates the proportion of revenue left over after paying for variable costs: Operating margin = operating income (net sales minus all operating costs)/net sales (total sales minus any returns). Multiply by 100 to arrive at a percentage. It indicates your ability to control costs efficiently.

    If the margin increases year on year, then your business is earning more money per sale and going in the right direction.

- **Return on capital employed (ROCE):** This is a great way to measure the overall performance of a business because it tells you how much you've made, or the *return,* on the amount you've *invested,* or the capital you've employed, in any given year: ROCE = operating profit/the total of share capital + long-term borrowings. Multiply by 100 to arrive at a percentage. The higher the percentage figure the better, and it should be compared year by year.

- **Gearing ratio:** The more your business borrows versus the money invested in it in capital for equity shares, the more highly geared it is. A highly geared business is exposed and vulnerable to any sharp shock in the economy, such as a recession, and to rising interest rates adding unplanned-for costs to running the business. Most businesses in the growth or expansion stage carry too much debt and are too highly geared. They're often funded more by creditor's funds instead of the business's turnover or the owner's funds. Funders are put off by this. Something between 25 and 50 per cent is normal for a well-established business.

Gearing ratio = debt (long-term borrowings or liabilities)/short-term debt + shareholder's funds or capital employed. Multiply by 100 to arrive at a percentage.

In addition to ratios, which all funders use, a bank does its own assessment of you, your business and whether the deal makes sense from the bank's point of view. Banks use something known as CAMPARI – and no, not the drink we all know and love with ice – to assess your **c**haracter and **a**bility to run your business prudently and with robust financial controls, the correctness of your business **m**argin, the **p**urpose you'll put the money to, the **a**mount you want, the **r**epayment potential and the **i**nsurance (or the security) you can offer to guarantee a loan. I talk more about CAMPARI and banks in Chapter 12.

For some useful information on all things ratio related, have a look at www. ibusinessbuzz.co.uk or www.smetoolkit.org.

They Rely on Credit Scoring Files

Whether they tell you or not, all funders use some generic, universally accepted and acknowledged sources of credit scoring. Become familiar with some of them, including:

- **Experian Credit Reports and Equifax:** Both look at your individual credit history, financial history and any court cases, and have rating scales (0–1000 for Experian; 0–750 for Equifax) ranging from 'very poor' to 'excellent' that indicate the level of risk involved to a lender. The cost of the reports varies from a one-off for up to £10 to a monthly subscription for around £15 per month, which allows you to easily stay on top of any changes.

- **Delphie Rating:** A Delphie Rating looks at a variety of indicators and data on your business, and uses a traffic light system with a corresponding numerical scale of 1–100, from red to green accordingly, to rate your business creditworthiness. Green is a good place to be and goes from 70–100, for example, with 1–30 being red, and the bit in the middle, amber.

  The variables in Delphie include the strength or weakness of your industry or sector, your company history and performance, the most current information on your balance sheet and P&L (profit and loss statement) that's on file, and all credit activity and previous credit history.

Every industry sector has a Standard Industrial Classification code, or SIC *Code,* that provides a description of your company activities as shown on the Companies House register of companies. It's important that you use the right code for your business because if you get classified under a code for an industry that's underperforming, it may have a negative impact on your funding applications. A condensed list of SIC codes can be found at www.gov.uk.

They Classify Your Business

Funders classify your business in a number of ways, such as industry type, age, credit profile and risk profile, in much the same way they classify you in your personal funding experiences.

Even if you pass the test on all the standard indicators and look like a good bet, debt funders have one more unspoken hoop for you to pass through – known in the trade as the *5 S's* – which go like this:

- **Stake:** How much of your own money have you put in?
- **Serviceability:** Can your business make the loan payments?
- **Security:** What can you put forward as security against funding given to your business? Property? Shares? Art? Jewellery? Insurance policies? Personal guarantees?
- **Secondary option:** Better known as your *Plan B* – what you'll do if your forecasts and projections don't go to plan.
- **Suitability:** If you can tick the box on the other four S's, you also face this very subjective indicator as to whether or not your business is suitable for funding. This can cover anything from being in a high-risk sector to being in an industry where the funder already has too much exposure.

The good news is that although you may not be right for one funder, you may be just the ticket for another, so keep knocking on doors.

They Investigate Your Background Fully

Business owners are often surprised to hear that a funder does a background check not only on the business but also on the principals. If you consider that a funder is either lending or investing in a business run by people who claim to be responsible with finances and who more often than not are acting as guarantors or putting up security in case something goes wrong, it begins to make sense.

To make sure you know what's out there on you, and before you approach someone for funding, do your own due diligence on yourself. (I explain due diligence in Chapter 4.) It's very easy to check your credit file online for about £10 (www.experian.com). You can see all your credit history from phone bills to credit cards applied for and used, and any county court judgements and whether they were satisfied.

The report may throw up information you didn't know was out there. Checking your report gives you a great opportunity to put right any incorrect data, tidy it up and prepare for what may confront you at a funding meeting. Knowledge is power, and in this case, it's wise to check yourself before you wreck yourself.

How to Get the Best Rate

It won't come as a shock to you that most banks don't tell you that they want all your money – your savings, mortgage, current accounts, individual savings accounts (ISA) and so on – and if you give them all your money, you're more likely to get a better rate when you approach them for funding. If you're a top-of-the-class customer when it comes to maintaining a well-conducted bank account – consistently putting money in and managing the outflow, and have more assets to your name than liabilities – you're more likely to get the best rate.

If you aren't getting the best rate you think is possible, it's worth looking at the problem from a different angle. For example, see whether some fees can be waived on setting up your overdraft – which may help to ease the pain of the rate you're paying.

Of course, your ultimate trump card is taking your business elsewhere, and depending on the bank's internal targets for retention of accounts and services, this threat can prompt a positive response. It can be quite time-consuming to get through the exercise to see what you can get elsewhere, but it's a good idea to review your arrangements periodically in any event, and it may uncover a deal that gives you significant savings.

On the same theme, but not directly linked to a rate, you may also want to shop around when it comes to getting the best terms on an equity investment. Each investor or investment fund has its own terms and conditions, and what they offer you may be different to what they offer another business because of the risk it poses to their portfolio. You can sometimes get feedback that explains this in more detail, but this isn't always the case, so don't go mad spraying your application out to dozens of investors, and then praying for the best deal and playing potential lenders off against one another.

The investment community in the UK is very tight, and everyone knows everyone, so this will get around. However, have more than one interested investor to make sure you get the best deal.

How to Improve Your Credit Profile

Unless you were born after the crisis of 2008, you're very risk averse, super prudent with finances or very lucky, you've probably had a brush with a questionable credit profile. You may even have had a full-on knock 'em down, drag 'em out ruckus, where you came out worse for wear and the other guy – the companies and organisations that help to build your credit profile – escaped unharmed or with only a few cuts and bruises in the form of customer complaints and decisions being overturned.

Your credit profile is comprised of and affected by a number of things, and one of them is your track record in managing previous credit agreements. Lenders look to your credit profile, explained in the earlier section, 'They Rely on Credit Scoring Files'. Internal bank mandates may trigger an automatic decline or acceptance when a certain profile presents itself. These standards tend to be set in stone, and you're generally powerless to change a decision based on them, so it's best to do all you can to clean up and/or maintain a strong credit profile.

You can swear on a stack of Bibles that you're great at managing other peoples' money, or can make all the repayments based on the budgets and forecasts you provide, but your version of reality and a funder's version based on your profile may be two very different things. The lending process has been tightened up significantly since 2008. Banks are now being told by the Financial Conduct Authority (FCA) to be more diligent when assessing customers. All the new lending platforms have a duty of care to their investors and lenders, and so they have their own version of a credit profile, which you may or may not be aware of, as well.

So make your payments on time, always pay off as much as you can as quickly as you can when it comes to credit cards and short-term debt, even if you use it little and often, list yourself in a public place that gives you a confirmed residence and stability (such as the electoral register) and stay out of courtrooms whenever possible.

Chapter 20

Ten (Plus One) Terms You Need to Know before Raising Start-Up Capital

....

....

*Y*ou won't necessarily use all the terms here every day, but you will encounter each one of them someday, so file away these definitions for future use.

Profit and Revenue

You can be excused for thinking that these two terms have the same meaning, because so many people use them interchangeably – incorrectly, I may add. The two words have distinctly different meanings. *Revenue* – also known as *sales income, fee income, income* – is the money you get in for the sale of goods or services. *Profit* is what you earn on those sales after taking away the cost of doing business. You need to have the terms straight in your mind before you start looking for funding.

Gross Profit Margin

Getting the money in is one thing, but ensuring that you make a profit is your top priority. In basic terms, profit equals revenue less expenses or costs. However, typically you calculate a couple of measures of profit on your business and in your income statement, which are gross profit and net profit.

(The German word for large or big is *gross,* and this is how I remembered which was which when I started out.) Your gross profit shows the total revenue minus the direct costs of materials and/or labour to generate that revenue – these are costs that you cannot change. The percentage representation of your gross profit is what's known as gross profit margin. This margin is an indication of how cost-efficiently you produce your basic goods and services. For example, if you have £100 worth of sales with a direct cost of £30, you have direct costs of 30 per cent of the sale value to create the sale.

Each industry has an optimum gross profit margin or percentage, and it's up to you to do some research and find out what it is for your business. Your trade association or professional body may have this data, and your accountant is always a good resource. The many private organisations that publish this data are not impartial, so tread carefully.

Critically, if your gross profit is out of line with the rest of your industry, it should set off alarm bells because it's a strong indication that you're either paying too much to generate your sales, or you're not charging enough for your product or service – or a bit of both – and you're in danger of not making an overall profit.

You can generate tons of revenue, but if you don't have your costings right it's impossible to run a profitable business. Your gross profit margin is a key indicator of your business profitability and a risk indicator to a funder.

Once you have your gross profit, you need to look at the impact of all your general operating or variable costs – the costs you can control – on this income to determine net profit (before you look at tax) for a given period.

Cash Flow

Cash flow is the actual cash your business generates from your services or products, investments, sales of assets and interest payments received, and the cash your business spends on providing your service or product, operating the business, servicing debts and purchasing assets. Cash flow is essentially the life source of your business. It keeps money circulating and tells you whether you're running a healthy operation or not!

A cash flow budget or forecast highlights the following figures:

 ✔ **Revenue from the sale of your product or service:** The combined sum of all the sales you make

> ✔ **Development expenses:** Costs associated with product, service or technology improvements and developments
>
> ✔ **Cost of goods:** The direct cost of all the materials and labour to produce your goods and services
>
> ✔ **Capital requirements:** The cash you need to start your business operations

Cash flow projections for your start-up are based on your projected sales income for the next year combined with your payment terms, as these determine when your business actually receives the cash for each transaction. Cash flow projections include your anticipated expenses as well.

One way to calculate cash flow is to split the sales for each month into cash sales and credit sales. Cash sales can be entered into the cash flow statement in the same month they're generated, while credit sales come under the term *accounts receivable* and are logged into the cash flow statement when you receive the payment.

Accounts payable is money your business is due to pay in the future for purchased on credit terms, bills falling due and loan repayments, which you have agreed to pay within a set period of time.

For example, Ms Johanna Smith buys 30 toys from Mrs Jane Doe, who has a 45-day payment term. Johanna logs this as accounts payable in her cash flow statement, while Jane log it as accounts receivable to show she is expecting the cash from that sale to flow into the business within 45 days.

The next line on the cash flow statement is *other income.* This refers to any money received from interest on loans your company extended, revenue from dissolving any assets and cash received as an investment into your business.

The total income in your cash flow statement is a sum of sales revenue, accounts receivable and other income.

After you log all your income, you need to log all your expenses and costs. A golden rule here is to include all your business outgoings. Even the little things can add up over time, and if you don't include everything, your cash flow forecast won't be 100 per cent accurate.

Direct labour costs to produce your goods are logged in your cash flow statement the same month that they're accrued. Material costs are a little different in that they need to be logged within the period of time it takes to convert the raw material to products for sale and then receive payment for that sale.

After you log all of your costs into your cash flow statement, add them up to arrive at a total figure for your expenses. Then take away the total expenses from the total income to find your cash flow, which may be either positive (in surplus) or negative (a deficit).

Working Capital

Working capital refers to the cash available for your day-to-day operations. Working capital can affect your ability to buy assets, pay bills and obtain favourable credit terms from other companies. In a cash flow statement, working capital is detailed as operating cash flow. It can be determined from operating expenses including payroll and fixed overheads (outgoings).

The simplest way of calculating working capital is: Current Assets – Current Liabilities = Working Capital.

A positive working capital figure means that your current assets are more than your current liabilities, but a negative figure means that your business is spending more cash than it's currently bringing in! It's crucial to keep an eye on this figure.

Capital equipment costs can be logged under the heading *capital*.

Break-Even Analysis

A *break-even analysis* tells you how much you need to sell in order to cover the monthly running costs of doing business. This is really useful if your product or service requires you to spend money in order to sell to your customers. Every product you sell generates a cost, so the more you sell the higher your expenses.

The calculation for your break-even analysis uses three key figures:

✔ **Average per-unit revenue:** The average amount of money you receive for every product or service sold. Be sure to include any discounts or promotions so that you can figure out the average selling price across your business.

A simple formula to calculate this is: Total Product Price ÷ Number of Products = Average Per-Unit Revenue.

For example, Ms Delph sells five different products, at the following prices:

- £10,000
- £12,000
- £15,000
- £30,000
- £50,000

Her average per-unit revenue is the sum total of all her services, divided by the number of services on offer (5) which equals £23,400. Her average per-unit revenue is £23,400.

✔ **Average per-unit cost:** How much it costs you to sell your product or service to customers. Usually, this figure doesn't include things like payroll and so on. For example, if a carpenter sells various wooden furniture products, the average cost per unit can be calculated using the formula for average per-unit revenue when she tallies up costs, such as the wood sourced to make her furniture.

✔ **Monthly fixed costs:** Regular running costs that you expect to incur on a monthly basis. These are the *operating expenses* of the business and can include things like business insurance, office rent, utilities and payroll.

Balance Sheet

The *balance sheet* is a summary of a business's assets, liabilities and equity at a given point in time. A business has to pay for its assets by either borrowing money (incurring a liability) or taking cash from the equity in the company. Think of the balance sheet as a statement of how your business balances itself out financially.

The calculation used for the balance sheet is: Assets = Liabilities + Equity.

Investors commonly use the balance sheet to calculate what a business is worth using this formula. Investors may analyse a balance sheet to determine how much working capital a business has, how much it currently owes and what is left over for the shareholders.

For example, Karen has obtained a small business loan for her start-up – this is a liability but it also increases her assets as she now has cash. Karen uses this money to buy a minivan for her delivery business; this reduces her cash assets but is balanced by her new asset – the minivan. Karen starts using her van to make deliveries and makes a profit. She records this as retained earnings, which belongs in the equity section of her balance sheet. The cash from her deliveries is recorded as an asset, which Karen then uses to make repayments on her loan, which reduces her cash assets but also reduces her liabilities.

The balance sheet doesn't offer the whole picture of the financial performance of a business, so investors usually compare this with other financial statements.

Valuation

Arriving at a valuation for your business has been likened to art meets science meets finance. In dictionary terms, business *valuation* is a generally accepted process and set of procedures used to determine what a business is worth. Although this sounds easy enough, getting a business valuation done right takes preparation and a good deal of thought.

Business valuation results depend on your assumptions. For one thing, there's no one way to establish what a business is worth. That's because business value means different things to different people. A business owner may believe that the business connection to the community it serves is worth a lot. An investor may think that the business value is entirely defined by its historic income.

The circumstances of a business sale also affect the business value. A big difference exists between a business that is shown as part of a well-planned marketing effort to attract many interested buyers and a quick sale of business assets at an auction.

The three approaches to measure what a business is worth are:

- **Asset approach:** This method seeks to determine the business value based on the value of its assets. The idea is to determine the business value based on the fair market value of its assets less its liabilities.

- **Market approach:** This approach establishes the business value in comparison to historic sales involving similar businesses.

- **Income approach:** This method determines the value of a business based on its ability to generate desired economic benefit for the owners. The key objective of the income-based method is to determine the business value as a function of the economic benefit.

  Economic data, such as the seller's discretionary cash flow, is capitalised, discounted or multiplied to perform the valuation.

Return on Investment

Return on investment (ROI) refers to the benefit gained (or, in some cases, not) as a result of an investment or financial deal. ROI is a common way of measuring the profitability of a deal and the performance of a business. One of the most common ways to determine ROI is to divide your net profit by your total assets.

For example, ABC Tech Ltd has a net profit of £10,000 and its total assets are £30,000. Divide £10,000 by £30,000 to equal 0.33. Expressed as a percentage, the company's ROI is 33 per cent.

Be careful not to confuse ROI with profit. ROI refers to money invested in the company and the return on that investment, whereas profit relates to the performance of the business.

ROI can be useful for measuring a number of things in your business – for example, whether money spent on marketing is worthwhile.

Return on Equity

Return on equity (ROE) measures the ability of your business to generate profits from shareholders' income; in other words, how much profit a company can generate with cash invested by shareholders. This measure is expressed as a profitability ratio: Net Income ÷ Shareholder's Equity = ROE.

For example, Penny's Purses receives £2 million from shareholders to grow her company. With this investment, she goes on to generate £1 million in revenue. £1 million divided by £2 million is 50, so Penny's Purses has a 50 per cent ROE.

ROE is a good indicator of how well a business can use money invested by shareholders to make a profit and grow the company. Don't forget, though, that ROE is a profitability measure from the investor's perspective based on her investment in a company – it doesn't reflect a company's investment in assets or anything else.

Investors want to see a high ROE because that shows that your business is capable of using funds wisely to generate strong returns. Most industries have common levels of ROE.

EBITDA

EBITDA is defined as a company's net **e**arnings **b**efore **i**nterest, **t**axes, **d**epreciation and **a**mortisation are subtracted. It can be used to assess and compare profitability between two or more companies because it excludes the effects of financing and accounting decisions.

EBITDA is essentially a sum of revenue minus expenses, allowing a company to include or exclude particular items. It was commonly used in the 1980s to determine whether companies would be able to pay for their debts. Today, however, EBITDA is used as a measure of company's performance and financial health.

EBITDA doesn't represent cash earnings, and because business owners can alter what's included in this measure, investors often look at other measures to determine whether your company represents a financially viable investment.

A negative EBITDA may highlight that a business is struggling with profitability and cash flow. On the other hand, a positive EBITDA doesn't always mean that a business is generating money, as the figure depends on what numbers have been included and excluded.

EBITDA doesn't account for changes in the working capital of your business.

Personal Guarantee

You may be asked to provide a personal guarantee for a loan, either in full or in part. By definition, a *personal guarantee* is almost always unsecured. This means it isn't tied to a particular asset you own, such as your home.

If you make a personal guarantee, you put yourself and your personal assets on the line if the business fails to pay back the loan as per the agreed terms.

For banks and other financial institutions, lending to small businesses is risky business. That is why many request a personal guarantee – it minimises the risk of providing capital to your business.

Index

• M •

Notes

Notes

About the Author

Helene Panzarino is a passionate and proactive entrepreneur, educator, mentor and commercial advisor with nearly 20 years' experience helping thousands of small-and medium-sized businesses become investment ready. A frequent round-table participant, media guest and event speaker, Helene combines hands-on experience with theoretical know-how.

A former banker and a successful serial entrepreneur, Helene is a frequent judge for a variety of technology funding initiatives and specialist group programmes. She has been a judge and mentor for a number of organisations, including Mass Challenge, the Peter Jones Enterprise Academy and Innotribe. Helene was nominated for a Prowess Award for inspiring women in business in 2011 and for ITV Woman of the Year for inspiring in education in 2012.

She has been called 'relentless' in her pursuit to help British businesses scale and succeed, and is known for banging on about getting all areas of the business world working together on a truly global basis.

Author's Acknowledgements

I'd like to thank everyone at Wiley for the opportunity to write this book as well as for their encouragement and feedback throughout the process. I'd been looking for the right place to share my many years of experience in a way that would give confidence and encouragement to business owners, and the *For Dummies* series seemed the perfect vehicle. I'd also like to thank the UK financial community for its support in my quest to raise awareness of funding options for SME owners – CrowdBnk, GLI Finance, MarketInvoice and Syndicate Room, in particular. Lastly, I'd like to thank Kevin Davey for his insight, intelligence and ability to always see the bigger picture.

Publisher's Acknowledgments

Acquisitions Editor: Annie Knight

Project Editor: Rachael Chilvers, Iona Everson, Tracy Brown Hamilton

Development Editor: Kathleen Dobie

Copy Editor: Kerry Laundon

Technical Editor: Colin Barrow

Art Coordinator: Alicia B. South

Production Editor: Kinson Raja

Cover Image: ©Maxisport/Shutterstock

Take Dummies with you everywhere you go!

Whether you're excited about e-books, want more from the web, must have your mobile apps, or swept up in social media, Dummies makes everything easier.

Visit Us

Like Us

Follow Us

Watch Us

Join Us

Pin Us

Circle Us

Shop Us

FOR DUMMIES
A Wiley Brand

BUSINESS

978-1-118-73077-5 978-1-118-44349-1 978-1-119-97527-4

MUSIC

978-1-119-94276-4 978-0-470-97799-6 978-0-470-49644-2

DIGITAL PHOTOGRAPHY

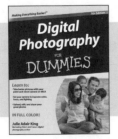  

978-1-118-09203-3 978-0-470-76878-5 978-1-118-00472-2

Algebra I For Dummies
978-0-470-55964-2

Anatomy & Physiology For Dummies, 2nd Edition
978-0-470-92326-9

Asperger's Syndrome For Dummies
978-0-470-66087-4

Basic Maths For Dummies
978-1-119-97452-9

Body Language For Dummies, 2nd Edition
978-1-119-95351-7

Bookkeeping For Dummies, 3rd Edition
978-1-118-34689-1

British Sign Language For Dummies
978-0-470-69477-0

Cricket for Dummies, 2nd Edition
978-1-118-48032-8

Currency Trading For Dummies, 2nd Edition
978-1-118-01851-4

Cycling For Dummies
978-1-118-36435-2

Diabetes For Dummies, 3rd Edition
978-0-470-97711-8

eBay For Dummies, 3rd Edition
978-1-119-94122-4

Electronics For Dummies All-in-One For Dummies
978-1-118-58973-1

English Grammar For Dummies
978-0-470-05752-0

French For Dummies, 2nd Edition
978-1-118-00464-7

Guitar For Dummies, 3rd Edition
978-1-118-11554-1

IBS For Dummies
978-0-470-51737-6

Keeping Chickens For Dummies
978-1-119-99417-6

Knitting For Dummies, 3rd Edition
978-1-118-66151-2